# HENRY FLAGLER

# HENRY FLAGLER

The Astonishing Life and Times
of the Visionary Robber Baron
Who Founded Florida

**DAVID LEON CHANDLER**

Macmillan Publishing Company

NEW YORK

Macmillan Publishing Company
866 Third Avenue, New York, N.Y. 10022
Collier Macmillan Canada, Inc.

Library of Congress Cataloging-in-Publication Data
Chandler, David Leon.
Henry Flagler : the astonishing life and times of
the visionary robber baron who founded Florida.
Bibliography: p.
Includes index.
1. Flagler, Henry Morrison, 1830–1913.   2. Pioneers—
Florida—Biography.   3. Businessmen—Florida—Biography.
4. Florida—History—1865–    .   I. Title.
F316.F56C45   1986        975.9'06         86–152
ISBN 0-02-523690-3

Macmillan books are available at special discounts for bulk purchases
for sales promotions, premiums, fund-raising, or educational use.
For details, contact:

Special Sales Director
Macmillan Publishing Company
866 Third Avenue
New York, N.Y. 10022
10 9 8 7 6 5 4 3 2 1

Designed by Jack Meserole

Printed in the United States of America

To my wife, Mary

# CONTENTS

# ACKNOWLEDGMENTS

Despite his staggering accomplishments, Henry Flagler has been overlooked by history. The credit for rediscovering him goes largely to Edward T. Chase, editor of this book, and G. F. Robert Hanke, Flagler's great grandson and vice president of the Flagler Museum in Palm Beach, Florida. Sometime in the late 1970s or early 1980s (they don't remember just when) they began talking about the possibility of a Flagler biography. Out of those conversations grew the momentum for this book, only the second biography to be published on Flagler in the 115 years since he joined John Rockefeller to start America's first industrial giant, the Standard Oil Company.

They didn't stop with just mapping the idea. They remained ready and available to help throughout the writing of *Henry Flagler* and I called upon them often.

The actual mining of information began at the Flagler Museum. Over the years, the museum has become the central repository for the various collections of letters, newspaper clippings, photographs, paintings, business records, railroad logs and official documents that constitute the facts and feelings of Flagler's life.

For the biographer, even more information can be gained from the setting of the museum itself, it being located in Flagler's magnificent winter mansion, Whitehall. The museum has restored it to Flagler's original setting—the same furniture, paintings, colors and dinnerware.

Museum director Charles Simmons and archivist Joan Runkel were invaluable guides through the hundreds of thousands of documents, artifacts and photographs which needed to be sifted before the writing could even begin.

That wasn't the end of it. After the original research was done, during the year or more it took to write the book, Charles and Joan cheerfully and patiently responded to almost daily requests for photographs, documents and arcane questions on every facet of Flagler's life.

The help didn't stop there. Professor Harold Martin, Flagler's original biographer, is retired now in Valdosta, Georgia, after a distinguished career as an educator, a career which included the presidencies of Emory University and Valdosta State. He provided invaluable insight on Flagler's problems with his second wife, who had become insane.

Most of the St. Augustine material was provided by the St. Augustine Historical Society and its museum curator, Page Edwards.

A lot of published misinformation on Flagler's third wife, Mary Lily Kenan, was corrected by her cousin, Thomas S. Kenan III, an authority not only on the Kenan family but on Henry Flagler himself, Tom Kenan having been a board member of the Flagler Museum.

Additional information was provided by Sallie Bingham of Louisville, Kentucky, granddaughter of Robert Worth Bingham, the man Mary Lily married following Flagler's death.

All of the above were especially generous in their time, their courtesy and their knowledge, and a great pleasure of doing this book was the opportunity to meet them.

I also want to thank the Rockefeller Archives in Tarrytown, New York, the Drake Well Museum in Titusville, Pennsylvania, the Historical Museum of South Florida in Miami, the Dutchess County (New York) Historical Society, and the hard-working staff of the Jefferson County Public Library in Evergreen, Colorado. The latter, using the interlibrary loan system, came up with some hard-to-find books and magazine articles.

Last, but certainly not least, I want to thank William Oddo, the official historian of the Bellevue, Ohio, area where, nearly 150 years ago, Flagler matured from a 14-year-old boy to a 40-year old man.

When this book began, that large chunk of Flagler's life was missing. Very little had been printed anywhere on Flagler's formative years. Even the collection at Whitehall had little to offer.

Bill Oddo, however, had found it. He found it by basic research, by going through virtually every local record and newspaper still existing from Flagler's time. And I thank him for sharing it.

# HENRY FLAGLER

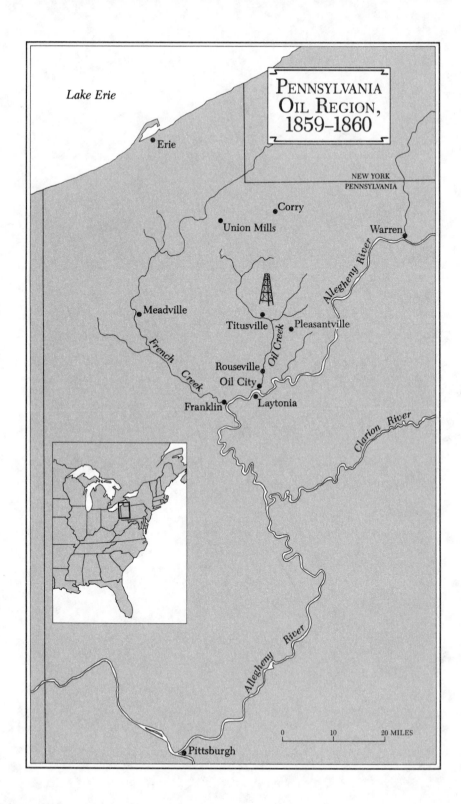

Lake Erie

PENNSYLVANIA
OIL REGION,
1859–1860

• Erie

NEW YORK
PENNSYLVANIA

• Corry

• Union Mills

Warren •

Allegheny River

• Meadville

Titusville • • Pleasantville

Oil Creek

Rouseville •
Oil City •

French Creek

Franklin • • Laytonia

Clarion River

Allegheny River

0        10        20 MILES

• Pittsburgh

# CHAPTER 1

# Henry Flagler

"When you thought about it, in the old days, could you close your eyes and see it finished?"

"Yes." He spoke in a matter-of-fact tone.

"Did you actually vision to yourself the whole thing? I mean, did you, or could you, really close your eyes and see it all? The derricks? The pipelines? The refineries? Did you see the men working? The tracks? The trains running? And hear the whistles blowing? Did you go as far as that?"

"Yes."

"How clearly?"

"Very clearly."

—Interview with Henry Flagler at age 76

THE lucky part of Henry Flagler's success was the timing of his arrival in Ohio.

It was the middle of the 1800s and a thing called rock oil, or petroleum, was just beginning to happen. It had, of course, been used in minor ways for hundreds of years. American Indians soaked it up from streams with blankets and used it as a medicinal balm, or set it afire for magic shows, or mixed it with colors to make paint.

In the late 1700s, shortly after the opening of the western territories of Pennsylvania, Ohio and Kentucky, oil proved to be a nuisance to the farmers and trappers who found it on the surface of springs and streams. As more and more crude oil appeared, however, people began to wonder if it might not have some value. In Burkesville, Kentucky, where oil was first found in abundance, it was skimmed and bottled under the name American Medicinal Oil and sold as a liniment not only on the frontier but also in New York, Boston, Philadelphia, and to European cities such as Paris, London and Prague where it was used as fuel for lamps.

The oil site causing the greatest excitement in the mid-nineteenth

1

century was a creek wandering among wooded banks and small farms
in the Allegheny Forest, 100 miles northeast of Pittsburgh.

Oil had been reported in this region for more than a hundred
years. As early as 1768, the Alleghenies missionary David Zeisberger
had begun selling oil for medicinal purposes and as a lamp fuel.[1] On
a map of Pennsylvania made in London in 1755 the word "petroleum"
was written across the territory of what would become the famous
site of Oil Creek, or "Oyl Creek," as it was identified on a 1791 map
of Pennsylvania.[2]

Thus, when the nineteenth century began, it was known in America, England and France that a substance called petroleum flowed
from springs scattered throughout the Appalachian forests. Oil had
medicinal value, burned freely, gave off a strong but smoky light and
was useful as a grease. But, because its odor was so offensive, many
doubted it would ever be widely used. This problem was solved in
the late 1840s when Samuel Kier, who owned some salt wells in
western Pennsylvania, discovered that different components of rock
oil had different boiling points. By controlling the distillation, he could
remove much of the odor and smoke problems, and obtain kerosene,
naphtha, lubricating oils and other products. Kier's laboratory became
the world's first refinery.

Kier had found a use for oil. It would illuminate the world. Com-
pared to lamp oil derived from coal and other sources, petroleum was
superior in every way. It was cheaper, it burned clearly and brilliantly,
and it would last much longer. It was also the best lubricator for
machinery ever known. It didn't congeal in any weather and, unlike
other oils, didn't become filthy through use.

The only snag was that the product was in short supply, obtainable
only by the various skimming methods.

It was, that is, until August 1859, when the history of the world
was changed by a 40-year-old jack-of-all-trades named Edwin Drake.
Drake's accomplishment was to use salt-mining equipment and drill
a well beside Oil Creek, 15 miles above its confluence with the Allegheny River. From somewhere below ground, he pumped up oil
and as far as anyone knows, it was the first time ever that man had
tapped a subterranean supply of petroleum. It was a vast step forward.
It meant that oil could be secured in large quantities, and men flocked
to the oil fields. Drake's discovery created a storm of excitement and
lured a swarm of oilmen, roustabouts, wildcatters and get-rich-quick

artists who built a forest of derricks in the desolate region. The boom was on and fortune hunters poured forth in streams.

AT THE TIME Drake struck oil, 30-year-old Henry Morrison Flagler was living in central Ohio, about 100 miles west of Oil Creek, two days' travel.

Now, curious as to what it was all about, he stood on a hill gazing down at the creek.

In the spring of 1859, Oil Creek had been bordered by meadows strewn with wildflowers. By winter 1859, when Henry arrived, Oil Creek had turned brown-gray and along a two-mile stretch of it were hundreds of wooden derricks jammed together over oil wells. The spread of wooden derricks and open vats and flimsy shacks almost crowded the farmhouses out of existence. The oil, wasted by primitive drilling methods, had laid vast sheets of shimmering scum over the creeks and lakes.

Henry walked down the hill to talk with the oil men.

He was a lean, handsome figure. A young captain of cavalry, you might say, trained to ride the field. Excellent head; strange violet-blue eyes; short dark hair parted on the side; straight, classic nose; cleanly shaven face. Picturesque as a stage idol. But a likable man despite his good looks; a ready and brusque talker who seasoned his ways with philosophy, reflection and a fine sense of humor. A man uncommonly in sympathy with human nature.[3] But there was also a distance.

There was a curious sense of difference rather than mere aloofness. There was no superciliousness, no impatience, no hint of superiority; yet you were subtly made aware that he was alone, by himself.

After becoming acquainted with him, you would find a man who talked freely, yet never freely enough; who answered everything, but volunteered nothing. Unlike his friend John D. Rockefeller, Henry Flagler was not a man perennially on his guard. He was calm and kindly; never distant—yet always at a distance.[4]

As he stood on the hill gazing down at Oil Creek that winter day in 1859, Henry Flagler was thinking that business could be done here. His expression was a perfect portrait of confidence.

DURING the next several years, Henry's fortunes would vary greatly, mostly because of the Civil War. But in 1867, he and Cleveland refinery owner Rockefeller joined to create a company which would set a standard of quality and practices in a chaotic industry. Appropriately, they called their company Standard Oil.

Handsome, roguish Flagler and his dour but fascinating friend Rockefeller were capitalists, pure and simple. "It was our idea," Henry said, "to work night and day, making good oil as cheaply as possible and selling it for all we could get."

Within a few years, Standard Oil was the largest monopoly in America, growing on its competitors, devouring them like an insatiable monster. Flagler, in typical understatement, explained that it was simply survival of the fittest: "As other little refineries sprang up, we bought them. Our business was developed rapidly."

There is much to be examined in those words. It was the age of the robber barons, and Henry Flagler and Standard Oil were at the forefront of the pack. The "little refineries" that sprang up were more often squeezed out of business than bought up. And Standard's success in making oil cheaply was largely obtained by Flagler making under-the-table deals with railroad owners who would give Standard Oil cheaper rail rates in return for guarantees of large shipments of oil. Standard would ship at lower rates, sell in the East at lower prices, make more sales and increase the volume of railroad traffic.

Standard's competitors were denied the lower rates. The rail companies didn't want to incur a boycott from their largest customer.

At the beginning, in 1867, the Rockefeller and Flagler company was only one of a number of refining firms in Cleveland. By early 1872, Standard had swallowed virtually all the rival refineries in that city. By 1879, Standard controlled between 90 and 95 percent of the refining capacity of the world, including Europe, Asia and the Middle East.[5]

The expansion of Standard Oil was engineered and controlled by a business innovation known as "The Trust," a board of trustees which could operate across state and international boundaries. When Rockefeller was asked if he had conceived the idea, he answered, "No, sir. I wish I'd had the brains to think of it. It was Henry M. Flagler."

STANDARD was an awesome achievement, but the most remarkable thing about Henry Morrison Flagler is not Standard Oil. It is what came after. Flagler and Rockefeller had perfected their money machine. And at that point, Henry said, *deal me out boys. There are other worlds to conquer.* He looked down to Florida, which was then a jungle—a pond of Spanish bayonet, sawgrass and unpopulated coasts 100 miles wide and 300 miles long. He planted his foot in St. Augustine and said, *boys, I am going south. From here, I will build railroads and hotels, farmlands and cities. I will build them all the way down to Key West.* And so he did.

He took a frontier wilderness sparsely populated by scattered settlements of farmers, fishermen and ship scavangers, and changed it into a twentieth-century superstate.

It seems he did this because of three women—one dead, one insane and the other doomed.

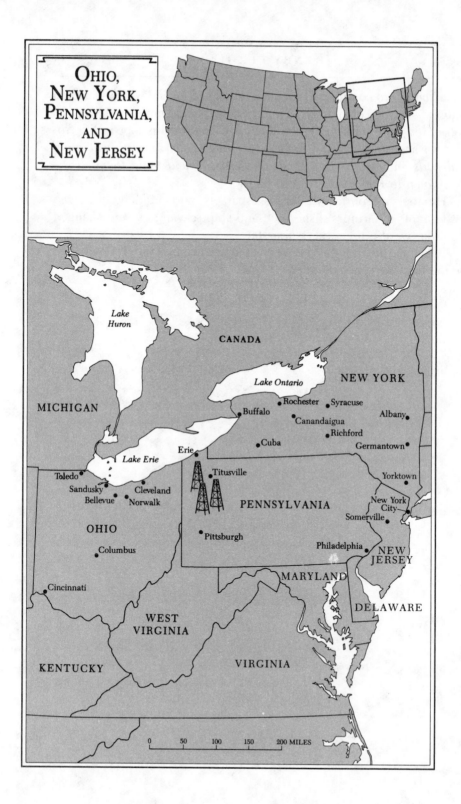

OHIO,
NEW YORK,
PENNSYLVANIA,
AND
NEW JERSEY

CANADA

Lake
Huron

Lake Ontario

NEW YORK

MICHIGAN

Rochester    Syracuse

Buffalo

Canandaigua          Albany

Richford

Germantown

Cuba

Lake Erie    Erie

Toledo                    Titusville           Yorktown

Sandusky    Cleveland

Bellevue    Norwalk          PENNSYLVANIA          New York
                                                     City

                                              Somerville

OHIO                        Pittsburgh

Columbus                              Philadelphia    NEW
                                                       JERSEY

Cincinnati                         MARYLAND

                                                     DELAWARE

WEST
VIRGINIA

KENTUCKY          VIRGINIA

0    50    100    150    200 MILES

# CHAPTER 2

# Ohio

"All the training I ever got at school was obtained
before I was 14 years old. At that age I concluded that
my mother and sister needed the lean pay which my
father received by preaching. So I left home and walked
nine miles to the town of Medina, carrying a deep, country-
style carpetbag in my hand. I got aboard a freight boat
on the Erie Canal and went to Buffalo."

Wasn't there a packet?

"More than one, but I wanted to save my money."

And at Buffalo?

"I took a vessel for Sandusky, Ohio. I was on Lake
Erie for three days in a dreadful storm. I was seasick,
lonely, and very wretched. My mother had put some
lunch in my carpetbag and of that I ate, when I ate at
all, during my gloomy journey over canals and lake."

—HENRY FLAGLER

LITTLE is known of Henry Flager's youth. He was tempera-
mentally averse to reminiscences.[1] But Flagler himself said that
he went to the district school through the eighth grade and
learned all there was to be learned there; also that he left home at
14 because he thought it was his duty not to be a burden to his father.
He knew no trade and probably did not fancy any.[2]

Henry was born in Hopewell, New York, on January 2, 1830 into
an already crowded household which included three half sisters and
one half brother. His sisters Mary Esther, aged 16, and Jane Augusta,
14, had been born to his father Isaac's first wife. His sister Caroline,
three and a half, had been born to Isaac's short-lived second wife.
His brother Daniel Morrison Harkness was the child of Henry's mother,
Isaac's third wife, and her second husband. Dan was seven years
older than Henry.

In September 1831, when Henry was 18 months old, his father, an itinerant minister, was assigned to the Presbyterian church in Hammondsport, New York, a winemaking center on Lake Keuka, one of the long, slender "Finger Lakes" between Rochester and Syracuse that point like warnings at Lake Ontario.

Henry was born at a time when the new United States was feeling the rumble of events which would shape its history for the next 150 years.

One of these was race.

When the Flagler family arrived in Hammondsport, Virginia, posses had just captured and hanged the black revolutionary Nat Turner who, believing himself divinely inspired, had led a band of slaves which killed 55 whites. The Turner rebellion led to harsher slave laws in the South and effectively killed off the Southern anti-slavery societies—the nation's last hope for a peaceful and orderly freeing of the slaves.[3]

Another primary event of the times was the emergence of technology. Important advances were being shaped most especially in Albany, New York, in 1831, by the physicist Joseph Henry. In the single year of 1831, Henry invented the electric motor, the electrical relay, the electromagnetic telegraph and the electric bell.[4]

ISAAC FLAGLER himself exemplified another important aspect of the American character, the wanderlust. He served in New York churches, with his daughters Mary and Jane in attendance, until the winter of 1832–1833, when he seems to have abruptly quit. His last recorded sermon was December 1, 1832. Shortly afterward, in the spring of 1833, the two older daughters moved to Chapinsville, New York, probably to stay with friends.[5]

For the next two years, Isaac drifted from place to place, dragging along his wife, his stepson Dan and the two smaller children. In 1836, they turned up in a booming Ohio coal port called Toledo. There, Isaac exhibited a risky passion for racial equality. We are given a contemporary account by a Toledo attorney named John Osborn.

In his diary entry for May 22, 1836, Osborn reports a scandal had arisen because of "the marriage of a mulatto, named Richardson, to a white girl from Norwalk, the first recorded case of the kind occurring in Toledo. The ceremony was performed by Rev. Isaac Flagler, pastor of the Presbyterian Church, and the affair caused intense excitement, and no little feeling against the officiating clergyman. The groom was an industrious, respectable man, and the bride (supposed to be the chief promoter of the union) seemed to act upon clear convictions as to the propriety of such a connection, she being of a respectable family, and having a brother, a 'student' at Oberlin College," the most pronounced anti-slavery school in the country.[6]

Osborn reflected that "Mr. Flagler no doubt acted conscientiously in the matter, but evidently against the prevailing sentiment of the community and a large portion of his own Church."

Not content with thumbing his nose at Toledo's bigotry, Isaac struck an even riskier blow by campaigning against drink. He was the leader of Toledo's first temperance meeting, held in a school house on January 14, 1838. He was elected president of the Toledo City Temperance Society and pledged not to use or traffic in intoxicating liquors himself. (The society and Isaac Flagler were not without political clout. Three months after its formation, the Toledo City Council passed an ordinance restricting the sale of alcoholic drink.)

How such outrages and the attending notoriety affected young Henry and Dan is not known, but apparently they weren't too impressed. Within a few years, both of them would be happily guzzling beer, and as young men would operate a highly successful distillery. As for racial equality, neither ever showed evidence of worrying about it.

In the meantime, Isaac's family split apart.

According to Presbyterian church records, Mary Esther and Jane were permanently settled in New York State. His wife, Elizabeth and the two youngest children, Henry and Caroline, were enrolled in the Rock Hill, New York, Presbyterian church in April 1838, some three months after Isaac launched his temperance venture.[7] Dan left the family in the same year of 1838 and went to live with his uncle, Lamon Harkness, in Bellevue, Ohio.[8]

Isaac's church, and all the other Presbyterian churches in the Maumee River valley surrounding Toledo, dissolved themselves in September 1840 because of internal dissensions. Like so many things concerning Isaac, his role in the churchwide dispute is unknown. But after 1840, his name disappears from church records and documents. He seems to have severed formal connections for almost 20 years. There are rumors that he went west to Illinois and then beyond the Mississippi to do missionary work.

How Henry reacted to the breakup of his family and his father's absence is not known. Henry rarely mentioned his father, and as far as can be told from letters and other documents, Henry ignored him for virtually all his adult life. When Elizabeth Flagler died in September 1861, Henry made elaborate funeral arrangements and had her buried in a brick vault. When Isaac died 15 years later, Henry didn't bother to attend the funeral.[9]

Because of the age differences, Henry's two older sisters had little influence on his life. However, as a boy, Henry's playmate was Caroline and his idol was Dan. Dan's bolt to the Harkness side of his family in 1838 would have a profound effect on Henry's life. It would bring him his first important job, his first business, his first fortune, his first wife and the humiliation of his first business bust.

By 1839, Henry and his mother were settled in Medina, New York, some 25 miles east of Niagara Falls. There, Dan and Henry began to exchange letters. It is unclear whether Isaac was with his family at this time. Judging from Henry's remarks about "lean pay which my father received by preaching," we can fairly infer that Isaac lived either at his father's home or nearby and had some income, probably from substituting for other pastors. To bring in extra income, during school summer vacations, Henry tried odd jobs as farm hand, store clerk and stable boy. For a time he worked as a deck hand on one of the Erie Canal boats running out of Medina, but that, too, didn't last.

Henry's thoughts were turning westward, to Ohio. Dan Harkness had written him that he would like it, and that there were opportunities for fortune.

Like many boys, Henry felt he had already been educated to the point of absurdity, so he studied Dan's letters instead and dreamed of Golconda, of the Seven Cities of Cibola. Why, with a little luck, he would win vast treasures of gold and emeralds. He would come back in a couple of years and lift his family from the weight of toil and the never-ending harassment of creditors. My, would he cut a figure then. . . .

We don't know how Henry won the approval of his mother to quit school, but she probably agreed only on the promise that he continue his schooling later. He would promise, of course, knowing full well that a hundred thousand classes could assemble and graduate before he'd ever again drag books and slate to a schoolhouse door.

Henry had made his decision. And on an early spring night, with tousled blonde hair and those clear, almost lavender eyes, he would have watched his mother rocking in a chair on the porch. In her right hand, leathery and prematurely aged, she would hold a soft, leafy willow branch to swat the bugs, the chiggers and gnats, mosquitoes and horseflies which tormented her to distraction.

His bag in hand, he took a last look at his home. The stone fireplace with its heavy oak mantel. The faded rugs, preserved by his mother from better days. The horsehair sofa and chairs, more of his mother's heirlooms, each with its starchy white antimacassar. His father once had wanted to sell the couch and chairs, but his mother had made a strong objection. She had said they were an investment, to be used by the daughters during courting. And two of them were now well married. In his mind's eye, Henry could see Elizabeth in the parlor now, rocking and knitting in her chair. Lit from within, with a kind of light which, in his adoring eyes hid the gray hair and the lines and splotches of age and hard work. She was beautiful, forever young and blonde and glowing.

Softly, he closed the door behind him. Dawn had just arrived. The morning was clear, cool and smelling sweet. His joy returned and happily he went off, down the road.

Although Medina was an interesting little canal town, Henry lingered there just long enough to make plans for his journey on to Buffalo, some 30 or 40 miles down the Erie Canal. Within a few hours he found a small boat headed for Buffalo which needed an extra crew member. Arriving in Buffalo late at night, he was required to unload the boat as part of the payment for his fare. From there, he booked passage for a boat to Sandusky.

It was early in the morning on Henry's second day away from home that the boat slid away from the dock. At last the whistle blew, and the huge side wheel began to turn. The boat thrashed out into the broad, rain-swollen lake, to the shrill squealing of pigs, the frightened cry of horses and not a few drunken hurrahs.

Once at sea, the entertainment fell into three divisions, none of which the boy could afford. The first was eating, in the boat's small dining room, which served breakfast from dawn to 10 in the morning and dinner from dusk until 8 P.M. The second entertainment, between meals, on the upper-deck, consisted of the gentry firing off pistols at objects in the water, with prodigious wagers riding on each round.

The third pastime, after the dinner tables had been cleared and the dining room became a saloon, was poker.

Henry would have loved to use the dining room, but he had to take his meals from his knapsack. He found the shooting games imbecilic. But he liked to watch the poker games, enjoying the warmth of the cabin, the smell of cigars and the good-natured bantering between the whiskey-drinking, red-faced men.

The journey across the lake took three days and nights. On Henry's trip the weather was rough and he was terribly seasick. Also homesick. "I remember," he would later recall, "that I went ashore early in the morning. Weak and dizzy, I staggered along the wharf, between long piles of cordwood, and was mortified to think someone might see me and believe I was drunk. I paid twenty-five cents for a hot breakfast and felt better."[10]

The boy had landed in the Western Reserve, a huge tract of land in northeastern Ohio on the southern shore of Lake Erie which was opened to American land claims in the 1790s. The open land, part of the old Northwest Territory, included half a million acres of rich farming soil called The Firelands.[11]

This Ohio country was set up to test the declared ideals of the new United States. Established under the federal Ordinance of 1787, the territory was comprised of the country around the Great Lakes north and west of the Ohio River. Gradually it divided into the states of Ohio (1803), Indiana (1816), Illinois (1818), Michigan (1837), Wisconsin (1848) and Minnesota (1858). The area was known as the "valley of democracy" in which the pioneers saw a chance to better their condition on the fertile flatlands.

The laws forbade slavery and gave the vote to all men, regardless of race or creed, who fulfilled age, residence and land ownership requirements. (In the spirit of the times, however, other adults, such as women and propertyless males, weren't allowed to vote.)

Education was emphasized. All land grants contained a "section sixteen" allotment which set aside one-sixteenth of every square mile of land for the benefit of public schools. Otherwise, the land was free for the taking, and a flood of settlers followed the trail of buffalo and deer, Indian, priest, and trader into the clean, unused forests and prairies.[12]

The country was being pushed to the west by irresistible forces. The wagons had been on the move for decades: first beyond the

Hudson, then beyond the Alleghenies, then beyond the Mississippi, then on beyond to Oregon. Every day carts and covered wagons could be heard rumbling along the roads. Everything was in ferment. In the decade of Henry's birth, half a million immigrants had poured into the new nation. In the 1840s, the amount would triple. And not only was the country moving because of foreigners. There were other shiftings about. Girls were leaving the farms to go to mills in nearby towns. Grain fields were moving west. New cities were sprouting in Ohio, Indiana and even remote Missouri and Kansas. The rule of the old New York patroons was over, and new men had taken over, Andrew Jackson's men of the soil and log cabins and industrial ambition. The country was atremble with the rustle of life, and the wind of the future was blowing over the land.

YOUNG HENRY had landed at one of Ohio's loveliest sites. Sandusky, at the mouth of Sandusky Bay, anchors an archipelago of dreamlike beauty, mapped by French geographers in the seventeenth century but not settled until the 1830s, a village of ivy-covered churches and houses made of blue limestone.

But Henry, broke and intent on finding his cousin Dan, had little time for such attractions. He spent but a day and a night in Sandusky before starting the last lap of his journey—a 34-mile walk from Sandusky to Republic. Enroute, he stopped for a day or so in Bellevue, which was about halfway in between, to introduce himself to his employer, Lamon Harkness, uncle of Dan Harkness.[13] The 43-year-old Lamon was the younger brother of his mother's second husband. Formerly a physician, who had dropped his practice in favor of real estate and other commerce, Lamon was a prominent landowner and co-founder of Bellevue. His company, Chapman & Harkness, employed Dan at a branch general store in Republic.[14]

Republic had the standard rural American arrangement. A sawmill turned the local oak, chestnut, poplar and walnut into lumber. The local artisans built good houses. There was a shoemaker who made shoes, a tanyard which made leather, a saddler for harness and saddles, two tailors, a cabinetmaker for good furniture but no undertaker. Various seamstresses went from house to house making dresses, and all of these activities were advertised or otherwise reported in a local newspaper.

The blacksmith and wheelwright had a connecting door between their shops where they made plows, harrows, wagons and almost every farm tool. Within a few miles could be found local potteries making pots, crocks and jars. Farms produced wool for fabric, wheat and corn for bread, also pork, beef, mutton, chickens, ducks, turkeys, eggs, milk and butter, a variety of garden stuff such as apples, peaches, cherries and other fruits.

Henry had been given directions to Dan's house, and about ten minutes outside of town he found the road. It was more of a rockslide, really, cutting up a steep grade between thick woods of walnut and oak. After considerable huffing and puffing, he came into a clearing and there it was—a miserable-looking farmhouse. Its clapboard siding was warped and gray. The roof had holes in it and patches of shingles had been curled by the sun and ruffled up by the wind, looking sort of like dog's fur rubbed the wrong way. The doorsteps were gone, burned for firewood most likely, and the yard was full of rusty old kettles and tools. There were some faded pants and shirts on the clothesline.

It was bad enough to make a normal human being cry. But a teen-aged boy is a different species, and when Dan came bounding out of the house with a big "Halloo," Henry just about burst with happiness.

HENRY went to work immediately, imitating, he recalled later, "the man in the Bible who had but one talent. I went to work in a country store for $5 a month and my board."[15] He learned the business well, including

. . . some of the vanities and infirmities of human nature. We sold everything, from a pint of molasses to a corn planter.

There was a keg at the bottom of the cellar steps which was kept filled with brandy from a larger vessel. Three classes of people were in that region, but in separate communities—English, German and Pennsylvania Dutch. Out of that little keg, we sold one kind of brandy to the English at $4 a gallon, another kind to the Germans at $1.50 a gallon and still another kind to the Pennsylvania Dutch for what we could get. The keg taught me to inquire somewhat closely into the merits of that which is offered for sale. . . .[16]

Henry had a knack for salesmanship, and his reputation spread to other parts of northwestern Ohio. In nearby Rome (present day Fostoria) he came to the attention of C.W. Foster, who owned a general store. Foster took young apprentices into his store to learn the art and trade of merchandising and would not let them "gamble, mingle with women, nor marry, nor could they frequent taverns. They were to learn to read and cipher . . ."[17] Foster attempted to recruit Henry, but the youth declined, perhaps because of the restrictions that would have been put on his freedom.

Henry did, however, become close with Foster's son, Charles Foster, a future governor of Ohio, who liked to come to Republic and enjoy the beer and society offered by Henry and Dan Harkness. They became sort of a Three Musketeers.

In 1845, Dan, much to his surprise, was asked to move to Bellevue and join the partnership. Henry remained in Republic, managing the store.

The trio remained fast friends, however, and all was not grim labor. One weekend in 1847, with Henry and Charlie visiting in Bellevue, they had a few too many at the new Tremont Hotel, and the boys were asked to leave after running across tables and breaking dishes. They paid for the breakage and returned two weeks later for more of the same. The table running became sort of a regular thing.

In 1849, Henry was called to Bellevue and his salary increased to $400 a year—five times what he had been making. In Bellevue one could make a fortune. Founded by New Yorkers in 1815, the town had grown slowly until 1839, when the marvelously named Mad River Railroad was completed, linking Bellevue to Sandusky and Lake Erie. In 1852, a branch of the Toledo, Norwalk and Cleveland Railroad was built to Bellevue, further increasing its growth. The principal promoter of both railroad deals was the Chapman & Harkness company.

In Bellevue, Henry roomed with Dan and often accompanied him to the home of Lamon Harkness, where Dan was courting his first cousin, Lamon's daughter Isabella. Henry attended their marriage on August 23, 1849. There two younger Harkness girls, Mary 15, and Julia, nine, enjoyed keeping Henry company when he came with Dan. Julia had a crush on Henry, but it was Mary who would become his wife.

About this time, there arrived from New York a new Harkness on the scene: 31-year-old Stephen Harkness, Dan's older half-brother, the son of Dan's father's first wife. Stephen would prosper in Ohio and some 17 years later would provide the stake for the incorporation of the Standard Oil Company.

MEANWHILE, in Bellevue, Henry and Dan, blissfully unaware of the future, were in good, high spirits. A report on their activities, and the climate of the times, comes from a local historian, Thomas Latham, who found an old Stephen Harkness ledger book. Perusing the book at a meeting of the Firelands Historical Society, Mr. Latham reported that

We find in 1848 game after game of ten pins charged to Mr. Flagler, and in one instance ten glasses of beer recorded on the Doctor's [Lamon's] side of the account book. Evidently this was a treat for the boys . . . During the holiday season of this year business seemed to be brisk. I find a charge to D. M. [Dan] Harkness of three games ten pins, 30 cents, two cigars six cents . . . on January 22nd . . . it appears that Henry M. Flagler and Dan M. Harkness walked in and while discussing some very important business problem, had lunch; . . . two for 75 cents . . . while at the close of the business day Mr. Ziter, presumably the tailor of Mr. Harkness, is credited with cloth for a pair of pants, $3.50. . . . "[18]

The ledger book also traces the movements of Stephen Harkness.
"Along in the 50s, Stephen V. Harkness pulls stakes [from Bellevue] and moves to Monroeville, while Henry Flagler and Dan Harkness remain at Bellevue, operating under the name of Harkness & Company.
"In course of time, Mr. S. V. Harkness at Monroeville became a large operator in livestock, the account book showing large profits and again severe losses; this was when hog cholera struck the country . . ."
By this time, the 1850s, Henry had piled up considerable savings. In 1852, he was able to join with Dan and Lamon in buying out Judge F. C. Chapman's interest in the company. The new organization became known as Harkness & Company, and its first major enterprise was to build a distillery to service railroad workers and later to take advantage of the railroad for transportation of spirits to Cleveland and other markets. This opened a new outlet for grain.
In the meantime, Mary had turned from an awkward teenager into a beautiful, dark-eyed, dark-haired woman. She was frail, however, and each winter her father would send her to a warmer climate, usually to a boarding school in Savannah, Georgia. In a letter written

on January 28, 1852, 12 days after her eighteenth birthday, we find him scolding her for not reporting on her health.

. . . Though much pleasure to hear from you I confess I felt much disappointed that you neglected to say one single word in regard to your health which with us here at home is the all important subject and I felt the more disappointment because I had so often impressed in your mind my wish that you should be particular on that subject and let us know exactly how your health was from day to day . . .

. . . write me often and particular as regards your health and I will answer all your letters punctually. . . . Give my best respects to Madam and all my acquaintances in Savannah.[19]

On November of the following year, at a ceremony held in Lamon's home, Henry and Mary were wed. She was 20, in fragile health and about to spend her first winters since childhood in the north. He was 23, already prosperous, sturdy, and ready to take on the world.

They went to New York for their honeymoon, accompanied by another newly married couple, Mr. and Mrs. Charles Foster, the latter Henry's old friend. Foster, who would later become Secretary of the Treasury under Benjamin Harrison and two times governor of Ohio, recalled:

"Henry Flagler and I were married on the same day. I was married in Fremont and he in Bellevue. . . . We took the same train for our wedding trips east and with our wives were in a railroad wreck near a small town in Pennsylvania. The little tavern in the village was not half large enough to accommodate the passengers. I remember we sat up the balance of the night with our brides sitting on our laps to save space for the others."[20]

FOLLOWING the honeymoon, Henry and Mary returned to Bellevue where they rented a house. In six more years, however, Henry was able to present her with the showpiece of Bellevue, a magnificent Victorian residence on Southwest street called the Gingerbread House because of its hand-crafted ornamentation.

# CHAPTER 3

# Oil

John D. Rockefeller was a commission merchant in Cleveland, and I sent him a good many carloads of wheat, which he sold as my agent. I also had an interest in a distillery. It was immensely respectable in those days to manufacture and sell liquor. The distillery gave me an outlet for considerable grain. Nevertheless, I had scruples about the business and gave it up, but not before I made $50,000 in Bellevue.

—HENRY FLAGLER

A S Henry handed the keys of the mansion to Mary, the couple stood on the threshold of a magic moment in history—the uncovering of the vast natural resources of America.

It had taken a long time to happen.

Explorers from Virginia, probing for a pass, had penetrated across the Appalachian Mountains by 1671 and returned with stories of a fabled land. The passage, however, was lost and for two-thirds of a century no white man was known to have crossed.

In 1749, a lunatic, "wandering as was his wont during his paroxysms," crossed the dividing ridge and upon his return asserted that he had been upon streams whose waters flowed to the west.[1]

The next attempt came four years later, in 1767, when a North Carolina farmer named Finlay returned to his family after a long absence "with accounts of the marvellous beauty and riches of the country beyond the mountains."[2]

That same year, Finlay returned to the western lands with a party which included Pennsylvania frontiersman Daniel Boone. Boone would return with even more settlers.

The land across the mountains was a paradise the likes of which had not been seen in the New World or the Old. Watered by many streams, it was the Indians' legendary "Happy Hunting Ground," in

18

which roamed vast herds of elk and deer disturbed only occasionally by a hunting party. Here were buffalo in herds of thousands; buffalo which, within 60 years, would no longer exist east of the Mississippi. Here were forests unencumbered by brushwood, stretching like a vast park from horizon to horizon. Poplars and sycamores grew a hundred feet high. From the abundant earth burst forth springs and streams, vast meadows and numerous salt licks. Pheasant, grouse and passenger pigeons, delectable to eat, made the sky dark with their flight, putting the sun into eclipse.[3]

Also to be found was a strange substance floating on top of some of the streams. Oily and slick, it would burn if touched with a flame.

The earliest record of oil's presence in North America seems to have come from the pen of a Franciscan missionary, Father Joseph de la Roche d'Allion, who traveled through what is now western New York in 1627 and saw "some very good oil." It is generally believed that his reference was to an oil spring near the present site of Cuba, New York. Several Jesuit missionaries, visiting that region in 1656 and 1657, apparently found the same spring. They reported that it contained a "heavy and thick water, which ignites like brandy and boils in bubbles of flame when fire is applied to it."[4]

In the fall of 1700, the governor of New York sent His Majesty's chief engineer in America, Colonel Wolfgang Romer, to visit the Five Nations and, among other things, instructed him to "view a well or spring which is eight miles beyond the *Sinekas* furthest Castle, which they have told me blazes up in a flame when a light coale or firebrand is put into it; you will do well to taste the said water, and give me your opinion thereof and bring with you some of it."[5]

THE BURNING "WATER" that intrigued the governor had been described by Herodotus and other ancient writers. In building his ark, Noah was commanded to "pitch it within and without with pitch." DeSoto caulked his boats with "pitch." Greeks and Egyptians used petroleum to lubricate chariot wheels. In his will, George Washington described "burning springs" on his lands in Pennsylvania and West Virginia that were "luminous and inflammable by nature."[6]

Petroleum was used in mortar, for coating walls and boat hulls, and as a fire weapon in defensive warfare. In Europe it was scooped from the tops of streams or dipped from holes in the ground, and in the early nineteenth century small quantities of it were extracted from shale. As early as 1814, DeWitt Clinton—U.S. senator, governor of New York State and mayor of New York City—suggested that oil from Cuba, New York, be used for lighting cities. In 1815 several streets in Prague were lighted by petroleum lamps.

IT HAS BEEN a common notion that America and its riches lay ready for the taking, an open paradise of natural treasures. But when Flagler came to Ohio, America's natural riches were almost unknown. The tin makers of New York got their sheets from Europe. The rum makers of New England imported molasses from the British West Indies. American blacksmiths made horseshoes from iron, imported mostly from Great Britain. The first textile mills used imported cotton. It was only later that the Southerners took up the planting of cotton. America's chief wealth was in grain, which was found east of the Appalachians. The making of flour and whiskey was the chief manufacture of the country. There was a little iron produced, and slightly more coal. But not enough to amount to anything. Men had not yet begun to scratch under the surface of the mountains and valleys. Henry arrived when they were just beginning to do so. When the nation was just beginning to discover its strength.

America also was looking for a source of artificial light. Most people went to bed at sundown. But light was needed for the new factories, for railroad trains traveling at night, for steamboats on the rivers— all needed light.

The most popular illuminant was the glass-chimneyed whale-oil lamp and the tallow candle, both made from the oil of the sperm whale. The industry was headquartered at New Bedford, Massachusetts, where the men went out to the sea in ships to fetch their oil from the whale.

By the middle of the century, however, whales were being killed at such a rate that ships had to range ever farther in their hunt for them. Whale oil was becoming scarcer and more expensive.

The emerging source for light was gas distilled from coal. As early as 1823, Boston, New York, Philadelphia and New Orleans all had gas-lit streets, using gas regulators imported from England. Coal gas illumination was rare in the West, but some of the finer homes burned lard oil made in Cincinnati. New mansions in the South burned cotton-seed oil made at Petersburg, Virginia; along the Gulf Coast resin and turpentine were distilled for camphine, a rather dangerous illuminant.

Substitutes were avidly sought but none proved satisfactory until 1850, when a Scot named James Young patented a method for getting liquid hydrocarbons from coal and shale. By 1857, when Henry and Mary moved into Gingerbread House, more than 30 plants in the United States had adapted Young's process and were making coal oil to burn in lamps.

Henry Flagler, who was fascinated with technological advance, lit his new Gingerbread House with coal oil lamps.

The use of oil lamps was building a market which promised attractive rewards to those who could find a plentiful, inexpensive source for light.

Another innovator was Dr. Abraham Gesner, an engineer on Prince Edward Island, Canada, who had distilled a flammable liquid from coal shale. He called it *keroselain*, from the Greek term meaning "waxy oil." Later the term was shortened to *kerosene*. Refineries sprang up in the East using Gesner's technique. The days were numbered for the whale-oil businesses of New England.

Thus, by the time of the Gingerbread House there were two popular sources for illumination—coal oil and kerosene. Petroleum wasn't given much thought as a source for lamps but seemed to have medicinal value, particularly for gastric disorders and as a balm for wounds.

The best-known sources of petroleum were Cuba, New York, and the area in Pennsylvania bounded by Oil Creek, French Creek and other tributaries north of the Allegheny River. The latter area had been settled by farmers in 1796, the first town in the region being named Titusville after Jonathan Titus. At first the farmers regarded the oil they found as a nuisance, ruining the purity of the streams. But soon they regarded it quite differently, as buyers from Pittsburgh came up on foot or on horseback, taking away all the oil they could carry and reselling it as a medicine called Seneca Oil, named after the Indians of the area. Soon, the people of Titusville were selling all they could dip from their springs at a dollar a gallon.

One of the larger springs was located south of Titusville, on the land of Brewer, Watson and Company, a lumber firm. Every now and then the firm would sell off some of its oil. Ebenezer Brewer of the firm had a son back in Vermont, a physician, to whom he sent samples. After Dr. Brewer tried it in his practice and found it useful as a medicine, he came to look at the springs.[7] He was excited by what he saw, and soon afterward, on July 4, 1853, there was signed the first lease in the United States in connection with the development of oil, made between Brewer, Watson and Company and J. D. Angier of Titusville.

In return for a share of the profits, Angier agreed to maintain the Brewer production facilities. He would repair and keep in good order the old oil spring, and develop new springs from which to seep oil; when the expenses were deducted from the proceeds of sales, the balance, if any, would be equally divided. Rude trenches were dug to convey the oil and water to a central basin, and by the use of some crude and simple machinery, erected at a cost of about $200, the oil was separated from the water. The men collected three or four gallons a day. It was considered a goodly amount at the time, and the supply was believed to be inexhaustible.

Upon returning from the springs in the fall of 1853, Dr. Brewer carried a bottle of petroleum with him on a trip to Hanover, New Hampshire, to visit with relatives and friends. While there, he passed it to a friend at Dartmouth College for analysis. It was seen in the laboratory by a Dartmouth graduate, a young lawyer named George Bissell. He was instantly enthusiastic.

Bissell was to be the midwife of the petroleum industry. In the summer of 1854 he visited Titusville. Upon his return, to entice investors, Bissell drew up an historic letter describing the find:

A creek known as "Oil Creek" runs through a portion of Venango Co., Pa., having received its name from the fact that in certain places an oleaginous liquid rises to the surface of the water, especially when the bed is stirred up with a pole or otherwise. The portion of the Creek containing the oil runs through a low bottom land, and upon this land west of the Creek are various springs yielding the same oil in abundance. It is susceptible of proof that Seneca Indians who formerly owned the territory were in the habit of procuring this oil and selling it to the French who then had a settlement at Franklin situated at the outlet of the Creek upon the Allegheny River. It was called by them "Seneca Oil" which name it has always retained in that vicinity, although it has also received the name of "Petroleum" or Rock Oil. There still exist abundant traces of the Indian excavations and one spring has been worked almost uninterruptedly since 1756 and the yield continues undiminished. . . . [8]

Bissell convinced others to join him in forming the world's first oil exploration company, The Pennsylvania Rock Oil Company of New

York. Incorporated on December 30, 1854, it eventually evolved into the Seneca Oil Company, which in May 1858 dispatched to Titusville a railroad conductor and handyman, "Colonel" Edwin Drake.[9]

Drake would change history. He would invent a means to "drill" for oil. He would bore beneath the ground with a metal auger and literally rotate, or "drill," the oil up to the surface. Drake did not invent the technique of drilling, which was already being widely used in America and Europe to bring up salt. Nor did he invent oil wells. A year earlier, commercial wells had been dug in Romania—large pits in the ground which were allowed to fill with oil. Although apparently ignorant of the Romanians' advances, Drake, like them, was convinced that the way to get oil was to dig in the ground and "mine" it; dig a hole deep enough, he thought and it would fill with oil. Thus, Drake combined the American technique of salt drilling with the Romanian idea that if one dug deep enough one would find oil.

MEANWHILE, 150 miles to the west in Bellevue, the days were happy ones for Mary and Henry Flagler. They were among the town's leading citizens and were surrounded by brothers, sisters, uncles, parents and other relatives, each in their place also secure and prosperous. In 1855, Henry's parents had retired and moved to Bellevue to spend their last years. With them came Caroline Flagler, the half-sister who had been a favorite of young Henry. Henry, although only in his twenties, had already built an excellent reputation as a man and a businessman and a modest fortune as well. He was also building a family. His and Mary's first child, Jennie Louise, was born in March 1855. A second daughter, Carrie, was born some three years later in June 1858. In the meantime, Henry was adding to his business experience daily and compiling savings of $10,000 or more each year.

Socially, these growth years were quiet ones. The young couple usually spent their evenings at home with their daughters alone. They were members of the Congregational Church in Bellevue, as there was no Presbyterian Church in the community.

The Flaglers were particularly close to a couple nearer their own ages, Mary's sister Julia and her fiancé, Barney York. York was a newcomer to Bellevue and was employed in the Harkness-Flagler business.

During this time, too, a regular visitor to the Flagler house was a young, ambitious produce broker who sold grain on commission and had cultivated Henry as a customer. His name was John Davison Rockefeller.

ROCKEFELLER was headquartered in Cleveland, which by the mid-1850s had become a sprawling town huddled around the flats on the Cuyahoga River running out to Lake Erie. The first railroad had entered Cleveland in 1852, and growth had been rapid. Cleveland had two medical schools, a university, various academies, a museum, a library and several literary and music organizations. There were gaslights, plank roads, railroads, well-established banks, two-score churches and industry with great promise, which further attracted wealth and population.

There were paved and lighted streets and an air of prosperity. Theaters shared in the flush of good times. Organizations combed the country to bring the brightest names on the lecture platform to Cleveland. They included Henry Ward Beecher, Ralph Waldo Emerson, Horace Greeley, Edward Everett, Horace Mann and Bayard Taylor.

Among the newer arrivals in Cleveland were the Rockefellers from western New York state.

THE ROCKEFELLERS, like the Flaglers, were of Palatine German descent.

The family emigrated in 1722 when Johann Peter Rockefeller came from Sagendorf in the Rhineland to Somerville, New Jersey. The maternal side of John D. Rockefeller's family had been in America even longer, beginning with Christopher Avery, who had emigrated from Devonshire, England, to Massachusetts in about 1630.[10]

Ida Tarbell, a talented but relentless and hostile biographer of the Rockefellers, once wrote of John's father, William Avery Rockefeller, that he had "all the vices save one." He did not drink. Father William was possibly the most interesting and certainly the most mysterious of all the Rockefellers. He seems as far removed from John D. in personality as is possible. Where John D. was quiet, religious, conservative, restrained and proper to an almost painful degree, Father William was outgoing, boisterous, restless and careless of the conventions.

In the wild country, west of the Hudson, west of the Alleghenies, William made a very good living as a peddler of patent medicines and miraculous cures, often made of the same substance that would make his son the world's first billionaire. William spent many months of the year away from his home, swinging about the frontier with his wagon full of medical goods and with syrupy assurances of good health for each and every customer. No ailment was beyond his powers, to judge by his handbills which read: "Dr. William A. Rockefeller here for one day only. All cases of cancer cured unless they are too far gone and then they can be greatly benefited."

William loved to chase the girls, but married a lady of upbringing and high moral standards, Eliza Davison. They moved to Moravia, New York, in 1843 and then on to Owego in 1850, finally breaking the ties with New York three years later by moving to Ohio. Bill Rockefeller set up his family southwest of Cleveland, in a village called Strongsville. There Bill, an unlicensed "physician," established a new headquarters for peddling medicine, keeping it a secret in the town but working it on the road. Bill Rockefeller's move was motivated not so much by a desire to be in Ohio but by a powerful wish to leave New York State, where he had legal problems arising from debts and a paternity claim. There is nothing to indicate that the selection of Strongsville was anything more than a random choice.

John D. was 14 and his brother William 13 when the move interrupted their schooling at Owego Academy. There was no high school in Strongsville; indeed the closest was the one high school in Cleveland, and that was 15 miles away, too far for daily commuting by horse or foot. But William was determined that his sons would have schooling and he could afford it. So he boarded the boys in downtown Cleveland and enrolled them in Central High School.

The student enrollment at Central was small, high school being something of an educational luxury at that time. But John and William found themselves among interesting classmates, including 16-year-old Marcus A. Hanna and pretty, shy Laura Celestia ("Cettie") Spelman. Cettie would marry John D. Rockefeller, and Mark Hanna would become a U.S. senator, a president maker and, for a time, the most powerful politician in the nation.

Elsewhere, the land was likewise filled with obscure boys and young men who would lift America from a struggling nation of farmers and inventors to an economic miracle.

In Pennsylvania, Andrew Carnegie, barely 20, was getting $35 a month as a secretary in the telegraph department of the Pennsylvania

Road in Pittsburgh. Thomas Edison, a boy of eight, was a pupil at the village school of Port Huron, Michigan. William McKinley, Hanna's protégé who would become President of the United States, was a student at Union Seminary in Poland, Ohio. And John Sherman, whose financial tip to Henry Flagler's half-brother would indirectly finance Standard Oil, was a 32-year-old Whig congressman.

Philip Armour, who would be a meat-packing king of such efficiency that no "part of the pig would go to waste except the squeal," was working as a miner in California. The great railroad kings were struggling through various kinds of education. Jay Gould, just 21 years old, was making railroad surveys. Collis P. Huntington was in the hardware business in Sacramento. George Pullman, 24, was working in warehouses on the Erie Canal. E. H. Harriman was entering Trinity School, and John Pierpont Morgan, a youth of 18, was at school in Germany.

BIG BILL ROCKEFELLER had a simple and practical program for educating his sons: "I cheat my boys every time I get a chance. I want to make them sharp. I trade with the boys and skin them and just beat them every time I can."

John admired the fact that his father never carried less than $1,000 in his pockets—this at a time when a thousand dollars was a large sum to have even in a bank.

John, who had deep affection and respect for his father, acknowledged the efficacy of Big Bill's tutorials: "To my father I owe a great debt in that he himself trained me to practical ways. He was engaged in different enterprises; he used to tell me about these things, explaining their significance; and he taught me the principles and methods of business. He used to dicker with me and buy things from me. He taught me how to buy and sell."[11]

WHEN John started high school, Cleveland's population was up to 17,000. A Board of Trade was promoting the name of the town far and wide. There was already a medical school and two hospitals. The Lake fleet was famous and prosperous, bringing in the first iron ore that year. Stagecoaches arrived several times daily with new settlers, visitors and traveling men. But, despite the spread of commerce, Cleveland depended on two industries—the receipt of produce from Ohio farms and its transfer to the East; and the handling of the flood of travelers flowing in from the East, headed west. The Republican party was formed in Jackson, Michigan, in July 1854, to fight the further extension of slavery. In October of that year, the new party won the state election in Ohio.

John's preoccupations, however, were closer to home. He was absorbed with his studies at high school, and to further his weekend social life he enrolled in sunday school at the Erie Street Baptist Church. The church was later to be known as the Euclid Avenue Baptist Church, and John D.'s friends and contacts were to come from the sunday school rather than the high school. He seems to have been a normal, hard-working student, not otherwise noticeable except for an intense concentration on earning money. Mark Hanna once said that his old schoolmate Rockefeller was "mad about money, though sane in everything else."[12]

IN CLEVELAND, in Bellevue, throughout Ohio, the 1850s were prosperous years. Opportunities were many, and making money was easy for men like Big Bill Rockefeller and Henry Flagler. The golden days, however, already were being threatened by the increasing ferment between North and South. Ohio was the bridge between the slave states south of the Ohio River and the freedom which could be found in Canada.

Ohio barns, Ohio sheds and Ohio farmhouses constituted the stations on the hit-or-miss "Underground Railroad." Friendly Ohio abolitionists smuggled escaped slaves from station to station, usually at night. Defying the federal Fugitive-Slave Act, which ordered the return of the runaways, the abolitionists pursued their ideals at great risk. Among the leaders was Owen Brown and his even more radical son, John. Oberlin, seat of a newly established college, was a major center of the abolitionist movement.[13]

Cleveland citizens silently provided havens for the fugitives, and decades later basements and secret passages in fine old houses still bore the mark of confinement in slavery days. Trembling slaves climbed the long, steep ascent to the belfry of St. John's Episcopal Church on the West Side, where they found refuge until signal flashes caused them to embark on the final lap of their journey to Canada.

The city also was a hunting ground for professional slave hunters. Protected by the Fugitive-Slave Act, they prowled the cities like wolves among the fold, looking for runaways.

An arrangement provided for the ringing of the Stone Church bell when one of the slave hunters was seen in the city, and a five-dollar reward was offered by an ardent abolitionist to the first person sounding the alarm.

In 1855, Bill Rockefeller followed his sons to Cleveland and moved into a house at number 33 Cedar Street. It was a 12-room house with an indoor bathroom, a marvel which the family managed to show to all visitors. Bill advertised himself in the Cleveland directory as "Botanic physician," meaning a "doctor" who specialized in giving out medicines, herbs and elixirs.[14]

YOUNG JOHN received his high school diploma on July 16, 1855, when he was already at work in Folsom's Commercial College, where he spent the remainder of the summer. He concentrated on bookkeeping and learned the rudiments of mercantile practice, banking and exchange.

In late August, he began to comb Cleveland for a job. He refused to think of a clerkship in any shop, for he wanted a job that would lead to the establishment of his own business. "I went to the railroads, to the banks, to the wholesale merchants," he said later. "I did not go to any small establisments . . . I was after something big." The search went on for weeks. Rebuffs meant little. "I was not discouraged because I was working every day at my business—the business of looking for work. I put in my full time at this every day."

Rockefeller had no letters of introduction, for he knew no Cleveland businessmen. He instead went to the City Directory and copied a list of the important firms and went calling. Day after day he tramped the city streets in the humid summer heat. But despite the prosperity, there were no jobs for his particular skills and experience. After a month of being turned down, Rockefeller later reminisced, "one man on the docks told me that I might come back after the noon meal."

John departed in dignified manner, but once out of sight of the man, he skipped along the street in boyish exultation. "I was elated but in a fever of anxiety lest I should lose this opportunity," he would say. After what seemed a proper interval, he presented himself to the man, Henry B. Tuttle, and was told:

"We will give you a chance."

John became an employee of Hewitt & Tuttle, a wholesale commission and produce company with headquarters on the Cuyahoga

River. Tuttle and his senior partner, Isaac L. Hewitt, were well known in Cleveland. Hewett was a founder of the Cleveland Iron Mining Company, which had been organized in 1850 and was one of the first operations to bring out ore from the Michigan wilderness.

Hewitt, a pleasant and friendly man, introduced John to the office routine, explaining he was to assist Tuttle with the bookkeeping. He began work on September 26, 1855, a day Rockefeller always remembered.

He stayed there three and a half years. His principal employer, Isaac Hewitt (Tuttle retired in 1856) was kindly. The job brought John into daily contact with railroads, lake steamships, merchants, jobbers and primary producers. He received steady salary increases, rising from $15 a month to $25 a month; then to $500 a year; and in 1858 to $600 a year. Late in 1858, he asked Hewitt for a salary of $800. But the firm was "really bankrupt," as Rockefeller said later; it offered him only $700. Early in 1859, he began looking for larger fields. Another clerk also was unhappy over his prospects, a young Englishman named Maurice Clark.

The two decided to form a partnership as commission merchants in grain, hay, meats and miscellaneous goods, each investing $2,000. Clark, by industry and frugality, had saved his stake. Rockefeller had only $900 in savings. But his father had promised each child $1,000 at age 21, and John proposed that his father advance him the money at once, paying interest for the 16 months remaining until he came of age.

On March 18, 1859, Clark & Rockefeller opened their doors at 62 River Street. The firm prospered, making a gross of $450,000 in their first year.[15]

Their business was strictly grain and produce. (Cleveland was surrounded by truck gardens, orchards and vineyards. Hundreds of acres were planted in wine grapes, and Cleveland was the largest shipping point for grapes in the United States.) Oil was not yet a matter of interest, except to Drake and his handful of colleagues in Pennsylvania.

At about the time Drake started drilling, three small stills in Cleveland were refining a smelly, tarlike oil from coal at the rate of about a barrel a day. Citizens were oblivious of the activity to the east; indeed, the two main topics of conversation, judging by the newspapers, were the increasing tensions with the Southern states and the city's new chain-gang system, which used prisoners to clean the city streets. Prosperous citizens found guilty of infractions were laboring with pick, shovel and broom in silk hats and frock coats by the side of petty offenders and thieves. Heavy iron balls were chained to each member of the crew.

After the establishment of Clark & Rockefeller, John decided to try his hand at customer development. It was an imaginative departure from commercial practices of the day.

Said Rockefeller, "I began to go out and solicit customers—a branch of work I never before attempted. I undertook to visit every person in our part of the country who was in any way connected with the kind of business that we were engaged in, and went pretty well over the states of Ohio and Indiana. I made up my mind that I could do this best by simply introducing our firm, and not pressing for immediate consignments. I told them that I represented Clark and Rockefeller, commission merchants, that I had no wish to interfere with any connection they had at present, but, if the opportunity offered, we should be glad to serve them.

"After I stayed in the country a few weeks, I returned home and the consignments came in."[16]

It was on one of these expeditions, in 1858, that he met Henry Flagler in Bellevue, Sandusky County, Ohio, heart of lush corn and wheat country. The Clark & Rockefeller firm began handling consignments from Flagler regularly from the summer of 1859 onward.

That same summer, on Independence Day, 1859, four days before John Rockefeller's twentieth birthday, the abolition terrorist John Brown secretly bivouacked in a Maryland farmhouse with his "army of 21 men." They were training for the thrust that would "rally Negroes everywhere and end slavery forever."[17]

Almost due north of them, in western Pennsylvania, Ed Drake was drilling his well. By a coincidence, in that part of Crawford County where Drake was occupied, John Brown had homesteaded 30 years earlier and there had buried his first wife, Dianthe.

The techniques of drilling into the ground to extract liquids was already worked out. Men seeking saltwater to distill for salt had used drilling methods for some 50 years. Drake, over the months, brought in the tools, built a derrick and enginehouse, and found a driller. The local folks were generally inclined to scoff at his attempts. But Drake said he would stick with it until he proved, once and for all, whether one could produce petroleum in quantity by boring into the ground.

His answer came on August 27, 1859, when at 69-and-a-half feet he punctured a rock dome, and the hole he had made with his drill filled with oil. In the first 24 hours, he pumped about 25 barrels. At the moment, oil was selling at 40 cents a gallon, or $16 per barrel.

The news that Drake had struck oil was a signal for a rush such as the country had not seen since the California Gold Rush in 1849.

A few weeks later, a second well, dug by a Titusville tanner named William Barnsdall, was put down no great distance from the first. He used a hickory drill and found no oil in the first sand. But drilling 150 feet further, the drill struck a second sand, which was to yield 20 barrels a day. A month later a third well went in nearby and began pumping 70 to 80 barrels per day.[18]

The strike was further blessed by the fact Drake had drilled into one of the finest oil basins in the world. Unlike later finds, the Pennsylvania oil was pure and didn't require complicated refining. It was made of molecules that resist change even under heat and pressure, making it ideal as a lubricant.[19]

Drake's success triggered a boom, although the news came late.

On November 18, 1859, the Cleveland *Morning Leader* carried a brief item with an inconspicuous heading. It read that the "oil springs of northern Pennsylvania were attracting considerable speculation," and that there was "quite a rush to the oleaginous locations." It also noted that Drake's well "yielded 25 barrels of oil a day."

River Street was awash with the talk of oil. The coming of new wells confirmed the discoveries of Drake. Oil began to find its way to Cleveland. There was talk of erecting a refinery or two to handle the local trade. Several Cleveland businessmen met to look into the possibilities and appointed young Rockefeller to make the journey. In the spring of 1860, he set out to do so. He traveled by railroad to Meadville, then by team overland through the forest roads. As he reached the Oil Regions, he found the banks of Oil Creek, French Creek and the Allegheny River dotted with tall derricks and rickety engine houses with tall thin smokestacks, from which the black smoke poured over the once green farms of the creek. There was a steady stream of arrivals into the boom towns of Titusville, Oil City, Franklin, Meadville, Tidoute. Hastily constructed shacks were going up and rudimentary business streets were taken form, lined by small, rude, unpainted one-story affairs, roughly boarded stores, lawyers' offices, oil drillers, notaries, traders and many saloons. For each saloon, there seemed to be a church. Each day, one or more new wells came in.[20]

At Henry's Bend, men anchored a raft in the creek and began boring in the creek bed. At night, angry citizens cut the ropes of the raft. Fights followed. The raft went on with its drilling, its defenders camped at its edge with shotguns.

Rough men were coming in—floaters without money or plans, attracted by the tales of quick and easy wealth. The barrooms were crowded at night with boisterous, noisy adventurers playing cards, drinking whiskey, speculating and brawling. More serious men sat around the hotel lobbies—the American House, the Anthony Hotel, the Eagle House and dozens of others. The talk was of oil, oil, always oil, and sometimes about this new man Lincoln who had been named by the Republican party to run for President.

There were long lines of wagons, snaking in endless procession through the Regions. The nearest railroad station was at Corry, 16 miles from Titusville and Oil City. Meadville was 30 miles away and Erie, 40 miles. Pittsburgh became the first great oil market. It was reached by Allegheny riverboats. But Erie became the first important overland market. Oil was sent there and to railroad terminals by wagon.[21]

By the early 1860s, crude production had spread throughout five Pennsylvania counties lying between Erie and Pittsburgh.

The location and very nature of the product created the new industry's most serious problem—transportation.

Crude was heavy, flammable, bulky and difficult to contain by packaging. There were considerable losses from leakage. Compounding those problems was the location of the oil fields. By the early 1860s, the nation's rail network had expanded to connect all of the large commercial centers, especially those in the East. However, there was virtually no track to be found in the Oil Regions.

In the period 1859–1861, there were two alternate outlets for crude—one being the water route to Pittsburgh, and the second being by teamster to Corry, the nearest rail head. Either route began by hauling the crude to Oil Creek by mule, then loading the barrels on barges at Oil Creek, where it was either shipped directly to Pittsburgh or floated down stream for transfer to larger vessels for the trip down the Allegheny. In addition to hauling crude to Oil Creek, teamsters also had to haul thousands of barrels and empty barges upstream to reach the wells. Literally thousands of horses and mules met their death under the brutal strain of the work. Use of the small tributaries connecting the Regions to the river was both dangerous and expensive. Oil Creek was navigable only six months of the year; and, during the summer months, the water level was too low at spots to permit passage of the barges.

The first railroad constructed in the regions was the Oil Creek Railroad. Completed in May 1861, its track connected Oil City to Corry, Pennsylvania. From there, oil could be hauled east to New York or west to Cleveland. The railroad was financed primarily by oil-producing concerns in the Oil Regions.

Shortly afterward, the Pennsylvania Railroad ran a line from Pittsburgh to the Regions, thus providing a second connection to East Coast cities.

As early as 1850, the feasibility of pipelines to transmit gas and liquids had been recognized. Many cities already had developed gas and water delivery systems. The first pipelines in the Oil Regions, built around 1862, connected the wells to local refineries. But the expertise was lacking to carry the pipelines further.

Pipelines, which would later revolutionize oil transportation, were ridiculed when they were first introduced. Laying them was rugged work for tong gangs, so called because of the tool they used to carry lengths of pipe.

New fields were opening up and down Oil Creek and its tributaries, up and down the Allegheny River. The drilling spread throughout that section of Pennsylvania and into parts of West Virginia. At the same time, the country was learning, through the U.S. State Department, that oil was being sought in foreign lands. (As early as 1877, oil men from Titusville were drilling wells for the Chinese government among the headhunters who then inhabited Formosa.)

Ironically, and maybe tragically, one of the persons who benefited least from the boom was Ed Drake.

Drake had the means and opportunity to lease or purchase any quantity of land and was repeatedly advised to do so. But he rejected all counsel. When nearby wells were quickly struck, he realized his mistake. But it was too late, and after the bringing in of his own well he practically ceased to be a factor in the petroleum industry.[22]

Before the public and the press had absorbed Drake's achievement, it was relegated to the background. Seven weeks later John

Brown and his men rocked the country with their attack at Harper's Ferry. But Harper's Ferry rallied no Negroes; it only hastened the coming of the Civil War.

THERE IS no evidence that either Henry Flager or John Rockefeller gave a damn about the coming civil struggle. They were, perhaps rightly, tending to their business—John selling grain in Cleveland and Henry, along with his partners Dan and Stephen Harkness, making liquor in Bellevue.

They were not, however, oblivious to the oil boom.

There were three great divisions in the petroleum business: production, transportation, and refining. Furthermore, they were so intertwined that if any one party controlled a single division, he would have a fair show at controlling everything.

In the next few years, John would tackle the refining aspect and Henry would take on transportation.

# CHAPTER 4

# Civil War

Henry Flagler was a lively, though generous youth,
and in later years, a useful and progressive citizen. He
did not go to the front when war was declared, but he
provided canteens for the "squirrel hunters" who were
recruited to defend Cincinnati from invasion. . . .
—JACOB WALDECK, newspaperman[1]

AS 1860 opened, the air was full of the ugly talk of war. A
presidential election was looming. Cleveland, the largest city
on the lakes, was the last stop on the Underground Railroad.
The boats used to hustle runaway slaves to Canada were just a few
blocks from Rockefeller's place of business. By summer, 37 Ohio
citizens were in the county jail on charges of aiding runaways.

In the slums of Cleveland, there lived a day laborer named Samuel
J. Andrews, a man so poor that he was supported by his wife, who
went out among the families of Cleveland as a sewing woman. Although Andrews had no money in his pocket, he did have brains in
his head and set up a small still in the garage behind his home. He
tried one experiment after another in crude oil and soon became
convinced he could produce a good lamp oil. After the first year he
netted a profit of $500, more money than he had ever had in his life
before.[2]

The Rockefeller family had moved to 33 Cheshire Street. The
Flaglers remained at the Gingerbread House in Bellevue where Mary
was suffering from increasing illness. Henry had accumulated $50,000,
but his interest in the liquor business seems to have waned. He was
looking for something else.

Henry would not join the war. His wife was frail. His family
needed him. And, as both a serious reader of history and a practical
man, he saw no sense to it.

One wonders if he wasn't right.

35

From the founding of the Virginia colony in 1607 and the Massachusetts colony in 1620, there had existed on the continent two subnations, known then and later as the "South" and the "North." Differing in political, social and economic attitudes, each spent the next two centuries contesting a wide variety of issues, including taxes, fiscal policies, the rights of local government versus central government, foreign relations and slavery.

In the case of slavery, it wasn't that the South had an unnatural desire to enslave people. Or that the North was a more moral community. Slavery had been part of all of the original colonies. In the northern climates, however, slavery eventually proved unprofitable and, with compensation to the slave owners, had been phased out by the 1820s. In the South, with its economy and politics ruled by the plantations dependent upon slaves, there was no abolition.

What was at work, of course, was not morality, but the power of ideas. The idea that blacks should be as free as other Americans had power. And over that issue, North and South locked into combat— the former middle-class, industrialist and mercantile; the latter, feudal and agricultural. The welfare of the blacks was the objective of the battle but not the cause of the war. The cause was the natural collision between two differing economic and social systems, and the ambition of their leaders, competing for the same market.

Being very practical men, neither Henry Flagler nor John Rockefeller saw any convincing reason to risk their lives for such a cause.

Henry favored very strongly a compromise with the South and saw no reason why some workable plan could not be adopted, such as what had been done in the Northern states. Meanwhile, having no personal quarrel with the Southerners, he was not about to take the risks involved in military service.[3] He would instead tend to business.

THE GREAT industrial muscle of America was beginning to flex, and nowhere was the transition more vivid than in Cleveland, where horse-drawn barges still ambled through the canals; the white-sailed schooners still sailed into the harbor; heavily laden wagons and stagecoaches still rumbled and squeaked over the cobblestone streets.

Cleveland's population, however, had increased to 43,417, more than 44 percent of the residents being of foreign origin. The New

England element, the first settlers, represented a distinct minority although they were the leaders in the professions, in business and in industry.[4]

Elsewhere in the nation, Matthew Baldwin was building 100 locomotives a year. Robert Hoe was making rotary presses for Europe as well as America. Up in Hartford, the Colt Arms Factory was inventing a thing called mass production. Colt superintendent E. K. Root was doing away with handwork; he tooled up his machines and put everything on platforms and jigs and cranes. Businessmen said he was crazy. Social workers said he was an enemy of the people. But Colt paid him the staggering sum of $25,000 a year.[5]

The age of iron and the age of invention had dawned. From American minds came the telegraph, the cylinder printing press, the penny newspaper, the Atlantic cable, the sleeping car, the sewing machine, the passenger elevator and above all a process for the mass production of steel which allowed for the manufacture of stronger machinery, tools, wire and the structural framework of skyscrapers. Great factories were arising everywhere. McCormick was making reapers. Case was making threshing machines. Studebaker wagons were everywhere. Deere had invented the iron plow, which opened the prairies for farming. Epoch-making steps were thus being taken in American industry, and even the arrogant English appointed a commission to study American methods.

Motion—powerful, surging motion—churned the nation. Waves of new peoples flowed in from Europe; the immigrant trains moved endlessly westward, filling the Midwest prairies and crossing the Rockies. Increasing numbers of immigrants were attracted by the nation's prosperity. Germans predominated, followed by English, Irish, Scots and Welsh.

The vast natural resources of the continent were being uncovered—gold and silver and iron and copper and coal; the vast grain fields of the West and Northwest; the seemingly limitless timber.

Henry Flagler's Ohio was at the vortex of this economic churning which soon would be fueled by a civil war.

SLAVERY was the issue in the election of 1860. *The Plain Dealer* supported the Democrat Stephen Douglas, while Lincoln was strongly supported by *The Leader*. Lincoln carried the city and stopped in

Cleveland on the way to his inaugural. Citizens gave him a welcome, said the New York newspapers, larger than that of any other city on his tour.[6]

Then came the war.

It began at dawn on Friday, April 12, 1861. Confederate General P.G.T. Beauregard's force at Charleston, South Carolina, opened fire on the Union troops at Sumter, catching the harbor fort in heavy cross fire. Lincoln announced on Monday, April 15, that "combinations too powerful to be suppressed" existed in the South without the expansion of the national army. He issued a call for state militia volunteers. Ohio's quota was set at 10,153.[7]

Bands played "The Girl I Left Behind Me" as many of the volunteers went to camp in shirt sleeves; arms and equipment were scarce. At camp the volunteers had their first taste of war's privations—beans and coffee for supper and "the soft side of a pine board" for a bed.[8]

In the beginning, there was no draft, as Ohio and the other states faced a common problem of turning away thousands of volunteers clamoring for a chance to fight. Anxious company commanders wired that they could not hold their men together any longer without definite marching orders. Men frequently deserted to companies fortunate enough to have been ordered to battle.

The initial outpouring of volunteers far outstripped the government's ability to arm and equip the eager recruits. The Dayton *Journal* told Ohioans to be patient, for "uniforms, arms, equipments cannot be spoken into existence—their production requires time." The problem of inadequate food and clothing was particularly acute for Ohio troops. Word came from Philadelphia, where units were being assembled from several states, that "Ohio troops now here have been on our streets as beggars for food."

When Lincoln called for volunteers in 1861, Dan Harkness was among the first to go to Sumners Hall in Bellevue and enlist, but Flagler did not feel so compelled. He heard no moral call to become one of the dead or maimed. He was not alone. Other men of his circumstances didn't enlist, men such as Philip Armour, John Rockefeller and John Wannamaker. They, like Flagler, attended to business.

When the Civil War began, business profits rapidly rose for Flagler and the Harknesses. They dealt in salt, mess pork, breadstuffs

and other commodities needed by the Union armies, in clover seed
and timothy seed, in farm implements and materials; they became
agents for distant businesses. Their business was further increased
by the heavy demand for foodstuffs in Europe, especially England,
where the harvests of 1860–1862 were poor.[9] With Dan in the army,
Henry's work in Bellevue was heavy, routing grain purchased by the
government to the federal troops, a transaction which meant large
financial returns for him.[10]

DESPITE the profits, the year 1861 was a tragic one for Mary and
Henry. His mother died, to the grief of both. An even crueler blow
fell just before Christmas. The couple's daughter Carrie died on December 7. She was barely three-and-a-half years old.

To add to his preoccupations, Henry was considering selling his
liquor and grain business in Bellevue and moving elsewhere. There
were pressures from his wife's family, however, not to do so because
the company was shipping large quantities of wheat and fortified wines
to Cleveland where John Rockefeller, their commission agent, was
selling them at handome notes.[11] John D.'s dealings with Henry made
it possible for the two men to know each other well while they built
fortunes.

BUT there was more to war than profits. War ate men.

After the first flush of bellicosity came a bloody and humiliating
defeat at Bull Run on July 21, 1861, and the young men of the North
were no longer rushing to join the war.

Still a draft wasn't called. Newly appointed Secretary of War Edwin
Stanton, an Ohio man, was confident and predicted imminent Union
victory. But in April 1862, General Ulysses Grant lost 13,000 men at
Shiloh; three months later the Union's primary army, McClellan's on
the Virginia peninsula, was in retreat. The Union desperately needed
more men, and the desolated Stanton set in motion the machinery
for a national draft.

The national draft of 1862 was the first of four drafts which would
extend to the end of the war. It authorized the states to compel
military service of physically able men, aged 18 to 45, a range which
easily embraced Flagler and Rockefeller.[12]

Although the majority of eligible men complied with the law, or
the attention of the local draft officials, tens of thousands resisted

violently and non-violently. Hundreds of draft officials were beaten, and scores were killed in their attempts to round up recruits.

Others hired substitutes, paying the government $300 and the substitute whatever necessary, to replace them in the draft. New words were being added to the American language as other resisters "skulked" in desolate rural or crowded urban areas, working and living normally except when the draft enrollers came around. Then they would vanish. Still others "skedaddled" to Canada or the far West, as did Mark Twain who went to the Nevada Territory. Many resisters directly bribed draft officials, and many more feigned physical disability or claimed exemption on grounds of religious scruples or foreign birth.

Automatic exemptions went to telegraph operators, railroad engineers, workers in crucial occupations such as salt mining, and several specific occupations such as mariners in the merchant marine. Exemptions also were given to powerful political lobbies such as members of the judicial and executive branches of the federal government; congressmen and their aides; and customhouse and postal officials. Physical disability could be certified only by physicians specially appointed in each county by the governor. Provost marshals were hired to arrest all draftees who otherwise avoided service.[13]

The most controversial aspect of the draft law was the one that allowed a draftee to avoid service if he could hire a suitable substitute.[14] This was the law used by Henry Flagler and John Rockefeller to stave off the draft. As far as is known, Henry never felt the need to defend his action.

Rockefeller, on the other hand, did. He later explained he had a growing business on his hands, moving toward the immense wealth he so desired. "I wanted to go in the army and do my part," said John. "But it was simply out of the question. There was no one to take my place. We were in a new business, and if I had not stayed it must have stopped—and with so many dependent on it."

Henry's buy-out was simple. He appears to have paid $300 for a single substitute and taken no other action. The younger John, on the other hand, made more elaborate preparations. At the time John had $10,000 in cash tucked away in a strong box. As allowed by the draft laws, he paid the government $300 to allow him to be replaced by a substitute, then guaranteed to give the families of 12 soldiers each $300 a year until the war was ended, thereby pledging his entire assets.[15]

By avoiding service, men like Rockefeller and Flagler would make fortunes. More importantly, they would stay alive and thus be able to alter the direction of history.[16]

IN THE MEANTIME, Dan Harkness, who had volunteered in 1861, was garrisoned in Savannah. His wife, Isabella, and their two children remained in Bellevue. She and Dan had been married in 1849. They had had five children but three had died in infancy. When Dan went into the Union army in 1861, he left a despondent wife, who had never fully recovered from the loss of her babies.

Dan's army experience was, for the most part, that of brigade quartermaster for the 72nd Regiment under Gen. R. P. Buckland. While serving with Buckland, in the army of General William Tecumseh Sherman, false rumors arose that Dan had been arrested for selling government stores on the black market. The rumors were printed in a letter to the Fremont (Ohio) *Democratic Messenger.*

Dan was immediately and energetically defended by Henry Flagler, who arranged for a body of Dan's army comrades, including his commanding officer, General Buckland, to write testimonials as to the untruth of the accusations. When the *Messenger* refused to print the rebuttals, Henry arranged for publication in other local newspapers.[17]

Dan was discharged in late 1863 and returned to Bellevue. Shortly afterward, in February 1864, his and Isabella's only daughter, Kittie, died at the age of eight years and six months. The sad event was followed by Isabella's death in July of the same year. Isabella was 34 years old.[18]

After the death of his wife, Dan sold his share of the liquor and grain business and retired. A man of ample means, he spent the remainder of his life in local politics and as a powerful figure in the Ohio State Republican party.

During the war, Dan and Henry's half-brother, Stephen Harkness, opened a liquor distillery and grain store in nearby Monroeville. The half-brothers and Henry worked separately as two organizations but cooperated to their mutual benefit. Indeed, Monroeville claimed Flagler as a resident because he spent so much time there.[19]

As THE WAR INTENSIFIED, so did Henry's restlessness. In the summer of 1862, he opened a grain-purchasing warehouse next to the railroad station in Norwalk but turned over the day-to-day operations to his Norwalk partner, George Vail.

During the Christmas holidays of 1862–1863, Henry, Mary and pretty seven-year-old Jennie Louise dropped all other matters to attend the marriage of Mary's youngest sister, Julia, to Barney York. The marriage thus brought a third son-in-law into the Lamon Harkness family.

Two months later, in February 1863, Henry abruptly sold all his business interests, including the Bellevue distillery and the Norwalk warehouse.

He moved to Michigan to buy into the war-fueled salt industry. It was a move indicative of Henry's attitude at the time—a move prompted in part by his desire to avoid the army but even more so by a hunger to *make it*, to be rich.

Salt, discovered in the Saginaw area in 1858, had been boosted by the Civil War demand into a boom industry. Prices were high, taxes low and the Michigan legislature had passed an act paying a bonus of 10 cents a bushel for salt produced in the state. The law also made salt-producing property tax-exempt.

Thus encouraged, a group of businessmen organized the East Saginaw Salt Manufacturing Company, whose founders included Henry's father-in-law Lamon Harkness. Aware of Henry's restlessness, Lamon had encouraged Henry and Barney to make a change to the salt business, offering any financing that might be necessary. One of Lamon's motives, apart from profit, was that the salt industry would exempt his two sons-in-law from the draft.

Flagler, Mary and Jennie Louise moved to East Saginaw in the spring of 1863, taking along Barney and Julia. Both men scraped up $50,000 each, with Barney borrowing his share from Lamon. They started a firm called Flagler & York, producing salt at Salina, now on Saginaw's south side.[20]

Incorporated in 1857, East Saginaw was already an attractive place with a host of tall old trees, nineteenth century mansions, street-corner water pumps, roaring sawmills and the Saginaw River, which flowed through the center of town, choked with logs.[21]

The Flaglers lived at 718 South Washington; the Yorks four blocks away at 1102 South Washington.[22]

Henry liked Saginaw, and although Mary continued in poor health, the presence of Julia kept her from becoming despondent among strangers. The Flaglers took an active interest in the community, including church, Henry becoming superintendent of the Congregational Church Sunday school, and a member of the board of trustees.

Flagler & York made money for two years, but it wasn't easy. Forced to learn the salt business from the ground up, they found the competition hotter than they could handle. In 1865, with the war ending, salt prices collapsed. The two lost their $100,000 initial investment, and Henry lost another $50,000.

Borrowing $50,000 from Lamon Harkness, at 10 percent interest, Henry paid off his creditors and left Saginaw at the age of 36. When he came back to Bellevue from Michigan, in January 1866, he and his family boarded with Sam Kingsley and his wife on East Main Street, a far comedown for a man who, less than three years earlier, had owned the town's most imposing mansion. For the first several months of 1866, Flagler worked in downtown Bellevue with a man named John Burger, selling felt wool. The Flaglers were so poor, and Henry so proud, that he secretly avoided eating lunch so that there would be food on the table at night for his wife and daughter. His secret was discovered, however, by an old friend named Peter Brady, later mayor of Bellevue and Ohio State treasurer. Brady began carrying a large lunch of his own upstairs to Flagler's desk. Sociably, he would insist on sharing his lunch with a protesting Flagler each day.[23]

Flagler had returned more or less a wounded warrior carried home on his shield. It was possibly the most humiliating time of his life and he never referred to the Bellevue interlude in the many newspaper and magazine interviews he gave later in life.

His standard comment simply omitted the Bellevue years, such as in this 1909 interview: "At the end of three years, I had lost my little fortune and owed $50,000 to about 50,000 Irishmen who had been working in the salt factory. My relatives by marriage and a half-brother loaned me enough money, at 10 percent interest, to pay my debts, and I removed to Cleveland and engaged in the grain and produce commission business."

IRONICALLY, Flagler's departure to Michigan to seek a fortune may
have cost him two fortunes. While he was away, Ohio was the scene
of major opportunities. Two examples: his half-brother Stephen Harkness made a killing in the liquor market; his former grain broker,
John Rockefeller, discovered that there was gold in oil.

Harkness's opportunity had come in the unexpected disguise of
the first comprehensive Internal Revenue Act of July 1, 1862. Among
other things, the law included a tax upon malt and distilled liquors.
The act was under the personal stewardship of U.S. Senator John
Sherman of Ohio, powerful member of the Senate Finance Committee. Like all the Harknesses, Stephen was a zealous supporter of the
Republican party and a longtime financial backer of Sherman, a personal friend.

Sherman was a good friend to have.

Born in Lancaster, Ohio, in 1823, John Sherman, brother of the
Union Army general William Tecumseh Sherman, was an organizer
of the Republican party in Ohio and presided over the first Republican
state convention in 1855. Elected to the U.S. House of Representatives in 1855, he served three terms there and moved on to the
Senate where, as part of the powerful Ohio congressional delegation,
he became instantly one of the Senate's most influential members.[24]

When it was certain that the liquor tax act would pass, Sherman
warned Harkness who immediately set forth distilling and stocking
up his alcohol supply. By the time the tax was announced, he enjoyed
a $2 a gallon advantage over his competitors.

This advantage wasn't easily won. To build his inventory of pre-
tax alcohol, Stephen dipped into deposits of the Perkins & Company
bank in Monroeville, which he owned. Indeed, he secretly used every
available dollar until the bank was almost completely looted.

Rumors began, and farmers who had funds on deposit became
alarmed. Harkness employed a decoy, a man named Hiram Latham,
to stand on the street and assure the anxious farmers that old Steve
Harkness was all right and was as good as gold.

The tension was fierce; for example, a man entered the bank and
demanded the cash for a couple of loads of corn amounting to $79.
Harkness talked to the concerned agriculturist about the prospect for
rain, while a Mister Gillett, the cashier, disappeared through the

back door to borrow this sum from S. B. Martin, a druggist, in order to meet the demand.

It was at this time, desperate for cash, that Harkness addressed the firm of Rockefeller & Andrews, commission merchants, Cleveland: "Why in hell don't you remit for the last car of corn I shipped you? Unless I get it soon I will bust."[25]

The law eventually passed, however, and Harkness was stocked from cellar to ceiling with all sorts of whiskey and wines made and stamped before the tax applied. He sold out his stock at the advanced price without having to pay the tax and made over $300,000 clear profit. This money would later become part of the investment funds which started Standard Oil.

THE STORY of the second opportunity missed by Flagler begins with John Rockefeller's entry into the oil business. During the war, the demand for petroleum rose rapidly, especially in Europe. Great Britain had been the first country to import American-made kerosene in large quantities, followed by France and Germany. In February 1863, a merchant in Frankfurt-am-Main was reported to have ordered 9,000 barrels of refined oil, selling it all in a German district which ten months earlier had never even seen the product.[26] By 1864, the citizens of Cleveland had begun to be aware of a nuisance along a stream called the Walworth Run. Little refineries had appeared there to distill petroleum into kerosene. From his store, John D. could see the unpleasant scum trickling down the run into the Cuyahoga River. Citizens complained, but nothing was done. Occasionally young Samuel Andrews would come over to Rockefeller's store. There were a couple of connections between Andrews and Rockefeller. For one, Andrews came from the same town in England as Rockefeller's partner, Maurice Clark. A second tie was the Erie Street Baptist Church of which both the Rockefeller and Andrews families were members.

By now, Andrews had a little refinery, a small affair of 10 barrels' capacity. Although Andrews was among the first in Cleveland to see that kerosene would supplant coal oil as an illuminant, he was desperately poor and totally devoid of business ability. He had gone into oil refining from candle making—a natural drift. He devised methods for getting a higher yield of kerosene from crude oil than his competitors and was the first to find a use for the residium as a fuel for his still. He continually pressed Rockefeller to join him, needing John's money and business expertise.

Although oil prices were dropping and the industry carried big risks, Rockefeller decided to join with Andrews. He persuaded his partner, Clark, to invest several thousand dollars and establish the firm of Clark and Andrews. Rockefeller invested a similar amount, but kept his own name out of it. Thus, entering by the side door, John D. Rockefeller was in oil.[27]

Clark and Andrews built a refinery on the high south bank of Kingsbury Run, the still-wooded tributary of the Cuyahoga, about a mile and a half southeast from the Public Square of Cleveland. Lying near the point where the run emptied into the Cuyahoga, it had water transportation to the lake, while it abutted directly on the tracks of the Atlantic & Great Western railroad.

In Cleveland, the demand for kerosene was growing. The old coal-oil business was swept away. The trade to Europe was growing. In 1862, Europe took 11 million gallons. In 1864, it took 27 million.

Flushed with new riches, young John married Cettie Spelman, his high school sweetheart, in August 1864. The couple moved into a house at 27 Cheshire Street, next door to his father's home.

JOHN was not yet wholly an oil man. His main business was still in dealing grain, and oil refining profits had tailed off due to dwindling supply. The change came—a momentous change—in January 1865, when a farmer named Thomas Brown found himself a hazel twig and went hunting for oil near the Allegheny River. Blissfully ignorant of the learned gentlemen of the universities who said not oil nor water nor any other commodity could be found with spirits and divining rods, farmer Brown walked the woods along Pithole Creek with his mystic twig and where it dipped he put down his drill. A few days later he hit oil, the well bringing in 200 barrels a day.

The news burst across the Regions like a gas explosion, and immediately prospectors began flocking to the spot. In January, when Brown started to drill, the neighborhood consisted of an old farmhouse and two unprofitable farms. By May, the countryside was sprouting derricks. In June, a town had been laid—two entire streets had been built, lined on both sides with shops, offices, dance halls and saloons. Pithole, the "magic city of Petrolia," had sprung almost full blown out of the forest.

By summer, Brown's well was producing 800 barrels a day, and the property was estimated to be worth $3 million. By October, the Oil Regions as a whole were producing about 10,000 barrels of crude a day, and Pithole was supplying 6,000 of them. By Christmas, the new city had a population of 15,000. Seven months before it had been a clearing in an unpeopled wilderness.

The city grew faster than order and government could hold it. Within 10 months, it had 50 hotels, three of them of the palatial sort. Its streets were lined with buildings, many of them good ones— schools, churches, banks and stores. But in Pithole and the other boom communities there were dance halls, saloons and gambling halls. The Union Army was being demobilized. Soldiers flocked to Pithole and the other oil towns. Creek settlements were filled with lieutenants, captains, colonels and even a few generals. As for the rank and file, released suddenly from the iron discipline of the army with pay in their pockets, they reveled in the style of Pithole's free and easies.[28]

The discovery of oil at Pithole caused John Rockefeller to abandon all other business and devote himself wholly to oil.

In the meantime, he decided to dump his partner Clark.

Andrews and Rockefeller had hit it off well together and decided to make a go of it by themselves. Clark, however, wished to keep the Clark and Andrews oil business, and proposed to buy out Rockefeller. The partners met to discuss it. Clark appeared with his lawyer. Rockefeller went alone. It was decided to collect all the cash assets of the oil business, pay the debts, and sell the plant and goodwill to the highest bidder. Someone said, "Let us sell them now and let the lawyer act as auctioneer." This suited all parties and the auction began. Clark bid $500. Rockefeller promptly raised the ante to $1,000. The bidding went back and forth. Rockefeller was surprised at the price Clark was willing to pay. But he had formed his own opinion of the value and he continued to top Clark's bid each time. Finally Clark said $72,000.

"Seventy-two thousand five hundred," replied the unhesitating Rockefeller. Clark threw up his hands with the exclamation: "The business is yours!" He generously added that Rockefeller need not write a check at once. "Settle at your convenience." They shook hands and parted.[29]

IN MOVING into the oil business, Rockefeller saw that competition was complicated by two powerful forces. One of these was the flood of raw materials pouring out upon the nation. The other was the widening of the markets. The country was producing with ease far more oil than it could use, thus the wild scramble of producers to sell and the utter collapse of price. Moreover, the railroads had now made almost the whole country both a market and a competitor for oil and oil production. A man was not only competing with his rivals in the town, but with innumerable rivals in other towns and states. Rockefeller saw the problem, but he was unsure of how to deal with it.

While pondering this, he paid what he called "attention to little details." He instituted economies in his operations. He began to make his own barrels. He did his own hauling. He bypassed jobbers and brokers and bought his oil directly from the wells. Soon, he was selling kerosene at lower cost than any refinery in Cleveland.

Rockefeller's private life was austere, although there were rumors he was a secret womanizer. As far as is definitely known, however, his life was wrapped around his family and his church. He had few friends, Flagler being perhaps the closest. From 1863 until early 1866, however, Flagler was involved in Michigan and later with his debts, and the two were not in contact.

Ida Tarbell, the biographer, historian and investigative reporter, talked with many men in Cleveland who knew Rockefeller and Flagler in the 60s. They told her that Flagler was the charmer, but perhaps the harder of the two. Flagler would smile, while breaking your back with a deftly worded contract. Rockefeller, on the other hand, rarely smiled and almost never laughed. The only sign of hilarity he ever gave was when he struck a good bargain. This would make him clap his hands. Let it be a very good bargain and he would throw up his hat, kick his heels and hug his informant.

In matters of money, Flagler was taciturn and undemonstrative. Rockefeller, on the other hand, sometimes couldn't contain his glee at a good deal. One time, Miss Tarbell recounts, he was so overjoyed that he kicked his heels and hugged himself and said: "I'm bound to be rich! Bound to be rich! *BOUND TO BE RICH!*"

# CHAPTER 5

# Cleveland

John D. and William Rockefeller and Samuel Andrews
had started a small oil refinery in Cleveland on the side
of a hill. When the second refinery was built, in 1867,
Stephen Harkness, who was related to me by marriage,
backed me for $100,000 in a partnership with Mr.
Rockefeller and his associates. Other little refineries sprang
up and we bought them. Our business was developed
rapidly. . . ."

—HENRY FLAGLER

NINETEENTH-CENTURY Cleveland, the city which was to
make both Rockefeller and Flagler rich beyond their dreams,
was an example of a strange but persistent phenomenon in
history: the sudden eruption of multiple genius at a specific time and
place. It happened in Periclean Athens, in Medicean Florence, in
Elizabethan England and in Jefferson's Williamsburg. When it strikes,
it roars through events like a forest fire with everything conspiring
to feed the flame. In a decade, or a generation, it burns itself out
and intellectual life returns to normal. Historians have offered no
convincing reasons as to why it happens but they argue persuasively
as to *how* it happens: contagion. And some, reducing it to a miniscule
scale, have traced it to instances of spontaneous combustion within
our own experience. At the mundane level, we see it in sport where
an athlete's powers can ignite a whole team. On grander sweeps of
the horizon we have seen it in a body of literature, such as in nineteenth century Russia which spawned such contemporaries as Dos-
toevski, Tolstoi and Chekov; or in music, such as the classicism of
Haydn, Mozart and Beethoven.

A similar explosion of genius, a conflagration of industrial and
entrepreneurial vision, burst forth in Cleveland in the latter half of
the nineteenth century.

CLEVELAND is among the oldest inhabited sites in the world, being situated in a basin of rich archeological finds, some of which date back more than 10,000 years.[1]

The first white settlement at the mouth of the Cuyahoga River was a trading post established in 1747 by the Irishman George Croghan, first British agent in the area. Among other early white settlers were David Zeisberger and John Heckewelder, Moravian missionaries who built a village for friendly Christian Indians on the present site of Cleveland.[2] Later, the land was bought and surveyed by the Connecticut Land Company, led by General Moses Cleaveland who held meetings with the Mohawk and Seneca representatives of the mighty Six Nations. After shrewd bargaining, the Six Nations relinquished their claim to the lands east of the Cuyahoga in exchange for 500 pounds New York currency, two beef cattle and 100 gallons of whiskey. It was not quite as good a deal for the white man as Manhattan, but almost.

Instructed to found a "capital town," Cleaveland laid out two main streets (Superior and Ontario) as broad as they are today. The 49 settlers endured the winter of 1796 and then forsook their capital by the frozen lake.

They returned a year later, and shortly after that the settlement's name changed from Cleaveland to Cleveland. The reason for the dropping of the "a" is disputed by historians.

When the first Great Lakes steamer, *Walk-in-the-Water*, steamed into Lake Erie in 1818, Cleveland was the smallest of 14 towns in the Western Reserve. Then, in 1832, the Ohio and Erie Canal was completed with Cleveland as the terminal, and in 1836 the city became incorporated, with 5,000 citizens. Mid-century, the railroads brought the first loads of Lake Superior ore and bituminous coal from the East. Cleveland was on its way.

From about 1860 onward, Cleveland was to be the center stage for a cast of characters gathering from all over the country for the coming gaudy drama of American business, the coming of the Gilded Age.

The men and women of Cleveland were destined not to merely pile up vast fortunes. They would create a civilization.

Until they came, the chronicles of American fortune building had not been very noble ones. In America's first 100 years, the way to get rich was to grab land and hold onto it, doing nothing, waiting for others to develop it and give it value. Most of these early fortunes were built by bribery or monopoly by people like John Jacob Astor, who amassed land and sat idly upon the acres while great cities grew around him through the energies of other men.

The fortunes of the next generation were for the most part acquired through downright frauds or stock-jobbing operations closely bordering upon fraud. The Jay Gould fortune was reared through a career of almost unparalleled security frauds. The great railroad fortunes of the West—of Huntington, Leland Stanford, Crocker and Mark Hopkins—were chiefly the fruit of gigantic frauds upon the government, upon the public through stock issues and upon stockholders through schemes directed against their own companies.[3]

Most of the fortunes of Flagler and Rockefeller's wealthiest contemporaries were made through stock manipulations, including those of J. Pierpont Morgan and Edward Henry Harriman.[4] In the Civil War, millions of dishonest dollars were made through political connections, such as those seen in the story of Stephen Harkness. Such fortunes were parasitic, collected without the performance of any important or necessary service to society.

In Cleveland, the Cleveland of this story, it was, for the first time, beginning to be different. The fortunes to be made would be derived from hard work, insight and contribution to society.

In the summer of 1866, Henry Flagler left his wife and daughter in Bellevue, and with Barney York drifted to Cleveland. Henry carried with him a patented horseshoe which he had invented and hoped to manufacture. Nothing came of it, however, and his despondency was such that he remarked to a friend one day that if he ever paid off his debts and got $10,000 ahead, he would retire from business.[5] Henry and Barney boarded with a family named Russell, and eventually they took a job selling barrels to Rockefeller and other refiners, putting their hand to anything they could find to do.[6]

Maurice Clark, Rockefeller's ex-partner and still a grain commission merchant in Cleveland, heard that Henry was having a hard time and offered him a job with his firm, Clark and Sanford. Henry cheerfully took the job and met with success from the start. Within a few months the firm began to show a noticeable increase in business, and the commissions enabled Henry to rent a house and bring his wife and daughter up from Bellevue. The good times continued. In 1867,

Henry made a lucky speculation, enough to pay off $20,000 of his debt to the Harknesses and to buy Clark's company.

Unbeknownst to himself, Henry's fortunes had permanently changed. Never again in his life would he be poor.

Once more he had money, possibly as much as $50,000. The Flaglers rented a larger home on Euclid Avenue. There were nine rooms in the two story structure, some of them often occupied by relatives.

Now, with his confidence and reputation restored, he began once again to drop by Rockefeller's desk to talk over the deals he was putting through and to listen to Rockefeller talk about oil. Flagler was a sympathetic audience—and more. With his sharp, practical imagination, he came forward with suggestions. Rockefeller meanwhile studied Flagler. He liked what he described as Henry's "vim and push."

In his *Random Reminiscences*, Rockefeller makes it clear that of all the men with whom he was associated through the years, none meant more to him than Flagler. He "was always an inspiration to me."

Flagler, in turn, said a friendship founded on business was better than a business founded on friendship.

When Rockefeller, in his 70s, was casting backward glances over his years and writing about his old-time colleagues, it was Flagler to whom he gave the most attention. Said Rockefeller of Henry: "He invariably wanted to go ahead and accomplish great projects of all kinds. He was always on the active side of every question and to his wonderful energy is due much of the rapid progress of the company in the early days . . . For years and years this early partner and I worked shoulder to shoulder; our desks were in the same room. We both lived on Euclid Avenue, a few rods apart."[7]

EUCLID AVENUE was the home of kings. Beginning at the southeast corner of Public Square, where stands the brooding Soldiers and Sailors Monument, it was described in the nineteenth century by the American writer Bayard Taylor, as "the most beautiful street in the world . . . the only honest rival of the Prospekt Nevsky in St. Petersburg, Russia. . . . "[8]

Bordered on each side with a double row of arching trees, and with handsome stone houses standing at intervals on large, broad lots, the vistas reminded one of the nave and aisles of a huge cathedral.

One of the grandest houses on Euclid was that of Rockefeller's partner Sam Andrews. Money had gone to his head, and he had built a home he considered fit for royalty. Contemporaries were divided about its grandeur. Some said it was the most elegant house ever built in Cleveland. Others said it was an overwhelming monstrosity. Done in the Victorian style, it cost a million dollars; its 33 rooms were laid out in a haphazard arrangement of a master suite, six apartments (one each for Andrews' six daughters), three kitchens and an assortment of stairways, dumb waiters and laundry and utility rooms which confused everyone, most especially the imported English servants.

Despite the confusion, it was grand enough. The first floor had six mammoth rooms, with a skylighted court in the center entranceway, lit by stained glass windows. Spiral staircases wound up on each side of the court.[9]

To live on Euclid Avenue was to be a member of a private club. Fashions were copied from New York, and a local editor reported sorrowfully that "duty compels us to announce that the days of big hoops and bulging crinolines are coming back. The narrow skirts of the past six months, pinned back so that the wearer had to go mincing along with dainty steps, were certain to be followed by excess in the opposite direction. . . . A lady will fill an opera box or a carriage and three will crowd a street car."[10]

The families along the elegant row were formidable members of the local society, and they demanded formidable houses as a mark of their station. All the homes were set back from the sidewalk with a pretty expanse of shady parkland for front lawns and smooth driveways to carry the carriages up to the front steps. Most were in the Victorian tradition, lavished with architectural bric-a-brac, with gables and towers, high-ceilinged rooms and tall windows. Others were of an antebellum–Greek Revival type, mansions with imposing high white pillars. It was an eye-stretching experience to stroll Euclid Avenue in its heyday.[11]

Although horses and carriages were the transportation mode of the day, the avenue invited walking, with its broad sidewalks overarched with massive shade trees. Both Flagler and Rockefeller have described how they left their homes at the same time each morning

in order to walk downtown together, passing stately homes owned
by men with whom they had frequent contacts in the course of a day's
business.

Both men had their offices in the new Case Block, on Superior
Street east of Public Square. It is a considerable distance to cover on
foot, and doubtless there were times when they went back and forth
by horse and carriage, or on horseback. Whatever the mode of transportation, they used the time profitably. "Free from office interrup-
tions," Rockefeller said, "we did our thinking, talking and planning
together."

The men who walked Euclid were the kings of Cleveland, a ferment of creative and energetic men which included not only Flagler
and Rockefeller, but Mark Hanna, who would elect William McKinley
president and make a fortune in coal and shipping; Jephtha H. Wade
in the telegraph and real estate business; Sherwin Williams in paint
and Otis in steel; Charles F. Brush, who would light Cleveland's
Public Square with carbon arc lamps and later give America its first
electric streetcars; and A. L. Erlanger, whose Klaw & Erlanger Theatrical syndicate would control 800 theaters in the United States. [12]

Flagler's friends in Cleveland were influential men, and among
them was Stephen Harkness, who had sold his Bellevue and Monroeville businesses in 1867 and moved to Cleveland to take up the
oil business. He regarded Mary, his first cousin, as his favorite kins-
man, and as her physical infirmities grew worse with the years, Stephen shared her husband's concern over her condition. He was a
regular visitor in the home and enjoyed the Flagler hospitality many
a winter evening.

Flagler himself engaged in little social activity. Even his religious
activities were limited because of Mary's increasingly poor health.
Occasionally, he would take the family to the country for a picnic.
He was an ardent member of the Cleveland Board of Trade and of
the Manufacturers Association of Cleveland, but neither took much
time away from his family.

Flagler was an active Republican. Believing it to be the party most
protective of his business interests, he made generous financial donations to it. However, unlike many—perhaps most—Republicans
he had no enmity toward the South. To the contrary, two years after
the Civil War he persuaded the Board of Trade to donate money for
the destitute of Georgia, where rapes, arsons and lootings had been

forcibly imposed upon the civilian population by the troops of General William Tecumseh Sherman, brother of Stephen Harkness's senatorial benefactor.[13]

More and more, Flagler began to be intrigued by the oil industry, which was rising like a whirlwind. The invention of a more efficient refining-still, the use of torpedoes in drilling, replacement of the clumsy flat car with the wooden tubs by the tank car, and regular use of pipe lines helped the business. But not all of the refiners could use these economies. Small concerns either had to increase their capital to about $500,000 or else combine with some larger unit.[14]

Flagler recognized the shift toward capital. By the spring of 1867, he had paid off the last of his loan from Lamon Harkness. Instead of building a house, as his rising station required, he began saving cash for investment in the new industry.

Rockefeller, too, looked to the larger market. He began building up a trade with wholesalers in the West and South. He saw the export side of the business growing. In 1865, the year he entered oil full time, American refiners sent 30 million gallons abroad. By 1867, it was 97 million. Very little of this came from Cleveland, however, and very much of it came out of New York.

In 1867, John made his move toward bigger things. He began by opening a sales office in New York City, then the center of the world oil industry. He induced his brother William to quit the produce business and go into oil, move to New York and become a selling agent for oil produced by the Rockefeller and Andrews refinery.[15]

Rockefeller began to look about for more capital and became angry with Andrews for spending a million dollars on his mansion. (Rockefeller had spent a mere $40,000 on his more modest home.)

He needed only $100,000 to finance his expansion plans, but the extravagance of his partner Andrews had alarmed Cleveland bankers and they advised him instead to go and interview John Gardiner of Norwalk. He did so, but Gardiner considered it too speculative and of the wildcat order and turned it down, to the everlasting dismay of his heirs. Not dismayed, Rockefeller hastened to see Stephen Harkness. Within an hour, Harkness decided to go in, and put up the money, with a single stipulation: Henry Flagler should have complete control of the investment.

Thus, in 1867, began the momentous partnership of Rockefeller, Andrews and Flagler.[16] Andrews would soon fade, but Rockefeller and Flagler would build the greatest industrial empire of the age. Prior to 1867, Rockefeller had simply been one of many Cleveland refiners. Flagler was one of many grain brokers. Together, however, they were vastly more than the sum of their parts. Their combination—Rockefeller's "attention to detail" and Flagler's ruthless strategies—triggered an explosion of creativity.

The firm's main product was kerosene, and soon it was penetrating every place "that wheels could roll or a camel could put its hoof." They packaged the kerosene in a distinctive and useful five-gallon tin can, which soon was considered as valuable as the contents. The dependable, leakproof can played a vital part in the success of Rockefeller, Andrews & Flagler. Used for a variety of purposes all over the world, storing liquids and grain, it was the decisive factor in turning back domestic competition from American refiners and overseas competition from Russian and Romanian oil.[17]

Two other decisions were important to the early success of Rockefeller, Andrews & Flagler. The first was the building of a second refinery, operated under the name of William Rockefeller and Company. William remained in New York as selling agent for the company, the new refinery merely being labeled with his name so as not to alarm competitors watching the expansion of Rockefeller, Andrews & Flagler.

The other move was more momentous. Flagler and Rockefeller went to Amasa Stone, vice president of the Lake Shore and Michigan Central Railroad, and asked for a "rebate", a rate reduction to be kept secret from other refiners.

It was a bold move, because on the surface there could be no conceivable advantage to the railroad to lower its price. Furthermore, Stone, the richest man in Cleveland, was known to actively dislike young Rockefeller, and such a rebate would give Rockefeller, Andrews & Flagler a significant competitive edge over other refiners in Cleveland.

In the meeting with Stone, Flagler did the negotiating, pointing out that there was a trade war between the cities and if Cleveland were to survive as an oil center, and a transporter of incoming crude and outgoing refined, then Lake Shore must help.

Indeed, there was a battle of the cities. There were about 250 refiners of oil scattered throughout the country. They competed first against each other in their own cities, and second as cities against other cities. The use of kerosene was general throughout the nation and the world. The chief refining centers were, in order of volume, New York, Erie, Philadelphia, Pittsburgh, Cleveland and the Oil Regions around Titusville. Baltimore, Boston and Buffalo refined only small quantities, but were important shipping points.

The refiners in the Oil Regions enjoyed the greatest advantage since the oil was produced at their door. They needed to make but a single shipment, refined oil to the seaboard. New York refiners, too, had to pay freight on but one shipment, but that was crude oil and hence bulkier and more costly to ship than refined. New York also was closest to the population centers and strategically located to negotiate foreign sales. The same was true of Philadelphia.[18]

Pittsburgh and Cleveland were at a distinct disadvantage. They had to import the crude from the Oil Regions, a long haul. Then refine it. Then ship the refined oil to the East. They had a geographical advantage for capturing the thinly populated western and southern trade, but were seriously handicapped in the race for the richest trade of all—the oil markets of Europe.

Even in the Pittsburgh–Cleveland competition, Pittsburgh was in a better position. It had better railroad connections and the advantage of cheaper river transportation.

The only way Flagler and Rockefeller could compete was through a freight concession. And they were in a strong position to demand a lower rate. Cleveland was growing as a refining center and the business could make or break Stone's railroad. Rockefeller, Andrews & Flagler was the largest of the refiners in Cleveland. Flagler pointed out that other railroads were favoring other cities, and that Rockefeller, Andrews & Flagler might move their refinery to the Oil Regions unless they received a rebate.

The railroads serving the oil industry were headed by some of the greatest robber barons of the age. Commodore Cornelius Vanderbilt controlled the New York Central. Jay Gould had the Erie. J. Edgar Thompson ruled the Pennsylvania, assisted by the handsome, dashing, powerful Tom Scott, who through campaign contributions, business deals and bribes virtually controlled the Pennsylvania legislature and many of the Pennsylvania courts. None of them, however, would prove a match for Flagler and Rockefeller.

In the battle between the cities, the railroads favored their own routes and thus had their favorites. The Pennsylvania threw its power on the side of Pittsburgh and Philadelphia. The New York Central favored Cleveland. The Erie supported Buffalo and New York. The Oil Regions seemed to have no railroad friends. The interest of the roads was in hauling bulky crude out of the Regions, not in developing refineries there.

Stone quickly saw where his interest lay and agreed to a rebate of 36 percent below the published freight rate for crude shipped from the Regions to Cleveland. The rebate was secret, and other refiners in Cleveland would continue to pay the published cost.[19]

The firm used the advantage successfully. By 1869, a mere two years later, Cleveland had passed Pittsburgh and become the largest refining center after New York. Cleveland's surgence was owed to the Rockefeller, Andrews & Flagler refineries, which had a capacity of 1,500 barrels a day—the largest in the world. They had their own warehouses in New York and owned their own wooden tank cars to ship the oil. They employed about 100 men in the Cleveland refineries and another 800 men making barrels. The firm loaded and unloaded its own tank cars and employed several chemical and mechanical experts to improve its processes of manufacture and make a greater use of the by-products of crude.

By day, the energetic, popular Flagler was active in civic and business organizations like the Board of Trade, associating with the city's leading men. In the fresh hours of the morning, Rockefeller made it a habit, as he has said, to stop in at Flagler's house from where the two "walked to the office together, walked home for luncheon, back again . . . and home again at night."

When they didn't go home for lunch, they dined at the Union Club, walking home together at night and discussing every policy. Rockefeller said later that they never quarreled but once, and then, "only for a moment."[20]

It was Flagler who first mentioned the possibility of combining with smaller refineries. He brought up the matter one morning while he and Rockefeller were walking to work. Rockefeller thought about the idea and replied, "Yes, I'd like to combine some of these refineries with ours. The business would be much more simple. But how are you to determine the unit of valuation," to determine how much to offer for each plant? "How are you going to find a yardstick to measure the value?"

"I'll find a yardstick," said Flagler with assurance.[21]

That afternoon, Flagler went hunting for refineries and found an operator on the lakefront who was about ready to quit. The man said that the oil game had proved too much for him, and he was convinced he would never make any money at it. Flagler bought him out for $4,700.

It was the first step toward Standard Oil. By 1869, Rockefeller, Andrews & Flagler had outdistanced all other refineries in Cleveland. In all these purchases, Flagler used his yardstick. He determined the value of the refinery and set the price which Rockefeller, Andrews & Flagler would pay for it.

From his office window, Flagler could see the Cuyahoga River, once a pretty view. But the scenes were fading. Cleveland was being changed by the mighty flow of oil drawn from the Pennsylvania oil fields. Refineries were springing up all over town. The smell of oil was in the air, and it was beginning to discolor the waters of the Cuyahoga flowing past the Rockefeller, Andrews & Flagler offices.

# CHAPTER 6

# Standard Oil

In 1870, we organized the Standard Oil Company.
We worked night and day, making good oil as cheaply
as possible and selling it for all we could get.
—HENRY FLAGLER[1]

IT was especially noticeable on starless, moonless nights.

Cleveland glowed like an inferno, the low clouds mirroring the hot orange furnaces of the city's industry. It was a city saturated with oil. The river and lake were smeared with it. Oil wagons rumbled through the streets day and night, and oil fires kept the firemen at work around the clock. The smoke from the railroads and industrial development was becoming a blight in the city. When Lily Langtry, loveliest of the English stage stars, praised Cleveland for its beauty, the *Plain Dealer* replied that she could hardly have seen it because of the smoke. It added, "Our streets are hog pens of filth and unsightliness."[2]

But there were new opportunities arising daily for those who had had none. For example, the newly available kerosene lamps, replacing the feeble, flickering candles and whale-oil lamps, had created a new home business, with women working late at night to sew clothing, either by hand or by use of Isaac Singer's sewing machines.

Traveling through Ohio by train, women's rights champions Susan B. Anthony and Elizabeth Cady Stanton were astonished at the number of homes in which lights shone during the late hours. Learning of the cause, they endorsed it as a means of liberating women and distributed handbills bearing suffrage information on one side and sewing machine advertisements on the other.[3]

The city hummed with energy.

On an early spring morning smoke begins to rise from the chimneys of the mansions along Euclid Avenue. The massive houses, made of brownstone and brick, squat behind vast lawns and gardens which are still bare and gray. Smart rigs stand in the carriageways of some of the houses. Here and there a baron is already on his way downtown, driving behind a spanking team. These are the new gentry, the men of iron and oil and ships.

The whispers begin when the kings of the hill emerge. First comes a tall gentleman, in frock coat and silk hat, leaving his bulky, mansard-roofed mansion. Almost immediately he is joined by another, silk-hatted, frock-coated companion who greets him familiarly. The two, with canes swinging, walk briskly. The taller man is John Rockefeller. The other, Henry Flagler.

Rockefeller has a stoop in his shoulders and a shamble in his gate.

Flagler is more erect, handsome, older, more distinguished looking. He walks straight, with head and chin up, his chest out and the air of a man through whose veins pump healthy blood, whose nerves are not unstrung by dissipation, who feels younger than his years. What is sometimes considered brusqueness is simply the natural buoyance of temperament. He is a man of sunny disposition who decorates his lapels with flowers.

To Flagler, now in his 40s, increasing age means an increasing awareness of one's limitations. Not a diminishing of limitations, but an awareness of the boundaries.

The oil business was profitable from the start, and the minds of these two men had grasped its vast possibilities. Business was booming at Rockefeller, Andrews & Flagler, and investors flocked to the company. "We soon found ourselves able to raise a million dollars as more money was needed," said Flagler.

Watching the growth of the company, Flagler pondered replacing the firm of Rockefeller, Andrews & Flagler with a joint stock "corporation." A simple partnership held too many risks for a large enterprise. The death of a single partner could throw a business into confusion and years of litigation.[4]

He moved cautiously, however, because corporations were a relatively new business tool. At the time, virtually all businesses in the United States were owned by individuals or partnerships. Flagler, however, saw that corporations had distinct advantages.

Unlike individuals or partnerships, civil liabilities applied only to the corporation, not to the individual officers or stockholders. This limitation of risk made it easier to raise money for corporations. Corporations could sell shares or "stock" (percentages of ownership) in the business to raise money, which was called capital. Buyers risked only the cost of the stock. Should the officers of the corporation drive it into debt, the stockholders would not be exposed to further losses, as would be the case in partnerships or individually owned businesses.

Opponents of the device said it gave a few men control of such large amounts of money that it represented a step toward monopoly. Critics also objected that corporation directors, with a built-in goal of providing profits and dividends for their stockholders, were less sensitive in using their capital for improvement of the company and unsympathetic to labor. Corporations, such as those held by Jay Gould and Daniel Drew, also had been outrageous in manipulating stocks to defraud stockholders.

The proposed Standard Oil corporation, a closely held enterprise which did not plan to offer stock for public sale, was exposed to none of those objections except the one concerning labor.

On January 10, 1870, at Flagler's urging, the company incorporated. Flagler, who had no formal legal training, drew up the act of incorporation, a marvelous bit of brevity and a lesson for lawyers everywhere. It did not exceed 200 words.

It stated the name of the concern—the Standard Oil Company of Ohio. It declared its purpose to "manufacture petroleum and to deal in petroleum and its products." The stock was put at one million dollars, divided into shares of 100 dollars each. The signers and incorporators, and the shares subscribed for were: John D. Rockefeller, 2,667 shares; Henry M. Flagler, Samuel Andrews and William Rockefeller, 1,333 shares each; S. V. Harkness, 1,334 shares; O. B. Jennings (a new investor), 1,000 shares. The firm of Rockefeller, Andrews & Flagler took an additional 1,000 shares. They defined their plant and business as worth $400,000.

The leading partners in the arrangement were Flagler and John Rockefeller. Each directly voted 2,667 shares—Flagler having full control over the shares of Stephen Harkness.

Later, during federal hearings on the Standard monopoly, John D. Rockefeller was asked on the witness stand if it was he who had conceived the idea of Standard Oil. He answered: "No, sir. I wish I'd had the brains to think of it. It was Henry M. Flagler." The driving force of the arrangement, Rockefeller said, was Flagler. "He was the man of the most imagination in the firm." He was, said Rockefeller, blessed with an analytical mind and was the "lawyer" of the group.

He could grasp the essentials of any transaction and reduce them to a simple statement. He was the oldest of the group and though he spoke in a soft, velvety pleasant voice, he was a resolute man. Rockefeller said he leaned on Flagler's advice more than on that of any other man.[5]

Finally, it was Flagler who offered the solution to the problem which had bedevilled Rockefeller since 1865—namely: How to bring stability and order to the oil industry so that prices of crude and refined remained stable.

After analyzing the problem, Henry saw but one solution.

Monopoly.

Because of Rockefeller and Flagler, Cleveland had become the largest oil refiner in the world, and if the Standard could monopolize the refineries in Cleveland, it would be in a position to virtually dictate railroad rates on crude, refined and other products, such as cans, to any destination in the country.

Henry's big advantage was already in hand—the Lake Shore rebate from Amasa Stone and the Lake Shore Railroad. This allowed Standard to sell oil cheaper and within a year, Standard forced four of the 30 other Cleveland refiners out of business.

As his fortune mounted, Henry bought a house on Euclid Avenue. Within months, it was filled by relatives—old and new. Father-in-law Lamon Harkness retired from his business and came to live with Mary and Henry. Sometimes Isaac Flagler camped in for long visits. And on December 2, 1870, a son was born in the house.

Henry Harkness Flagler was the boy both parents had hoped for, and they made great plans for his future. However, the birth taxed Mary's strength and she became increasingly invalid. The devoted Henry spent the long winter evenings at her side, reading aloud to her for hours at a time. Stephen Harkness was a frequent visitor. John and Laura Rockefeller dropped in often to cheer her up.[6]

In the meantime, 36 miles away in Akron, Doctor Benjamin Franklin Goodrich built the first rubber factory west of the Alleghenies to make fire hose and carriage tires. Although none of the Standard men were aware of it, a foundation was being laid for something called the automobile industry.[7]

Flagler and Rockefeller found themselves being overwhelmed by the details of Standard's growth. As a solution, they created a management innovation which would become the model for big business in America. They called it the "committee system." Unique at the time, it became the hallmark of the Standard's administrative methods. The original bylaws provided for an executive committee composed of two members, Rockefeller and Flagler. Later, a third member was added, the position being rotated between Sam Andrews and O. H. Payne, a new investor and friend of the Rockefellers.[8]

THE STANDARD'S MOVE toward monopoly did not go unnoticed.

On February 21, 1872, the Cleveland *Plain Dealer* reported:

A gigantic "little game" has been going on in oil circles in Cleveland to the effect that a single firm has bought up or got control of all the refineries in the city and proposes to monopolize the business, having allied itself with the oil-carrying railroads as well as a similar monopolizing firm in Pittsburgh. Rockefeller, Flagler and Andrews of the Standard Oil Works are credited with being the shrewd operators in Cleveland.

The Standard men were alarmed—not by the criticism, but by the news leak.

Indeed, the move toward monopoly had created an atmosphere of secrecy and conspiracy which would become another hallmark of Standard Oil. The paranoia contrasted with the general friendliness of the place. All of the officers, including Rockefeller, were well liked. Flagler was held in great esteem by all employees. In fact, he was familiarly known and referred to as Uncle Henry.[9]

But there was a frightful competition in the oil industry. Spies were everywhere, so much so that Flagler, who did virtually all the contract negotiations, held meetings mostly in hotel rooms, always in different cities. Employees, low and high, were sometimes followed by Pinkerton detectives. The Standard men had to be sure of everyone in the office.[10]

This was particularly true in the early days when the Standard was establishing its monopoly. One of its goals was to control the price of oil produced in the Oil Regions, the Titusville area wells which constituted the world's largest oil production fields.

On February 22, 1872, the *Petroleum Centre Record* blew the whistle on the Titusville scheme, reporting a "rumored scheme of gigantic combination among certain railroads and refiners to control the purchase and shipment of crude and refined oil from this region."

A *Plain Dealer* reporter arrived at the Standard Oil offices and tried to draw out Flagler.

"Do you suppose," the reporter asked Flagler, "any one firm exists which can obtain control of all refineries here?" Even as he asked the question, he knew that Standard had in its pockets all the refineries in Cleveland.

Flagler smiled and replied, "You tell me."

"What is the South Improvement Company?" asked the reporter.

"I don't know," replied Flagler. He of course did know. South Improvement was the company formed by him and Rockefeller to control the Oil Regions.

The reporter pressed on, asking if Standard Oil "might have some connection with it and if you could tell me."

Flagler laughed. "Do you suppose I would be fool enough to tell you?" he replied, and walked the reporter to the door.

FLAGLER AND ROCKEFELLER both held shares in the South Improvement Company, but denied any active role. Despite the denials, however, the scheme had all the earmarks of a Flagler operation.

The gist of the plan was that the South Improvement Company would secretly bring together the key refiners and shippers of the Oil Regions to force the railroads to give special rebates and thus gain an advantage over competitors elsewhere in Ohio, Pennsylvania and New York.

South Improvement Company was set up to do throughout the entire oil industry what Standard Oil had done in Cleveland—exterminate or absorb all competition.

On February 26, 1872, five days after the news leak appeared in the *Plain Dealer*, the South Improvement Company signed agreements between all railroads in the Regions, giving rebates to the South Improvement Company.

When details of the arrangement leaked out, the independents of the oil-producing regions, those who hadn't been invited to join South Improvement, went into a rage. They would be undercut on shipping rates and be given no choice but to join the South Improvement Company or face bankruptcy. Rockefeller and Flagler were burned in effigy and denounced in dozens of newspapers as "monsters" and "anacondas."

In early May 1872, Flagler and Rockefeller appeared on the streets in Titusville. They talked with the refiners, attempting to convince them that the South Improvement Company represented no threat; that they, the Standard men, had joined simply as a protection and that the protection could be extended to all refiners.

Public meetings were held on May 15 and May 16, during which Flagler acted as spokesman for the Cleveland refiners. He said the South Improvement Company would embrace all refiners and was a scheme to save the oil industry rather than to monopolize it. It would present a united front to deal with the railroads, pipelines, government and other entities. Yes, the parent would be Standard Oil but all refiners would be stockholders and elect the board of directors. Some prominent independents, such as John Archbold and J. J. Vandergrift who would both later join Standard as top executives, were swayed by the speeches and persuaded to join the South Improvement Company. But the vast majority of the audience was hostile and hooted down the embarrassed Flagler.

Flagler and Rockefeller returned to Cleveland beaten men. The publicity had tipped off their plans and allowed the opposition to organize. But their defeat was only temporary. South Improvement Company would be abandoned, but Flagler and Rockefeller would return in the guise of other companies and eventually control all oil production in the Regions.

IN THE MEANTIME, Standard was making moves in other directions.

Through purchases made between November 1871 and the middle of the following March, the Standard acquired the largest buyer of crude oil and refined products in the New York area (J. A. Bostwick & Company) and absorbed another New York selling agency, six tar distilling plants and 18 refining units, including one in the Oil Regions. Payment was made in stock or cash or both. Standard thus acquired leases, equipment, trademarks, patents, market connections and such able executives as Oliver Payne and Jabez Bostwick.

Each of the deals was negotiated by the precise-minded Flagler, a man who in these years lived in near monk-like austerity.

His personal habits had always been simple. Weather allowing, he walked to his office daily for years, even after he was a millionaire; not from excessive frugality so much as from absorption in his work and from that curious half-shyness, half-modesty of his. Every night, when his work was done, he went home. He would read to Mary; or, if she were too fatigued, he would sit in the adjoining room and read to himself. In 17 years this man, who was a charmer and well liked by his fellows, spent but two evenings away from his home. Two nights in 17 years. His distraction from business cares was found in books read aloud to an invalid and silently to himself.

A magazine editor wrote of Henry:

At first blush, it seems curious that this man, with his genius for detail, his broad grasp of essentials, his remarkable sense of fundamentals, his vivid imagination, and a very highly developed creative impulse, a man who never was really selfish nor self-centered, found more pleasure in things than in men. But if you think about it, it is not strange at all. Unessentials never entered into his scheme of things. He found men ready made; and saw industrial processes in embryo. He said to me: "I never want to leave a thing unfinished"; and he was very busy with his Standard Oil Company.[11]

His wife was dying, leaving him only with work and a fence of solid gold, exactly man high.

Rockefeller insisted that Flagler had more common sense than anyone he met.

In putting up refineries and other buildings, Henry always insisted on sound structures. He would not allow a flimsy shack to be built.

Everyone was so afraid that oil would disappear and that the money expended in building would be a loss that the meanest and cheapest buildings were erected for use as refineries. This was the sort of thing Mr. Flagler objected to. While he had to admit that it was possible the oil supply might fail and that the risks of the trade were great, he always believed that if we went into the oil business at all, we should do the work as well as we knew how; that we should have the very best facilities; that everything should be solid and substantial; and that nothing should be left undone to produce the finest results.[12]

Flagler also insisted on fairness to the workers, a rare consideration in that age.

In addition to absorbing the employed workers, Standard Oil was attracting many immigrants and it was reported almost every Czech man had spent some time "making barrels for the Standard."

At Flagler's instigation, the Standard encouraged its workers to invest in their stock, but most declined, waiting for a safer place for their savings. The decision would cost the men, and their descendants, small fortunes.

Both Flagler and Rockefeller were energetic promoters of Standard Oil stock, being convinced, correctly, that it was better than money. Whenever a competitor was approached to sell out to Standard Oil, they were given the choice of accepting cash or stock in the firm. Rockefeller and Flagler always recommended that the competitor take stock instead of cash. But usually they refused, sold out for cash and retired from the oil business in disgust.

Flagler tells about one victim of a "freeze-out" as follows:

When I was selling flour and grain in Cleveland, I had a certain German for a customer. He owned a bakery in the suburbs, and I often trusted him for a barrel of flour when collections were slow and money was scarce. One day I met him on the street, and he surprised me by saying that he had sold his bakery and was running a little oil refinery. Usually Mr. Rockefeller and I walked downtown in the morning to talk over private matters. Next day I told him about the little German baker who had gone into the oil business without my knowledge. We bought the refinery for $5,200. The German owed $5,000. At my suggestion he took $2,700 in money, with which he pacified his creditors for the time being, and $2,500 in Standard stock. We made him superintendent of our stove department and sent him into the woods, where he arose to a salary of $8,000 a year. I was pleased later to ask him for his $2,500 in stock and to issue in its stead $50,000 of stock in the larger corporation. Still later he received $10,000 more in a stock dividend.

Their business was increasing by geometrical proportions, but the partners did not rest on their profits. Instead, they found ways to use the by-products of petroleum. For instance, no market for gasoline had yet developed, and while most refiners were trying to find a place to dispose of it, Rockefeller and Flagler used it as fuel.

The key to their success, however, was transportation. Any refiner who had the advantage in transportation usually had the advantage in petroleum. Henry assigned himself to the task of out-maneuvering competitors. Accordingly, he looked at the railroads.

In the late 1860s, there were three different railroad systems in the Oil Regions. The Atlantic and Great Western, which in 1868 was absorbed by Jay Gould into his Erie system, shuttled into Titusville and Franklin. The Lake Shore and Michigan Southern, which later became a part of the New York Central, tapped the regions at Oil

City. The Pennsylvania controlled the Allegheny Valley Railroad, terminating at Franklin; and the Philadelphia and Erie served Franklin and Titusville.

Playing one railroad against the other, Flagler got Jay Gould's Erie system to become the second railroad to favor the Standard with special rates and rebates.

Then came the great panic of 1873 which, while ruining many, provided new opportunities for the Standard.

During the Civil War and the years following, the nation had raced through one of the most feverish orgies of financial and public corruption and social extravagance in its history. Suddenly on September 18, 1873, the great banking house of Jay Cooke and Company in Philadelphia closed its doors. It had been caught in the wreckage of the Northern Pacific Railroad stock scandal. A wave of fright ran through the entire business world. For the first time in its history, the New York Stock Exchange closed its doors. The panic of 1873 was on. All over the country businessmen talked in excited gestures of the great disaster. Stocks and bonds fell to ridiculous figures. Banking houses, brokerage houses, manufactures went into bankruptcy.

Grain rotted at the sides of railroad tracks. Ships laden with wheat stood idle in harbors. Banks quit paying in currency and substituted their own promissory notes, called scrip. Hundreds of thousands of people were thrown out of work. Bread lines formed in cities. Collections were accelerated in churches. In Cleveland, every day brought news of new failures. Some 200 business houses closed their doors that year. Rockefeller and Flagler, with notes for great sums in every bank, kept a close eye on events, and on their books.[13]

But the strong feed on depressions.

Standard now nailed down two important advantages, both of which arose from problems caused by the panic.

The Standard had been shipping oil tank cars over the New York Central to a Standard-owned depot at Hunter's Point, Long Island. There it was put into barrels for shipment to eastern refineries. The barrels were made in Standard's own cooperage. The Erie Road had a similar plant at Weehawken, New Jersey. Now, however, its investments hurt by the panic, the Erie called on Standard to get some of the eastern shipments.

"Why," said Rockefeller, "should I ship oil to your plant at Weehawken when I have my own plant at Hunter's Point? However, I will give you a portion of our oil if you will turn over your Weehawken plant to us so we can handle our own barreling and shipping."

"But," said the railroad, "what will we do about the oil of our other shippers which we now handle at that plant?"

"That will be quite simple," said Rockefeller. "We will do the work for all other shippers. We will make the same charge you now make and out of the profit pay you a profit of 10 cents on each barrel."[14]

It was a way out for the financially strapped Erie, and Erie's directors quickly agreed. Standard thus controlled the terminal facilities of two railroads in New York—the Erie and New York Central.[15] That was the first advantage.

But witness the profound shrewdness of the move beyond that. Every barrel of oil shipped east by the Standard's rivals passed into Standard hands at Weehawken. Thus, Standard came into possession of full information about the volume, character and destination of their rivals' sales. Advantage number two to Standard.

PLAYING one railroad against the other, Flagler increased his concessions until his refineries enjoyed a significant price advantage. When other refiners complained, it was for naught. The railroads replied if they would ship as much oil, then they could have the same prices. It was a case of survival of the fittest.

Prior to 1872, Standard Oil was one of a number of refining firms in Cleveland. By 1872, the group controlled most of the refining capacity in that city. And by 1878, there was no major American refining city in which Standard did not control the majority of refining capacity. By 1884, Standard had imposed a virtual national monopoly in the transportation of crude oil.[16]

Critics, such as Ida Tarbell, have since explained Standard's dominance by ruthless predatory practices. Modern biographer and historian Allan Nevins, on the other hand, attributes the success to enterprise and efficiency.

Standard was indeed on the move to monopoly. Standing directly in its path, however, were the producers and refiners of the Oil Regions, the men who had defeated the South Improvement maneuver.[17]

They were constructing pipelines to bypass the Standard's advantage in rail rates.

Pipelines from the Oil Regions began to have a small effect on oil transportation in 1865 and by 1877 had grown to a significant role. In that year, Standard began to acquire the pipelines. On March 22, 1877, Standard acquired the United Pipeline Company, the largest in the regions, along with four smaller independent lines. This left only the Empire Transportation Company to provide competition.

The Empire decided to fight.

Joseph Potts, the president of Empire, feared a Standard takeover and, he later testified, "We therefore suggested to the Pennsylvania Railroad that we should do what we did not wish to do—become interested in one or more refineries," to provide an alternative to Standard refineries for sale of their crude.

The Pennsylvania Railroad liked the idea and promptly acquired a large refinery in New York and another in Philadelphia, thus giving Empire an outlet for the crude it carried from the Oil Regions. Standard retaliated by withdrawing all shipments of refined oil over the Pennsylvania in March 1877. Standard also began to cut off crude supplies to the Pennsylvania Railroad, and at one point the Pennsylvania Railroad actually paid eight cents a barrel to ship crude to New York City. Losses were so heavy that eventually pressures from stockholders forced the Pennsylvania Railroad to divest itself of its refining capacity. Standard's victory was complete when the Pennsylvania Railroad then bought out the Empire and sold its pipelines and refineries to Standard. This gave Standard control of all pipelines in the Regions.

As the takeovers increased, Standard Oil became the target of an investigation by the Ohio legislature. Appearing before the investigative committee, Flagler blithely justified the takeovers:

"With the aggregation of capital and business experience, and the hold upon the channels of trade such as we have, it is idle to say that the small manufacturer can compete with us and, although it is an offensive term, 'squeezing out' has happened. It is a competitive world."[18]

The consequences of Standard's monopoly of the pipelines soon became abundantly clear. The railroads were totally dependent upon Standard's pipeline system for crude shipments. On the very day that Standard bought the Empire, October 17, 1877, the railroads began paying the Standard a 10 percent rebate on crude shipments. This was in addition to a 22.5 cents per barrel rebate on all crude received from Standard's pipeline gathering system. Further rebates were added in May and July of 1878. Under the arrangement, Standard plants could serve the New York market, for example, far more cheaply than New York refiners, who had to import their crude at published freight rates.

Standard enjoyed this advantage until June 1879, when the Tidewater long distance pipeline was completed, connecting New York City to the crude oil-producing regions in Pennsylvania. The president of a new company, the Tidewater Pipe, turned a valve that started oil flowing through a 110-mile pipeline from rich fields in western Pennsylvania to a railhead at Williamsport, Pennsylvania.

There had been earlier pipelines, some of them owned by Standard Oil, but none as long as the Tidewater or with such direct connections to the eastern refineries. Acting quickly, the Standard men built an intricate system of pipelines, linking every significant producing field to virtually every Standard refinery. The lines ran from the Pennsylvania oil fields to Bayonne, to Philadelphia and Baltimore, to Buffalo, to Pittsburgh and to Cleveland. To supply refineries on Long Island, a branch line was built from Bayonne under the Hudson River, across Manhattan Island at the southern end of Central Park and under the East River.

Pipeline construction in the 1880s became one of the heroic trades. Men worked in gangs of 28 men, equipped with long-handled tongs, and could join together and bury in a ditch 6-inch pipe stretching more than two-thirds of a mile each day. At pipeline tank farms, one of the workers' duties was the manning of small cannon, which were kept on hand to puncture burning tanks in case of fire. A fireman at a pumping station might shovel two-and-a-half tons of coal to keep the pumps turning on a single tour of duty. A line walker, who patrolled for line breaks, could cover 28 to 30 miles in two days.

Standard Oil boasted it would run a pipe to the well of every oil-producing man who wanted one and would provide storage tanks for all oil taken from the fields.

When a producer requested a run from the tank at his well, a Standard Oil gauger "strapped" or measured the tank, and then telegraphed the measurements to his district headquarters, where clerks referred to tables on which the dimensions and capacities of all tanks in the area were recorded, noted the run in barrels and returned the credit balance for the well owner. Teams of clerks, bookkeepers and accountants kept track of oil received, of gathering and storage charges and of oil forwarded to refineries. Telegraphers along the lines kept the chief pipeline offices in touch with operations and tapped out daily reports to Standard headquarters in New York. Few Americans realized that this vast, buried transportation system even existed.

Crude was moved over the Tidewater pipeline to New York at 30 cents a barrel, far lower than the published rate of $1.40 and even the net rate of 88 cents paid by Standard refiners in New York.

Once again, war ensued. In 1880, the Standard completed a 102-mile, five-inch pipeline to transport crude from the regions to Cleveland refineries.

In the same year, Barney York died. Flagler, in New York, received a telegram from Dan Harkness in Bellevue announcing the sudden death of their brother-in-law. York had suffered from heart trouble for some time. He was survived by his wife, Julia, and three children.

Standard proceeded, in the period 1880 to 1883, to connect all the major refining centers throughout the East to the Regions through a network of long distance pipelines. Transportation costs changed every time a pipeline was completed.

During this time, Flagler and Rockefeller continued to plot endlessly, interrupted by nothing. They pressed on to monopoly.

One of their targets, the firm of Scofield, Shurmer and Teagle, included John's younger brother Frank Rockefeller. One day, John warned Frank, "We have a combination with the railroads. We are going to buy out all the refiners in Cleveland. We will give every one a chance to come in. We will give you a chance. Those who refuse will be crushed. If you don't sell your property to us it will be valueless."[19]

Frank was furious, and would remain a lifelong enemy of his brother. But his firm decided that Standard was in earnest and agreed to sell.

As Ida Tarbell later remarked, "a business proposal from Rockefeller or Flagler was regarded popularly as little better than a command to 'stand and deliver.' "[20]

The two oil men—Rockefeller and Flagler—kept at it until every refinery in Cleveland, save two or three small ones, sold out. A kind of terror got abroad among the refiners as they talked in whispers about the thing that was wiping them out of business. They despaired at their helplessness.

The story of Frank A. Arter was the story of many. He owned a refinery which had cost him $12,000 to build. He said:

It was a hard blow when Standard's appraiser valued my plant at $3,000. I had a debt outstanding of $25,000. But what could I do? When conditions were so bad in the oil business that a small refiner could not make money, his plant was worth only what it would fetch as material. So I sold out for $3,000. I had my choice of cash or Standard Oil stock. I asked Rockefeller and Flagler which I ought to take. They both spoke at once, "If you will take the stock and hold it some day you will get back the full price you asked for your refinery." I had a hard pull carrying the $25,000 indebtedness for the next four years in order to hold that stock. Sometimes I got worried. One day I met Mr. Rockefeller and asked him: "How are things going?" He asked, "Are you still holding your stock?" I said that I did in a way, that I had it what you now would call in hock and was trying to follow his and Mr. Flagler's advice. Rockefeller leaned over and in an undertone said, "Sell everything you've got, even the shirt on your back—but hold on to that stock. "[21]

Rockefeller, too, justified the takeovers, saying,

The Standard Oil Company assumed all the risks and at a time when it was evident that the larger number of its competitors could not continue to compete with it in the struggle for existence. What did it do? It turned to these men with whom it had been in sharp competition and said to each: "Come with us, and we will do you good. We will undertake to save you from the wrecks of this refining business and give you a return on the capital which you have in the plant and land, or, if you prefer, we will take the business off your hands."

The Standard men were sassy, but they were also aware of clouds on the horizon threatening their kerosene market. The year 1878 saw the first industrial use of Brush electric lights. It also marked Ohioan Thomas A. Edison's patent of the incandescent lamp. Referring to his own achievement, Charles Brush said, "It was this invention that made arc lighting from central locations commercially possible. I think it may justly be regarded as the birth of the electric lighting industry. . . ." The first Brush plant was sold in December to light a Boston store. One of the lights was hung over the sidewalk, in front of the store, and became the first electric light used on Boston streets.

Another system went up in Wanamaker's store in Philadelphia. The new lights were exhibited in London, and English businessmen organized a corporation and started a large plant.

At the Cleveland debut of Brush's lamps, one gentleman examined the lights for perhaps a half hour and pointed at the wire and asked, "How large is the hole in that little tube that the electricity flows through."[22]

By 1878, barely 10 years after they began as partners, the grand scheme of Flagler and Rockefeller was realized. Virtually the entire oil business of America—refining and gathering—was in their hands, the most complete monopoly that had yet been built in American industry.

New York was rapidly becoming the center for Standard Oil activity. Flagler and Rockefeller, using two private freight cars to carry luggage and furniture, began spending their winters in New York, the rest of the year in Cleveland.

They preferred Cleveland. It was their home. Rockefeller had purchased a large tract of land in East Cleveland, what he considered a "good investment," at a thousand dollars per acre. This was his famous Forest Hill estate, a family playground where he developed roads and paths for driving, walking and bicycling; constructed a lake; planted trees; and built a half-mile track on which he exercised his fast trotters. His and Flagler's mansions, with heated stables, provided the two men with their sport—the driving and racing of fast horses. The horses and their carriages were shipped back and forth twice a year, along with pianos and other furnishings. In those years, many wealthy Americans delighted in such horses. White-haired Commodore Vanderbilt snapped the whip above his trotters in Central Park. Henry Cabot Lodge has told how the solid men of Boston sped along the Charles River Drive. The Standard men maintained stables in both New York and Cleveland. Rockefeller recalled later that whenever he was worn out, an hour's fast driving—"trot, pace, gallop, everything"—with a rest and dinner, would rejuvenate him. "I was able to take up the evening's mail and get the letters off."[23]

Flagler had a number of fine trotting horses, which he purchased for the use of himself, his family and their guests. He built a quarter-mile track, and this attracted much attention.[24]

THEIR DAY-TO-DAY WORK was intense and sustained. But at one hour of the day, at noon, the leaders met in a more relaxed mood. This was the famous Executives' Lunch.

The lunch table for officers began in 1876. Regular seats were assigned. The men arrived in the stiff business dress of the day: high silk hats, long coats and gloves. Briskly, they took their places. Rockefeller had courteously given the head of the table to his senior, Charles Pratt. On Pratt's right was Flagler. Next to Flagler sat Rockefeller, then Archbold and Bostwick. All who lunched in the room were of high consequence in the organization. To be asked to join the table was a high honor. The great function of the gatherings was to provide a cordial relationship, flow of ideas and opportunity for friendly persuasion. The New York office at 26 Broadway and the Cleveland office were both composed of all-male personnel. Flagler was always immaculately attired and presented a fine and impressive appearance, especially whenever wearing his favorite set of black pearl studs and cufflinks.[25]

IN THE YEARS from 1877 to 1883, Flagler and Rockefeller, their families, their partners and principal executives moved twice a year between Cleveland and New York.

The drift of the Standard toward New York did not go unnoticed in Cleveland, nor did it go unresented. Rockefeller in particular was vilified.

As Rockefeller biographer John Flynn later noted, "The name of John D. Rockefeller was the most execrated name in American life. It was associated with greed, rapacity, cruelty, hypocrisy, and corruption. . . . Theodore Roosevelt denounced Rockefeller as a law breaker. William J. Bryan, his fellow Christian, went up and down the land demanding that he be put in jail. Tolstoi said no honest man should work for him."

The vilification included rumors that John was a womanizer. His main mistress was supposed to be a woman who lived in Bellevue.

The editor of the Bellevue *Gazette*, hearing rumors that Rockefeller had been surprised by the mistress while his wife and family were in New York, published a paragraph of calculated naivete. Said the *Gazette:*

Mrs. C.B. Reed of Topeka, Kans., a guest in the home of Mr. and Mrs. J. H. Brinker, together with Mrs. Cora Higbee and Mrs. Cornelia Sinclair, two former Bellevue residents, went to Cleveland and called on John D. Rockefeller at Forest Hill, by request. The ladies were met at the entrance by Mr. Rockefeller's coachman and conveyed to the residence where they were welcomed in a most cordial manner by their host. Mrs. Reed also had the honor of being extended an invitation to take a spin in the host's auto, enjoying a drive through the grounds for an hour and a half. To most people it is counted a great pleasure to stand on the outside of the boundary fence and view the beautiful grounds, but to be extended an invitation to be the guest of the owner is an honor which many wish for but few receive and one which will be long remembered by those present.

The coming years, 1878 to 1884, saw new combats between Standard Oil and its competitors. During that time, the Standard added several more firms and executives to the combination.

One of the most influential men in the Standard Oil combination from 1874 until his death was Charles Pratt (1830–1891). Below medium height, with a thin face adorned by a goatee, he possessed tremendous energy and a foundation of confidence in his ability as a refiner and marketer. Following six years of participation in a paint manufacturing partnership, he turned to refining and marketing petroleum after 1864. He specialized in a high-quality kerosene which he widely advertised as Astral Oil—"It will not explode." He built a substantial market for his products at home and for export.

Oliver H. Payne (1839–1917) was one of the leading figures in the original organization of Standard Oil. Wealthy by birth and the only member of the early top management to have attended college, he had an excellent record in the Union army before becoming a refiner in 1864. He and his partners built Clark, Payne & Company into Standard Oil's most formidable Cleveland competitor before the former was merged into the latter in 1872. He then became a member of the Standard's executive committee.

Pratt had been one of those absorbed in Standard's expansion. And he did not resent it. Whenever the Standard Oil men felt it necessary to apply pressure as a means of persuading a rival to sell, they showed no hesitancy in using the sharp competitive practices prevailing in the industry. On one occasion or another, they preempted all available staves and barrels, restricted as completely as possible the available tank cars, and indulged in local price cutting. They meticulously watched and checked on competitive shipments and sales, sometimes in cooperation with railroad men, and diligently negotiated for secret discounts on railway rates, even to the point of receiving cash payments on rivals' shipments. All acts were kept secret as long as possible.

Despite all the criticism of the Standard men, they were careful to stay within legal boundaries. The sole major indictment against them in the robber baron years came on April 29, 1879, when the grand jury of Clarion County, Pennsylvania, took offense and indicted Flagler and Rockefeller for criminal conspiracy, along with Jabez Bostwick, William Rockefeller, Daniel O'Day, William Warden, Charles Lockhart, Jacob Vandergrift and George Girty, the last the cashier of Standard Oil. There were eight counts, including conspiracy to secure a monopoly of the oil industry; to oppress other refiners; to injure the carrying trade of the Allegheny Valley and the Pennsylvania Railroad; to extort unreasonable rates from the roads; and to fraudulently control the prices of crude and refined oil.

The case was delayed by Standard for years, however, and never went to trial. Indeed, Standard absorbed most of its critics, including the prosecutor and his chief witnesses, who later became stockholders of Standard Oil.

Sweet as life might have seemed for the Standard men, all their problems weren't yet solved. Flagler and Rockefeller talked constantly about the need to legalize their out-of-state holdings.

The Standard Oil Company of Ohio, the nucleus of the business, was chartered only to own property and to do business in Ohio. The Standard faced heavy attack from its many rivals and enemies if it attempted to assert ownership of non-Ohio properties. It had no legal existence in other states. It had no legal right to own plants in other states, or to hold stocks in other companies. If, as was happening, the Standard were to expand on a national scale, there would have to be some way to form, in effect, a national corporation. But how to do it?

As early as 1872, in the purchase of the New York-based Bostwick & Company, Flagler had devised a simple solution. Relying on English common law, he created a "trustee" to hold the property and administer it on behalf of Standard.

The trustee concept was ancient and derived from the English practice of appointing guardians or other persons to be the trustees of property owned by children. The trustee held the property "in trust" with a charge that it should be administered for the benefit of the owner.

Several times between 1872 and 1878, Flagler and Rockefeller used the device as an expedient to protect the Standard. Flagler was usually the appointed trustee to administer the properties on behalf of Standard Oil.

The arrangement was formalized in 1879 when Flagler prepared a formal trust agreement which dispensed with single trustees for each company and property, and instead named a small body of trustees for all of the Standard properties. The main duty of the trustees was simply to divide profits annually in proportion to the number of Standard Oil shares held by each of the 37 stockholders.

At the time, Rockefeller was the principal holder of stock, with 8,984 of the 35,000 shares. Flagler stood next with 3,000 shares; S. V. Harkness with 2,925; Charles Pratt with 2,700; O. H. Payne with 2,637; J. A. Bostwick with 1,872; and William Rockefeller with 1,600.

John Rockefeller's holdings were estimated at the time to be worth at least $18 million, Flagler's at $6 million.

The agreement was revised and signed on January 2, 1882, setting up all the properties of Standard Oil under a board of nine trustees, headed by Rockefeller and Flagler. The trustees were to have their offices in New York. They were charged to set up Standard Oil companies in other states and territories. The trustees controlled nearly 90 percent of the nation's refining capacity, and Standard-owned property in 13 states and several foreign countries.

IN EFFECT, though not in law, one great national company, the Standard Oil Trust, had been created. It showed how, at a time when interstate holding companies were outlawed, an interstate business could be efficiently established and managed. Other trusts were soon to follow, and in the end the states abandoned their unworkable prohibitions.

From a single office, the Standard Oil Trust controlled most of the oil-refining and oil-marketing machinery of the world.

The nature of the trust was kept secret from the public as long as possible. When Standard men first mentioned it, in testifying before a New York State Senate committee in 1883, it was described as a trusteeship in the good old sense. Flagler, explaining the successive creation of Standard Oil of Ohio, of Pennsylvania, of New York and of New Jersey, said the trust was "an agreement of individuals who have created a trust and placed it in the hands of trustees. It holds bonds and stocks for individuals."

Of its control and managing of the bulk of the world's oil, he said nothing. Furthermore, he refused to give any information whatsoever upon the close relations among the various Standard companies. When asked several times if the trust were an interstate monopoly centrally directed, Flagler and the other officers simply denied its existence; and in fact, legally it had none.

It is fair to say that the Standard by 1884 was the largest and richest manufacturing organization in the world. It was ruled by an executive committee composed of Rockefeller, Flagler, Pratt, Warden and Archbold. Strong men all, they did not work by orders, but by suggestions and consensus. In a letter of the early 80s, Rockefeller speaks of having a hard time to "hold my own" in the executive committee.

In general, the Standard paid better salaries than most other businesses and added bonuses for especially efficient officers. It made a point of looking after the physical and moral welfare of its principal employees.

The Standard put into practice benefits that would not become a regular part of American business for nearly another 100 years. Upper-level personnel transferred to a new city were given aid in finding a house. Pains were taken to provide the best in office facilities. Officers were encouraged to hire assistants to look after details, so that they could themselves attend to large policies. Employees were rigidly forbidden to have conflicts of interest, for instance in speculating in oil stock.

Meanwhile, the native creativity of Cleveland continued. A local grocer who received a barrel of Mexican chicle instead of nuts gave it to William J. White, an obscure popcorn salesman. White added flavoring to the "worthless" chicle, thus inventing chewing gum. In 1884, White further endeared himself to all future generations of American kids and dentists when he invented cracker jacks, complete with a trinket dropped in each bag.

In 1882, Standard Oil Company of New Jersey, the future main holding company of the Standard Oil Trust, was incorporated. Quickly it acquired a refinery, barrel factory and paraffin works at Bayonne, a refinery at Communipaw, and docks at Weehawken. The first president of the new company was Flagler.

In the meantime, the Standard headquarters was moved to New York.

In the downtown New York of 1882, the dominant feature of the skyline was the steeple of Trinity Church. A few blocks northeast of the church, near City Hall, a new shape was forming on the skyline— Brooklyn Bridge, still under construction. The city's important streets were paved with Belgian block, which resounded continually under the iron rims of thousands of wagons and carriages. A few steps south of Trinity Church, across the street at 26 Broadway, was the headquarters of Standard Oil.

The New York *World* described it as

. . .one of the most superb edifices on Broadway. . . . It is magnificent in dimensions, aesthetic in adornment, the very essence of convenience in all physical facilities, for ingress, egress, occupation. There, hand in glove with the railroads, owning the producers, controlling the refiners, they sit absolute masters of the situation, recognized in every financial center of the earth as a power, as a power of financial strength with foundations broader and deeper and apparently more enduring than those of any corporation known in the present day . . . [26]

It was at this time that the efficient, tightly knit trust entered the retail trade field, its wide-flung network of interlocking companies providing a ready-made channel for reaching every part of the country. Soon, neat Standard Oil wagons, always pulled by good horses, became familiar sights on city streets and country lanes. Kerosene for light, and later, for cookstoves, was trundled to the doorways of America.

This was the Gilded Age, and the golden glow of the kerosene lamp became the heart of every American home. The technology of the little lamp had changed an American life-style which had survived for 200 years.

The hearth was the heart of every room until the mid-nineteenth century, and the kitchen fireplace with its open hearth was the center of the house. Now the kitchen hearth was no longer the main room of the house. Now, supper was over early, and after the dishes were cleared away the dining room was the gathering place for the family. A "turkey-red" cloth was spread on the table and an oil lamp placed in the center. Under its glow the children did their lessons and played. The wife and mother caught up with her mending. And the husband and father read aloud to the family from Tom Sawyer, Uncle Remus, or newspapers and magazines.

The home itself was slowly becoming mechanized. In 1882, one could buy for twelve dollars a kerosene-powered magic lantern and project sliding pictures on a sheet hung against the wall. Most middle class households had a foot-treadle sewing machine, a hand-cranked clothes washer, a carpet sweeper with revolving brushes, and a geared egg beater.

Almost all men's clothing was factory-made in the 8os. It was a golden age for inventors. The typewriter, phonograph, trolley car, Kodak camera, motion pictures, fountain pen, enameled bathtub, skyscraper, automobile and airplane all belong to the kerosene era.

Much of the credit for the changes could go to Rockefeller and Flagler. Nevertheless, the Standard Oil Company became a prime target for the muckrakers. Two books, Henry Demarest Lloyd's *Wealth Against Commonwealth* and Ida M. Tarbell's *The History of the Standard Oil Company,* attacked the company. So did many newspapers and national magazines. Four principal accusations were made against the company:

- It secured railroad rebates not available to competitors.
- It secretly owned companies which pretended to compete with it.
- It cut prices to drive out competition, but raised them once it dominated the market.
- It spied on competitors.

The Standard men shrugged off such criticism. In their day, competition was cutthroat, best characterized in a maxim from *David Harum,* a popular novel: "Do unto others as they would do unto you—and do it first." Henry Flagler kept a copy of the axiom on his desk.

By 1884, the goal of Flagler and Rockefeller to monopolize was complete. Standard had its pipeline network, and transportation rates were stabilized in the Standard's favor. For all other shippers, railroad rates on crude from the Regions were set equal to rates charged by pipelines. The rate on crude to New York City was 45 cents a barrel; Baltimore and Phildelphia were charged 40 cents a barrel. Standard, because it owned the pipelines which supplied the railroads, could ship at cost—12 cents per barrel to New York and 10 cents per barrel to Baltimore and Philadelphia. It thus shipped crude at about one-third the cost paid by independent refiners.

The shipping cost advantages allowed Standard to expand via merger. Independents had the choice of joining the corporation and enjoying the cost advantages, or competing at disadvantage as independents.

By 1884, Standard's position was virtually impregnable. The corporation owned the entire pipeline gathering system in the Oil Regions. With the exception of the Tidewater, it also controlled all long distance crude lines. Its virtual monopoly of transport made it difficult for independents to compete in any and all markets. For all practical purposes, Standard had monopolized the entire American oil industry. It would not face serious competition again until its hold on transportation was broken by the discovery of new crude oil fields in the Midwest and Southwest.

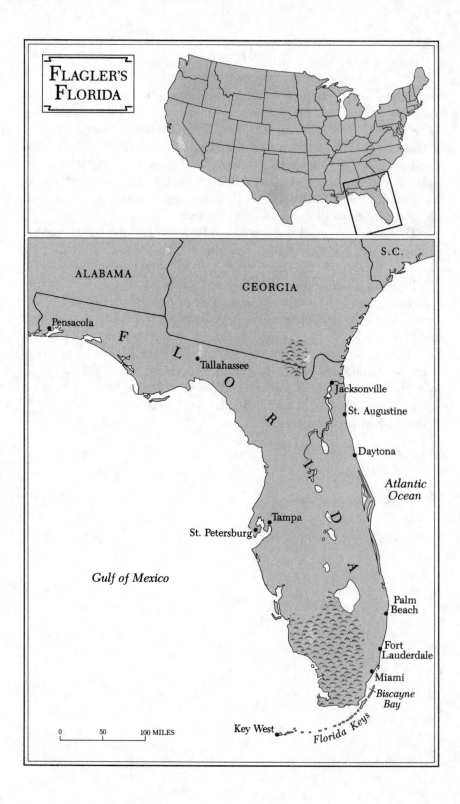

FLAGLER'S
FLORIDA

ALABAMA

GEORGIA

S.C.

Pensacola

F
L
O
R
I
D
A

Tallahassee

Jacksonville

St. Augustine

Daytona

Atlantic
Ocean

Tampa

St. Petersburg

Gulf of Mexico

Palm
Beach

Fort
Lauderdale

Miami

Biscayne
Bay

0      50      100 MILES

Key West

Florida Keys

# CHAPTER 7

# Florida

AS the Standard Oil fortunes soared, Henry spent less and less time with his family and more and more time in New York, staying at the Buckingham Hotel. By 1874, he was listed in the city directory as secretary of Standard Oil, his office at 140 Pearl Street, his home "in Ohio." His trips home were becoming an increasing interruption in his normal life, which more often was the conducting of the business of Standard Oil.

Family members, too, were shifting to New York. In the spring of 1876, on April 26, Jennie Louise married a young financier, John Arthur Hinckley, in Cleveland. After a honeymoon, the couple made their home in New York.

About the same time, Mary moved to New York. Her breathing crippled by bronchitis, she was a respiratory invalid, incapable of any regular activity or movement. Perhaps sensing her impending death, she refused to be separated from Henry. She arrived in New York in the winter of 1876–1877, the first time she had ever been there, and set up house with Henry and young Harry at the Buckingham.

In the same winter of 1876–1877, Mary's doctors advised Henry that he take her to Florida, where the sunshine, warmth and fresh sea air might work their healing. Since the Civil War, the northern and Panhandle areas of that state had begun to enjoy a slim reputation as a rest-cure area. The remainder of Florida, however, the entire peninsula of it, was virtually an unpenetrated wilderness. Wrenching himself away from his business routine, Flagler took the family there, including Jennie Louise, who was then 22, her husband, John, and seven-year-old Harry.[1]

Reluctantly, the future developer of Florida prepared for his trip expecting the worst. He was not to be disappointed. Florida was awful. The land that awaited them had only recently become a state, in 1845, and was the most primitive of all U.S. territories in North America or abroad.

The first Indians had walked into northern Florida from Georgia 10,000 years earlier. Later, other Indians, island-hopping across the Caribbean, came up from Cuba and South America. It was these later Indians, Caribs, which Columbus encountered when he bumped into the Bahamas while trying to figure out where he was.

Florida, with its vast unexplored interior and a few underpopulated coastal fishing villages, passed back and forth between Spain and England for nearly the next 300 years until 1783, when England ceded all of Florida to Spain. In the next several years more than 15,000 English fled to the West Indies, abandoning their coastal plantations to Indians, robbers and the quick-growing tropical jungles.

In an effort to resettle the plantations, Spain induced Americans to colonize, and the land-hungry "Yanquis" poured over the border by the thousands. The Americans, however, were obstreperous and almost immediately began demanding independence. In 1812, they formed a Republic of Florida, and an agreement was made with the Spanish authorities granting local self-government to northeast Florida.

Any further pretense of Spanish authority was shattered by General Andrew Jackson's two invasions. In 1814, he struck at Pensacola, explaining that it was being prepared as a base to attack the United States. After taking the city by storm, he retired. In 1818, however, he made another punitive expedition, this time striking down the main stem of Florida, burning many Indian towns and seizing several forts, on the argument once again that they threatened American security.

Wanting no more of Andrew Jackson, Spain, on February 22, 1819, sold Florida to the United States for $5 million. In March 1822, the Territory of Florida was created. Twenty-three years later, in March 1845, Florida became a state.

At the time of the Flagler visit, Florida had a population of less than 250,000, mostly in the northern tier of counties bordering on Georgia. It was the most backward of the then 38 American states. Key West was the largest city, with a population of about 10,000. Jacksonville, the chief city on the mainland, had 7,000; Tampa, less than 1,000. The principal towns on the east coast, between Jacksonville and Key West, were St. Augustine, with 2,300 inhabitants, and Daytona, with 321 inhabitants.[2]

The deepest harbor in Florida, in fact the deepest one south of Norfolk, was at Key West. The trip to Florida promised to be a great adventure. But, as we shall see, Henry was preoccupied with business and in no mood to appreciate it.

New York to Jacksonville was then a brutal trip involving several changes and indifferent equipment. The first leg began by railroad from New York down to Savannah and was relatively comfortable. Then the horrors began. Savannah was the last outpost of civilization before jumping into the Florida campaign.

There were two choices of conveyance to Jacksonville. And the local joke was that whichever you chose, you would be sorry you had not taken the other. Choice one was the night train which, without sleeping cars—meaning you would pass the night sitting straight up on benches—would bring you to Jacksonville in about 16 hours. Choice two was the steamboat line, more picturesque and far more comfortable because sleeping compartments could be arranged. It went inland nearly all the way, behind the barrier islands. The problem with it was that it might land you in a day, or you might run aground and remain on board for a week.

Out of concern for Mary, Henry chose the steamboat.

Upon landing at Jacksonville, they found primitive hotels but a wonderful climate. It was pleasant there, soft blue sky mingling with fragrant orange groves. But there was nothing to do save walk among the few rambling hotels. There was not even a beach, for the ocean was several miles away.

To relieve the boredom, Henry decided to move the family to legendary St. Augustine, proclaimed to be the oldest city in the United States. Again they took a steamboat, sailing down the wide St. Johns River, which was a nesting place for that rare and most beautiful of birds—the swallow-tailed hawk, with its gray back and wings, snow-white breast and exquisitely graceful flight. The Flaglers sailed through a virgin forest of cypress, maple, pine and live-oak. At every turn in the river, the tall forms of the blue and white heron would rise from the shallow waters. Thousands of ducks fed among the water plants. Along the banks lay the torpid bodies of huge alligators.[3]

From the river landing, a lackadaisical horsecar carried the Flaglers over narrow rails into St. Augustine. There, the magic of the river vanished, to be replaced by a grim mosquito-plagued reality.

St. Augustine was a pesthole.

"We came," Flagler said later, "for Mrs. Flagler's health. I did not form a very favorable first impression, I must admit. We came from Jacksonville by way of the river and the Tocoi Railway and got here just at night. The accommodation was very bad, and most of the visitors here were consumptives."[4]

Florida was the land of wild game but rarely did said game ever come to the refreshment of the Flagler tables. Said another visitor at the time:

Fresh nutritious meat there were not. It was the land of early vegetables, but no friendly hand ever strove to put them on our table. In place of wholesome, well-cooked food, we were served with canned meats, canned vegetables; and, as if in compensation, all sorts of fancy tarts and meringues. Orange trees were not very plentiful in the city, although the perfume of the blossom often enough greets one as we walk through the streets.[5]

"I didn't like it," said Henry, "and took the first train back to Jacksonville."[6]

Henry likewise found Jacksonville "awful." After a few weeks, he decided he must return to New York. Against his arguments, Mary and the children went with him.

The Flaglers changed their New York residence to the Windsor Hotel and, with the exception of several long visits to their home in Cleveland, remained at that hotel. Mary's bronchial trouble grew steadily worse, aggravated by the cold weather, and her doctors advised that she leave New York and begin spending her winters in Florida. She refused, however, to go alone and Flagler wouldn't go with her, saying he couldn't be that far away from the business of Standard Oil.

AND there we have it. The life of Standard Oil was more important to Henry than that of his wife. Unfortunately for the historian, there are neither letters nor diaries of Henry or Mary explaining his harsh decision. There is only the decision. Henry is told by doctors that Mary must move to Florida to survive, and he refuses. He didn't refuse for money. Already, he had more than he, Mary and the children would ever need. No, he refuses because he cannot tear himself away from the *game*, the power and excitement that he has at Standard Oil. In these decades, the years of the 1860s and 1870s, the kindly "Uncle Henry" of later days hasn't been born. What stands in his place is a cold, remorseless Flagler—the dark wizard who makes the contracts and thinks up the various combinations of interest which gave Standard Oil its monopoly over the oil industry. Remember that it was Flagler who suggested devouring all the little refineries that would form the Standard Oil Trust.

MORE AND MORE, Henry's time was spent at 140 Pearl Street, an old-fashioned building which contained his headquarters. While all other directors had separate offices, Rockefeller and Flagler continued to have their desks together. Flagler was attached to no department. He was the "lawyer" of the crowd. What was known as the Standard Oil Company consisted, in fact, of 40 corporations. There were refineries at Buffalo, Philadelphia, Cleveland, Baltimore, New York, Portland, Pittsburgh, Hunter's Point, Bayonne, Rochester and in all the cities of the Oil Regions.

Flagler and Rockefeller were the co-rulers of the empire. Andrews had quit in 1880, saying the vast acquisitions were too much for him. He turned over his stock for a million dollars in cash.

The name of the Standard was a household word in every quarter of the globe. It was spread throughout Europe, the Middle East, India, Siam, Sudan, Liberia, Morocco, the Congo and China. It did business, and obtained franchises, from kings, presidents, emperors, mandarins and warlords.

The Standard can was a familiar object in every village of Europe, Asia and Africa. The Standard delivery service was as familiar along the Nile and the Ganges as it was in America. Camel trains carrying Standard cans crossed the desert of the Sahara. Even elephants in India wore caparisons showing the ubiquitous Standard Oil white-and-red symbol.

Standard Oil was Henry's life, and he loved it like a father.

In the meantime, he and Mary decided that a New York hotel was not a good place to raise young Harry, nor was it a proper address for one of the nation's most successful businessmen. In 1880, they bought a house at 685 Fifth Avenue, a large brownstone very near the similarly designed mansion of John Rockefeller. They also purchased a stable nearby for Henry's horses, at 121 West 55th Street.

In addition to those projects, Henry also was in charge of construction of a new, $1 million Standard Oil headquarters building at 26 Broadway.[7]

While the brownstone was being renovated, young Harry was sent back to Ohio to be cared for by his Aunt Carrie. Harry also was a regular companion of his grandfather, Lamon Harkness, who remained in the Cleveland home. Although letters from his father were rare, the boy regularly received cheering mail from his ailing mother.

Typical was this letter posted November 29, 1880.

My darling Harry

I received your letter this morning. Was very glad to hear from you. And to know you are having such a good time. I hope you will not take cold playing in the snow. We miss you very much and just think when you come home I shall have a *ten year old* boy. I think I shall miss you more on your birthday than you will me. I have not sent your birthday gift. But it will keep until you get home. Tell Jennie and Carrie they must kiss you and *spank* you for me. I know Jennie will enjoy the spanking part. Good night with a kiss from Mama.

Barely two weeks later, on December 11, 1880, Mary's father, Lamon Harkness, died in the Cleveland home. Funeral services were held in Bellevue, where he was buried.[8]

It was now, on the trip to Ohio for the funeral, that Henry realized the inevitable. Mary's condition was critical, and it was too late for the curative powers of Florida sunshine and warmth. Doctors, furthermore, advised against any traveling. Mary became so weak that Henry hired a full-time companion, a former actress named Ida Alice Shourds.

Despite his millions, Henry could only stand by and wait for Mary's death, which came on May 18, 1881.[9]

Curiously, we find no indications of Henry's feelings. In his later sorrows—the insanity of his second wife, the estrangement from his son—we find letters and other references in which he expresses guilt, or at the very least anguish. In Mary's death, we find no such records. Nor does Henry's conduct indicate any great melancholy. Instead he reverted to bachelorhood, persuading his half-sister Carrie to come to New York, preside over the new home, and take care of

Henry's son Harry, a youth of 11. Jennie Louise also helped care for the boy.

Flagler's abrupt turn from austerity and family activity is a peculiar thing because it suggests a callousness not previously expected or demonstrated. Even during his most intense intoxication with Standard Oil, Henry spent nearly every night with his ailing Mary. And judging from all indications from friends and relatives, he showed her a constant love.

So why the changed behavior?

There are at least two possibilities to consider. One is that his shame over her death was so traumatic that he buried it within deep layers of his psyche, a guilt so heavy and deep it would not emerge for 25 years when, indeed, he developed lapses of black depression and unexplained weeping.

The other possibility is harder to entertain but is nevertheless a valid hypothesis. And that is that he had ceased to care for her. That he was tired of the burden of an invalid wife and was glad to be rid of her. This, too, could explain the mysterious guilt of his elderly years.

Unfortunately, we have no record of his emotions at the time. What we have instead is a track of his conduct. It is a track of a new Henry Flagler, a man who leads Florida out of the wilderness and a man who, along the way, becomes a humanitarian.

JUST PRIOR to Mary's death, Henry had rented a large house at Mamaroneck on Long Island Sound.[10] Situated on a narrow extension of land, almost surrounded by water, Mamaroneck was accessible by both water and rail from New York, being about 20 miles northeast of downtown Manhattan.[11]

The 32-acre estate had been named Satan's Toe and included a 40-room mansion plus guest houses. Following Mary's death, Henry spent most of his summer weekends with the children and Carrie at Mamaroneck. His weekdays and nights were spent at his Manhattan hotel so that he could be close to his office.

For the first time in his life Henry began to go to restaurants and shows and, to the gossip of his friends, was often seen in the company of his wife's ex-nurse, Ida Alice Shourds. Increasingly, Satan's Toe became the scene of glamorous full-dress parties, and Ida Alice the queen of the balls.

THE FEW PHOTOGRAPHS of Ida Alice show a rather unpleasant-looking woman with a too-small face. Apparently, she wasn't photogenic because contemporaries described her as exceptionally attractive. And even Henry's son, who disliked his stepmother, said Ida Alice was a spectacular-looking woman with red hair and green eyes.

Born in 1848, she was 18 years younger than Henry and came from a shattered family. She was a former actress who had turned to practical nursing to make a living. Her father, an Episcopal minister in Philadelphia, died when she was a child. Her two brothers, Charles and Stephen, were sent to Kansas as "indentured," or apprenticed, farm laborers. She and her mother moved to New York, where she finished the eighth grade and then went to work in various occupations including sewing and, at some point, stage work.[12]

Ida Alice filled up the year of Henry's life following Mary's death. At the end of that year, it seems that Henry decided to disengage from Standard Oil so he could begin enjoying his millions. It was a decision which would lead to his great work in Florida, but it began as an hedonistic act and, in fact, he was led to Florida in the pursuit of pleasure, not opportunity.

Shortly after the anniversary of Mary's death, Henry bought Satan's Toe for $125,000, then pitched in another $200,000 for massive renovations of the house and grounds. The appointments were lavish and unlike anything Henry had done in the past. The interior was completely redone, new furniture installed and custom-designed chandeliers hung. One, of Henry's own design of brass and crystal, weighed half a ton. He built a private breakwater, extending 200 yards into Long Island Sound. And he imported sand from New Jersey to transform the rocky, muddy shores into a smooth bathing beach. The house became his permanent summer home and its wide verandas and big halls the scene of more and more social functions.

Realizing that the business of the Standard Oil Company had been perfected, largely by his own energy and imagination, Henry began to spend less and less time in the active work of the company. It may have been that the death of Mary had taught him there was more to life than making money.

Flagler began to distance himself from Standard Oil. Although he would remain an active director of the company until 1911, he was rapidly turning over his daily duties to John Dustin Archbold, a young, aggressive executive. As he entered his 50s, Henry said, "I had the sense to see the younger men in the company could run the business better, if they had the chance."

The money-making machine of Standard Oil was not only perfect; it was permanent. The only concern of its engineers was now personal: What to do with the profits? The yearly incomes of Flagler and Rockefeller were in themselves a princely fortune—and growing princelier. Outside investments were being sought. John D. Rockefeller seemed determined to become the richest man in the world. Flagler, however, was beginning to see clearly and think in straight lines that led in a different direction.

In the meantime, he was finding comfort in the arms, affection and body of Ida Alice. [13]

In the winter of 1882–1883, however, Henry was hospitalized with a liver ailment. Reading more than 10 newspapers a day, his attention returned to Florida and land deals being put together by a Philadelphia industrialist named Hamilton Disston.

It seemed that in the federal Swamp Land Act of 1850, Florida had been given title to 13 million acres of undrained federal land. The Civil War, followed by legal and financial problems, prevented the state from doing anything with the bonanza. Indeed, by 1880, the state was near bankruptcy and had opened land offices in major eastern cities to sell the land at 50 cents an acre. There were, however, few buyers. The state was looking for a bailout, and the only hope seemed to be a huge land deal.

The state made a deal with Mr. Disston, selling him a tract almost twice as large as Connecticut—four million acres for 25 cents an acre.

Disston proceeded to drain two million of the acres. His engineers completed about 10 miles of drainage canal, and money poured in for projects aimed at production of sugar cane, rice, fruit, vegetables and cattle. The town of Kissimmee grew into a "magic city."

All this was read by Henry at Satan's Toe. And there was more. Rail construction was spurred, and during 1881–1882, more miles of track were laid than during the entire previous history of the state.

HENRY decided that it might be time to have a second look at this state which was virtually giving land away in exchange for develop-

ment. He hoped to see the Disston development, but his doctor
restricted him to St. Augustine. To Henry's surprise, the town wasn't
the hellhole he had previously experienced.

He told a St. Augustine friend,

When my liver became disorderly, I told my physician that I was coming
back. He at first demurred, but said that if I would come to St. Augustine
I might. This promise I gave with a mental reservation. Therefore I telegraphed for rooms for myself and friends, not because I wanted to come
here, but just to ease my conscience of the promise given the doctor.

I was surprised when I got here. There had been a wonderful change in
the former state of things. Instead of the depressing accommodations of the
years before, I found the San Marco one of the most comfortable and best
kept hotels in the world and filled, too, not with consumptives, but that
class of society one meets at the great watering places of Europe—men who
go there to enjoy themselves and not for the benefit of their health. . . .

I liked it well enough to stay, and since I couldn't sit still all the time,
I used daily to take the walks down St. George Street, around the plaza to
the club house, and back to the hotel again. I found that all the other
gentlemen did the same thing, with the same apparent regularity and then,
as now, that was all there was to do for recreation and amusement.

But I liked the place and the climate, and it occurred to me very strongly
that someone with sufficient means ought to provide accommodations for
that class of people who are not sick, but who come here to enjoy the climate,
have plenty of money, but could find no satisfactory way of spending it. . . .[14]

FLORIDA was a wilderness sparsely populated by a few families in the
north and a scattering of settlements of fishermen and ship scavengers
in the south. The interior of sawgrass, swamp, Spanish bayonet and
desertlike plains was largely unexplored. Lake Okeechobee, the nation's sixth largest fresh water lake, wasn't even mapped.[15]

It was the last American wilderness, and that appealed to Henry.

# CHAPTER 8

# St. Augustine

ON June 5, 1883, Ida Alice Shourds and Henry Morrison Flagler were married at the Madison Avenue Methodist Church in New York City. Mysteriously, Henry declined an immediate honeymoon, saying he was in the midst of several business deals that would not permit him to leave the city. This suggests that the date of the wedding, and perhaps the wedding itself, was Alice's idea, not Henry's.

If Henry had wanted a honeymoon, he wouldn't have scheduled the marriage in June 1883. The year was as crucial as any before for Standard Oil and, like it or not, Henry was up to his neck in unavoidable Standard business. He was still secretary of the Standard Oil Trust and president of the new holding company, Standard Oil of New Jersey. As such, his signature was on immediate demand for the many negotiations going on in 1883, most especially Henry's own project, the takeover of Tidewater Pipeline Company, the last obstacle to Standard's monopoly of the oil transportation industry.

It is reasonable to assume, therefore, that the timing of the wedding was set by Alice, not Henry, a rush job as it were.

Consequently, trunks containing Alice's personal belongings were delivered to the house at 685 Fifth Avenue on the day after the wedding.

The new bride was greeted sullenly by the family. Within the week, Carrie Flagler left. She who had mothered young Harry and looked after the house for two years spent the remainder of the summer in Europe with a friend, and upon her return bought an apartment elsewhere in Manhattan.

Alice did not succeed in her role as stepmother to young Harry. Years later, he said that she tried earnestly, but the resentment of his mother's replacement was too strong for him to overcome.

These things—the departure of Carrie, the resentment of Harry—
did not seem to weigh too heavily on Alice. Her interest was focused
almost exclusively on the new style of life made possible by Henry's
vast wealth. With a virtually unlimited bank account, she launched
a spending spree that would have astounded lesser millionaires. Within
a few months, her wardrobe contained some of the most beautiful
and elaborate clothes in New York.

During the summer and fall, Henry was occupied with Tidewater
Pipeline, the successful takeover being completed in late 1883. He
spent November wrapping up details.

Henry and Alice's delayed honeymoon began in December 1883,
in St. Augustine. In choosing it, Henry, it seems, was still chewing
on his idea that the place attracted a lot of rich people with nothing
to do.

The Florida weather was delightful, and shortly after the couple's
arrival a cold wave struck the north, making their stay even cozier.
In New York it was 10 below. In St. Louis it was 23 below; in Cleveland 14 below. The Flaglers, accordingly, prolonged their trip among
the orange blossoms and didn't return to New York until March 1,
1884.

That summer at Satan's Toe saw more rounds of parties in the
country, dinner and theater in the city—a social season which extended into the fall. The following winter, in February 1885, Henry
and Alice returned to Florida. After a week in Jacksonville, Henry
heard that a new hotel was being built in St. Augustine which he was
anxious to see.

He and Alice arrived to find that considerable changes had occurred in the short 12 months of their absence.

They stayed at the San Marco Hotel, a huge six-storey wooden
structure located just outside the old city gates across from Fort San
Marcos.

Henry by now was exploring the possibility of building a hotel in
St. Augustine and was met immediately by Osborne Seavey and James
A. McGuire, the manager and the builder, respectively, of the San
Marco. He also met Franklin W. Smith, a Boston architect whose St.
Augustine winter home, the Villa Zorayda, was one of the first cast-
in-place concrete buildings in the United States. Designed as an exact
miniature reproduction of one of the palaces of the Alhambra, the

Villa Zorayda was built with a new kind of material made from a mixture of cement and coquina, a soft whitish rock made up of sea shell and coral.

WITHIN an hour of registering at the San Marco, Henry was on the street studying the Zorayda. Its exterior was square and massive but the interior was soft and well lit with windows, doors and balconies opening onto a large, flowery courtyard. The hotel's Spanish style appealed to him.

Flagler had been perplexed by the task of building a large modern hotel in a style befitting St. Augustine's old Spanish character. He believed he had found his answer in the poured concrete method used by Smith in his Villa Zorayda. The Zorayda was the way to build in St. Augustine. The building was new and strong, but the red and gray colors of its cement walls and Spanish tiled roof allowed it to blend inconspicuously with the remainder of the city.

That year, the city of St. Augustine put on a special costume show for its winter visitors, in observance of the landing of Ponce de León. Highly impressed with the show, Flagler at last made his decision: He would build a hotel in the midst of the city, and he would name it the Ponce de Leon.

Before leaving, he was approached by Dr. Andrew Anderson, a prominent local landowner and politician with whom Henry would form a lifelong friendship.

Anderson was a practicing physician with considerable real estate holdings. Born in St. Augustine in 1839, when Florida was still a territory, Anderson had inherited a considerable amount of land in New York City, and had used the funds to invest in Florida ventures.[1] Among other properties, he owned the Markland orange groves, one of the best in Florida, which provided him with a handsome income. He and Henry hit it off immediately, forming a friendship based on mutual business interests and trust.

Flagler told Anderson that to build his hotel he would need paved streets and sewers, improvements which would enhance not only Henry's hotel but property values for the entire city. Anderson said he would do his best to get the passage of bonds to finance the improvements.

By the time Henry departed on April 1, 1885, he had purchased several acres of Anderson's Markland groves, portions which by then had become unprofitable for oranges but were ideal for Henry's hotel. Henry also appointed Anderson to serve as his agent in all his matters in St. Augustine, a remarkable bit of instant trust which was never betrayed.

Upon Flagler's return to New York, he contacted a young architect, Thomas Hastings, whose father—like Flagler's, a Presbyterian minister—was a close friend of Henry's. He engaged Hastings and his partner, John Carrere, to design the Ponce de Leon in the Spanish manner. (Later, Carrere and Hastings would design the New York Public Library, the interior of the old Metropolitan Opera House and the U.S. Senate Office building in Washington.) Louis Tiffany was hired to decorate the hotel. His stained glass windows graced the Ponce de Leon and founded his reputation.

In May, Flagler returned with Hastings and a building consultant, Benjamin Brewster. The three closeted themselves with Anderson, working in all-night sessions to draw plans for Flagler's hotel. They intended, simply, to make it the best in America.

No expense would be spared, said Flagler; he announced that his policy had always been to make a " 'big grind for small grist'—to give as much as possible for as little money. It defies competition, gives satisfaction to the customers and the bulk of business thus secured will pay greater dividends in the end."[2]

The news of Flagler's interest in St. Augustine hit Florida, and the nation's financial circles, like an explosion. Unlike in later years, Flagler was then as well known as Rockefeller, a celebrity of high finance. And any interest of his was reported and speculated upon.

Flagler told newspapermen:

I have two stories, to tell to every one who asks me my reasons for building the Ponce de Leon Hotel . . .

I was coming downtown in an El road car in New York recently when a friend said to me, "Flagler, I was asked the other day why you were building that hotel in St. Augustine and replied that you had been looking around for several years for a place to make a fool of yourself in, and at last selected St. Augustine as the spot."

The other story that I used to illustrate my position is this: There was once a good old church member who had always lived a correct life, until well advanced in years he got on a spree. While in this state he met his good pastor. After being roundly upbraided for his condition, he replied, "I have been giving all my days to the Lord hitherto, and now I'm taking one for myself." This is somewhat my case. For 14 years I have devoted my time exclusively to business, and now I am pleasing myself.[3]

People began to speculate in land throughout northeastern Florida and Flagler was deluged with offers. He turned all of these over to Dr. Anderson.

Flagler made Anderson his agent throughout all of Florida and gave him free access to his purse strings. No task was too great or expensive. Anderson represented Flagler's interests not only with local businessmen, but also with local and state government. On numerous occasions he went before the St. Augustine city council to represent Flagler and in the popular mind was known to be his representative. In 1886, Anderson was elected mayor, a victory generally interpreted as a ringing endorsement of Flagler by the citizenry.

As time went on, the Flagler–Anderson relationship became increasingly personal. James Ingraham, later a close business associate of Flagler, noted that "perhaps no one possessed Mr. Flagler's entire confidence and esteem to a greater extent than Dr. Anderson. . . . Mr. Flagler told me that in a great part of this work, much of his inspiration and help and suggestion came from Dr. Anderson."

For the rest of Flagler's life, he and Anderson were the closest of friends. Flagler's records show a constant stream of personal letters between the two, usually initiated by Flagler. At the turn of the century, Anderson began to travel extensively abroad. This development alarmed Flagler, who tried to keep constant track of Anderson's whereabouts so he could communicate with him. In those years, the tone of the letters at times reaches near desperation and shows a strong dependency on Anderson's friendship.

As his workers broke ground in St. Augustine, one of Flagler's concerns was malaria. The disease was uncontrollable at that time because it was unknown that mosquitoes spread the disease. It was known, however, that malaria struck in moist, warm climates which contained swamps or other land with standing water. Flagler feared that digging the hotel foundation might create a malarial sinkhole in St. Augustine. Anderson, however, being a physician, assured him that if lime were freely used by the workmen while digging, the possibility of creating such sinkholes would be minimized. Whether lime had anything to do with it or not, there was no malaria.

Flagler was greatly helped by the cooperation of the city fathers and other businessmen. The president of the local Jacksonville, St. Augustine and Indian River Railway volunteered to extend his line further into the city so that the materials could be hauled right up to the hotel site.

Permission was also promptly granted by the city for the use of coquina from nearby Anastasia Island, provided Flagler could obtain approval of the U.S. government, which owned the quarry. Flagler was a personal friend of the Secretary of the Navy, William Whitney of New York, who secured permission through the Treasury Department for Flagler to use as much of the coquina as he needed.[4] Said Flagler,

On the first day of December, 1885, we commenced the digging of the excavation for the foundation of the Hotel Ponce de Leon in St. Augustine. At that time St. Augustine had a population of from 1,500 to 2,000 persons. There were but 12 houses on the line of the railroad between Jacksonville and St. Augustine. There was no house, no habitation, between St. Augustine and what is now Palatka . . . Ormond may have had 150 inhabitants, Daytona 150.[5]

Flagler explained that although he was a novice, he intended to build a hotel which had quality and permanence.

I am not a hotel builder. I have just completed an office building for the Standard Oil Company in New York that cost over a million dollars. But the Ponce de Leon is an altogether different affair. I want something to last all time to come and have no doubt made the walls much more expensive than necessary, but I had much rather spend $50,000 too much than $50,000 too little. I take a great deal of pride in it, and watch its progress with much interest. I do not care whether it pays in five, ten, fifteen or twenty years, but I would hate to think that I am investing money that will not bring a return in the future. I will, however, have a hotel that suits me in every respect, and one that I can thoroughly enjoy, cost what it may. I tell my friends that when they stop at the Ponce de Leon it will cost them a good deal of money, but guarantee them that they will get its full return in value.[6]

Although the hotel was inspired by the Spanish style, it was not precisely Spanish architecture. Done as an adaptation of the Spanish and Italian Renaissance, it is a monolithic structure of concrete composed of six parts of coquina shell to one part of cement.

"It is not even exact to say the hotel was built," said architect Hastings. "It was cast. The coquina, found almost on the very spot, was a suggestion of nature not to be overlooked."

Electricity was provided by four Edison direct current dynamos. Water came from artesian wells 500 feet deep. Because the water stank of sulphur, it was piped through several fountains on the hotel grounds so that it could be aerated before being pumped into the four large iron holding tanks located near the roof of the hotel. In 1892, a pipeline to a fresh water pond west of town was built so that the hotel guests would not be required to drink sulphur water, although such water was recommended by physicians of the day for its supposed healthful properties.

In only one respect did Flagler and his architects fail to anticipate public demands—the matter of toilets. In the standards of the day, public toilets were considered sufficient, one for each floor. The Ponce opened with only one private toilet, that in Flagler's suite. Almost immediately, however, it would become necessary to add private baths and toilets to the rooms of the hotel.

Flagler paid personal attention to each detail. In one instance, he eliminated a wall so that his telephone operator could have natural daylight.

He often walked about the unfinished building smoking a cigar. There were "No Smoking" signs placed here and there for the attention of the workers. One day, Flagler tried to enter the building, smoking his Havana, when he was stopped by a watchman. Henry quickly informed the watchman that he was Flagler, the owner of the hotel and he could damn well smoke where he wanted to. The watchman was unimpressed. "There have been a great many Flaglers trying to get in here lately," he said. He was still arguing with Flagler when one of the contractors, James McGuire, came by and rebuked the guard for not recognizing his boss. Flagler recovered sufficiently to compliment the young man on his efficiency, then huffed and puffed his way into the building under a full head of steam.[7]

When suites of furniture arrived late for the hotel's scheduled opening, Flagler took off his jacket, got beside his hired hands and smashed open the crates. When the pouring of cement became a problem, Flagler had his agents recruit 1,200 Negroes from the countryside and brought them in to tamp the liquid coquina gravel into the wooden construction forms with their bare feet while musicians played lively music.

The Ponce was finished on May 30, 1887, but the opening was delayed until the next year on January 10, the beginning of the new season. Spanking new and costing $2.5 million, the Ponce opened as cooly as if it had been part of the landscape for 300 years. There were no formal ceremonies. The hotel unlatched its doors, guests arrived and registered, and within 30 minutes there were nearly a thousand people crowding the spacious rotunda and corridors of the hotel, spilling out eagerly into the Tropical Court. The "band discoursed sweet music, and the scene was grand enough of itself to impress the average mind with a sense of awe and admiration," wrote a wide-eyed travel reporter.[8]

The first dinner began with two choices of soup, moved on to hors d'oeuvres and Croquettes of Shrimp; dallied over Broiled Shad and Parisienne Potatoes, then settled in for a run at three main courses. First there was a choice of roast beef with mashed potatoes and stewed tomatoes; turkey with cranberry sauce, sweet potatoes and onions; or ham with Madeira sauce and vegetables. That course was followed by either lamb chops with peas or sauteed Chicken à la Espagnole. Then came something called Rock Punch, followed by broiled Golden Plover on Toast. Afterward came coffee and a choice of desserts— pudding, vanilla soufflé, apple pie, coconut pie, chocolate eclairs, fruit cake, assorted ice creams, fruit and cheeses.

The opening menu set the pace for the remainder of the century. The staggering array of choices, varying only in type but not in quantity, was standard fare for lunch and dinner. Breakfast was a little easier, but not by much.

Across from the Ponce de Leon, separated by a landscaped garden occupying a full city block, was the Alcazar, a second hotel begun by Flagler for guests who were not quite so wealthy. Construction had begun in early 1887 by the same contractors—McGuire and Mc-Donald—and the same architects—Carrere and Hastings—as had been used for the Ponce.

Not quite as large as the Ponce, the Alcazar's facade was a reproduction of the Alcazar Palace in Seville, Spain. The hotels were alike, however, in their Moorish style, castellated towers and roofs of rich red terra cotta tiling.

One of the Alcazar's features was a swimming pool 120 feet long and 50 feet wide, ranging in depth from 3 feet to more than 12 feet. A constant supply of water from an artesian well poured into the pool. A skylight overhead provided a sunny atmosphere in the deepest part of winter.

Dressing facilities for gentlemen were located in the east end; those for ladies in the west. The water extended into the rounded portions of the rooms, and from the men's side it was possible to dive underwater and swim out into the main pool. The ladies' side was closed off so that they could swim in privacy if they desired.

A gallery overlooked the swimming pool from which guests could watch the swimmers or dance to the music of the two orchestras located at either end. During the day, it was an ideal place to meet for tea or a game of cards.

The casino also had the first steambaths built in Florida. Attendants were quartered on the third floor in order to be available to guests at any time. In the beginning massages were for men only, but in later years certain days were set aside when female masseuses ministered to ladies only.

Of the Alcazar, Flagler said,

[It] will furnish superior accommodations for those who do not wish to stay at the other hotel. Amusements will be provided, and the vicinity of the hotel made as attractive as possible. The Methodist Church, which I am constructing across the avenue on the north, will be the finest church edifice south of the Potomac. The Casa Monica [a hotel designed by the Zorayda's Franklin Smith and purchased by Flagler] is very near, and it is a handsome structure. These, with the big hotel and the Alcazar will make a beautiful group.

The hotels were bordered by an avenue called the Alameda, a street which Flagler had paved with asphalt. In St. Augustine, it had long borne the name of Lover's Lane, because of the great live oaks which sheltered it with great branches and made a shadowy and cool archway during even the hottest summer days.

The nation's press was in awe. A hotel superior to the Palmer House in Chicago, the Palace in San Francisco and the Fifth Avenue in New York had been built in an isolated Florida hamlet of fewer than 4,000 inhabitants. At a time when resort hotels, from Maine to California, were furnished with a standard brass bed, a rocking chair, a dresser, a wash basin and a chamber pot, the Ponce offered the luxuries of Babylon. There were 540 rooms and, as advertisements pointed out, each cost $1,000 or more to furnish and was lit by electric lights.

Rooms at the Flagler hotels, however, did not come cheap.

Julian Ralph, a *Harper's* magazine writer, visited what he called Flagler's "Riviera" and found

. . . a woman and her lady friend and maid were paying $39 a day for rooms and meals; where an Astor and his bride had paid the same sum per day during a week of their honeymoon; where one lady took a room solely for her trunks at $10 a day; and where an economical young woman told me that she was filling her mother's closets and her own with dresses, while the mother put her things on the chairs. "Mamma has had her day, you know," said the maiden, "and she doesn't care."

There was one little party that occupied three bedrooms, a bathroom and a parlor, taking up a whole corner of the hotel on the ground floor, whose bill at the hotel might easily have been $75 a day. And in all these instances the extras are lost sight of—the $5 to the head waiter, the $2 or $3 a week to the waiter at the table, the fees to the bellboys and the ice-water boy and the bootblack.[9]

At the time, the average factory worker made eight dollars a week and a school teacher six dollars.[10]

The operation policy of the Ponce de Leon was the same as Flagler's construction policy, namely, the best of everything. He felt that a fine hotel or restaurant was bound to lose a certain amount of money before it established itself as a place of bona-fide quality. In the 1890s, as the Ponce continued to be crowded with fashionable guests and to lose money at a nice rate, a new manager decided to economize. Unaware of the deficit policy, he wired Flagler in New York for permission to discharge the costly French chef and an equally costly dance band.

Flagler wired back: "Hire another cook and two more of the best orchestras."

With the opening of the Ponce de Leon, the Flaglers established a suite at the hotel and made St. Augustine their permanent winter home. They commuted back and forth to New York in a private railcar, which Henry named Alicia, in honor of his wife.

Together they were very private, very intimate, very personal. St. Augustine was the happiest time of his life.[11]

But it was not to last.

A sorrowing blow was about to descend.

In March 1887, 31-year-old Jennie Louise divorced John Hinckley on grounds of adultery, after 11 years of marriage and no children. Seven months later she married dashing Fredrick Hart Benedict, a Wall Street broker, explorer and son of Chicago industrialist E. C. Benedict, head of the Chicago Gas Trust. Contemporaries described Jennie as a beautiful woman with a retiring disposition. Her courtship with young Benedict was noted in the newspapers as being "as exquisite as any of the tales of fiction."

Jennie made a will after marriage in which she bequeathed all her property to her husband, while he on his part gave her everything that he had. Henry Flagler made a wedding gift of $1 million in Standard Oil stock.

On February 9, 1889, the Benedicts' first child, a daughter named Margery, was born. Complications set in, however, and the child died within hours.

Jennie's condition also worsened, and her doctor recommended that she be taken to Florida for rest and recuperation. Her father-in-law, a well-known yachtsman, offered his finest schooner, the *Oneida*, for the trip. Her doctors felt that the luxurious care she would receive on the yacht would be less strenuous, and the ocean air more healthful, than the trip by rail, even if made in Henry Flagler's private car. She sailed, accompanied by her husband and her younger brother Harry. Several days after the yacht put to sea, however, she developed high fevers and entered a coma. Before the yacht could reach Charleston, the nearest port, she was dead.

At the time, Henry was in St. Augustine with Ida Alice. He hurried to Charleston and led the party back to New York, where Jennie was buried in Woodlawn Cemetery.

Flagler was desolate and his friends feared the blow was too great for him to endure.

Henry rebounded by beginning plans to commemorate Jennie and Margery with a monument. He would construct a domed church, in the style of the Venetian Renaissance, to be called the Memorial Presbyterian Church. When completed in 1890, the monument became one of the chief adornments of St. Augustine. (In 1904, Henry

added a mausoleum to the church, having the bodies of Mary Harkness Flagler, Jennie and Margery reburied. Upon his death, Henry
Flagler, too, was buried in the crypt.)

MEANWHILE, trouble was developing with Alice.

Flying into red-hot rages over small matters, her explosive temper
was becoming notorious. And, being something of a social climber,
she was perceptive to the fact that Flagler's friends, and the New
York set, considered her a fortune hunter of no pedigree and cold-
shouldered her accordingly. Being snubbed and snobbed by others
is a great spur to social ambition; fashionable acceptance became an
obsession of her life.

It seemed Alice could not sate her thirst for luxuries. Henry tried
to provide her with everything that might make her happy. She liked
yachting and boating, and at one time they owned two yachts, the
sloop *Eclipse* and the schooner *Columbia*. Those were succeeded by
perhaps the finest yacht the Flaglers ever owned, the *Alicia*, named—
like the private railcar—in honor of Alice. It was a beautiful craft and
very fast. It was 160 feet in length, yet it was easy to handle. Although
seen often in Florida waters, the *Alicia* was used more during the
summer when the Flaglers were at their Mamaroneck home. They
often used it to visit friends in the fashionable summer resort of New
London, Connecticut.[12]

To provide a social base in Florida, Henry and Alice built a winter
home, called Kirkside, in St. Augustine. It was near the Ponce de
Leon Hotel and specially designed for winter living. Pure colonial
architecture prevailed throughout its 15 rooms, and its exterior was
painted white with pale green blinds. The downstairs rooms were
extra large and fitted for entertaining. The salon, the main room, was
worthy of Versailles. Custom-designed chandeliers furnished electric
light, with the electricity piped in from generators at the Ponce.

The steady outflow of cash, however, was beginning to tell on
Flagler's bank accounts, and for the first time he found it necessary
to sell off some of his Standard Oil stock. In December 1890, he sold
2,500 shares to John Rockefeller for $375,000.[13]

Lavish balls, with guests numbering in the hundreds, became a
regular feature of the Flaglers' winter seasons in St. Augustine. Perhaps the peak of the flood came in 1893 when *The Tatler,* St. Augustine's social newspaper, listed five formal affairs given by the Flaglers

between January and March. Many small parties given at Kirkside were not listed.

Alice Flagler usually wore extravagant gowns of extremely revealing décolleté at these functions. On March 23, 1893, she gave a dance at the Ponce which *The Tatler* called the "Pearl Dance" because of the unusual size and beauty of the pearls Alice wore.[14]

To Alice, St. Augustine was a personal playground. But by now her gait was proving too fast for Henry, and he began to withdraw from the frenzied social activity. In the very act of withdrawal, however, he found a new interest.

Among the guests at several of the Flagler balls was a young Southern woman named Mary Lily Kenan, a 24-year-old, unmarried daughter of the distinguished Kenan family of North Carolina. Attractive rather than pretty, she had what was considered the ideal figure of her day—small, barely over five-feet tall, with narrow waist, large bosom, and thick, dark hair which could hang down to her waist. Mary Lily had met Alice and Henry Flagler in 1891 at the Newport, Rhode Island, home of Mr. and Mrs. Pembroke Jones, mutual friends of the Flaglers and the Kenans.[15]

HENRY was becoming attracted to Mary Lily, and increasingly distressed by his wife. According to those who knew her, Alice Flagler could be vastly entertaining, or hard to take. She was self-centered to an exceptional degree and interested largely in matters that pertained to her own social status and personal appearance.

She was subject to quick temper flares and sudden crying. She also was given to making cutting remarks about friends, family and most often Henry.

Henry attempted to overlook her excesses until her willfulness nearly caused a maritime disaster. She was entertaining a group of friends with a yachting party off the coast of New England when a gale-force storm arose suddenly, reaching a velocity of more than 60 miles an hour. Despite the pleas of the captain, the only man on board, and her many seasick friends, Alice refused to return to port, and the yacht lashed around in heavy seas for six hours. They were driven further and further out to sea and were eight hours overdue before Alice allowed them to return. Flagler, waiting at the dock at Mamaroneck, was in a rage and later mentioned to friends his concern about her peculiar and dangerous actions.[16]

There were other problems for Henry.

In 1892, his son Harry had dropped out, or had been asked to drop out, of Princeton. Flagler invited him down to St. Augustine to help with the hotel work. Young Flagler went reluctantly. It was the father's plan for Harry to learn the hotel and the railroad business and gradually succeed him in the work. An indifferent student, Harry proved equally indifferent to hotel work. After nearly two years of frustrating conflict with his father, he returned to New York.

He enrolled at Columbia University and shortly afterward, on April 24, 1894, married Annie Louise Lamont, heiress of financier Charles Lamont. After ceremonies at the Madison Avenue Baptist Church, the couple's wedding supper was held at Delmonico's, at 555 Fifth Avenue, a short walk from the Flagler family mansion. Both Henry Flagler and Ida Alice attended the wedding and supper— showing that the rift between father and son was not yet complete. [17]

It was about this time that a Baltimore man named Isaac Fuld patented something he called a "Ouija" board, from the word "yes" in French (oui) and German (ja). The device consisted of a small, three-legged board, called a planchette, which moved over a larger board enscribed with the letters of the alphabet and "yes" and "no" boxes. The user places one or more fingers on the planchette, attempts to relax and awaits a question from someone else in the room. Then the planchette begins to spell out the answer, moving either by the involuntary muscular action of the user or through some other agency. The other agency, of course, is believed to be a spirit. Spiritualists and mediums loved the Ouija board. They particularly liked to use it with clients who were rich but dissatisfied and who desired help from the occult.

In 1893, someone brought such a board to Alice.

# CHAPTER 9

# Transitions

O N Tuesday, January 2, 1894, we can see Henry Flagler arise promptly at his accustomed hour of 7 A.M. He takes breakfast alone in the dining room at Kirkside. Alice is upstairs in their bedroom, disheveled in her nightgown, tossing fitfully in her sleep, hung over from many glasses of champagne. Elsewhere in the house, the servants are already hard at work, cleaning up from last night's party. Henry suffers no ill effects. He left his guests early, after seeing to his duties as host, and he drank, as usual, in moderation. His sole indiscretion, he feels, may have been the too solicitous attentions he paid to young Miss Kenan. There is no question that he is attracted to her and likes her company.

It is his sixty-fourth birthday, and though he may not know it, he is at the third great watershed of his life. It is a natural time for him to reflect upon his life. On this birthday, Flagler had written to his son: "It will take 30 more years to complete my projects in Florida, but I have only 20 more years to live.

"I will live to be 84," he predicts with near uncanny accuracy.[1]

By his sixty-fourth year, Henry Morrison Flagler had known fortune and success. He had had years of happiness—with Mary in Ohio, with Standard Oil, with Alice in the first several years. There had been, too, great grief. The deaths of his daughters Carrie and Jennie Louise and his granddaughter Margery; the inability to communicate with his son.

Lurking behind all was the death of Mary.

Had he yet, at this senior age in life, faced his responsibility in that? Judging by the written record, he hadn't. His letters, his journals, his interviews are all strangely quiet on his loss of Mary.

Yet it is impossible to accept that he had not dealt with it somewhere in his mind. The facts were too clear. His refusal to bring her to Florida had hurried, maybe even caused, her death. Scary as it was, it was not the sort of thing that Henry's straightforward nature could have ignored forever.

The *degree* of his responsibility was the question and one which should not be guessed at by biographers. That judgment belongs to Henry, and it is fair to assume that somewhere, in his conscious or subconscious mind, he had arrived at a figure.

He had, in the years following Mary's death, done what she had asked. He had disengaged from Standard Oil, and he had moved to Florida where he was poised on the brink of great enterprises and philanthropies. He had moved forward like a man impelled. And the question is how much he knew of his own motivation. Was he running away from his role in Mary's death? Or had he accepted it? Was Florida his escape? Or his atonement?

WHATEVER the explanation, Florida would cost him. Each accomplishment of his past had extracted its payment. The first, the launching of himself as a boy to find a life in Ohio, cost him the sole stability of his childhood, the presence of his mother. The second, transforming his Michigan humiliation into the creation of Standard Oil, may have cost the health of Mary. Had he attended to her with the thoroughness and attention he paid his business, she probably would be alive today. Indeed, had he paid attention to young Harry, he might have him, too.

He had yet to be billed for the price of the third, his plan to raise up Florida from tropical swamp to a productive land. But he knew the expense would be dear.

It would be normal for a man of his age to retire. At the time he owned about one-sixth of Standard Oil, and his shares could generate more millions than even Alice could spend.

But he would not do that. He would become instead the developer of great cities and vast farmlands. His greatest successes lay ahead.

But before that, there was the trouble with Alice.

IT began simply enough.

When in the summer of 1893 Alice received a Ouija board, almost immediately she became infatuated with it, holding seances with friends, consulting mediums and spiritualists, and paying handsomely for their advice.

A curious part of it was that her social conduct, always cutting, turned vicious. She spent hours alone in her room using the board to communicate with astral spirits. She would at times shun her husband's attentions and began confiding to disconcerted friends that she had plans to kill him.

She became irritable and erratic, and gossiped constantly about the immorality of her socially prominent friends. When Flagler's friends began to avoid her, she related her gossip to hairdressers and manicurists, once tipping a manicurist with one thousand roses.

The Ouija board, she told friends, had informed her that the Czar of Russia, whom she had never seen, was madly in love with her and that they would be married upon Flagler's death.

She paid $2,000 to Tiffany's to have her miniature painted, set in diamonds and sent to the Czar. She told a friend about the gift, however, and it was intercepted and returned to the patient Henry.[2]

During the summer, she convinced several friends that Henry was mistreating her. The gossip spread and began to damage Henry's reputation. A family friend and prominent New York physician, George Shelton, became suspicious of Alice and made it a point to be around her, inviting her to his house for teas, to his office for medical advice and attention. Soon, she began to tell him, too, of Henry's mistreatments.

At a pivotal occasion, at Mamaroneck, Shelton was astounded to hear her repeat the remarks at a large gathering of family friends. Embarrassed, Shelton retreated from the salon, but Alice followed him to another room where she told new tales of scandal, of prominent New Yorkers and European aristocrats and sex orgies. As the doctor again attempted retreat, she drew him by the arm to her bedroom where she opened a jewelry case and handed him three plain pebbles. She asked him if he could not see certain marks in the pebbles. When he said no, she flew into a rage and jerked the stones from his hand.

"Of course you cannot see them. There are only three people in the world who can, and only members of a secret society possess them and the power to interpret them. They are talismen and are very, very old!"

She showed the stones, one by one. "This one has cured many forms of paralysis. This one will produce pregnancy in a barren woman . . . The other one," she said with an eerie laugh, "I am going to send to the Czar."[3]

The thoroughly alarmed Shelton quickly got out of the house and not long after reported to Henry that he feared Alice was ill. Henry related other incidents, and Shelton suggested that Henry move the household from Mamaroneck to the Fifth Avenue mansion where Shelton could keep a closer eye on Alice. The move was made, and Alice was encouraged to contact Shelton with the smallest problem. She saw him often, usually on complaint of a "slight headache."

Her conversations with Shelton fixed upon the general infidelity of men, most especially Henry but also other prominent New Yorkers. Her suspicions of infidelity may not have been total delusions, as we shall see. In the meantime—in Shelton's presence—she would fall into conversations with imaginary people and laugh and joke with relatives who were not there.

A year passed in this fashion. By October 1895, Alice began to tell anyone who would listen that she had a great love for the Czar, explaining that she had been informed by her Ouija board that the Czar was also madly in love with her. She would marry him, she said with ominous looks, as soon as Henry died.

Shelton advised Flagler not to share the same bedroom with her for fear she might try to kill him. Henry refused because, when they were alone, she was affectionate and tender. He also felt that if they did not occupy the same bedroom it would lead to her total mental collapse.

Fearing for Henry's safety, Shelton obtained permission for Alice to be formally interviewed by himself and two other doctors—Allan Starr and Frederick Peterson, who were specialists in the field of mental disorders.

The three doctors arrived at the Fifth Avenue house on October 24. Upon learning their intention, Alice immediately flew into a violent rage and after a china-throwing tantrum locked herself in her room and barricaded the door. After an hour or so, Peterson enticed her out by a ruse. She emerged, hysterically protesting that the house was full of Russian spies and that Henry was trying to poison her.[4]

THE interview was punctuated with homicidal threats to Henry. When it ended, Alice ran to her room and locked the door. The three doctors conferred in private and agreed that she had "delusionary insanity." Peterson, in addition to his private practice, was president of the

Lunacy Commission of New York State and thus empowered to commit Alice on the spot. Shelton produced papers he had prepared for her confinement at Choate's Sanitarium in Pleasantville, New York, in Westchester County, about 20 miles north of downtown Manhattan.

Two nurses—one male and one female—were waiting in the carriageway outside and were summoned to accompany Peterson to Alice's bedroom. When she opened the door, they grabbed her and, while she screamed for Henry's help, Peterson read her the commitment papers. She was then hauled down the stairs by force and put in a waiting carriage at the door.

Flagler was miserable. Throughout Alice's madness, he seemed to have never feared for his safety, although it was the homicidal threats that spurred Shelton into action. Flagler truly hoped that Alice might be cured. Meanwhile, he took Shelton's advice to go to Florida for the winter where he would have the friendship of Dr. Anderson for support.

It was, however, a restless winter. He would spend a few weeks in Florida, then go back to New York, then back to Florida. On Shelton's advice, he steered clear of the sanitarium, but Shelton himself made two visits at Henry's request. Alice was no better. She cursed Shelton and repeated her love for the Czar. She said she despised Shelton and would get even with him for putting her in "this hole." Realizing his visits did nothing but rile her, he quit going.[5]

In a letter to Anderson in December, Henry said it was the most agonizing time in his life. Alice's madness, he said, was worse than the death of Mary or their child Jennie. It was compounded by the "desertion" of Harry. Henry wrote:

I thank you for your thoughts of me and for your hopes in my behalf. Not a day passes but that I call myself to account for what I fear my friends may think is unmanly weakness. I summon all the philosophy I am capable of. I reason about it. I realize that mine is no exceptional case, but it is no use. You have known me, my dear friend, in one great sorrow; when it was comparatively easy to think and speak of Heaven. Now it is not so. This is something immeasurably harder to bear than death. I need God himself; His personal presence and I am devoutly thankful that He has not deserted me. For all this, I am grateful to you for your tender sympathy, for it helps me.

Harry's desertion of me has made my burden much heavier. And I constantly wonder why this additional sorrow was necessary. God knows and I must trust Him.[6]

Four months later, Flagler talked with his doctors about his wife's release.

In May, an examination was made, and Alice was found to be better than expected. She talked freely about her delusions and only once did she revert to an abnormal state. She said she loved her husband and was distressed by the trouble she had caused him.

The doctors agreed to release her, but warned that she might have a relapse in two to six months. Flagler, optimistic, wrote Anderson, "I shall try to keep up courage and make the best fight in her behalf that is possible."[7]

Alice was brought home to Mamaroneck on June 5, 1896, her and Henry's thirteenth wedding anniversary. Alice was allowed only a few visitors that summer but was given full liberty of action otherwise, to ride or go on the yacht—provided Henry was with her. She seemed to be totally recovered, and Flagler wrote Anderson, "It seems too good to be true."

In July, Eugene and Eliza Ashley of Lockport, New York, both close friends of Henry, arrived at Mamaroneck for an indefinite stay. Eliza, Henry said, was just about his favorite niece, and he and Eugene, a prominent lawyer, had many business interests in common. It was Flagler's hope that the Ashleys, whom Alice liked and trusted, would divert her attention from her troubles.

The plan didn't work. Alice became fidgety and begged Henry to get her another Ouija board. When he refused, she offered a bribe to one of the servants to find one for her. After several weeks, Alice returned to her delusions, expressing her love for the Czar, complaining of Henry's infidelities and her loss of respect for him.

As her condition worsened, friends advised Flagler to return her to the asylum. He refused, saying he would do so only as a last resort. "I shall not let her leave home until it becomes absolutely necessary," he wrote Anderson.

In October, Alice finally obtained a Ouija board from a neighbor and secluded herself in her room. Almost immediately, her condition degenerated to absolute madness. The three doctors—Shelton, Starr and Peterson—decided to confine her at Mamaroneck. The house was converted into an asylum as a full-time staff of male and female nurses were hired. Henry moved to the Manhattan Hotel in town.

He "looked very bad," said an associate. "The strain upon him was great indeed. However, now that the shock [of Alice's relapse] has come, he looks more composed. The feeling that he can now sleep without any apprehension must afford his mind some relief. It is indeed a sad case."

During the long winter at Mamaroneck, Alice turned homicidal. It became necessary to hide such articles as knives and forks. Despite such precautions, she attacked one doctor with a pair of scissors she had hidden on her person. She bruised the doctor about the face and badly lacerated one of his hands before he could escape from her room.

On March 20, 1897, she was recommitted for a second and final time. Henry saw her being led away, the last time he would ever see her. In 1899, the courts ruled her officially insane and appointed Eugene Ashley to be the guardian of her property. Dr. Carlos MacDonald, operator of the asylum, was named her medical guardian.

For her care, Flagler set up a fund of $1.4 million in Standard Oil stock, providing an income of $120,000 per year, which grew through the years. At MacDonald's sanitarium, she lived in a private cottage with her own maids. She had her own carriage and later her own car, and took regular outings in the company of MacDonald or other personnel. She lived longer than any of the other principals in Flagler's life except his son. Alice Shourds Flagler died at the asylum, of a cerebral hemorrhage, in July 1930. She was 82 years old, and her wealth had grown to more than $15 million.

PART of Alice's rage may have had foundation. Henry Flagler's infidelities seem not to have been imaginary.

A divorce suit, filed in Syracuse, New York, and naming Henry as co-respondent, claimed that he had kept a married woman as his mistress, from at least December 1896 through December 1897, or later. The dates include the time when Alice was in isolation at Mamaroneck and Henry was registered at his New York hotel.

In the suit, the plaintiff, C. W. Foote, claimed that his wife of five years, Helen Long, began an affair with Flagler in December 1896, and that Flagler established her in an apartment from that time until June 1897.

During June and July, said the suit, Helen and Henry spent considerable time on his yacht, the *Alicia*. In July, Henry bought a house for the woman at 27 East 57th Street and also gave her $400,000 in Standard Oil stock.[8]

Henry didn't reply to the suit, and later his name was dropped as co-respondent. The divorce was granted.

There is no conclusive evidence that Flagler was involved with Mrs. Foote. But the details of the suit are so explicit, and the denials so absent, that it is fair to assume that Henry bought his way out of the litigation.

Such an arrangement would not have been unusual for men of Henry's class, and most especially for the men of Standard Oil. Rockefeller was rumored to be something of a womanizer. And Flagler's own private secretary, Warren Smith, later wrote that the top echelon of the Standard had regular matinees at fancy houses near the company headquarters.

The randiest of the lot seems to have been Flagler's chief of staff in New York, W. H. Beardsley. Smith said that Beardsley and

. . . two very close associates, Berwind and Shonts, the coal and traction magnates, were known as the Three Musketeers.

Frequently they imbibed too freely, and were wont to go to a house [a brothel] on Pineapple Street, Brooklyn Heights, operated by a Mrs. McCaffrey. On one occasion, Mr. Beardsley fell, entering 26 Broadway. Mr. Flagler told him that any repetition would end his position. There was no recurrence.

Mrs. McCaffrey had a daughter, a late teenager. Mr. Beardsley had an operation performed on the young lady, correcting a "crossed eye." She moved to a New York hotel. She became the constant companion to Mr. Beardsley. He lavished the most expensive jewels upon her. Every anniversary, he heeded the slightest whim, a diamond or something equally precious. There was no attempt to hide this liaison.

It was common knowledge to the office. He left at noon every day in his private car and chauffeur. During the baseball season, often bringing an office boy along, he'd pick up Dora, then go to the ball game. He phoned the office for whatever stock market news he was interested in at the time.

One brother of Dora's worked in the office awhile, but left. Another brother, a Roman Catholic priest, was a regular visitor. Likewise he was the recipient of Mr. B's generosity. . . . Beginning in October, by private car, he made monthly trips to Florida lasting about 10 days. He inspected everything in the system. He was available to every employee. He had full knowledge of every action going on. At those times, Dora, accompanied by a companion, went to Atlantic City. She kept in daily touch with Mr B by phone. Dora used the name of Mr B's daughter.

It is a laugh, in a grim sort of way, that when Mr B lay dead in his own bed, in his own home, in New York City, his wife held his hand and said, "Papa was a good man, he was home every night." She apparently never knew that he had left the office every day at noon.[9]

Flagler himself was seen regularly in this period with young Mary Lily Kenan, although it is unknown exactly when their affair began.

Unlike Mrs. Foote, whose husband also claimed two other co-respondents in his divorce petition, Mary Lily was no trollop. She was a close friend of Eliza Ashley, and Flagler was often in the company of both young women.

Mary Lily was an attractive, full-figured girl from a socially prominent North Carolina family. Born June 14, 1867, she was nearly 38 years Henry's junior. One of four children of William Rand Kenan and Mrs. Mary Hargrave Kenan of Chapel Hill, she had an engaging personality and elegant bearing and manners. She was also an exceptionally talented pianist and singer, having studied music at the Pease Institute in Raleigh.[10]

It was said she was always popular with men, never without an escort, and her suitors were struck with her grace and charm and her taste for beautiful clothes. Flagler was impressed with her from the start, and Alice Flagler, too, had admired her for her pleasing personality and her elegant manners.[11]

In the beginning, when they first met in 1891, Flagler's interest in Mary Lily seemed fatherly. He lavished attention on her and Eliza, and took them on frequent trips to exotic sites in Florida. His attention to Mary Lily, and the trips, preceded the confinement of Ida Alice.

During Alice's time of troubles, Mary Lily sang for him, and it was generally agreed among mutual friends that she was chiefly responsible for lifting him out of his heavy depression concerning his wife's illness.

Soon afterward, gossip spread that Flagler and Mary Lily were in love.

At Flagler's invitation, Eliza Ashley and Mary Lily spent the early months of 1897, the height of the Palm Beach season, at his Reef cottage, on the Atlantic shore.

During 1898 the two women accompanied him to New York and Florida. He always provided them with a private railroad car and every imaginable luxury.

It seemed obvious to many that Flagler was using Eliza as a "beard," a disguise to protect his involvement with Mary Lily.

# CHAPTER 10

# Railroading

SOMETIME in the late 1880s, before his trouble with Alice, Flagler had sailed his yacht south down the Florida peninsula and happened onto a slender, sandy island, which at no point was wider than three-quarters of a mile and in some places was only 500 feet.

What the island lacked in width, it made up for in length, running for 18 miles along the Atlantic coast. Brushed by the Gulf Stream, which touched closer to the shore there than at any other spot in America, the island, which would be called Palm Beach, had exceptionally mild weather, usually in the 70s and 80s in the winter and seldom hotter than 95 degrees in the summer.[1]

Bordered on one side by the ocean and on the other by a navigable ocean inlet known as Lake Worth, Palm Beach was perpetually cooled by offshore breezes. It was a barrier island, but what set it apart from other such islands was its superb stands of coconut palms. Abundant fishing, the palm trees, the breezes, a fresh water lake and the Gulf Stream made the island nearly a tropical paradise for the three or four families who lived on its north end.

The palm island formed part of the Lake Worth basin, more than 100 miles of shoreline inhabited by a total population of less than a dozen families.

Charles Lang, a Civil War draft dodger, is generally considered to be the first white man to have built any sort of a permanent residence in the area. When the war began, and the Confederacy began drafting soldiers, Georgia resident Lang jumped into his small sailboat and headed south along Florida's east coast to escape conscription. He finally happened upon an inlet and steered inside a shallow pass to explore it. There he found a beautiful tropical lake, the shores of which were lined with overhanging trees, jungle vines

119

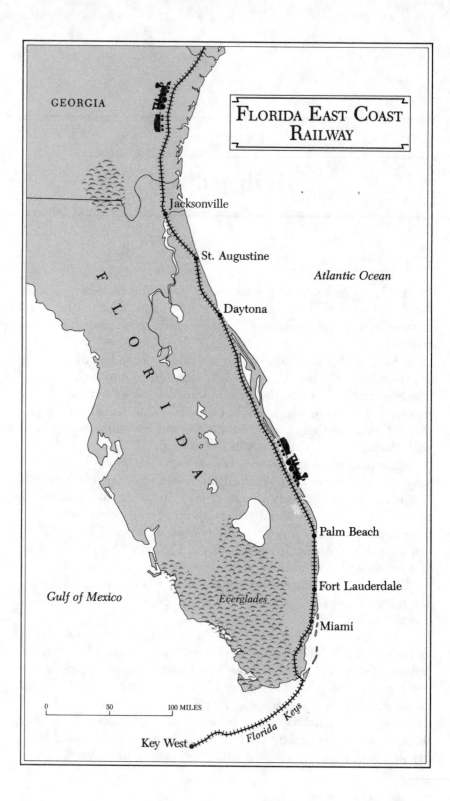

GEORGIA

FLORIDA EAST COAST
RAILWAY

Jacksonville

St. Augustine

Atlantic Ocean

Daytona

F
L
O
R
I
D
A

Palm Beach

Gulf of Mexico

Fort Lauderdale

Everglades

Miami

0        50        100 MILES

Florida Keys

Key West

and foliage. It was a natural wonder, virtually untouched. There were no inhabitants, neither white people nor Indians. Lang steered his boat to rest on the western shore of Lake Worth, directly across from the island scouted more than 25 years later by Flagler. There, on the site of the present city of West Palm Beach, Lang built a small palmetto-thatched cabin.[2]

It wasn't until 1867 that another visitor, George Sears, discovered the hidden inlet and docked his boat at Lang's cabin to tell him, among other things, that the war had been over for two years. Lang departed promptly, and Sears settled in.

Others followed, and by 1873 there were four families settled at various points along the coastline. Among them was that of Charles Pierce, who had come down as a boy from Chicago. He later recalled:

My father, H. D. Pierce, and uncle, William Moore, bought a boat at the waterworks in Chicago in 1871, in which to move to Florida. Immediately the big Chicago fire came and burned everything in sight but our boat.[3]

We found spars and rigging and started sculling down the Chicago River on our way to Florida . . . [After an eight-month journey, from November 1871 to July 1872, they passed down the Illinois and Mississippi rivers, into the Gulf of Mexico, and navigated along the coast until they reached Cedar Keys, near the mouth of the Suwanee River, north of Tampa.]

We sold the boat and went by train to Jacksonville. That old railroad was the most southern railroad in Florida at that time.

. . . Eventually we arrived at Hypoluxo Island, on the south end of Lake Worth.

Only five other people were on the lake when we came. Mr. and Mrs. Malden lived 12 miles north, up at the inlet. Charlie Moore lived on the old Lang place, about nine miles north on the lake. My uncle and William Butler were with us on Hypoluxo Island.

The first years on the lake, the people lived off the country and the beach. The beach furnished us a lot of stuff. Beach combing was practiced by everybody.

. . . Mr. Malden on the north side of the inlet [on Palm Beach Island] did nothing but hunt for a living. He got some lumber off a shipwreck and built a house. No doubt Mrs. Malden was glad of that for they had been living in a tent.

The first settler in Palm Beach was a man named Lang. He was a German, lived on north Indian River. When the Civil War came he ran away from conscription. He was not a deserter, neither was he a criminal. He was a draft dodger.

He planted coconut trees, citrus fruit, oleanders and a flowering tree called the "Geiger," which was a crooked ungainly tree, but bore beautiful small clusters of flowers with hardly any leaves. When he heard that the Civil War was over, he left. . . .

Charlie Moore took the Lang place in the winter of 1872. The house was built of pine logs. He never had to pay for it, there was no one to pay. Charlie kept the place up, taking care of the trees and flowers, that Lang had planted, and making improvements on it.

There were ample stands of palm trees on the island prior to 1878. However, thousands more trees were added that year when the bark *Providencia* ran aground.

The drunken crew—there were more than 50 sailors aboard—lost control of the ship while en route from Havana to Barcelona with 20,000 coconuts and 100 cases of wine. The ship broke up, strewing its cargo across the beach. The islanders salvaged all they could carry, including the coconuts, selling some and planting others.

In his memoir, Pierce recalled the *Providencia* wreck.

About 200 bearing coconut trees were growing along Lake Worth before the wreck of the *Providencia*. . . . All the settlers along Lake Worth planted coconut trees.

The coconuts from the *Providencia* had grown easily without any care, burying themselves in the sand and sprouting shoots from their sides.

But, said Pierce, the Palm Beachers

. . . did not receive the coconuts gratis. My father bought 700 nuts from the ship's captain and no one got them for nothing.

. . . There were no mangoes, sapodillas or tropical trees here. They had all been introduced by the settlers. . . .

We often saw Indians in the early days. When the steamer *Victor* was wrecked at Jupiter in 1872, seven canoes of Indians appeared immediately on the scene.

Morally, the old time Indians were the best people you'd want to meet. They were thoroughly honest in every way, whenever they told you anything you could depend upon it absolutely. . . .

At that time the woods were full of deer, and the bear lived in the beach hammocks. Every few feet you could see bear wells, water holes dug by bear, especially on the east shore of Hypoluxo Island. It seemed that every time a bear wanted water he dug a hole . . .

Logger head turtles came upon the beach during the spring and laid their eggs in the sand. The bear hunted these eggs, and wouldn't eat anything else as long as they could find them.[4]

Among Pierce's neighbors was Captain Elisha Newton Dimick, sometimes known as the founder of Palm Beach, and at various times mayor of the town and state legislator. He reached that island in 1876 and built a house on land purchased from the state at approximately $1 an acre.[5]

Despite the near-perfect living conditions, there was no great land rush to the area. Palm Beach island and the Lake Worth coast remained a well-kept secret for the next 15 to 20 years.

THE secret began to end in 1888 or 1889 when Flagler, without revealing his identity, went ashore on the island, made notes of who owned what and returned to St. Augustine. He delighted in such adventures. As his Florida plans developed, Henry would repeat his visits as a mysterious stranger, make his reconnaissance and return later for the raid.[6]

Henry had decided he was going into the Florida business—and in a big way. He was going railroading.

For about 15 years after the Civil War, no new railroad construction had taken place in Florida because the state-owned lands were tied up in litigation due to the bankruptcy of early railroads as a result of the war. By 1884, there were a few railroads along Florida's Atlantic coast, but each had different track widths. Trains that would run on one track could not run on the others unless their wheel and axle widths were adjusted, a time-consuming project. Zigzagging down the Florida coast, none of the early railroads could interchange rolling stock because of the different sized track. This required unloading and reloading for cargo shipment between lines. Consequently, the Florida railroads were not prosperous.

To service his projected resorts, Flagler needed standardized track and a dependable railroad. When existing lines failed to meet his needs, he purchased the Jacksonville, St. Augustine & Halifax River Railroad. While the Ponce de Leon was being built, he had the railroad widened to standard gauge and began construction on a bridge across the St. Johns River, which ran between Jacksonville and St. Augustine.

It was something of a feat, recalled an associate.

One of the first great works he [Henry] undertook was the construction of a bridge across the St. Johns River at Jacksonville. While the work was being planned, his engineers came to him one day and told him that there was no precedent for the construction of a center pier on a caisson in 90 feet of water, that nothing of the kind had ever been done before, and they rather intimated some doubt of the practicability of it. Mr. Flagler looked at the gentlemen for a few moments and said: "It has never been done before? Well, why not? Cannot you build that pier in 90 feet of water?" They looked at him for a few moments and they said: "Yes," and they did it and the bridge is standing and they established a precedent for construction of that character.[7]

This was a turning point in Flagler's career—and in the history of Florida. Had the previous owners of the Jacksonville–St. Augustine line improved service to supply Flagler's needs, he might never have gone into the railroad business—and it was Flagler's railroads, not his hotels, which opened up Florida.

Following his purchase of the Jacksonville, St. Augustine & Halifax, Flagler rebuilt a short local line and renamed it the Jacksonville and Atlantic Railway. He extended it to connect Jacksonville Beach, Atlantic Beach and Mayport with the city of Jacksonville. At Mayport, he constructed large coal and lumber docks so that his road would serve as a vital link between the beach town and Jacksonville. This line enabled Jacksonville to become a major port. Then he turned south, running his railroad into a land of pinelands broken by occasional marshes and cypress hammocks. Cabbage palms grew thickly along rivers and creeks, and the undergrowth was often dense and impenetrable. Track was laid through sandy ridges, forested with black-jack oaks, and skirted cypress ponds, the dark waters studded with tiny yellow flowers. Across the grasslands, there were small white mounds thrown up by salamanders.

As the railroad moved south, Henry did not neglect St. Augustine, buying the hotel Casa Monica and renaming it the Cordova.

Flagler also donated funds to build the Memorial Presbyterian Church, a Methodist church and a hospital, and to rebuild the Catholic Cathedral when it burned down. He underwrote the construction of the City Hall and a segregated school for colored children, the paving of the city's streets, and the first installation of electric lights and public water works.

Flagler swept further south, acquiring in 1887 and 1888 the St.

Johns & Halifax River Railway and the St. Augustine & Palatka Railway. Those two additions were widened to standard gauge and gave access to Ormond Beach and Daytona Beach.

The first of these new stops, Ormond Beach, was a quiet town with pleasing houses and well-kept gardens, established in 1875 by the Corbin Lock Company of Connecticut as a health center for its employees threatened with tuberculosis. At Ormond, Flagler purchased a large frame hotel, which had been built in 1875 on the wooded banks of the Halifax River. Henry rebuilt it with rambling wooden verandas, painted it bright yellow with green trim, added an 18-hole golf course, and named it the Ormond Beach Hotel. It was immediately popular. John Rockefeller built his winter home, The Casements, across the street.[8]

The next stop on the Flagler line was Daytona Beach, settled about 1870 when a man named Mathias Day, of Mansfield, Ohio, paid $1,200 to the state for the site of the present town and named it after himself. Flagler brought the first train into Daytona in 1887, and the population spurted from less than 100 to more than 2,000. Daytona and its beaches, more than 23 miles of hard, white sand, became one of the nation's leading tourist resorts.[9]

By 1890, Daytona Beach was the southern terminus of all standard gauge rail in the United States. It was possible to board a Pullman in New York and ride all the way to St. Augustine, Ormond Beach and Daytona Beach without changing trains.

Flagler believed that such through service was the key to Florida's tourist success. "The average passenger," said Flagler, "will take a through car ninety five times out of a hundred in preference to making a change."

With through service in operation, Florida's appeal to tourists multiplied. One of Flagler's most celebrated visitors was President Grover Cleveland, who journeyed to Jacksonville and then on to St. Augustine where he stayed at the newly constructed Ponce de Leon.[10]

UNTIL this time, Flagler had merely acquired and improved existing railroads. Now he became a railroad builder, driving south into the jungles and undeveloped coastlines of eastern Florida.

After Daytona, Flagler linked his trains with the steamer traffic to haul fruit and produce from the Indian River, a long saltwater lagoon, extending 150 miles from New Smyrna Beach south to Stuart, where it turned into the Atlantic. Far into the twentieth century, it was the major means of travel for the pioneers who had settled along its banks.

Even as picturesque steamboats plied the river, landowners from below Daytona petitioned Flagler to extend his railway to Rockledge, some 80 miles further to the south. The owners offered Flagler free land for the right-of-way, and in less than a year the railroad had made its way to Rockledge, halfway down the Florida coast from Jacksonville and just across the lagoon from Cape Canaveral.

As a railroad man, Flagler was thrown into competition with Florida's other spectacular builder, Henry B. Plant, a Connecticut-born Yankee who first came to northern Florida in 1853 as a 34-year-old land speculator. He returned following the Civil War and during the 1880s bought up several narrow gauge railroads operating from Savannah to Jacksonville. Turning southwest, he crossed the mainland of Florida to Sanford and Kissimmee, ending up at Tampa on the coast of the Gulf of Mexico. In 1885, Plant created the port of Tampa by building a causeway and constructing piers in deep water. With a capacity for berthing 26 ocean steamships, he inaugurated a steamship service to Key West and Cuba.

In early 1891, Plant completed the building of his Tampa Bay Hotel, extravagant in size, plan and furnishings. An outspoken rival of Flagler's, Plant had said he would outdo the east coast developments and, accordingly, had spent more than $3 million on the hotel. Plant said he was prepared to spend even more to make Tampa a fashionable winter resort.

The Tampa Bay Hotel was a thousand-foot long brick structure with Moorish horseshoe-arched windows, a design that was repeated in the intricate woodwork of the lengthy veranda. Its silvered domes and minarets, emerging from tropical shrubbery on the bank of the Hillsborough River, evoked an Oriental quality.

The opening of the hotel in 1891 was a social sensation, attended by 2,000 guests, among them princes, dukes and duchesses, and celebrities of financial, theatrical and literary worlds. A symphony orchestra and grand opera artists entertained the guests, who toured the 20 acres of garden in rickshaws. It was a remarkable event for a city of less than 6,000.

Plant did not rest on his laurels but instead planned an extension of his railroad line to Fort Myers and then to Miami. In 1892 he sent a favored employee, James E. Ingraham, and a party of 21 to explore a route across the Everglades.

But Flagler's plans were even more ambitious. Poised at the half-way point on Florida's east coast, he decided he could drive his railroad all the way to Key West, 400 miles to the south, with virtually all of the distance unexplored, much of it swamp, and a considerable amount of the last 150 miles across open ocean. Flagler was planning an engineering feat considered impossible at the time.

With a certain amount of ironic impudence, Henry first broached these plans to Jefferson Browne, state senator from Key West and president of the Florida Senate, at the opening festivities of the Tampa Bay Hotel. Browne recalled:

I had just been elected to the state senate and was at the Tampa Bay Hotel in January or February, 1891. Mr. Flagler was there, and invited me to call on him. In the course of the conversation he mentioned several matters of state policy, and among them the advisability of refusing to extend franchises that had been granted to build a railroad to Key West, "to get them off the statute books," as he expressed it. There were three such franchises at the time. . . .

Mr. Flagler said that the promoters of these railroads had no financial standing, nor did he think they would be able to raise money to build the road, but the existence of these franchises would tend to discourage anyone with a bona fide desire to build a railroad to Key West. In the course of our conversation he made this statement, which so burnt itself into my memory that I have always been able to quote it verbatim. Said Mr. Flagler, "The ultimate end of all railroad building in Florida is to reach deep water at an extreme southern terminus, and Key West is the only place that fills that requirement." . . .

I quite agreed with him that these promoters' franchises might hamper one with a bona fide intention to build a railroad to Key West, and told him I would dispose of them all if I possibly could.

He further said that sooner or later communication with the Pacific Ocean would be opened, either by a canal using the De Lesseps route, or at Nicaragua, or by the Eads' ship railway at Tehauntepec, and sooner or later an enormous trade would come to the United States from Central and South America, which would seek the nearest deep water point—Key West.[11]

At the legislative session of 1891, the usual bills were introduced to extend these railroad franchises for two years or more, and in each instance

I left the chair of the president of the Senate, which position I occupied, and opposed the bills and succeeded in defeating them.

An amusing incident occurred with regard to one of them. State Senator Delano, of Volusia County, was interested in one of the franchises and the day after the extension bill was defeated he appeared on the floor of the Senate and engaged in earnest conversation with quite a few members. He succeeded in having someone move to reconsider the vote by which the extension bill had been defeated, and was going from senator to senator, apparently soliciting their support. From my seat on the rostrum, I sent him a note to the effect that I was deeply interested in the defeat of all bills seeking to extend the franchise of proposed railroads to Key West, and that if he continued using the floor of the Senate to lobby for the passage of bills that I was hostile to, I would take the floor and offer a resolution to the effect that any person who used the privileges of the Senate for the purpose of lobbying for the passage or defeat of any message pending before that body, should forfeit his privilege.

Senator Delano and I were warm personal and political friends; in fact that very afternoon we went together to Lake Hall to a picnic . . . When the senator read my note, he looked up smilingly and shook his finger at me, but at once left the Senate chamber and the motion to reconsider was defeated.[12]

In 1892, with his legislative path cleared, Flagler combined all the roads under a single corporate title—Jacksonville, St. Augustine and Indian River Railway Company. (On September 7, 1895, the corporate name was changed to the Florida East Coast Railway Company.) Henry notified the state government that the final destination of the main line would be the island city of Key West. In the same year, he obtained a state charter to extend his tracks as far south as Miami.[13]

Flagler continued to drive south, into the region called Dade County, 7,200 square miles running south from the northern shore of Lake Okeechobee down to the end of mainland Florida and the beginning of the chain of islands called the Florida Keys, from the Spanish word *cayo*, meaning "small, rocky islet."[14]

At the time Dade County was barely inhabited, the whole vast area having a population of only 726 in the 1890 census. Happenings were of a primitive nature, as is indicated in the "guide and history" of sometimes newspapermen, sometimes fishermen C. M. Gardner and C. J. Kennedy who reported such entries as the one of July 23,

1894: "Wildcat attacks little daughter of W. E. Devers near Magnolia."

The capital of Dade County was a new settlement called Juno, a town which, like Mark Twain's Hadleyburg, killed itself through avarice. The tale is told well by J. E. Chillingworth, son of a pioneer family:

When Henry Flagler purchased the Jacksonville, St. Augustine and Indian River Railway in the early summer of 1892, he announced that he would continue the road southward without stating the exact terminus. As construction proceeded, there was great speculation among the people of the lower east coast as to what course the road would take in coming south from Jupiter.

We all knew that the flatwoods several miles back from the coast were frequently inundated to the depth of several feet, and it was the general belief that Mr. Flagler would never try to build a road through that low inundated land because of the danger of the roadbed being swept away by water.

Early in 1893, Mr. Flagler had made his first purchase at Palm Beach. Exorbitant prices were asked by the landowners at Juno, feeling they had him in a fix. It so exasperated Flagler that he built his roads across those very flatwoods, bypassing Juno.

Although the road was washed out several times, Flagler spent a million dollars draining the flatwoods to make the road dry and safe. And in the meantime, Juno withered on the vine. Many people at the time believed that if Juno hadn't of been so greedy, it would have become Flagler's staging area, the city of West Palm Beach would never have been built, and Juno would have developed into a premier city of Florida, rather than a flattened scrubland. [15]

Flagler wasn't the only tycoon on the go. Not to be outdone, Plant, whose steamers were skirting the Atlantic coast from Nova Scotia to Florida, built himself a palatial mansion at Tampa. To keep the pace set by the younger Flagler, money was spent in immense sums, and as Flagler added hotels and railroad mileage, it must be said of old Plant that he, too, had something new in the form of a new steamship line to Jamaica, and a new steamship, the *Grand Duchess*, built to accommodate 700 passengers.

While both Flagler and Plant were watchful of each other, neither wanted a head-to-head competition. Some of Flagler's branch lines reached inland and tapped rich agricultural lands or commercial points on the St. Johns River, but none extended very far out of the east Florida area. Flagler seems to have had no desire to go west of the St. Johns River and Lake Okeechobee. The Plant System, on the other hand, extended throughout West Florida, but did not attempt to intrude on Flagler territory.

Nevertheless, Flagler was wary.

As Henry headed south, he ordered the head of construction to take precautions.

With a good summer resort at Ormond, we might some day decide to strengthen the draw and run at least excursion trains to the beach . . .

It has recently occurred to me that if our friends of the Plant System should hear of our proposed ocean pier and bridge across Lake Worth, they might seek to influence the War Department not to grant us permission to cross the Lake. I don't want to believe that they would do so; at the same time, the fear of it is an additional reason for making haste with the plans and securing the permission.[16]

Perhaps one of Flagler's most profitable pursuits was the acquisition and subsequent sale of large tracts of land throughout the east coast area. By May 1889, the State of Florida had given, through the Trustees of the Internal Improvement Fund, between eight and ten million acres to the various railroad companies. Thousands of acres of land had been granted to the various small railroads between Jacksonville and Daytona, which Flagler bought. After Flagler began his railroad building he claimed from the state 8,000 acres per mile of railroad. His total claims amounted to 2.04 million acres.

To exploit these land holdings, Flagler established a department of the Florida East Coast Railway Company to handle the sales and management of his land acquisitions. Later, the department expanded to become the Model Land Company, a separate organization of its own. This and subsidiary land companies would eventually control land from Jacksonville to Key West and would largely contribute to the agricultural and industrial growth of the east coast of Florida. The company and its group of experts gave liberally of time, money and experience in the development of the soil area. The Model Land Company and its associated companies employed expert agriculturalists, horticulturists and stockmen to give years of attention to the practical development of the east coast country.[17]

In October 1892, Flagler hired Henry Plant's star employee, James
E. Ingraham, to run the Model Land Company. Ingraham, announced
the Jacksonville *Times Union,*

. . . says he will at once go to work in securing settlers for the country lying
along the Jacksonville, St. Augustine and Indian River Railway, mainly permanent farmers and mechanics. . . . When the railroad is done there will
be some 240 miles length of unproducing lands that must be made to produce
something, or Mr. Flagler's railroad will not earn cotton waste and oil; for
the tourist business is only for three months, and the expense is so heavy
in operating a railroad to meet the increased travel that nothing is left for
the other nine months.

Consequently, the country must be opened up, and Mr. Flagler has
assigned that task to Mr. Ingraham. If farms do not flourish like green
bay trees, it will be the fault of the people, and not of Mr. Flagler or his
agent.

Mr. Ingraham has set up shop in St. Augustine and is awaiting visitors.

It was Ingraham's duty to advertise the east coast of Florida to
the people of the North and to entice them to take up residence,
either temporary or permanent, in that area. Ingraham published
booklets, pamphlets and a magazine called *The Homeseeker,* in which
he told about the advantages of the east coast and described the lands
which were for sale at most of the points. These lands were sold at
relatively low prices, ranging from $1.50 to $5 per acre. Special prices
were given on large tracts and land bought with cash, and to groups
of people wanting to colonize.

Ingraham had a splendid corps of assistants all along the east coast.
In some cases, railroad agents at various stations would serve as representatives for the Model Land Company in addition to their other
duties. They were well versed on soils, crops and production, and
gave out reliable information to persons in their vicinity.

Flagler realized the importance of bringing people to the east
coast because the freight and passenger traffic which they produced
would help his railroad. Flagler once said that every new settler along
his railroad was worth $300 to him since an inhabitant of the east
coast had to bring in everything he used and send out everything he
produced over the Flagler railroad.

Many of the settlements along the Flagler railroad grew out of
the efforts of small groups to plant colonies at various points. Settlements at Linton and Boynton were established by pioneers who pur-

chased land from the railroad. Another small colony, called Modelo, was established in the same vicinity. It was a Danish colony, and newcomers were mostly from Illinois, Michigan, Wisconsin and Iowa. Holland was another colony in lower Florida, which was settled during the 1890s.

Other settlements directly derived from the Flagler land policies included Delray, Deerfield, Dania, Ojus, Perrine, Homestead, Kenansville and Okeechobee, in addition to principal cities such as Fort Lauderdale, Miami and West Palm Beach.

Flagler made many concessions to people who came to colonize. In order to encourage and stimulate the planting of lemon, grapefruit and orange groves, he made a temporary reduction of 50 percent in freight rates on nursery stock shipped over his lines to points south of Titusville. The Model Land Company quite frequently gave a variety of seeds to people in the area.

At one time it was believed that tobacco could be raised with some ease in Florida, and in 1895, Sims W. Rowley, of San Mateo, raised 2,800 pounds of leaf per acre with plants donated by Flagler.[18]

Flagler himself undertook farming on a large scale in Florida at various places. He established a model farm at Hastings, which gave the town a good lead in the production of potatoes. At San Mateo, Flagler owned a large orange grove, in which he took much pride and interest; and just south of West Palm Beach, he had a large plantation on which he raised pineapples. Flagler's Model Land Company did more perhaps towards actually building up the Florida east coast than any of his other undertakings.

In the meantime, he had connected Florida to the rest of the United States.

By the end of 1893, a traveler could leave New York and within 36 hours be in St. Augustine after a pleasant journey and no fatigue. There, Moorish palaces awaited, said a Philadelphia newspaper:

He [Flagler] has built a 300-mile railroad, although back in 1825 Col. James Gadsden of the U.S. Army Engineer Corps reported that the construction of a wagon road between St. Augustine and Cape Florida was not advisable, as "the country south of St. Augustine was alluvial and had been formed by a succession of encroachments of the Atlantic." Even if such a road were constructed, Col. Gadsden said it could not be maintained. Mr. Flagler built the supposed impossible road with 2,000 men, and they are fond of saying

A wanderer and a somewhat mysterious man, Henry's father, Isaac Flagler. (*The Henry Morrison Flagler Museum*)

Isaac Flagler's second wife, Ruth Deyo Smith. (*The Henry Morrison Flagler Museum*)

The Gingerbread House in which Henry and Mary Flagler lived during prosperous days in Bellevue, Ohio. (*Courtesy of Wm. Oddo*)

Drake's second well, seen in 1860, is the old-est derrick in the world. (*Drake Well Museum*)

"Colonel" Charles Drake, whose work started the world's modern oil industry. (*Drake Well Museum*)

Henry with Mary Flagler (back) and sister-in-law Isabelle Harkness in Belle-vue in the 1850s. (*The Henry Morrison Flagler Museum*)

Henry Flagler in 1909. (*The Henry Morrison Flagler Museum*)

Henry Flagler, one of his favorite pets in hand, traveling on the grounds at Palm Beach. (*The Henry Morrison Flagler Museum*)

Flags flew and spirits were high when the first train pulled into Key West in 1912; Henry Flagler is at left front. (*The Henry Morrison Flagler Museum*)

in Florida that only one man in the total number contracted a case of fever during the period of construction.[19]

There was more to come. Flagler was looking still further south—to the place of his secret visit, the island called Palm Beach.

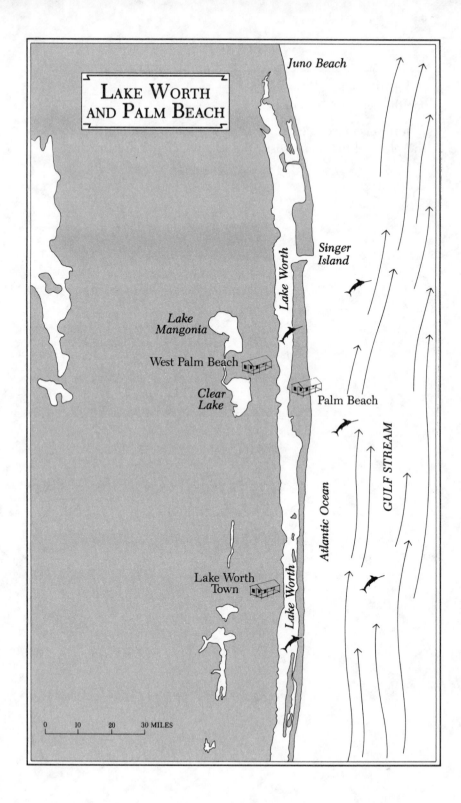

LAKE WORTH
AND PALM BEACH

Juno Beach

Lake Worth

Singer
Island

Lake
Mangonia

West Palm Beach

Clear
Lake

Palm Beach

Atlantic Ocean

GULF STREAM

Lake Worth
Town

Lake Worth

0    10    20    30 MILES

# CHAPTER 11

# Palm Beach

TRAVELING once again as the incognito Mysterious Stranger, Flagler returned to the island of Palm Beach in the summer of 1892. He had preceded the visit by dispatching an agent to sound out certain of the Palm Beach pioneers on selling portions of their land. Flagler was especially interested in acquiring a one-mile-square section which began about four miles from the northern tip of the island. On the western side of the section, on the shore facing Lake Worth, Flagler intended to build a hotel and a railroad bridge to the mainland. On the eastern side, the ocean side, he would build some cottages and perhaps another hotel.

He began negotiations with Robert McCormick, a horticultural enthusiast who had pioneered in the Biscayne Bay area in the early 1870s. McCormick had built a winter home on the palm island in 1878 and created a tropical garden which contained almost every tree, shrub and flower that could thrive in the area's soil and climate.

Rumors of Flagler's visit preceded him, according to Sarah Geer, a pioneer of the island:

In February, 1893, what then comprised Lake Worth was buzzing with excitement. It was being whispered about that the great oil magnate's representative had been in the vicinity and that Mr. Flagler himself was on his way. The rumors were confirmed by the arrival of the "great man" in March. Mr. Flagler's enthusiasm knew no bounds, and upon his return to St. Augustine he exclaimed, "I have found a veritable Paradise." He had purchased our former farm from its subsequent owner, a Mr. McCormick, for the stupendous sum of $75,000 and immediately announced his intention of erecting the largest resort hotel in the world and the extension of the Florida East Coast Railway to this section. He began to quietly acquire more land, and Palm Beach's first real estate boom was initiated, assuming proportions of an old-time mining town rush.[1]

FLAGLER also paid $50,000 for a point of land owned by general store operator E. M. Brelsford. Both the Brelsford land and the Geer land were on the sheltered Lake Worth side. He also bought land along the ocean beaches. At Brelsford's Point, Flagler would later build a winter home. On the old Geer homestead, he would construct the Royal Poinciana Hotel.

Flagler's purchase of land in Palm Beach was publicized far and wide. Real estate that had been virtually worthless on the market immediately jumped to $150 to $1,500 per acre, depending upon its proximity to the center of Palm Beach island. Homesteaders, and there were only 30 or 40 cottages scattered around the 100 miles of lakeshore, plus a couple of stores, suddenly found themselves rich. All because of Flagler, and the magic of his reputation.

To build the Royal Poinciana, Flagler's contractors, Joseph A. McDonald and James A. McGuire, immediately recruited hundreds of workers. As there were no housing facilities on the island, the men were put into a community of tents and shanties north of the building sites. For some reason lost in history, it was given the name The Styx.

During this period, Flagler was paying his chief contractors, McGuire and McDonald, $208 monthly; other executives between $35 and $125 monthly; the janitors $30 monthly; three white handymen between $1.25 and $1.50 per day; and a white driver $1 per day. Numerous laborers, all listed as "colored," were paid $1.10 per day. McGuire and McDonald's compensation was supplemented by bonuses. The wages paid to the other workers were higher than the national average of 70 cents a day for non-skilled labor and $1.44 per day for skilled workers.[2]

Unlike his previous hotels, which were built of stone and coquina, Flagler decided to use wood for the Poinciana. As he wanted it built with dispatch, Henry set up a race between his railroad men, who were extending his line to the Palm Beach area, and his builders, who were working on the hotel. Although all the hotel materials had to be transported by a series of transfers from barges and ships to a tiny narrow-gauge railroad, the builders won out.

Construction started on May 1, 1893, with more than 1,000 men working, including some of the best artisans of the world.

It soon became apparent that The Styx could not accommodate all the workers. However, there were miles and miles of open, well-watered land on the mainland, across Lake Worth, and Flagler saw the possibilities of establishing a town there. The new town, he said, would be "for my help." Palm Beach itself would be reserved for the exclusive use of its present occupants and the winter visitors.[3]

In April 1893, Henry purchased several hundred acres on the mainland, largely from Captain O. S. Porter, and laid out the town site of the city of West Palm Beach. He moved The Styx to the new town and West Palm Beach grew rapidly, resembling a mining town as more and more workmen poured into the area. Until the railroad bridge was completed, the workmen rowed across Lake Worth each morning to their jobs on Palm Beach island and then back across the lake in the afternoon.

Flagler built West Palm Beach out of whole cloth. As the months, and then years, passed, he tore down the temporary houses for his employees and replaced them with permanent structures. He contributed to funds for all of the new town's public buildings and gave land for cemeteries, churches and other uses. He also built the first Catholic church in the city, which served his contractor, Joseph McDonald, and many of the workers. Flagler also used leverage to separate the area politically from the remainder of Dade County and create a new Palm Beach County, which, both on a per-acre basis and on a total tonnage basis, became one of the leading agricultural areas of the world.

Inasmuch as Flagler built West Palm Beach, he didn't hesitate to crack the whip on the city council. The early town records are peppered with the notation: "A communication was received from Mr. Henry Flagler . . ."

That was all the signal necessary to make changes, even if the council had to reverse itself on some previous action. For example, the council gave alderman (and saloonkeeper) George Zapf permission to build a wharf in the lake near his Seminole Hotel. Construction was under way when "A communication was received from Mr. Henry Flagler . . ."

Down came the wharf.

Two men, with council approval, had built a fish house on the lake. "A communication was received from Mr. Henry Flagler . . ."

Down came the fish house.[4]

FLAGLER finished the Royal Poinciana, the largest resort hotel in the world, in record time. It opened on February 11, 1894, nine months after construction began. Occupying the old Geer homestead, it embraced more than 100 of the most beautiful acres on Palm Beach and was covered with perhaps the greatest variety of tropical growth found in Florida. Fronting on the lake, the building was a huge sprawling structure with six floors and 540 rooms. It opened with only 17 guests. But soon after, when all the wings were completed and the hotel expanded to 1,150 rooms, the accommodations for up to 2,000 guests were usually filled to capacity. Suites cost $100 per day, and a couple occupying a double with a bath would pay $38 per day—a lofty price at the turn of the century. Like most of Flagler's enterprises, the hotel's exterior was painted a vivid lemon yellow, the color which Flagler would use for all his hotels built after the ones in St. Augustine.[5]

The Royal Poinciana's interior color scheme was green and white. The furniture was upholstered in green velvet, and the carpet was light green. Walls and ceilings in the public rooms were of light green with white trim.

Immediately, the Royal Poinciana became the gathering place for wealth and fashion. It was known throughout the United States for its food and service. Its staff varied between 1,200 and 1,600. Normally, the servants occupied rooms on the upper eaves floors, but in crowded times those were turned over to paying guests and the help doubled up both in the two attics and in nearby barrack-type buildings.

The mirrored, chandeliered dining room was like a crystal palace and could seat up to 1,600 people. It was so big that humorist Ring Lardner claimed that communicating from one end of the main dining room to the other was a long distance "toll call."

During the season, from December through April 1, the hotel employed a chambermaid for every four rooms; a bellman in every hall; and 400 waiters, one for every four diners at capacity, not counting an exalted headwaiter who had a secretary and 26 assistants. There was a separate dining room for the lower echelons of hotel staff; another for the first officers; a third dining room for the second officers; a fourth for servants of guests; and a fifth for children. The staff had its own orchestra for their dances and other social functions. The head housekeeper had a three-room suite.

The Poinciana was the *in* hotel for the Northern social set. At the onset of each season, more than 100 private railroad cars, each luxurious in its own right, would arrive at the hotel with the masters obtaining suites while the servants slept in the cars.

The highlight of each social season was the Washington Birthday Ball, held each February 22. For the 1898 event, reported the Palm Beach *Daily News,* the ballroom had been converted into a

. . . fairy grotto filled with countless miniature electric lights, set in scores of gorgeous and immense Japanese and Chinese lanterns. The walls were lined with stately columns of palm leaves, ferns and pine branches. The ladies in fine silk gowns and white powdered wigs on the arms of gentlemen in white tie formal attire. Having dressed in the rooms of Whitehall's second floor, they descended the grand staircase to be greeted by Mr. and Mrs. Flagler in the Marble Hall. The entourage promenaded through the Music Room and St. Mark's Hall arriving in the dazzling ballroom all a-glitter with light dancing off the Baccarat crystals. Strains of music waff through the house as fourteen Palm Beach beauties began the minuet opening this most spectacular of the Season's affairs.

. . . One of the musicians became lost in contemplation and was spellbound, forgetting to strum his banjo . . .[6]

What so transfixed the musician was the sight of a couple of dozen of the nation's most powerful men, Flagler included, parading around in long dresses.

According to the newspaper account, a judge came as Marie Antoinette, complete with powdered wig and solitaire diamonds. Financier Fred Sterry was in a gown of hand-embroidered lace decorated with gold crests of the Royal Poinciana, worn over cream-colored satin. H. R. McLane wore a silk fishnet costume with rows of alligator teeth and a hand-painted ivory portrait of Izaak Walton. Joseph Jefferson, perhaps the most famed actor of the era, masqueraded as Rip Van Winkle.

The newspaper reported that the women were "insanely jealous" of such fineries.

Flagler—Henry Flagler of the thick shock of hair and ever-present cigar—was stunning in a dress of Florida East Coast Railway colors, "a Martha Washington combination of colors," said the newspaper, trimmed with bands of miniature silk flags and a palm leaf boutonniere. The list went on and on. The ladies' costumes were not mentioned—perhaps being outshone by the male plumage.[7]

At such times, it seemed that the Gay '90s were perhaps nowhere gayer than in Palm Beach.

THERE were many sports available at the Poinciana, including golf, tennis, fishing and boating. For bathers and swimmers, Flagler built in 1895 an annex, known as the Palm Beach Inn, about one-quarter mile east of the Poinciana on the ocean shore. To his surprise, the Inn became as popular as the Poinciana and was enlarged, with its name being changed to the Breakers.

Flagler and his executives had expected the Breakers to be nothing more than an annex to the Poinciana, but beach bathing became so unexpectedly popular that the former always had a waiting list, while the Poinciana was sometimes hard pressed to fill its hundreds of rooms. The Breakers was destroyed by fire in 1903, rebuilt in 1906, destroyed again in 1925, and immediately rebuilt again at a cost of $7 million. Its Italian Ranaissance design, buff stucco and twin towers became a visual and metaphorical symbol of Palm Beach as well as one of the finest hotels in the world.

To further boost business, Flagler brought in Colonel Ed Bradley to operate the Beach Club, a gambling house which, after Monte Carlo, became the most famous casino in the world.

Flagler and Bradley were already partners in another casino, the Bacchus Club, in St. Augustine and had possibly known each other earlier than that.

Born in Johnstown, Pennsylvania, in 1859, Bradley graduated to a varied career which included being an Indian scout for the U.S. Army and a noted horse breeder in Lexington, Kentucky. His Idle Hour Farm purebreds won four Kentucky Derbys, the first time that was ever done, and he was known as "One-Two Ed" because his horses so often came in first and second.

Bradley and his brother John had opened gambling houses at resorts in New York State and New Jersey, and Flagler had recruited them to open the Bacchus Club shortly after the Ponce de Leon was finished.

Although Flagler himself was not a gambler, he liked the style and burnish of the Bradley casinos and accordingly invited him to Palm Beach.

Membership in the Beach Club was for men only, although later the rules were relaxed to admit women, as guests only. Once inside, however, ladies mingled freely with gentlemen without regard to who brought them.

Roulette, hazard and chemin were played, but not anxiously, of course. Only those who, in the management's eyes, could afford to wager large sums on the roulette wheel or dice tables were welcome. Proper evening attire was a must. The finest food, served by outstanding chefs, was offered.[8]

THE success of Palm Beach was instant. A Philadelphia travel editor, quite pleased with his assignment, wrote from Palm Beach on January 28, 1895: "On Monday of this week nearly 100 men and women were in the surf here bathing at one time. On the same day, the average temperature in Philadelphia was 26 degrees. This will give a good idea of the difference of living in Philadelphia and in Palm Beach." [9] He also interviewed Flagler and found him "a very approachable man; and in speaking of the number of persons who call on him largely out of curiosity, he says that he does not blame them. 'I suppose they want to see the idiot who has spent all this money,' was his laughing remark on this subject."[10]

PUBLICLY, Flagler despised the press. Privately, he recognized its value to his enterprises in molding and informing public opinion. Quick to finance newspapers, provided his involvement could be kept secret, Henry was the leading newspaper owner in Florida and one of the leading press magnates in the nation.

He was quite duplicitous about such ownership. In 1890, when rumors circulated that he was to buy a Jacksonville paper, he replied, "There is not a particle of truth in the rumor that I am out to start a newspaper. If I had to take my choice between a den of rattlesnakes and a newspaper, I think I would prefer the snakes."

Less than a year later he was among the three buyers of the Florida *Times-Union* in Jacksonville and later acquired control of the Miami *Herald*, the *Metropolis*, the Miami *News*, the St. Augustine *Record*, as well as the Palm Beach *Daily News*. His ownership in many of the papers wasn't revealed until years after his death.

For example, shortly after construction began on the Royal Poinciana, Flagler established Palm Beach island's first newspaper, the

*Weekly Lake Worth News,* and installed a partner, Bobo Dean, as publisher. Within three years, the paper expanded into a daily and was renamed the Palm Beach *Daily News,* advertising itself as the "only daily newspaper published between St. Augustine and Key West, a distance of 500 miles." For 54 years, Dean was erroneously believed to have been the paper's sole owner and Flagler's connection to the Palm Beach *Daily News* wasn't revealed publicly until 1948 when it was disclosed in a sale.[11]

BY LATE 1892, Flagler had pushed his tracks to New Smyrna; in 1893 to Titusville, Rockledge, Cocoa and Eau Gallie; in January 1894 he reached Fort Pierce. Two months later, Flagler's crews laid tracks to a point just across Lake Worth from Palm Beach.

Mile by mile, he was chaining together the constituent parts of Florida.

Before the Flagler line moved south of West Palm Beach, the only method of getting mail from the settlement at Miami, a distance of but 80 miles, took two months, going first to Key West, then to the island of Cuba, and eventually to Palm Beach—a total of 3,000 miles. With the railroad at West Palm Beach, mail from New York could now be delivered in two weeks, the final leg being carried by mailmen often walking barefoot along the beaches.

There was a single small church on Palm Beach when Flagler arrived, so he built a grander one—the Royal Poinciana Chapel. A frequent lecturer was Henry's pastor, the Reverend E. B. Webb, who came to Palm Beach in 1895. Flagler engaged Webb to lecture weekly and built an annex to the Poinciana where people might assemble, regardless of religious affiliation. Webb, who became ill in 1897, was replaced by George M. Ward, who was at the time president of Rollins College in Winter Park, Florida. Ward became an intimate friend of Flagler and was his pastor for the remainder of Flagler's life.

The outspoken Ward said that Flagler provided him with

. . . the freest pulpit in the world. Early in my ministry, even before assuming the position, I said to Mr. Flagler, "I do not think I am so constituted that I could talk soft nothings to the guests at Palm Beach." His answer was prompt, "Who asked you to talk soft nothings? Speak as you think right." "Yes," I said, "but are you and I both disinterested enough and big enough not to be influenced at times?" "Try it and see," was his answer; and after

16 years of a very happy relation to this pulpit and people, I can say he never by word or sign indicated his difference of opinion . . .

Once, said Ward,

. . . I asked him his purpose in Florida. . . "What are you trying to do in Florida? Is this investment or philanthropy, or are you anxious to pose as a state builder?"

"That's pertinent enough," he said. "I believe this state is the easiest place for many men to gain a living. I do not believe any one else will develop it if I do not. This is a safe kind of work for me to do. I believe it's a thousand times better than your colleges and universities (that was rubbing it into me), but I do hope to live long enough to prove I am a good business man by getting a dividend on my investment." . . .

. . . When his whole fortune was at stake behind an incomplete work, he never flinched, but staked his all on the road's completion. A gentleman now dead, a railroad man, a member of the Board of Directors of a concern to which he had applied for a loan, said when asked his opinion on the wisdom of this loan, "I know nothing of the road and care nothing, but I am satisfied to lend anything he asked for to the man."[12]

Flagler contrived to hide his charities, not wanting to become a target for every supplicant in the land. Nevertheless, by the middle of the 1890s, he was renowned for his generosity. The New York *Herald* reported on several such gifts and concluded that Flagler might convert the word *millionaire* to mean a good thing.

It is narrated that on a recent New Year's morning he handed his New York pastor [the Rev. Dr. Paxton] a check for $100,000, to be distributed according to the clergyman's own ideas, no report of which was to be made this side the stream of Time. It is said he has given away in the past five years not less than $1 million in charity, not a report of which has ever been made, concerning which no flattering echo has rolled about his social circle. . . .

. . . One of his fancies has been to build up the town of Fernandina, Fla., and down there he is regarded with a reverence just this side of superstitious awe. . . . Having made up his mind that he wanted a certain plot of ground which was then occupied by a church, he offered the congregation $2,400 if they would have the building moved. It was done. Shortly thereafter, a meeting was held to raise funds for liquidation of the debt hanging over the church, and Brother Flagler was in the audience. A collection was about to be taken up when he, rising, said he would make up the deficiency, whatever the amount might be, after the collection was taken up and the amount ascertained.

They needed about $2,800, and the collection amounted to $400 or $500 only, whereupon, in addition to the $2,400 he had already given, he planked down his cheque for $2,000 more. . . .

. . . He cares nothing for outside show, yet he buys pictures of great value and statuary of note. Although careful and cautious in all business matters, his expenditures along the line of friendly entertainment are phenomenal. He cares nothing and knows less about horses, yet his equipages are very fine and his stables well stocked. . . .

. . . If giant monopolies produced this kind of man continually, much of the opposition now manifested against them in spirit and in fact would be killed. Unfortunately, Mr. Flagler is not a product of the Standard Oil Company. On the other hand, that cruelest, severest and least merciful of monopolies is his favourite child.[13]

Another example of his generosity and Christianity came in the winter of 1894–1895, when a freeze hit Florida as far south as Palm Beach and much damage was done to the groves, truck farms and pineapple fields.

Reports of desolation came from around the state. Major H. B. Lowery, quartermaster of the Marine Corps, returned from an inspection and reported, "The orange crop is ruined . . . The nurseries all ruined also, and this makes the condition of the orange growers all the worse, because they cannot set out new groves from natives slips. . . . Losses are in the millions."

A *New York Times* correspondent touring central Florida in February 1895, wrote, "all the vegetables are frozen. 'I had fine lettuce,' one farmer told me, 'which brought a good sale—and onions, turnips, beets, cucumbers, beans and carrots, but they are all gone.' . . . The loss to gardeners, and nearly everyone was gardening to make up for a lost orange crop, will be great."

Flagler's pastor Ward recalled:

The great freeze of 1894–95 wiped out of existence a hundred million dollars worth of property in a night, and men walked the streets with stricken faces and discouraged hearts. The tragedy of that day no one save a Floridian can ever know. In other sections of Florida men packed what they could carry of their earthly possessions and worked their way back North, leaving their houses to the bats and the owls . . . but in these sections a man was sent on a mission. "Find," were his instructions, "any and every case of real need where a chance to start again will be appreciated and see that they have that chance. The only condition I impose is that they do not know the gift comes from Henry M. Flagler."[14]

One result of the freeze was that Flagler arranged to obtain from the U.S. Weather Bureau advance information as to any predicted drop in temperature to the point of danger. "This information was transmitted through agents to the engineer on every train, who was instructed to sound six long blasts of the locomotive whistle at intervals of every three miles." When the growers heard the signal, they knew to prepare their fire pots and take other precautions to save their crops.[15]

FLAGLER'S consideration also was seen in personal matters.

In the summer of 1895, following the freeze, he learned that the daughter of his contractor, Joseph McDonald, was about to be married. He wrote to James Parrott, the head of his railroad, telling Parrott to offer the couple his, Parrott's, private railcar.

I suggest that you get yourself in communication with Mr. McDonald and offer the young couple your car, running it with an engine, special from West Palm Beach, leaving at a reasonable hour in the morning, and over-taking the regular train at Fort Pierce or perhaps at some station north of Fort Pierce. . . . Mr. McDonald will appreciate the compliment and I would be glad to have you render it.[16]

In another instance, Mary Elizabeth Anderson, the wife of Henry's friend Dr. Andrew Anderson, was spending sleepless nights because a switch engine on Flagler's railroad performed its work not too far from her bedroom window. Flagler was a frequent visitor at the Anderson home in St. Augustine and Mrs. Anderson prevailed on Flagler to spend the night, placing him in the guest bedroom next to hers. As she hoped, the offending switch commenced its raucous noise shortly after Flagler retired. Not surprisingly, after that night Mrs. Anderson was never troubled again by switch engines that went bump in the night.

AS BEFITS a giver, Henry's favorite holiday was Christmas. He spent each one in Florida from 1885 until his death at 83, in the spring of 1913, and many of them at the Ponce de Leon.[17] During one of those St. Augustine Christmases, he gave an FAO Schwarz train to Andrew

Anderson, son of his friend. With it went instructions, to Anderson senior, on how to build a table: "Have a table made five foot by seven, nicely planed on top and gotten up in good shape," Flagler wrote. "I hardly know what height to advise, but I would suggest two and a half to three feet. It wants to be low enough so Andrew can stand alongside of it and watch the performance."[18] Flagler also suggested that if Anderson still had trouble setting up the toy system that he call in Flagler's "men from the RR yards."

Every kid in St. Augustine was invited to the Flaglers' annual Christmas party at the hotel, and all got presents.

Immediately after Christmas, as a pre-birthday celebration for Henry, Ida Alice, and later Mary Lily, would arrange for the Ponce de Leon to set up in its rotunda a table with punch bowl service for all who desired to come in personally and extend best wishes. The punch itself was of a champagne variety and welcome to everyone.[19]

His son, Harry, was likewise given to holiday celebration, and during the 1890s Harry's exuberance was a source of repeated embarrassments to Henry.

One such scandal came on 1 A.M. Sunday, December 20, 1896, when New York Police Captain Michael Chapman, in command of the tough and notorious Tenderloin District, raided the fashionable Sherry's restaurant, where Harry and 20 friends were throwing a bachelor's party for one of their friends. Entertainment was provided by a group of professional entertainers, which included two male singers, a comedian and seven exotic dancers, including the star of the show, the famous belly dancer, Little Egypt.

In between acts, with some of the cast changing costumes, the zealous Chapman burst into the ladies' dressing room and announced a vice raid. One of the women was naked, being in the midst of a costume change, and told Chapman and company to clear out. He scolded her as "a disgrace to your sex" and proceeded to rave until the noise attracted the restaurant owner, who managed to calm him down. Chapman then watched part of the show, said his raid was "a mistake," drank a glass or so of champagne and left, after requesting and obtaining a photograph of the naked entertainer with whom he had had words. Little Egypt put on a raunchy performance. And a merry time was had by all.

Then the newspapers got hold of it.[20]

In the ensuing events, Chapman was charged, and exonerated,

of exceeding his authority; Harry and others were charged, and exonerated, of enticing Little Egypt into a lewd dance; Oscar Hammerstein made a burlesque of the farce, staging something called "Silly's Dinner," and was likewise charged and exonerated of lewdness; Little Egypt continued her career as an international superstar kootchy dancer; and although it was an innocent enough affair, Harry Harkness Flagler had driven another nail into his coffin as far as his father was concerned.

THE diversity of Flagler's interests is evidenced by the story of the first county fair held in the state of Florida. In 1897 a few residents of Dade County were anxious to exhibit the products grown in that region. The majority of them believed, however, that fruits or vegetables could not be grown in south Florida and certainly never on a commercial basis. Only a few had even a "kitchen garden." The enthusiastic growers, nevertheless, pledged and planned a few exhibits for a fair. They requested cooperation from James Ingraham, who headed the land department of the Florida East Coast Railway.

Anxious to foster growth and industry in Florida, the Flagler interests agreed to pay all expenses and furnish a tent for the event. Flagler personally offered a prize of $75 for the best display of vegetables.

The fair was a great success. Glowing accounts were written, and reassessments of the area's potential began to form. The fair was the impetus needed to initiate agricultural development that was to continue for many years in all of south Florida.

The Florida East Coast Railway continued to pay all expenses for the fair during the next several years until it became a self-supporting institution.

ANOTHER of Flagler's developing interests was the automobile.

In 1893, two brothers, Frank and Charles Duryea of Springfield, Massachusetts, had built a horseless carriage: a one-cylinder gasoline engine attached to an ordinary buggy to make it run. The vehicle went almost unnoticed at the time. But in 1895, when the Duryea "motor wagon" won a race sponsored by the Chicago *Times-Herald*, it set people to talking about the automobile. Other backyard tinkerers, including Henry Leland, Alexander Winton, Ransom Eli Olds and Henry Ford, were building them, too.

Leland, the New England toolmaker, introduced the idea of stand-ardized, interchangeable parts. Olds was the first to go into quantity production; in 1905 he turned out 6,500 of his famous one-cylinder, curved dash Oldsmobiles. Ford began to experiment with one model after another, and mass production was in sight. The first Model T Ford was delivered to the dealers in 1908.

In 1896, there were four automobiles in the United States that would run. Two years later there were 800.

In reaction to those developments, Flagler suggested to Rocke-feller that Standard Oil begin expanding its gasoline production. A few years later, when Flagler became president of a reorganized Standard Oil company, he made gasoline production a top priority.[21]

Ironically, Flagler himself did not buy a car fueled by gasoline. He felt they were not yet reliable. Instead, he bought a White Steamer, a car propelled by a steam boiler.[22]

He brought the steamer down to West Palm Beach by railcar and there, at the southern terminus of his railroad, he stood poised and ready to head even further south.

## CHAPTER 12

# Interlude: Biscayne Bay

FLAGLER had his eye on Biscayne Bay, an inlet of the Atlantic, which, although shallow, provided the best sheltered harbor between Jacksonville and Key West. If he could push his railroad to Biscayne, he would have the shortest sea route in America to the Bahamas, Key West, Cuba and the Caribbean.

Like Palm Beach, the bay was a hidden garden, waiting for cultivation. Unlike Palm Beach, it had somewhat of a history.

Forty-eight miles in length, Biscayne Bay was protected on its eastern shore by a string of barrier islands and on the west by the mainland of Florida. Since pre-Columbian times, a handful of people had lived on the bay, most of them settled near the mouth of a small, clear river later called the Miami.

There were even smaller rivers, creeks really, which flowed into Biscayne Bay and, like the Miami, they flowed from that strange topographical freak called the Everglades.

The Everglades was and is the dominant geographical feature of South Florida. With its saurian wildlife, hammock islands and subtropical plants, the Everglades looks like a swamp but in fact is a broad, 100-mile-long river of water and saw grass which flows southward from Lake Okeechobee to the Bay of Florida. What gives the river its swamplike appearance is its breadth—it averages 50 miles in width—and its sluggish flow of water caused by the barely perceptible decline from Lake Okeechobee to sea level.

Virtually all the fresh water in South Florida, including the Biscayne Bay region, comes from the Everglades. The Glades, and its runoff streams which flow down to the sea on the east and west coasts of Florida, save South Florida from being a desert and instead make it into something of a tropical Eden, as far as the nature of it goes.

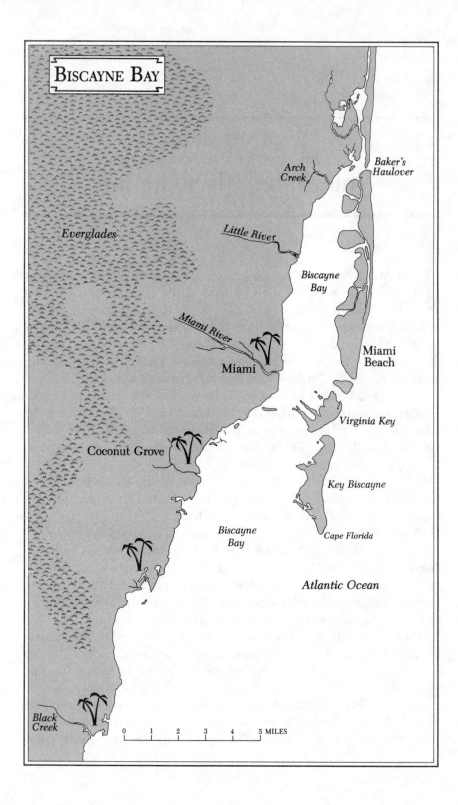

BISCAYNE BAY

Everglades

Arch
Creek

Baker's
Haulover

Little River

Biscayne
Bay

Miami River

Miami

Miami
Beach

Coconut Grove

Virginia Key

Key Biscayne

Cape Florida

Biscayne
Bay

Atlantic Ocean

Black
Creek

0   1   2   3   4   5 MILES

It is a land which deserves a better treatment than it has received from its inhabitants.

THE earliest map of the Biscayne area was published about 1514 and shows a Tequesta Indian village located at the river's mouth. The mapmaker calls the town Chequiche, and it is likely the earliest townsite of any city of the United States to appear on a map.[1]

The first white settlement is believed to have been a short-lived mission erected on one of the barrier islands in 1567 by Don Pedro Menendez de Aviles.[2] The barrier island was later named Miami Beach.

Attempts to settle the Biscayne Bay area were abandoned for two centuries, being resumed in 1773 by the Cape Florida Society, a group created in England to colonize east Florida. The colony was to be established on 6,000 acres of the Lord Dartmouth grant, located about 12 miles south of the Miami River.[3]

All this occurred before the name Miami came into use. On the maps of the 1770s, the river is called Rio Rattones, or "river of mice." Biskaino Island, a barrier island later to be called Key Biscayne, made its first appearance, the word *Biskaino* probably being a corruption of an earlier Spanish place name, Cayo Viscaino.[4]

The name *Miami* doesn't appear on maps until the 1820s, many decades after white settlement began. Even at this early stage, the region had begun to show its illusionary nature, a land of masks and disguise. We don't know who invented or adopted the word *Miami*, the Calusa Indian word for Lake Okeechobee, but as an advertisement it certainly was an improvement over "river of mice" (or rats).

The Cape Florida project never reached colony status but instead collapsed due to the lack of financing and the lack of Europeans willing to settle on Biscayne Bay. The first real colonist arrived in 1808, when John Egan, a white resident of the Bahamas who had become familiar with the coast while salvaging on the reefs, petitioned the Spanish government in Cuba for a land grant. The Spanish deeded him 100 acres of land on the confluence of the Miami River and Biscayne Bay.[5]

Egan and his family soon were joined by a family named Lewis, and a handful of other settlers followed over the years. In 1817, it was reported in newspapers that "two or three settlements of little consequence are about Cape Florida [i.e., Key Biscayne]. All of these southern settlements are from Providence, Bahamas."[6]

The future development of Biscayne would be atypical of the South, but typical of southern Florida. It would be done almost entirely by Northerners and, in the specific instance of Miami, it would be done largely by Ohioans, culminating with a prickly cooperation between Henry Flagler and a pretty Cleveland widow named Julia Tuttle.

THE REAL pattern of settlement began in 1821 when Florida became a territory of the United States. One of the first priorities of the United States government was to do something about the many wrecks on the Florida Reef. To this end, in 1825, a lighthouse was built on Cape Florida, at the southern tip of Key Biscayne. It was the first permanent structure in the Miami area.[7]

Of the 110 miles of shoreline, and the more than 100 islands that make up the boundaries of Biscayne Bay, there were in 1821 only 3,000 acres privately owned, those being held by the Egan and Lewis families. They built homes, cultivated their farms and began the chain of titles to the land that continues to this day.

In 1829, a certain Dr. Benjamin Strobel of Key West visited Biscayne Bay and wrote a description of what is today downtown Miami.

The point of land to which we steered our course was steep and perpendicular, consisting of a wall of limestone rock, 12 or 15 feet above the level of the water. At one of these we landed, and ascending a rude flight of steps, I found myself at the door of a neat palmetto hut which was seated on the brow of the hill. It was quite a romantic situation. The cottage was shaded on its western aspect by several large West Indian fruit trees, whilst on its eastern side we found a grove of luxuriant lemons, which were bowed to the earth under the weight of their golden fruit.

This was the residence of the old lady to whom I had been recommended and who was bordering on 80 years of age. I entered the house and made my devoirs. She received me graciously and placed before me some Palmetto and Icaca plums and after refreshing politely conducted me herself over her grounds and showed me a field of potatoes and corn which she had cultivated. She generally employed several Indians for this purpose, who for their labor received a portion of the products.[8]

In February 1829, James Egan, John's son, decided to sell his land and advertised in the Key West *Register* that he was selling 640 acres on the north bank of the "Miami River." Thus, one of the earliest recorded uses of the name *Miami* was in a real estate ad.

The land was purchased by a Key West resident, Richard Fitzpatrick, formerly of South Carolina, for $400. Fitzpatrick dispatched an overseer to develop a plantation and also dispatched colored slaves from South Carolina to do the work. Living in 12 wooden cottages—and cultivating sugarcane, corn, pumpkins, sweet potatoes, and groves of bananas, plantains, lime and coconut trees—these workers were possibly the only slave labor ever used in south Florida.

The plantation was destroyed by the Seminole Indian wars of the 1830s, which rid the area of all whites. They didn't return until 1836, when the army established Fort Dallas as its main base for raids into the Everglades against the Seminoles.

Fitzpatrick sold his holdings to his nephew, William English, who came to Biscayne Bay with the most ambitious plan since the Cape Florida Society. He platted the "Village of Miami" on the south bank of the river, perhaps the earliest use of the name *Miami* to describe the settlement rather than the river. One by one, settlers began to arrive. By 1856, there was a sufficient enough population, perhaps a dozen families, to warrant establishment of the Miami Post Office. The mailboat from Key West came once a month to service the area.

In 1857, in response to further Seminole raids, the army built the first road in South Florida, linking Fort Dallas with Fort Lauderdale. It was 16 feet wide with "causeways" built over swampland and a corduroy road, of sawed-off pine trees, laid through the marsh. The man who mapped and built the road was Captain Abner Doubleday, commander of an artillery company at Fort Dallas.[9]

The Civil War halted all development, but immediately afterward began the era of Reconstruction, which in 1870 brought in a handful of Northern settlers, including William Brickell and Ephraim Tanner Sturtevant, both of Cleveland, Ohio; the latter the father of Julia Sturtevant Tuttle, later to be known as "the Mother of Miami."[10]

Neither Sturtevant nor Brickell was precisely a carpetbagger, that is, one determined to exploit the helplessness of the South. They were, instead, businessmen who wanted only to homestead some land and operate a store. They figured they could make a pretty fair living selling whiskey to the Seminole Indians. Such sales were illegal, but, isolated in the wilds of Biscayne Bay, who was to say them nay?

Sturtevant, who would be state senator from Dade County in 1872–1876, was a Connecticut man, born July 28, 1803, and a Yale graduate. He had taught school for 20 years, mostly in Ohio, but had retired because of impaired health. He was working on his third marriage when he moved to Florida. Sturtevant had first come to Dade County on a scouting trip in 1870, when it had a population of 85, a gain of two over the Census of 1860.

Brickell, a generation younger than Sturtevant, was a native of Steubenville, Ohio, who had first seen Biscayne Bay in the 1850s while on a sailing ship.

The families of the two men arrived January 12, 1871, in a schooner loaded with lumber and furniture, and settled on adjacent lots on the south side of the Miami River, where they opened their general store.

Clearing the land, running the store and feeding his family was a hard task for the elderly Sturtevant who had only his 57-year-old wife for help. His two living adult sons by an earlier marriage (two other children had died by 1871) did not accompany the family on the trip. Nor did Julia, then 22, who remained in Cleveland with her husband and two small children.

Within a year, a quarrel of an unknown nature erupted between Sturtevant and Brickell, and the Sturtevants moved five miles up the Bay to a choice bayfront property that already had a house on it.

Mrs. Sturtevant wrote to a Cleveland newspaper about the quarrel and did not disguise her bias:

We purchased a comfortable house vacated by a New York lady, leaving behind the results of a year's successful labor with most of the comforts we had risked a winter sea voyage to secure in our new home, thus paying the forefeit, like poor Tray, for getting in bad company . . .

We will persevere in our pleasant work and have the oranges, lemons, limes, tamarinds, figs, bananas, pineapples, mangoes, alligator pears, Jamaica apples, Japanese plums, sugar apples, guavas, papaws, and dates in readiness for our visitors.

The Sturtevants raised only what they and their friends could eat. There was little reason to raise fruit for which there was no local market and no means of shipment. Only pineapples and limes could survive the long trip north by way of Key West without spoiling.[11]

Northern newspapers began to take an interest in southern Florida in the 1870s, viewing it as a wonderland. There were a few authors, however, who saw it with a different eye.

F. Trench Townsend's *Wild Life in Florida*, published in 1875, noted that

. . . the settlement of Miami, on Biscayne Bay, is represented as a sort of terrestrial paradise . . . It is in reality a very small settlement on a ridge of limestone, rising from five to 30 feet above the sea, with a loose sandy loam over it, only a few inches in depth, but tolerably fertile. The climate is equable, but very hot, the scenery is pretty but never approaches magnificence, while the multitude of insects make life hardly endurable.[12]

Another dissenter was Adam Richards, who reported after a visit:

. . . the scale of living was pretty low. People lived on potatoes and other easily grown vegetables, fish, birds and once in a while would have some venison when somebody would shoot a deer. It was inordinately difficult to obtain groceries, such as flour, coffee, sugar and canned goods, and anyway most people couldn't afford to buy them most of the time. Travel and communication were both difficult and dangerous, there being rivers with swift currents, wild animals, snakes and roaming beach tramps with criminal tendencies to contend with.[13]

The settlement at Miami River and Biscayne Bay had only a score or so inhabitants, including the Sturtevants and the Brickells. But there were slightly larger settlements at Lemon City, some five miles north, and Coconut Grove, some five miles south. All three were on what was called Coral Ridge, which wasn't coral at all but a rock substance peculiar to the region and known to geologists as Miami Oolite. This, with the pine trees and the thick growth of scrub palmettos and other undergrowth, made the land exceedingly hard to clear. Interspersed were the prairies, usually free from rock and thus tillable but which defied large-scale cropping. The prairies were dotted with hammock, jungle-like stands of tropical hardwood trees.[14]

On the higher lands of the Coral Ridge, to the west of the three bay settlements, lived most of the homesteaders. In all there were from 300 to 400 people scattered over perhaps a hundred square miles of Key Biscayne shoreline. Behind the settlements were the Everglades, alligators, crocodiles, bears, snakes, deer, panthers and Seminoles. No wilder or more dangerous country existed north of Panama.

Another of the early settlers was William Wagner, who had a farm about two miles west of Miami. Wagner's son Henry, born in 1871, later recorded the life-style of the bay region.

Most folks lived off sow belly and grits when they could get it, and off the land and water otherwise. Everybody made coontie starch [arrowroot] and a hard-working man could make maybe 75 pounds in two days.[15]

It was either traded at the local store or shipped to Key West and sold at auction for between 1.5 cents per pound and sometimes 5 cents a pound. At best, two days' wages amounted to about $3.75.

If you depended on getting your groceries from Key West you had to buy in quantities to last at least a month. The boat running to Key West was supposed to make a round trip every two weeks, but I have known it to take three weeks and even four to make a round trip.

Some of the settlers raised a few vegetables. The water from the coontie made the ground very rich and you could raise more than you could use with very little effort. The first fruit trees were planted around these coontie mills. There were three kinds of oranges—sour, sweet and bittersweet; avocado pears, mangoes, sapodillas, sugar apples, soursop, grapefruit, and bananas. In the vegetable line, most of the settlers raised only sweet potatoes and pumpkins. These need to be planted but once and continue to grow year after year. The Indians in those days raised sweet potatoes, Indian pumpkins and field corn which could be bought very reasonably from them. . . .

The first vegetables raised for market were tomatoes grown by Adam C. Richards. He tried it as an experiment, shipping them to New York, and proved it could be done if you had the nerve to take a chance—the chance being to get the tomatoes from Miami to New York before they rotted on the way.

The tomatoes were shipped to Key West by sailboat. A great deal depended on the speed of the boats from Miami to Key West.

They would leave Miami on Mondays, and the steamers left Key West for New York on Fridays, once a week, so if the Miami boat was late to Key West, the tomatoes stayed in Key West for a week . . . the best time that could be made from Miami to New York was eight days.

There were three general stores on the bay, one at Lemon City; Brickell's store at Miami; and Alfred Peacock's at Coconut Grove.[16]

From Lemon City to Miami there was only one road, a rocky road. It was just as bumpy as could be. There wasn't any way to get to the rest of the world except by boat.

That is the way things were on the bay when Mrs. Julia Tuttle came.

## CHAPTER 13

# Julia Tuttle's Deal

JULIA Tuttle, born January 22, 1849, in Cleveland, was the only child of Ephraim and Frances Sturtevant.

Frances was a teacher from the Indian school at Tallahassee and thus Julia's acquaintance with Florida was a natural heritage. After completing her education in the Cleveland schools, Julia was married on her eighteenth birthday, in 1867, to Frederick Leonard Tuttle. Her new husband was in the iron ore trade, his father having been among the pioneers of the American iron industry.[1] The father, Henry B. Tuttle, was also the man who first gave a job to John D. Rockefeller—a connection which would frequently prove useful to Julia.

On January 16, 1869, Julia and her husband became the parents of a daughter, Frances ("Fanny"). Two years later, on May 19, a son, Henry ("Harry") was born.

When her parents moved to Florida in 1871, Julia, four years into her marriage and with two children, remained in Cleveland. Furthermore, her blunt-tongued mother did not urge her to come to Florida, feeling the area was much better suited to tourism than to agriculture and raising a family:

This section of country is better adapted for handsomely fitting up grounds for commodious dwellings than for extensive plantations. For those having the dimes already in store, where they can bask in sunshine and where enfeebled children can live out of doors, and grow strong in that best of tonics, pure air, this might be the place.

Nevertheless, the Sturtevants were delighted when they learned that Julia and her children were coming for a visit in 1875. Julia and the children were accompanied by a friend, a Mrs. Davis. Despite her married status, Julia was discreetly courted by James Ewan, a

newly installed postmaster with whom she would one day become
romantically linked.

The ladies' arrival was recorded by a neighbor, George Parsons,
who wrote in his diary, March 18, 1875:

Ewan and I went out in the Pearly & found a boat of passengers, two ladies
included—something new for these parts. One a married daughter of Judge
Sturtevant, Mrs. Tuttle of Cleveland with two children and her friend Mrs.
Davis from the same place with one child. Mrs. Tuttle very goodlooking &
lively. We took them off to Mrs. Lovelaces where they stayed the night.
Ewan and I took the ladies around showing them the place & all objects of
interest and after supper, which was a woeful one, we visited some Indians
who were camped for the night near Brickell's and the ladies were quite
interested, though somewhat alarmed as the Indians were not very sober
and I had to take hold of one young buck to prevent his embracing Mrs.
Davis.[2]

In a later entry, Parsons confided that while he preferred Mrs.
Davis, Ewan preferred Mrs. Tuttle and thus began their friendship.

Julia returned to Biscayne two years later, this time accompanied
by her now ailing husband Frederick, hoping the mild climate would
improve his tuberculosis. She was immediately impressed by the
luxurious growth of both fruit and flowers along the bay. Nor was she
disappointed in the place as a health resort. Although her husband's
disease was too far advanced for a cure to be effected, the visit brought
about a decided improvement.[3]

In 1882, Julia's father died, and she returned to Miami for a third
visit, again accompanied by Frederick, who had been named executor
of the estate.

During the 1882 visit, the Tuttles spent more time at the fort than
at the family home in Biscayne. They were looking at land plats,
assisted by Ewan, who had by then been appointed the U.S. land
commissioner. Frances Sturtevant inherited her husband's property,
and Julia and her husband returned to Cleveland.

Tuttle, however, had roots and business obligations in Cleveland
and declined to leave.

Their life went on with Julia taking up charity work, including
volunteer jobs at the Euclid Baptist Church, whose membership included her father-in-law, her husband and a parishioner who had
recently become world famous—John D. Rockefeller.[4]

Then, on February 22, 1886, Frederick Tuttle died of tuberculosis, leaving Julia and the two children.

It took much of the year for Julia to settle her husband's estate. When it was done, she was left with a few thousand dollars and their house in Cleveland.

Weary, fearing that her children might have inherited a weakness for tuberculosis and wanting them to live in a benign climate, Julia sought aid from Rockefeller. Just five days prior to Christmas 1886, she asked him to use his influence to get her a job with Henry Flagler.

She wrote:

I shall need to do something to increase my income somewhat, and I have been thinking of getting something to do for a part of the year in a more genial climate.

Now if you think I am equal to such an undertaking, I think I would like the position of housekeeper with the new hotel Mr. Flagler is building at St. Augustine, and if you would be good enough to recommend me to Mr. Flagler I am sure your good word would do much to induce him to give me a trial. Of course you may not think this is a feasible project at all, but you can easily say so. As I understand it the building will not be completed until next season but I thought if one was going to get the position it was time to be moving in the matter.

I would like to take my daughter Fanny to a milder climate for she is not quite as well as I wish she was. There is nothing alarming but I want to avoid any trouble for her. If I am all wrong about this it will do no harm to know it, and perhaps you know of something else it will be better for me to do only I could not do what would confine me constantly indoors or at a desk.

Rockefeller's reply was dated December 27, 1886:

Yours of the 20th at hand and I will see Mr. Flagler as requested and advise you. If you are in good health I have no doubt you could fill the position referred to providing any other woman could, and I will say the same to him.

I will gladly communicate with you if anything in any other direction presents itself that might seem to be favorable for you. I congratulate you on your success in administering your own affairs. Hope you can so shape your investments as to give you the necessary income with less hard work.

Two days later, Rockefeller informed her of Flagler's blunt turndown: "I have spoken to Mr. Flagler. He will not give any personal attention to the running of his hotel when it is completed, and is of the opinion that his manager, Mr. Seavey, has arranged in respect to the position you refer to."

To soften the blow, Rockefeller added, "I wish I had at my command the postion you want. I may be in Cleveland within a few weeks, and if so, will try to see you."

Julia wrote Seavey, but nothing came of it.

In 1887, she traveled about searching for the ideal place in which to settle. She took her children to southern California but decided she preferred south Florida. Accordingly, she returned to Fort Dallas and, with the assistance of Ewan, bought the abandoned Fort Dallas and an adjoining 640 acres on the north side of the Miami River. During the next year, she commuted between Fort Dallas and Cleveland, making at least two round trips.[5]

On Julia's last trip to Cleveland, in 1887, her mother, Frances Sturtevant, returned with her and took up residence in the Tuttle house. Frances left the Sturtevant house and property vacant in Florida and appointed Julia her "lawful attorney," authorizing her to sell all the Sturtevant real estate in Dade County.

Julia, however, had no plans to sell real estate. Instead, she was more interested in acquiring and developing it.

Early in 1888, Julia offered a young Cleveland man, S. J. Kelly, and several of his friends 10 acres of Florida land, said a Cleveland newspaper, "in her large, undeveloped tract on Biscayne Bay if they would settle on it and take with them her cow. They agreed, but declined to take the cow."[6]

As the Kelly expedition made preparations for the trip, she seized on a rumor that Rockefeller was investigating land near hers at Fort Dallas.

In a March 6, 1888, letter to Rockefeller in New York, the 39-year-old widow asked for verification:

Yesterday in a letter from Florida I heard that you were about buying a tract of land in Florida but what most interested me was the fact that only a narrow river divides it from my own property—so I could not but hope it was true and that we might be winter neighbors; for another winter will find me & mine in Fla.

If you are thinking of investing down there do tell me about it. I think Fla. will become my headquarters.

At present my plans are in a most chaotic state. My mother's health has been failing all winter and now she is confined to her room and most of the time to her bed. I feel very serious about her for at her age (this month is so trying). Had she been well as in former years we should even now be in Italy but owning to her illness, I was obliged to change my plans. I have rented the property here [Cleveland], at least the house, and I am hoping for a rest and change after my long work time . . . I get very weary of it all sometimes and wonder if it all pays.

Well I shall know how to appreciate rest when it comes and that is what those who never work cannot do.

I hope your family are all quite well and that you enjoyed your trip abroad. By the way, I was much amused to read in a Painsville [Ohio] paper last summer that Mrs. Fred Tuttle was travelling with Mr. Rockefeller's family in Europe. How it got there remains a mystery, but then newspaper items often are mysterious.

To conclude I only hope it is time that you are going to invest in South Fla. I can think of no one that I would prefer for a neighbor.

Two weeks later, Rockefeller said his so-called Florida investment was but a rumor:

It was a mistake about my purchasing property in Florida. I hope your venture there will prove successful. I am just returned from Cleveland and regret to hear your mother was quite ill. I congratulate you on the success of your efforts to save your property and cannot say too much in your praise for the battle you have made. We hope to see you on returning to Cleveland after a few weeks and hope before this your mother is better, and that you will enjoy a good rest after your long and hard struggle.[7]

In the fall of 1888, the Julia Tuttle-backed Kelly expedition returned in tatters to Cleveland. They had been shipwrecked off the lower Florida coast and were forced to hike a hundred miles across unexplored Seminole country before reaching a white settlement. Weak, starved and scarred by insect bites, they wanted no more of Julia's Biscayne Bay country.

Julia, however, was made of sterner stuff. By the end of 1889, Julia decided to leave Cleveland permanently and make her residence at Fort Dallas. She again leaned on Rockefeller for help, writing him on December 7:

I hoped I should hear something from Mr. Cowles in reference to the sale of my property here [Cleveland] but I have not seen him or heard from him. Do you think I had best go to see him?

I am very sorry you were out when I called and had I known just when I could call should have dropped you a line—

I am as much troubled as ever about my business and I confess I do not quite see how it is coming out . . .

If you can induce Mr. Cowles to take up that matter I hope you will and please let me know if I am to call upon him or to wait his movements.

SHE WAS off to Florida and her spirits were high. As her future daughter-in-law, Corrie Fowler Tuttle, later recalled:

. . . She told friends who accompanied her to the railroad station in Cleveland, 'Someday soon you will be able to go all the way to my place by railroad.' At that time the only way to reach it was to sail down the Indian River, out Jupiter Inlet and down the coast to Biscayne Bay. After this hazardous trip, she found the only remnants of civilization at the Tuttle tract were two trading stores and the ruin of old Fort Dallas. This latter consisted of two buildings, a soldiers' barracks and the officers' quarters. She moved into the officers' quarters temporarily and later reconstructed it into a comparatively elaborate home. During the remodeling process, a ship en route from Barcelona, Spain, was wrecked on a reef below Key West. Divers salvaged the cargo, and thus she secured some exquisite Spanish tile with which she built a floor for her entire dwelling.[8]

As Julia herself told the story afterwards, the prospect was not inviting when she arrived in January of 1890. So dense was the jungle that before their boat could land, the trees and underbrush had to be cut down.

In the clearing thus made, we landed some Jersey cattle, cats and dogs, food and other articles necessary to equip a comfortable home. At this time the land surrounding Old Fort Dallas was an impenetrable thicket; where the city of Miami now stands was a pathless forest, through which ran only a narrow trail once used as the old Government Road to Fort Lauderdale in the days of army occupation.

She found the two stone buildings of the fort "in a bad state of repair" and entirely rebuilt the two-storey one with the exception of the walls. She also added a kitchen and outbuildings, built a workshop, windmill, stable, boathouse and wharf, and fenced in about 150 surrounding acres.

After she had lived on Biscayne Bay for a year, an old Cleveland friend, James Ingraham, the man who would later become Henry Flagler's land commissioner, sent word he would be visiting. Ingraham had been hired by the railroad man Plant to take a group of men

and push through the Everglades to determine the feasibility of bringing a railroad across the state from Tampa to Fort Dallas.

Julia prepared carefully for their visit and even erected a flagpole
in the hope that they would be able to see it at some distance and
thus find her home.

A week passed, then two weeks and still no word from the group.
She tried to restrain her fears for their safety, but when nearly three
weeks had gone by without word from the party, she confided her
uneasiness to Matlo, acting chief of the Seminoles. He had long been
one of her friends, bringing her gifts of venison and bear meat on his
frequent visits to the Tuttle home. So when she asked him, out of
friendship, to go into the Glades and find the white men, he assented.
She didn't know, said her daughter-in-law, Corrie, later, that conducting white men through Indian territory was a major offense in
the eyes of the Seminoles:

Matlo finally reached the fragment of the party that was left. A number of
the men had turned back—and he conducted Ingraham, and four others,
back to civilization. The men were worn out from 20 days in the Everglades
at the mercy of the insects, water moccasins and the heat. The arrival of
Matlo and his canoe had proved a godsend. After a few days of traveling,
Matlo stopped at a bend in the river and waited impatiently while he changed
his shirt and greased his hair. When he finished his toilet, they proceeded
around the bend to find they had been but a stone's throw from the fort and
Mrs. Tuttle.

For some weeks after that, Matlo failed to make his customary visits to
the Tuttle household, and when he finally showed up the lobe of one ear
was missing. He had been exiled on an island in the glades for escorting the
white men.

Julia had more than a humane interest in Ingraham's safety. She
wanted his help to open the almost virgin area to the outside world.
Even before moving from Cleveland to Miami, she had sought, un-
successfully, to interest Henry Plant's railroad in expanding to Miami.
Now, with Ingraham as her guest, she pressed her advantage, seeking
his help in persuading his boss, Plant, to extend the railroad. Ingraham carried the message, but Plant again declined.

She then turned to Flagler who was continuing to build south.[9]

THE Rockefellers had introduced Julia to Flagler and Ida Alice in
New York in 1889 and now, prevailing upon that acquaintance, she

wrote Henry saying that in exchange for his bringing the railroad to Miami, building a first-rate hotel and platting and building the streets of the town, she would turn over to him half her lands, much of it on the bayshore.

In a letter dated April 27, 1893, Flagler for the first time revealed his intention toward Miami. He said he was reluctant to commit himself to a railroad because he planned to build a canal linking Lake Worth and Biscayne Bay. With such a canal, he didn't need a railroad, nor did she.

He was obviously tired because the historic letter reads fuzzily; it is not in his usual crisp, concise style. He begins with the traditional American complaint of bad postal service.

I returned last night, from a trip down to the end of the railroad, and found your letter of the 13th, a sad commentary upon the mail service between our respective post offices.

Before entering upon a discussion of the matter, I ought to say that I am in no fit condition, mentally or physically, to consider your proposition. I am tired out, and a mole hill seems a mountain . . . I never have read your communication of Nov. 14th but once before today. . . . I observe that it is based upon the extension of the East Coast line to Miami, a distance Mr. Ingraham says will probably not fall short of 80 miles, and which, as I build railroads, will cost me, including stations and equipment, upwards of a million of dollars.

It seems to me an unsafe committal on my part to agree to expend so large a sum of money without any personal knowledge of the country through which the road will pass, or a personal knowledge of the terminal point. Under these circumstances, I don't feel qualified to form an opinion as to the liberality of your proposal. I can only look at the outlay, and guess as to the results. Upon general principles, it would seem as though you had made a very liberal offer.

I am very reluctant to send you an affirmative answer to your proposal; on the other hand, I am almost as reluctant to decline it, for, if my life and health are spared, it seems to me more than probable that I will extend the road to Miami within a very few years. To accept your proposal now, and not build the road, would result in no pecuniary loss to me, but it would tie up half of your property, and be a disappointment to you. The problem I am trying to solve is to see if there is not some way by which our interests may be mutually advanced, without my agreeing *now* to construct the road.

Flagler proposed instead constructing a canal to Lake Worth, and a line of steamers to Miami.

. . . do you not think that your object would be accomplished as well as if the railroad was built? I think I would be willing to accept your proposal based upon the canal instead of the railroad, leaving the latter for future consideration, for I should certainly build it as soon as the development of the country will justify it, but with all my present undertakings, I dare not make the positive promise, no matter what inducement is offered.

I think I told you that the East Coast Line from Jacksonville to Lake Worth is a piece of personal property as much as my umbrella. I cannot construct as cheaply (by that I mean at as little cost per mile) as roads are built; if I cannot have everything right, I don't want it at all. All this means the investment of a very large sum of money, and I want to finish and operate the road to Lake Worth in a reasonable length of time, before approaching the question of a further extension. . . .

Mrs. Flagler joins me in a kind remembrance.[10]

In the meantine, Flagler was completing his railroad to Palm Beach.

HENRY felt a personal responsibility toward his employees and many stories are told about his kindness. It was not uncommon for him to give a faithful helper a home, a sum of money or a farm. There was one case of an employee who had done his best to hamper building operations at Palm Beach. Later, the disgruntled man was incapacitated by a serious on-the-job accident, and during his period of forced inactivity his wife and children suffered from insufficient care. At a time when such victims were often dismissed by their employers, Flagler paid all the expenses until the wage earner was able to take his place again on the road.

He gave financial help to individuals, but only after personally determining the worthiness of each request. When one young woman requested a $60 loan to complete a stenographic course, Flagler informed an aide to look into it, saying that although it was "but one of hundreds received by me, 99 percent of which I turn down, there is something about the letter which commands my attention . . . If the young girl is energetic, intelligent and deserving, I do not know but I would make the small loan." After the aide reported the woman was of good character, Flagler sent the money.

He firmly believed in reciprocal responsibilities between employer and employee. He paid well, he paid promptly and he kept his railroad camps well stocked with food and medicine. In return, he expected a full day's work and was quick to fire any man he discovered loafing.

FLAGLER viewed his responsibilities as including the entire east coast of Florida. In the winter of 1894–1895 when the state was hit with some of the coldest temperatures in its history, property damage was in the millions. Thousands of people who had come to Florida to raise fruit and spend the winter packed what they had left and trekked back north.

Confidence dipped to zero. During the freeze, Flagler issued free seeds to farmers hurt by the cold, and hauled fertilizer and other materials free on his railroad. He sent Ingraham into the area with $100,000 in cash, instructing him: "Use it as necessary. I would rather lose it all, and more, than have one man, woman, or child starve."

The Biscayne region, however, was untouched by the freeze. Flowers bloomed fully, and not a single orange tree had died.

At that point, an enduring legend settled in.

According to the legend, and a lengthy list of histories, biographies, and newspaper and magazine articles, it goes like this:

At the height of the freeze, Mrs. Tuttle wrapped the fresh stems of some choice flowers in damp cotton and sent a bouquet of orange blossoms to Flagler in St. Augustine.

He was so impressed that the day after he received the orange blossoms he was on a launch headed south. At New River, near Fort Lauderdale, Flagler and his companion, James Ingraham, transferred to mules and continued south.

Three days later they arrived at the confluence of the Miami River and Biscayne Bay.

Leading his mule by the reins, the mustached Flagler, a dandy from the North, looked like a tramp. His tie was long ago discarded, his shirt and trousers were dripping wet with sweat, and his coat was tied to his saddle. But his eyes were bright as they swept the horizon and saw the turquoise promise of Biscayne Bay and its coconut palm beaches white as sugar.

Henry and the equally bedraggled Ingraham marched to the gates of Fort Dallas. Mrs. Tuttle came out to inspect them.

"Madame," said Flagler with a broad bow and courtly sweep of his soiled Panama hat, "I am Henry Flagler and these must be the shores of paradise."

Within the hour, Flagler and Mrs. Tuttle signed an agreement for land development.

As legends go, the story is not that far off the mark. There were orange blossoms. There was a meeting.

One of those present was 18-year-old Joseph Killian Dorn, a native of Germany, who came to central Florida when he was six. A friend of Julia Tuttle, he was on her front porch and listening to her talk with Henry Flagler when she asked:

"Mr. Flagler, why don't you build your railroad down here?"

Dorn recalled that

. . . Flagler just sat there and drew a long puff on his cigar. Figuring that Flagler might have to check with a board of directors, Mrs. Tuttle leaned forward and asked, "Mr. Flagler, just how much of that railroad do you own?"

Flagler looked at the cigar in his hand, looked across at Mrs. Tuttle and smiled, "Just as much as I own this cigar."[11]

A larger perspective on the story is added by Julia's daughter-in-law, Corrie, who remembered that Julia had contacted Henry Flagler at St. Augustine a number of times.

. . . hoping to persuade him to bring the railroad south to Miami. Finally, following the big freeze, she sent him a collection of orange blossoms and other tropical flowers to prove her point that the disaster had not touched Miami. This impressed him greatly and a meeting was arranged. By this time, Mr. Ingraham had left the employ of Mr. Plant to work for Mr. Flagler, and he was of great help in working out the details for this historic meeting.[12]

More details are added by one of the principals, indeed a central one: James Ingraham.

Ingraham, too, said orange blossoms were involved. He added that once Flagler got to Miami, in April 1895, he made instant selections of where his new hotel would be, where the rail terminal would be, and issued orders on the spot to arrange for workers and construction materials. But the rest of Ingraham's story differs from the legend:

Sometime before Mr. Flagler finished his railroad to Palm Beach, I met at a dinner party in Cleveland, Ohio, Mrs. Julia D. Tuttle, who told me that she was about to remove her family and effects to Miami, and during the evening she said: "Some day somebody will build a railroad to Miami. I hope you will be interested in it and when they do I will be willing to divide my properties there and give one-half of them to the company for a town site." "Well," I said, "Mrs. Tuttle, it is a long way off, but stranger things have happened, and possibly I some day may hold you to that promise."

On December 24, 1894, occurred the first of the great freezes, which was a tremendous disaster, at first supposed, to Florida, ruining the orange groves in the orange belt, touching to the heart of the Indian River and nipping trees in the coconut groves as far south as Palm Beach. As the orange industry was the principal industry at that time in Florida, it seemed as if this freeze was a fatal thing and could not be overcome, and in almost every family dependent upon the orange industry it seemed as if death and disaster were in their daily lives.

Shortly after this freeze I came to Miami, and I found at Lauderdale, at Lemon City, Buena Vista, Miami, Coconut Grove and at Cutler orange trees, lemon trees and lime trees blooming or about to bloom without a leaf hurt, vegetables growing in a small way untouched. There had been no frost there. I gathered up a lot of blooms from these various trees, put them in damp cotton, and after an interview with Mrs. Tuttle and Mr. and Mrs. Brickell of Miami, I hurried to St. Augustine, where I called on Mr. Flagler and showed him the orange blossoms, telling him that I believed that these orange blossoms were from the only part of Florida, except possibly a small area on the extreme southerly part of the western coast, which had escaped the freeze; that here was a body of land more than 40 miles long, between the Everglades and the Atlantic Ocean, perhaps very much longer than that, absolutely untouched, and that I believed that it would be the home of the citrus industry in the future, because it was absolutely immune from devastating freezes. I said: "I have also here written proposals from Mrs. Tuttle and Mr. and Mrs. Brickell, inviting you to extend your railroad from Palm Beach to Miami and offering to share with you their holdings at Miami for a town site."

Mr. Flagler looked at me for some minutes in perfect silence, then he said: "How soon can you arrange for me to go to Miami?" I said: "If you can give me three days in which to get a messenger through to Mrs. Tuttle, advising her of your coming, so that she may prepare for you and get a carriage and horses to Fort Lauderdale, I will arrange to have the launch meet you at West Palm Beach, take you down the canal to Fort Lauderdale and from there by carriage to Miami. How many people will you have in your party?" Mr. Flagler thought for a minute and said: "There will be Mr. Parrott, Mr. McDonald . . . , Mr. McGuire, yourself and myself."

The trip was quite easy to schedule, and when we arrived in Miami we found the most perfect moonlight that I have ever seen. After some discussions, Mr. Flagler had accepted the proposition for the extension of his railroad, had located the site of the Royal Palm Hotel and told Messrs. McGuire and McDonald to build it and had authorized Mr. Parrott to extend his railroad from West Palm Beach to Miami, and had told me to go ahead and make plans for [the] Miami town site, clear up the town and get it ready. He selected, too, the sites for a passenger station, freight yards and station, and told Mr. Parrott to put advertisements in the State papers that labor of all kinds could find employment for many months at Miami in the construction of the railroad, hotels, and other classes of work.

He sent for the steamers that had been running on the Indian River to the canal to establish railroad heads for the construction work, carrying men, material and supplies. He arranged to have an additional dredge put on the canal to hurry the completion of the work between Lauderdale and the head of Biscayne Bay, that supplies might be pushed into Miami. [13]

Upon his return to St. Augustine, Flagler confirmed the agreements in writing. His April 22, 1895, letter to Julia was in essence a contract creating modern Miami:

My dear Mrs. Tuttle,

The mail leaving Lantana this morning should carry a letter addressed to Mr. Brickell in reply to his offer sent me by Mr. Ingraham. Even if he should delay his reply until the mail leaving Miami on Friday, I ought to receive his answer not later than Tuesday [April 30th].

I expect to leave for New York on Thursday [May 2nd]. Before doing so, and to avoid any possible future misunderstanding, I venture to recapitulate my understanding of your proposal to me regarding the building of a Hotel at Fort Dallas, and an extension of the railroad to that point.

1st,—that you will give me one hundred acres of land, reserving your home lot . . .

2nd,—that you will give me one half of the remainder of the Fort Dallas property . . .

3rd,—"A water privilege for the Hotel, Railroad and Steamboats, reserving the right for the supply of the town." Just what you mean by this expression, I forgot to ask you. If, as I suppose, you mean that my right should be limited to the Hotel, Railroad, Steamboats and any improvements I make on the hundred acres, it is all right. In addition to this, I understand that you will grant me the right to lay a pipe line across your land, & will secure from other owners, a similar right to lay pipe line between the west (or north) line of the hundred acres, and the Glades at the head of the river— that if I am compelled to erect a pumping station at or near the Falls [of the Miami River], you will give me a small piece of land, say an acre, for that purpose. I am in hopes that there is fall enough to run the water by gravity, to a pump located much nearer the town site than the Falls. If steam is required to run the pump, the delivery of fuel to a pump station, will become a very important consideration, as it must be carried by the river or by a railroad spur: hence my desire to locate the pumping station (if one is necessary) as near to the town as possible . . . Do you not think that we can get enough water for drinking and cooking, by sinking wells near the Hotel? It probably will be necessary to put up a telegraph or telephone wire to the pumping station, wherever it may be, so, in securing the right of way for the pipe line, it will be necessary to include a telegraph line. At the proper time, I will send you a blank form.

4th,—that if future development makes it necessary to connect the railroad tracks on the west side of your Home lot with my bay frontage, I shall have the right to lay not exceeding two tracks along the river front across your Home lot, locating same as near the river as is practicable to do so; upon this point, let me say that I shall not avail myself of this privilege until it becomes a commercial necessity.

5th,—you ask for the "privilege of water and sewer connections, and electric lights when they shall come." I don't know what was in your mind when you wrote this sentence. So far as sewer connections are concerned, for your Home lot, that I should cheerfully accord. If "water connections" means to give you the right to use all the water you may desire for the grounds of your Home Lot, I should be entirely willing that you should have it, but if you mean to extend this privilege to your portion of the land outside the ten acres, it may become a serious tax on our Hotel water supply, and thus prove inequitable. Please advise me what you mean by "electric lights." If you mean that you reserve the right for an electric plant for the town, it is all right.

6th,—a hundred ft. right of way for the railroad through all the lands you own between Lake Worth and the Gulf of Mexico. [Flagler apparently means Cape Sable, the southern tip of the Florida mainland.] Also, a right of way across your land somewhere north of the Fort Dallas Reservation, and as may hereafter be thought best to locate. Also ground for a railroad station at Biscayne.

Closing the letter, Flagler informed Julia Tuttle that he would take every bit of land that she offered—and more.

It was, I think, during my first visit to Fort Dallas, that in alluding to your original offer, I told you that I thought it was unfair to you. I refer to your proposal to give me substantially half of the Fort Dallas Reservation. At the time I made that remark, I had no idea that you owned so much land in Dade Co.; consequently, I did not realize that you would be so largely benefited by the construction of a railroad. It was not your fault that I did not have the information. I mention this now, because I have come back to your original proposition, and having looked over the situation with a good deal of care, I have come to the following conclusion,—under the most favorable circumstances, it will be years before the extension south of Lake

Worth can be made to pay more than running expenses and cost of maintenance . . .

In view of all that I have said, which I believe to be true, I do not now feel any hesitancy in accepting all that you have offered me in the way of land, and even asking for more . . .

Flagler asked for 100 extra acres, explaining that he had received 100 acres from the Brickell family which was also asking his railroad to come to Miami.

You mustn't think it strange that I have "cheek" enough to ask at least as much from you in that vicinity, not that I expect to build up a town at [the Brickell property], but I think it is good farming land, and I should hope to recoup myself to some extent, by the sale of property given me in that neighborhood . . . I assume that it will be at least sixty days before we can determine the extent of the land donations, but it seems to me that I shall be able to decide, one way or the other, by the first of July, and if I feel sufficiently encouraged, I believe we can complete the Road to Miami River by the first of February; perhaps it will take a month or two longer, although I doubt it. We ought to get there in time to make an outlet for vegetables grown next winter.[14]

Julia Tuttle had made her deal. Flagler's railroad would be at her front door by February 1896.[15]

# CHAPTER 14

# Miami

FLAGLER's interest in Biscayne Bay had in fact long preceded his correspondence with Julia Tuttle.

In the early 1890s, Flagler began traveling incognito, using a hired carriage to drive down from West Palm Beach to Lemon City, a dusty, tedious 12-hour journey. At Lemon City, he stayed all night at Mrs. Carey's boardinghouse, got up early and walked to Bay Point, a promontory of 10-foot elevation overlooking Biscayne Bay. The point was and is among the most beautiful on the bay, and one can see for miles to the north, east and south. After some time there, Henry would return to West Palm Beach.

Unaware of Flagler's identity, the townspeople speculated upon the strangeness of the visitor's actions, especially when they were repeated again and again.

The last such visit came in early February 1895 and on this visit Flagler identified himself.

"It was a pretty day," recalled Charles Schmidt, who came to Lemon City from Germany, via Jacksonville, in 1894.

I was fishing off the dock of Mr. L.W. Pierce, the town postmaster and the man who owned Bay Point, which was then called Pierce's Point. The trout were biting good. Mr. Flagler and Louie Pierce came walking to the dock. Flagler was arguing, Louie was watching me pull in a four-pounder. I heard Mr. Flagler say he wanted to buy Pierce's Point to build a big hotel on for Yankees to come to in the winter, and also run his railroad on down to Lemon City. "How about my offer?" he asked.

Louie Pierce, however, couldn't agree on anything, except that it was a fine day to fish. "Build your hotel down on the Miami River," he suggested good naturedly. "I'll give you all the land you want for a railroad right-of-way through Lemon City. Pardon me a moment, Mr. Flagler. Say Charlie, what kind of bait are you using?"[1]

Thus, some several weeks before receiving the orange blossoms and visiting Julia Tuttle, Flagler was already looking for a railroad terminus on Biscayne Bay.

Six months later, following Julia Tuttle's deal, hundreds of imported laborers, artisans and businessmen streamed through Lemon City southward to lay out Miami.[2]

Julia Tuttle's young friend Dorn later recalled that

. . . in the early part of 1896, I returned to Fort Dallas and lived in a palmetto hut not far from Mrs. Tuttle's residence. It had leaked out that the railroad was to come to Fort Dallas, and hundreds of people came from all over the country. Our bay was literally covered with dozens of small sail boats. A [stagecoach] line was started from Palm Beach to Fort Dallas and they brought many more people. Palmetto huts and tents were erected everywhere in a most impenetrable forest. Days passed, weeks passed, and no railroad. The people were becoming impatient; their money was about to give out; food was getting scarce.

Finally, one afternoon, we who were on the bay front sighted a boat approaching from the north. Soon Joseph A. McDonald [Flagler's prime contractor], John B. Reilly and John and Everett Sewell stepped from the boat onto our small dock and announced that the work of clearing the grounds for a hotel would begin immediately, and that the railroad would be here in 30 days. The hotel was to be erected on the point of the Miami River which was, at that time, a large Indian mound covered with an impenetrable forest.

Their announcement brought a great deal of joy to all of us. The old sternwheeler, *St. Lucie*, arrived a day later with lumber and all kinds of implements for clearing the ground.[3]

Many of the workers were convicts leased from the state at $2.50 a month and keep. The convicts were controlled by foremen with long black whips, notched with deep indentures to make them more effective. Gamblers and women followed the workers, and quarrels and bloodshed ensued.

"I was a kid in school nearby," said Miami's Jerome Sands, "and every time we heard drunken shouts and sudden shots Miss Merritt let out school for the day. We had about 20 holidays that year!"[4]

The rails were completed in just 10 months. Flagler's surveyors, meanwhile, had laid out the streets of Miami and Fort Lauderdale. Plans for the towns of Linton and Boynton soon would follow.

On April 15, 1896, the last rail was laid tying Miami to the outside world, and the first little wood-burning locomotive chugged into the town with a load of building material. Seven days later the first passenger train arrived.[5]

Herbert S. Rogers was the engineer, driving a high-stacked 15-inch-type Schenectady. Built by the American Locomotive Works, it was a woodburner, pulling a tender, mail coach, baggage car, first- and second-class day coaches, and a parlor chair car.

"Ed Steinhauser was the conductor," said Rogers, "and as near as I can remember we arrived at Miami about 9 P.M. There was no station, of course, and we pulled up at a small platform with a telegraph office built at one end. This was located at or near what is now Flagler Street."[6]

Passengers on the first train included George Betton Massey:

It was a miserable ride and one I'll never forget. It was hot and dirty and as primitive as the transportation facilities that fed western boom towns. The engine on the train was a high-stacked wood burner and when she thundered down the track at a few miles an hour, cinders, soot and dirt would fly back over the open coaches.

At that time civilization actually extended only as far south as Fort Pierce [145 miles north of Miami] and when you left there it was like jumping off into a wilderness.

If the train got too hot you could always get up and wade through banana peels and lunch boxes thrown on the floor to reach a water cooler and a community drinking cup at the end of the car . . .

When we pulled into town, all 300 persons, who were mainly employees of Henry M. Flagler, turned out to greet us.

It was a strange settlement, as raw as any boom town. But strangely enough, since no saloons were allowed, much quieter. . . .

Horses and buggies whisked up and down the streets and the only real buildings in town were three or four brick structures, the partially completed Royal Palm hotel being built by Flagler, and the rest were just shacks.[7]

Three months later, on July 28, 1896, the settlement was incorporated. There was strong public sentiment to call it "Flagler," but Henry persuaded the city council to use the old Indian name of Miami.

The new city had an estimated population of 1,500, including 502 registered voters. This was a considerable size inasmuch as the whole southeastern coast, with the exception of Palm Beach, was a frontier. Traveling from north to south, Melbourne was a village of handsome cottages. Fort Lauderdale consisted of a post office, a hotel and a store. West Palm Beach, the city Flagler built for his help, had a population of only 1,200.

Almost overnight, Miami took shape. New settlers arrived daily. Flagler's workmen felled trees, cleared land and erected buildings. Flagler's hotel, the Royal Palm, was under construction.

John Reilly, son-in-law of chief contractor McDonald, was elected the first mayor.

"The city began to grow," James Ingraham recalled. "There were hundreds of people who had come into this territory to engage in trucking, vegetable gardening, putting out nurseries of young trees, who had been brought in by the railroad and encouraged to settle in this community."[8]

Among the newcomers was W. M. Burdine, a retired Confederate officer who had been running a store in Bartow. He wrote a friend that, "Miami is a tourist town and large numbers of people will be coming from the north every winter."

He sold overalls, white duck pants and sneakers to railroad workers. And shirts, socks and gaudy calicos to the Seminoles. Eventually, under the name of Burdine's, his business would expand into one of the most prestigious department store chains in America.

THE CENTER of Miami evolved from a cabbage palm patch.

A landscaped park for the Royal Palm hotel fronted the intersection at the southeast, and it was from there that the city began to grow.[9] Across the bay from Miami was a barrier island, later to be known as Miami Beach. Where Palm Beach had been a paradise, Miami Beach was the opposite. It was mostly swamp, and was filled with mosquitoes, snakes, mangrove thickets, and Spanish Bayonet— dark, spiny cactus-like plants which can easily run through an unwary human's hand or foot.

Lula Elizabeth Lummus was on the scene when Miami started, and she was as excited about it as any person in her 20s would be. In 1896, she was 23 years old and the new wife of J. N. Lummus. They had been married in 1894 and moved from Sanford, in central Florida, to open a grocery store to service the rail line.[10]

They arrived in April 1896, "in a boat from Fort Lauderdale."

The Lummuses, along with J. R. Dewey, rented a rickety structure, which was immodestly called the Hotel Miami, from Julia Tuttle for $400 a month. Hastily built by Julia to take advantage of the boom (and thus furthering a Miami tradition), it was the only large hotel in Miami at the time—the Royal Palm not yet having been built. Lula conceded that while it might be called a hotel, it was a "crudely-built one."

In May 1896, with the city of Miami but a few weeks old, Lula sat on the porch of her hotel and wrote an article for the Sanford *Chronicle,* designed to make her new digs look good to her old neighbors:

We now live at Miami, Fla., the terminus of the East Coast Railroad. I feel like I am in another world, but the novelty is fascinating and interesting. Miami is situated on the Miami River and beautiful Biscayne Bay. It is decidedly a "boom" town . . .

Everything is crude and we have few comforts of civilization, but I'm enjoying living near to nature's heart. Twenty business houses are going up, and in a few years everyone predicts this place will be equal to Tampa. Boats run three times per week from Key West, and crowds arrive on every train to see the much talked of place.

I had the thrill of my life when I stood and watched the first train come in . . . The climate is ideal, and sometimes when sailing down the beautiful bay in a launch to Cape Florida, I can imagine I'm in some far away, lovely Oriental country.

Up and down the banks of the Miami River, and on the bay, the coconut trees grow in wild luxuriant profusion, and are now laden with fruit. Oranges, limes, bananas and guavas grow wild.

They are cutting them down everywhere to make streets for Miami, as yet, it is very close to nature.

The pineapple crop is abundant this year; the air is so sweet with delicious odors, you can well imagine that it is a whiff from Paradise. One large pineapple was brought in the hotel office yesterday from Coconut Grove and it weighed 10 pounds.

Sitting on the hotel veranda, looking over the surrounding country, you can see dozens of tents where refined people live. Men are here from every state, almost, looking for work, or to invest, and make this their future home. It seems strange to me that only white men are employed as mechanics.

I have been in the Everglades of Florida and had a cool drink of water from a spring that flowed into Lake Okeechobee; and oh, the rare and beautiful ferns I have collected and gathered out of those dense woods.

Mr. Flagler is having the ground prepared for his new hotel. It will be built on a point facing the bay.

Mrs. Julia Tuttle's home, with its well kept lawns and lovely tropical flowers and luscious fruits, shows what can be done down here in Dixie land. The old Fort Dallas within her grounds is of much interest to sightseers. It is a picturesque sight crumbling away and covered with beautiful ivy.

The "Red Man" is at home in this country. At Fort Lauderdale, a few days since I saw a dozen or more. I used to have a romantic admiration for them, but on close inspection, recovered from my illusions.

I am glad to state that our beloved Bishop Gray of the Episcopal Church holds divine services and administers holy communion at the Hotel Miami twice a month. Mrs. Tuttle is a communicant and will give us two of her choice lots to build a church and rectory.

Mr. Flagler built the First Presbyterian and gave lots to the Methodist Episcopal Church, North.

Julia Tuttle, in the meantime, was constructing buildings and buying land faster even than Flagler. She quickly got into debt, however, and beginning in August 1896 began a series of requests to Flagler in New York asking for assistance in obtaining loans.

His replies shown a growing weariness with her dependency.

Dear Mrs. Tuttle, I have not been well for a few days, and this with the intense heat has kept me from the office where I am today but for a short time. I have three of your letters, but can answer only one of them today, the one in which you enclose to me a memo of your bills payable, which you state to be $30,000 . . .

Flagler agreed to cosign a $5,000 loan, but declined on signing for more and told her, "I am very much worried over the financial situation, and while I repeat what I said in a former letter, that I do not want to advise you, I hope that you will sell the Cleveland property and get yourself out of debt. . . ." [11]

She followed with another request, asking his aid in renovating Fort Dallas. Again, he declined:

"With regard to the improvement on the building at Ft. Dallas, it is utterly impossible for me to help you in this matter. . . ."

Buying land as fast as she could, Tuttle was unashamed in pressing Flagler for even more loans. In the fall of 1896 she had asked him to cosign $4,000 in a personal loan, saying that she was "suffering" from lack of money and faced the possibility of mortgaging her home. Responding in a letter of December 5, 1896, he refused and tried to wash his hands of her forever:

I had not . . . the faintest idea that you would ask me to become responsible for even one half the sum for which I already am. . . . The naked fact remains

that I haven't one dollar of security (for your loans) and it is not right that
the matter should be left in this shape. I note that it will be troublesome
to you to mortgage your property. I have not asked you to do it, but on the
other hand I cannot and must not increase my responsibility, and you should
not ask me to . . .

I do not want you "to suffer." But I cannot accept the responsibility of
your suffering. For months past I have advised against your becoming so
deeply involved in debt. . . . I return the $4,000 note without my endorse-
ment.[12]

Julia ceased her entreaties just prior to Christmas, the city's first.
With her grown children, Julia joined other Miamians in church
services, social gatherings and fine dinners. The traditional opening
of presents on Christmas morning, however, was devastated by a pre-
dawn disaster.

About 4 A.M., the fledgling city was struck by a raging fire, which
spread quickly to the wooden business establishments of the downtown district, destroying 28 buildings and killing one person. The fire
leapt across the streets, igniting homes, livery stables—everything
in its path. It ended at the Miami River, destroying the Lummus's
Miami Hotel.

The commerce of Miami stopped. There was no immediate money
to replace the buildings destroyed by the fire. The town's sole bank
had burned down, consuming thousands of dollars in uninsured deposits. The short boom was over. Hundreds of men were out of work.
Flagler stepped in with immediate help, remembered Charles A.
Mills, who in 1896 was a young timekeeper for the McGuire &
McDonald construction company:

[Joseph] McDonald, realizing the plight of our unemployed and their families, with the cooperation of Ingraham, induced Flagler to authorize the
construction of cottages near Flagler Street, mainly to provide work. . . .

They also convinced Flagler that it would be good business to dig a ship
channel from Cape Florida to the Miami docks, which meant more work for
local people.[13]

ON January 15, 1897, Flagler opened the lemon-yellow Royal Palm,
complete with 350 rooms, two electric elevators, a swimming pool
and an electric generator which provided lights for the hotel and the
city. He then spent $20,000 dredging a channel from the ocean into
Biscayne Bay, which converted Miami into a deep-sea port. Antici-

pating the city's rapid growth, he built a watertower sufficient to supply a population of 25,000. Passengers arriving to stay at his hotel had the additional comfort of having the train deliver them via a spur practically to the door of the hotel—a path through property still in the hands of, and homesteaded by, Julia Tuttle.[14]

Flagler's joy at opening the hotel was short-lived. Less than a month later, on February 7, 1897, Florida was hit with the second of the great freezes. The timing of the sudden cold couldn't have been worse. Trees were in bloom throughout the whole state. In many localities, vegetables were nearly ready to be shipped, and the losses were staggering, extending even to Miami and points south.

On the next morning, Flagler was nowhere to be found. In his absence, his top executives met in the company headquarters at St. Augustine.

Ingraham, who had guaranteed to Flagler that Miami was "forever free" of frost, recalled the details, and the surprising speed with which Flagler reacted:

At a conference with Mr. Parrott, Mr. Beckwith and our other officials, it was decided that the railroad company would issue seed free, would haul fertilizer and crate material free, but Mr. Parrott told me that that was as far as he thought the railroad company could go. I immediately got in touch with the seed houses, ordered supplies and seed to be given out free and bought all the seed beds of tomatoes that I could get my hands on for free distribution.

While we were talking in the afternoon a telegram was handed to me from Mr. Flagler, saying: "Come to Miami at once." I took the first train and arrived at Miami about 6:30 in the morning following, and found Mr. Flagler waiting for me on the steps of the Royal Palm. He took me by the arm, he did not say good morning or how do you do, but walked with me into Mr. Merrill's [the hotel manager] office, and turned around and putting both hands on my shoulders said: "Ingraham, tell me how bad it is." I said: "Mr. Flagler, it is a total loss . . . the mercury went to fourteen. Vegetables everywhere are killed; the pineries on the Indian River are killed and it is a hundred per cent of loss."

He said: "What have you decided to do?" I said: "After a conference with Mr. Parrott, he authorized me to issue free seeds and to haul fertilizer and crate material free. That is as far as he felt that we could go, and I have bought up all the seed I can get my hands on, and seed beds, for that purpose."

He said: "That is all right so far as it goes, but it does not go far enough.

These banks here in this territory are not strong, the banks will have to shut
down on the merchants and the merchants on the farmers, and they will
starve." He said: "Mr. Ingraham, I want you to get right into this territory.
These people are not beggars nor paupers and they must have money to go
on. In order to save time issue your own check and let them have such
money as they need at 6 per cent on their notes for as long time as they
desire. You can use $50,000 or $100,000 or $200,000."

Not only was Flagler quick to help the needy, but he had no
recriminations against Ingraham, who expected to lose his job.

There was never one word of reproach to me, who had been largely instru-
mental in attracting his attention to this territory, not one word, nor did he
have one thought in his mind I am sure, for the protection of this territory
when he authorized this issue of money to those in need. It was simply that
no woman and no child should starve.
    I was almost speechless when he told me. He said: "Now, get right out,
issue your own check and cover it by drafts on Beardsley, whom I will wire
about the matter."
    When I wired my associates and told them what Mr. Flagler had told
me to do, they were tremendously revived, their courage was restored, their
energies renewed and they realized what a great thing it was to do and why
they chose to stay by Mr. Flagler and work with him and for him rather
than independently. Within seventy-two days of the time that the first relief
check was issued, vegetables, tomatoes, snap beans began to move, first by
express, then by carload, then by trainload, and I want to tell you that the
season was so good a one as to price and quantity as to establish permanently
the trucking industry in Florida.[15]

Flagler didn't just bring the railroad, he built and ran the town.
He hired men, often black laborers, to lay out streets, build water
and power facilities and deepen channels. Within three months of
the railroad's arrival, Miami had a newspaper, The *Miami Metropolis*,
secretly financed by Flagler. While townspeople may have quarreled
with the not-always benevolent Flagler dictatorship, the railroad un-
questionably transformed a frontier hamlet into a burgeoning resort.
    In the ensuing year, Julia Tuttle sank ever faster in financial quick-
sand and once again sought help from Flagler. She wrote him the
day after Christmas 1897, saying she was so broke that she could use
any cash he could send her. She offered to mortgage her homestead
to him. He replied promptly, saying he had sent money, but claimed
with some cupidity that he himself was going broke:

Your letter of 26th reached me yesterday, but I was so overwhelmed with business affairs, it was scarcely possible to read it. I do so, however, but very hastily and telegraphed you that you might draw on me at sight for $2,000. This morning I received a message from the Bank of Bay Biscayne asking whether I would honor your sight draft for that amount, to which I replied "Yes."

I observe your intention of mortgaging your homestead, and I duly note your enquiry whether I would not make the loan. If you will remember the reasons I gave you for not complying with the request made in your former letter, you will see that it was not because of an unwillingness to help you, *but because I have no money* [emphasis added]. Besides I am heavily in debt myself.

Once again, Flagler let Tuttle know that he was tired of being her patron.

I do not see why your pecuniary difficulties should reflect upon me. Even if they did, I should not allow myself to worry about it, for my conscience acquits me of anything but the most liberal dealings with you. I assume that you have had a great deal to contend with, perhaps no more relatively than I. If your life and health are spared, I have no doubt but that you will pull through them. It may be necessary however, for you to exercise the most rigid economy for a few years. . . .[16]

Miami's economic depression was removed all at once in early 1898 when the U.S. battleship *Maine* arrived in the harbor of Spanish-held Havana, Cuba, to protect American citizens and property from an impending Cuban revolution. The *Maine* was blown up, by persons and agencies unknown to this day, and the Spanish-American War began.

The people of Miami were both joyous and shaken by the declaration of war with Spain. Its nearness to Cuba, the gunrunning, the refugees—all added to the excitement, and there was also strong sympathy for the struggling Cubans. The encampment of several thousand American soldiers on the bayfront brought the war close to home. People in Miami, like the world at large, had an exaggerated fear of Spain's power. A few so feared an invasion or a bombardment that they left town and pitched their tents at the edge of the Everglades.

Even before war was declared on April 25, 1898, panicky Miami petitioned for fortifications to protect the city. Although the waters around the city were not deep enough for true warships to enter, the government appeased the citizenry by building a fortification south of Brickell Point on the Miami River.

The Spanish-American War brought more than 7,000 soldiers into Miami. They were quartered in a tent city along Biscayne Bay.

During the summer months of 1898, the Royal Palm was head-quarters for a multitude of army and government officials and news-paper correspondents. The ensuing publicity helped break down the isolation of the little tropical outpost. After the war, many of the encamped soldiers returned with families to take up residence.

THE WAR boom caused the city's first telephone exchange to be opened in 1898, providing services to businesses for $30 per year. The ex-change was located in the rear of the Miami Drug Store, and lines were laid to Lemon City, five miles to the north, and Coconut Grove, five miles to the south. There were 25 initial subscribers, including Henry Flagler, the Royal Palm Hotel, the Miami *Metropolis*, and Julia Tuttle. The first operator was Miss Eunice Coons, who worked only during the day. The exchange was locked up at night along with the drug store.

On occasion, however, there were nighttime "programs" as op-posed to "service." The telephone company owner, John Dewey, would call all the subscribers and tell them he had arranged a musical program on a specified evening. On the specified night, a string quartet would gather before the switchboard. All the plugs would be inserted in the jacks. And the program would begin.

That summer of 1898, the summer of the Spanish–American War, Julia Tuttle did not go north as she often did. Her daughter, Fanny, had married the previous year and moved to Nassau. Julia's son, Harry, still a bachelor, was homesteading land about nine miles up the bay. Although Julia's headaches had become increasingly severe, when the troops came she stayed. More or less the city's official hostess, she was increasingly distressed by the disorderly conduct of some of the officers. One soldier committed suicide in her own gar-den. A couple of others were killed by a lightning storm nearby. Depressed and ailing, Julia stayed so close to home that when she did go out the *Metropolis* mentioned it in a news item, saying her health was improving.

It wasn't. On September 14, as she was trying to arrange for a private railroad car to take her to Asheville, North Carolina, in the

hopes that a change of altitude might end the terrible headaches,
Julia Tuttle died. She was 49.

Local medical opinion said she died of "inflammation of the brain,"
possibly a brain tumor. Few had realized how sick she was, and the
town was shocked.

The city was closed for her funeral, and she was buried in the
Miami City Cemetery, the twelfth grave to be dug there.

A month after her death, Julia's son married Corrie Rosetta Fowler, daughter of two Chicago doctors. For $33,000, Harry bought out
his sister Fanny's share of Julia's estate, estimated as worth between
$300,000 and $400,000, most of it in land. Within the next year or
so he sold his homestead and turned Julia's home, the old fort, into
an exclusive gambling casino, the Seminole Club.[17] Fanny returned
to Nassau where she proceeded to bear her husband seven children.
Angered over Harry's handling of Julia's estate, she refused to speak
to him for many years.

In the years that followed, Julia Tuttle's and Henry Flagler's Miami
saw great activity in winter. Northerners loved the warmth and sunshine, the flowers, the exotic trees in full leaf. Many a tourist found
the trees almost as much of an attraction as the climate. For the
sports-minded, there was golf, or sailing, or swimming, or, with local
guides, fishing for big ones in the Gulf Stream, or hunting gators and
wild boar in the backlands. Other tourists would saunter through the
streets or stores, their light, bright dress in gay contrast with that of
some grower or trapper just in from his daily chores.

Golf was almost an unheard of game at the time, but Flagler was
interested in luring rich tourists to the city and thus installed a circular
six-hole course on the hotel grounds. In 1898, Flagler purchased 75
acres of land in an area called the Tuttle prairie and built a regulation
18-hole course.[18]

Following the Royal Palm's lead, other hotels sprang up, ranging
from the exclusive Halcyon Hotel to the more modestly priced Green
Tree Inn. Another bank opened, so did a couple of grocery stores,
meat markets, pool halls, real estate offices, a bakery, a tailor, and
the first Burdine's, then billed as a dry-goods and specialty store.

Summer was a different story, when virtually everything closed.

South of Miami lay magnificent farmlands—large marl prairies,
where the rich, reddish muck soil, of almost claylike texture, was
excellent for fruit. From there, bounty poured forth to the tables of

the North. An article in the Cincinnati *Enquirer* of January 14, 1900, spoke with wonder of the products coming from America's newest city:

John Pillsbury, manager of the Cincinnati office of the Travelers' Information Company, had on his desk at the Grand Hotel yesterday an exhibit of green things that brought with it a suggestion of the soft air and sunshine of the Southland. There were ripe red tomatoes, green peppers, string beans and eggplant, all of which grew in the open in the gardens of Miami, Fla., the newest town in the United States at the terminus of the Florida East Coast Railway. Mr. Pillsbury says these are but samples of the season's products, pineapples, pears and various fruits being among other consignments of which he has been notified.

For many years Flagler had viewed Biscayne Bay as a springboard to the Caribbean, and in 1899 he built the Colonial Hotel in Nassau, the Bahamas. In the same year, he added another mainland hotel to his system, the oceanfront Hotel Continental, 21 miles east of Jacksonville.

The Continental was a wooden structure similar to the Royal Palm and intended to be a "summer Palm Beach," a cool summer resort for the wealthy people of the South. It was a loser from the start, however, and became Flagler's only failure in the hotel business. He blamed this failure on the lack of wealth in the South and bitterly noted in a memo "there is a *possibility* that before the building rots down, we may be able to make some money out of it, but I must confess that the prospect seems rather remote."

NEVERTHELESS, as the twentieth century drew to a close, Flagler's accomplishments were awesome. Indeed, said Ingraham, at the time they seemed impossible.

He had a wonderful vision of what this country would eventually be, a vision that was not shared by other prominent capitalists. I remember one time sitting on the broad piazza of the Royal Palm Hotel in conversation with the late Samuel Sloan, then president of the Delaware & Lackawanna Railroad. Our conversation turned upon Mr. Flagler and the wonderful work he was undertaking . . .

Sloan, who thought Florida "worthless," replied:

I do not want to criticise Mr. Flagler in what he is undertaking here, but I do say that it would be impossible for him to form a group of capitalists to build the Florida East Coast Railroad and make the other developments he is making in what I consider a worthless country, save its climate. A railroad must have a certain amount of business and there are but a few people in this southern section and no immediate prospect of the population increasing rapidly. Even though he fills this palatial hotel it will cut little figure in paying the expenses of the road. I do not think he can succeed, but should his dream prove true it will make him the greatest philanthropist of this or any other age.

Sloan, who had risen from a lowly position to the head of a great railroad, was one of many great financiers who honestly believed Flagler's great projects were doomed to failure.

Flagler once told Ingraham that many of his strongest friends had advised him to give up the Florida work. But, Flagler added, "there is an impelling force within me and I must carry out my plans." [19]

# CHAPTER 15

# Divorce and Marriage

WHAT was the force that drove Henry Flagler? Surely, he was driven. He himself spoke in many different words of being driven, of a lurking dissatisfaction, of a compulsion to do something with his life. But what fired the engine? Was it a desire to show off for Ida Alice, as some have suggested? Perhaps in the beginning it was. But most of the Florida accomplishments were done after she had gone insane.

Others have theorized that Flagler was in some strange competition with John D. Rockefeller. They say that despite Rockefeller's acknowledgment that it "was Henry Flagler's idea," the Standard Oil Company nevertheless bore the stamp of "Made by Rockefeller." By this theory, Flagler created a Florida domain so that he would have something important bearing his own imprimatur. It is an attractive theory, but has little evidence to support it. In fact, the evidence points in the opposite direction. Time after time, Flagler refused to stamp his name on Florida. The people of Florida asked him to put his name on towns, on lakes, on rivers, on cities, even on his own railroad. And in each instance he refused. He would not even countenance the sculpting of a statue or the design of a bust in his honor and, indeed, none were done in his lifetime.

A third hypothesis of why Henry was driven is that he was seeking some sort of immortality. It is noted that the Ponce de Leon, named after the seeker of the Fountain of Youth, was built by Flagler to last "beyond my lifetime." But that comment, made in 1886, referred to the quality of the building, not to Flagler's ambition. All of his subsequent hotels were made out of wood.

No, none of the above theories hold water. There is only one that meets the evidence of his track record and that is this: After Mary Harkness Flagler's death, he did what she had wanted him to do. He left Standard Oil. He went to Florida. And once there, he began to build. It was not easy. But with hard work and rare genius, he was able to transform his visions into reality. He kept building, and he would keep building until the end of his life. He was driven to do it; to create life in the form of towns and farms and colonies and cities and railroads and churches and schools. He, who may have believed he had killed Mary, became a giver of life, a tiller and planter in the land.

In the last quarter of his life, he was to attempt his riskiest stroke. He put everything he had gained—his entire fortune—on the line to build an "overseas railroad," an engineering challenge considered at the time to be second only to the Panama Canal.

In doing this, he was blessed in having the support and care of the most effective partner of his life—a woman named Mary Lily Kenan. If Mary Harkness was the great guilt of Henry's life, Mary Lily was his great love.

For Flagler, Mary Lily Kenan seemed to have everything—a compassionate soul; an intellectual development which included a broad, classical education (she had a beautiful voice and was an accomplished pianist); and a grace of style in personal and social matters.

With long, thick dark hair and blue eyes, and standing at a pretty, buxom, 105 pounds and five-foot one-inch, she was attractive and sexual. The latter was important for Flagler, who had by no means lost such interests.

Mary Lily came from solid stock. Her father, William, had been a captain in the Confederate service and was widely known socially in the Carolinas. She had been educated at St. Mary's College in Raleigh. One of her uncles lived there, who was a former colonel of a Confederate regiment, attorney general of the state for eight years, and later clerk of the North Carolina Supreme Court.

Contrary to many later legends about Mary Lily's background, the Kenans never knew even "middle class" poverty. Mary, born in 1867, was the oldest of four children. She had a sister, Jessie, born in 1870; a brother, William, 1872; and a sister, Sarah, 1876.

William, an engineer, had an independent relationship with Flagler, having met him in the early 1890s in New York City and being hired to design the power plant, laundry, steam heating and refrigeration of the Breakers Hotel.[1]

STRANGELY, for all her attractiveness and background, Mary Lily had never been engaged prior to Flagler and is not known to have had any affairs prior to him. She had some beaus, including a flirtation in the summer of 1884 with Sterling Ruffin, later to be the private physician of President Woodrow Wilson.[2]

Not much more can be learned about her early life. She can be tracked from birth through college. But after that, from about 1886, the traces vanish until about 1891, when she met Flagler at a series of social functions. Somewhere along the line she picked up a liking for bourbon whiskey and for laudanum, a polite Victorian word for opium.

For a woman of Mary Lily's class to use such drugs was not uncommon. Indeed, until 1909, there was no restriction on opiates sold in the United States. Cocaine was an ingredient of the new popular drink, Coca-Cola. Opium and morphine were widely sold in drugstores and were especially popular with discreet ladies who were otherwise respectable except that they were "on dope." In 1900, the profile of the typical drug addict matched Mary Lily exactly: white, female and middle to upper middle class. There was a higher rate of drug addiction in 1900 than in the 1960s and 1970s.[3]

It isn't known if Flagler knew or cared about her drug habits. He did, however, care about her reputation and managed for the first few years to keep their affair secret.

By 1899, however, they had been seen together so much that even society writers began to speculate. Mary Lily's family, furthermore, was uneasy about her association with one of the wealthiest men in the country, most especially since he was married. Her grandmother strongly advised her to end the relationship, not on grounds of morality but because the publicity was annoying.[4]

Despite the growing scandal, Mary Lily and Henry's niece, Elizabeth Ashley, continued to travel and visit with him, staying at one of his oceanfront cottages in Palm Beach. When in New York, they stayed at the Plaza.

In 1899, Flagler made his intentions known to Mary Lily while they were in Palm Beach. He wanted to marry her. As an engagement present, he gave her a magnificent strand of graduated Oriental pearls, the largest of which was the size of a robin's egg. It was held together with a 12-karat diamond clasp. To compliment the necklace, he added a diamond bracelet. Collectively, the jewelry was worth $1 million.[5]

Mary Lily talked to her family about the proposal. They were curious as to how Flagler intended to get a divorce. He was, as it happened, a legal resident of New York State, and the sole ground for divorce there was adultery—a contention hard to pursue inasmuch as the incumbent Mrs. Flagler was locked up in an asylum.

The Kenan family response was both practical and pragmatic. Mary Lily was a 32-year-old single woman. She had been having an affair with Henry Flagler since at least 1896. And now the newspapers had gotten hold of it. These were facts and problems to be dealt with. It was certain she had been compromised, and Henry Flagler owed her something.

In the meantime, Flagler, ever the negotiator, offered to ease the Kenans' uncertainties by forever providing for Mary Lily's future. The family debated and found the offer acceptable. Divorce or no divorce, he would take care of her. He instructed his architects, Carrere and Hastings, to design a "Cuban style home" for Mary Lily in Palm Beach, the town's first important mansion. Construction began a year later, the foundations being laid in the summer of 1900. But that was not all. On April 3, 1899, he transferred nearly $1 million in Standard Oil stock to Mary Lily. The transfer was handled by her brother, William Kenan, who was chief electrical engineer for the Flagler hotel system.[6]

Kenan, indeed, may have prompted the transaction. He was a hard and effective businessman. Flagler, who had his own ruthless side, rather admired him for it. "Will Kenan," he said, "got more for his dollar than any man I ever knew . . . Will Kenan was 21 years old when he was born."[7]

Now Flagler moved to get his divorce.

Step one came on April 23, less than three weeks after his proposal of marriage to Mary Lily, when he announced he was changing his legal residence from New York to Florida. He said he was doing it for business reasons, and Florida newspapers, such as the Florida *Times Union*, commented favorably on the "state's newest number one citizen." The *Times Union*, of course, was a newspaper owned by Flagler.

Step two came on June 28, less than three months after his proposal to Mary Lily. He petitioned for a ruling by the New York Supreme Court that Ida Alice Flagler was insane and incompetent. The court so certified.

Step three was one of preparation. Although Flagler was now a citizen of Florida, divorce was not allowed except in cases of proven adultery, similar to his situation in New York. But, where he felt blocked by the New York laws, he felt he could do something about the Florida laws.

Step four came on April 9, 1901, at the convening of the Florida legislature. A bill was introduced "making incurable insanity a ground for divorce . . ."

FEW BILLS ever sailed through both houses and were signed by the governor with greater speed. Rushed through, Standard Oil-style, it became law two-and-a-half weeks from the day it was introduced. The bill was introduced in the Florida senate on April 9 and passed on April 17 with little opposition. On April 19 it won approval of the House by a vote of 42 to 19, and on April 25 was signed into law by Governor William Jennings. After the divorce bill slipped through the legislature as if it were a greased pit, there were widespread charges of payoffs to legislators, but no official evidence of bribery was uncovered.

The Tampa *Herald* objected to that, saying, "It is a queer thing to see a state wake up so suddenly to the enormity of being a slave to Flagler. Scarcely a day has passed since he came into Florida that Flagler has not done worse and more atrocious things than cause a Legislature to pass a divorce law . . . He has had many newspapers at his feet, so to speak, and he has been a little tin god on wheels to an army of politicians . . ."

Rumors that he had bought the legislation, and the legislature, spread rapidly. The Tampa *Tribune*, on April 30, noted:

"The opposition to the measure doesn't seem to be directed at the bill itself, but to the unconcealed fact that it was passed for the special benefit of Mr. Flagler. And whenever the Legislature passes a bill that is supposed to benefit that distinguished gentleman, the average country editor always jumps at the conclusion that somebody, in some way, has gotten some money out of it. It's this idea that provokes the howl."

When Frank Harris, editor of the Ocala *Banner*, countered that the divorce law was sensible, he was roundly condemned by his fellow newspaper editors. "Harris needs the prayers of the brethren of the press," said the Palmetto *News*. "Has he shared some of the favors bestowed upon the Legislature?"

The Pensacola *Journal* accused Harris of selling out to Flagler because of a $20,000 gift from Henry to Florida Agricultural College (later to become the University of Florida). Harris was a trustee of the college.

Numerous legislators were defeated because of their support of the bill. It was a major issue in the 1904 governor's race, almost resulting in the defeat of Jacksonville's Napoleon Broward, who as a house member, had voted for the bill. Broward, who would succeed his friend, Governor Jennings, was shocked by the criticism of his vote: "I received nothing," he said. "No one solicited my support. I felt under conditions outlined in the bill it was a reasonable ground for divorce."

Flagler indeed had made payoffs, more than $125,000 worth. It was more than 70 years later, however, before researchers obtained access to the Florida East Coast files, which showed the disbursements. Flagler had paid former Governor Francis P. Fleming $15,000 for allegedly defending his insane wife. He had paid George Raney, an important member of the house, $14,500 to act as Flagler's attorney. He also had paid Raney $106,942, which was listed as "expenses incurred." Circumstances indicate that the latter amount was distributed to other legislators as bribes.

If Flagler was bothered by this sharp criticism in Florida and other states, he didn't show it. He was accustomed to obtaining what he wanted.

Nevertheless, even Flagler must have been shaken when yet another scandal was piled upon him in May. That was when C. W. Foote filed his divorce suit in Syracuse, naming 71-year-old Henry as correspondent—a circumstance which caused Henry's younger partner, John Rockefeller, who was nursing a bad stomach at Pocantico, New York, to shake his head mournfully. It is not known what reaction was had by Mary Lily and the other Kenans.

Public furor mounted sharply when on June 3, 1901, Flagler filed for divorce in a Dade County court. Represented by a prestigious New York law firm and a bevy of witnesses brought down from that state, Flagler was granted a divorce on August 13, 1901, two months after filing under the new law.[8]

UNDER TERMS of Henry's voluntary settlement, Alice received securities and properties worth about $2.3 million, which netted her an annual income of about $120,000. Her annual expenses were about $20,000.

Apparently, Alice Flagler never realized she had been divorced, living in her world of delusions and hallucinations. Confined in her sanitarium, Alice continued to excitedly discuss with a host of imaginary friends her approaching marriage to the Czar. She died of a brain hemorrhage on July 12, 1930.

By the time of Alice's death, and despite the stock market crash of 1929, her estate, comprised almost entirely of Standard Oil stock, had grown to $15.2 million, which was left to two nephews and a grand niece.

HENRY married Mary Lily on Saturday, August 24, 1901, a bare 10 days following his divorce. An elaborate ceremony was held in Liberty Hall, at Kenansville, seat of the Kenan family estates. There were only a few guests, however, most of them Mary Lily's relatives. For the event, the old ante-bellum mansion had been completely renovated and painted during the summer. The night before the wedding, Flagler brought the wedding party down on private railroad cars from New York. For wedding presents, Henry gave Mary Lily's brother and two sisters each a substantial block of Standard Oil stock. Flagler's gift to his bride was a certified check for $1 million and $2 million in registered government bonds.

ACCOUNTS of the event, which touched off international headlines, described Flagler as looking dignified in a Prince Albert coat with light trousers, "a happy man, his advancing years hidden behind a beaming countenance. He was a happy old man, and expressed his joy in the form of expensive gifts to the bride, certain members of the family, and the servants."

Mary Lily's wedding gown was white chiffon over white satin, trimmed with point appliqué with a veil of the same material, adorned with orange blossoms. She wore no ornaments, and a niece was her only attendant. The bride, leaning upon the arm of her father, Captain William Kenan, walked into the drawing room at noon, and was met by Flagler, who advanced with her to an altar under a bower of ferns, bamboo and other plants.

Soon after the wedding, the couple boarded Flagler's private train car at Magnolia, the nearest railroad point, and sped away to New York, to his summer home at Mamaroneck. From that point on, Henry Flagler spared no expense to give his bride anything she wanted that money could buy.

PUBLISHED accounts of the early days of marriage, at the time and afterward, state that Henry and Mary Lily were enthusiastic newlyweds and well matched despite the age difference of 37 years. But it appears that it was only the first few months that were romantic. After that, Henry began to tire and wanted to go to bed at eight o'clock. He wanted her to go, too.[9]

Indeed, although the marriage was later successful, it began as a bust. Less than two weeks after the marriage, Henry wrote to a stranger saying, "If it were not for the misery and wretchedness of mankind I think I might lead a happy life, in spite of all my own sorrows."[10]

And at Mamaroneck during the honeymoon, Henry was solicited for funds by a Philadelphia pastor whom he had never met. In a reply which rejected the charity request, Henry wrote a curiously detailed account of purposes and policies in his Florida "domain." For some reason, the reticent Henry chose to explain himself to a faceless stranger. Why? Perhaps he felt a need for self-justification, or self-verification, which he could not then share with his bride.

Here is one of Flagler's rare explanations of himself:

to Rev. Charles Stevens, Philadelphia,
September. 4, 1901
I am trying conscientiously to recognize the responsibilities of wealth. The statement may not surprise you when I say that I could give away in one short month the accumulation of a lifetime of industry and economy, and every dollar of it would go to some worthy person or object . . .

Aside from my regular contributions to the various public channels, I have a domain in Florida peculiarly my own. I am the sole owner now of a railroad in Florida, 462 miles in length; 300 miles of this road traverses a country which was entirely unoccupied when I built the road. My Land

Commissioner, through my instructions, has exercised a great deal more care as to the character of the colonists who go in, than their numbers. Consequently we have a class of people whose first need is a schoolhouse, next a church.

Acting upon the principle that we appreciate that which costs us something, I have in all these cases, required the colonists to raise all the money they could for such purposes, and then in some way they get the remainder, without knowing exactly how. I feel that these people are wards of mine and have a special claim upon me. It may seem egotistical, but it is nevertheless a fact, that I am doing this work in Florida wholly by myself, without making any appeal to others to assist me, and in doing so am paying out a great many thousands of dollars every year. The cause you present is a most worthy one, but it is to a certain extent local in its character, and under the circumstances, while I know you will be disappointed, I feel sure you will admit that I have given you a good excuse for not responding favorably to your appeal.

A few weeks after the marriage, Henry returned to business. At Miami, he assigned William Kenan to build a true electrical power plant, one capable of supplying a city of 25,000.

Electricity had first appeared in that city in 1897 with the opening of the Royal Palm Hotel, which was equipped with two 20-volt generators belted to a wood-burning steam engine. This provided electricity for the hotel and also to power a few feeble lightbulbs for nearby homes and businesses.

Kenan's new plant was far more powerful, but working at that plant wasn't the safest job in the world. "The switches were operated by a wooden board. The operator generally worked them with a piece of two-by-four, making sure that he had a clear space to jump if anything happened," remembered employee W. D. Avery.[11]

About this time, shortly after the Royal Palm was opened, Flagler inaugurated service of the steamship *Miami* between Nassau and Miami. "She was built flat bottomed because of the shallows at each end of her route," said Flagler's personal secretary, J. C. Salter. "For some reason the water ballast which had been planned was not used and in rough weather the *Miami* rolled badly. As a fitting addition to the Royal Poinciana, the Royal Victoria and the Royal Palm, the *Miami* was named the 'Royal Roller.' "

After a visit back home to Bellevue about this time, Henry was described as "a well-preserved man, his hair is silvered with the frosts of seventy-three winters, and his iron grey mustache gives a rather stern expression to an otherwise kindly countenance. He dresses quietly and in good taste and looks like a prosperous merchant rather than a capitalist."[12]

Mary Lily didn't accompany Henry to Bellevue but she did go with him on many trips to the Bahamas, Cuba and elsewhere in the Caribbean. In Palm Beach, they began planning a new residence. Mary Lily was dissatisfied with Henry's desire for a Cuban-style mansion. She wanted something grander, with columns. Accordingly, in late August 1901, Henry gave orders to a new architect, William Stymus, to commence design and construction of a Southern-style marble palace. He turned from his desk and asked Mary Lily to name it.

"Whitehall," she replied. "A house of marble."

# CHAPTER 16

# Days at Whitehall

HEN Henry Flagler undertook the Whitehall project, it seems he feared he hadn't long to live and that the work must be pushed forth with the greatest possible speed, regardless of expense. Whitehall might well have taken five years for its completion. Instead, Henry flooded the site with up to 1,000 workers at a time so that it was finished in 18 months. The total cost, including land, was $3 million, and that was before one stick of furniture was in place.

It was done not only as a gift for and tribute to his wife, but "as a demonstration of his taste. He was a frustrated architect in many ways."[1]

Like many a rich man before and after, Flagler could take a long view of the most massive transactions and expenditures while working up his blood over trivialities. Told that a federal court had just fined Standard Oil $20 million, a sum that would well affect his own fortune, Flagler brushed the matter off. "Have you got the plumbing estimates for the bathrooms at Whitehall?" he asked the messenger.

His secretary. J. C. Salter, recalled that in the early days of construction at Whitehall, Flagler occupied the dining room of a cottage in front of the nearby Royal Poinciana for his office, while Salter occupied the kitchen. On one occasion, Salter entered the dining room and found Flagler painstakingly removing a postage stamp from a spoiled envelope.

"Salter," he said, "if I can get this stamp the rest of the way off, we shall save two cents."

A few minutes later he went out toward Whitehall. The work was at a standstill.

"What is stopping the work?" demanded Flagler.

"We have no bricks," he was told.

"Have they been ordered?" asked Flagler.

"Three lots of 50,000 each," came the reply.

"Order a million," said Flagler crisply.

The man who took care to save a two-cent stamp had ordered a million bricks a moment later.[2]

Henry was involved with the smallest details, as a letter of December 1901 to architect William Stymus shows: "It has just occurred to me that I haven't a cuspidor for Whitehall. I wish you would order for me one for each office, two for the billiard room and one for the library. Mrs. Flagler says she doesn't want any elsewhere in the house."

AFTER feverish construction, a partially completed Whitehall was opened January 26, 1902, which signaled Mary Lily's first Palm Beach season as Mrs. Flagler.

The residential Parthenon featured a dozen blending tones of marble, $35,000 rugs, gold plumbing, 50 sets of dinner service and a hostess who seldom wore a dress twice.

Guests were received at monolithic bronze doors, which were balanced to turn on their massive hinges at the touch of a child's hand. They opened onto a marble foyer, or great hall, 40 feet in length and 110 feet wide. The foyer was, and still is, finished in seven shades of delicately veined marble, ranging from cream-yellow to dove-gray, and from sea-green to off-pink, rich brown and pure white. Sixteen bronze-topped pillars of solid marble supported a vaulted roof engrossed with paintings symbolic of such virtues as "Knowledge," "Prosperity" and "Happiness." A massive, nine-foot-high ornate clock, a masterpiece by Link of Paris, stood in the hallway. There was a profusion of tapestries and one rug, costing $35,000, big enough to accommodate a soccer field.

Upstairs there were 14 guest suites—each with its own bedroom, drawing room, dressing room, bath and foyer, and each with a different design that represented a different epoch in the world's history. The "modern" American room boasted Florida's first twin beds.

Mary Lily's personal suite was draped in silk damask, its bed canopied in gold cloth with panels of Cluny lace. Her bathroom measured 17 by 11 feet and had a sunken marble tub cut from a single prodigious piece of rare yellow Carrara marble. Breathless newspaper accounts said it was the first sunken tub in America, as indeed it may have been. Her dressing room was a massive array of glass-doored closets, cupboards and drawers designed to accommodate an even 100 dresses each.

Along with the hall, went a salon of the Louis XVI period, in French gray and silver leaf; an ivory-and-gold decored ballroom of Louis XIV period; a Swiss billiard room; a Renaissance library paneled with lion's heads; a dining room including some 26 dining chairs, each covered with its own individual Aubusson tapestry; and, finally, an antique-white music room of the Louis XV period.

The rest of the building, with rooms done in styles ranging from Francois I to American Colonial, was equally magnificent.

Despite the grandeur of it all, Flagler quickly made himself comfortable. He built himself secret stairwells so that he could easily slip out of parties and go upstairs to sleep or read. He had his office set up in a wing of the house which allowed him to come and go without notice.

Hard of hearing by this time, Henry was nevertheless still the music lover. He listened through a special device inserted in his ear and maintained a box at the Metropolitan Opera in New York during the season.

At Whitehall, Henry could be located on the veranda, listening to concerts with friends such as William Van Hester, owner of the Brooklyn *Eagle*. Afterward, tea would be served in the Coconut Grove of the Royal Poinciana Hotel.

Henry was in the habit of having young George Cooper, nephew of the White Hall housekeeper, ride him through the properties each afternoon in a special wheelchair. Twice a week there were baseball games on company diamonds between the teams of the Breakers and the Poinciana Hotels. A good deal of money changed hands between guests on the result of the games. An employee later recalled: "Mr. Flagler had a grandstand box for the season, but did not use it. Instead he'd look in at our Whitehall office and say, 'Boys, why don't you get out and see the game—and use my box!' Apparently not partial to spectator sports, his usual explanation was, 'Why should I watch some colored boys hitting a ball with a stick?' "[3]

He ran his Whitehall staff with paternal generosity.

Henry's young secretary Warren Smith recalled:

He was a director in the Western Union Telegraph Company, and would allow us to use his "dead-head frank" on any personal messages, by signing our own names, followed by the word "Flagler." The same was true with any railway express company shipments of fruit, etc. where he was also a director and we could use same, over his name for northern deliveries. The office staff were also allowed to use the launch *Kathleen* whenever desired.

If we were too busy to get to meals at lunchtime at the Royal Poinciana, where we were boarded, or when bad weather prevailed, he would have the kitchen staff make up a lunch, with a quart of good, plain eggnog on the side.

Mr. Flagler usually took an office nap during the afternoons. The Rev. George Morgan Ward would read to him. When en route by rail, Mr. Flagler always used FEC Railway Private Car No. 90. It was staffed by three colored attendants.[4]

Despite his reclusive tendencies, Flagler gave his all that first Whitehall season, and it was spectacular. At Whitehall's opening, on January 26, the Odell Pipe Organ Henry had installed was first played. The Palm Beach *Daily News* reported that a "musicale was given yesterday afternoon by Mrs. Henry Flagler. . . . Guests included Admiral and Mrs. George Dewey, Mr. and Mrs. Frederick W. Vanderbilt, Mr. and Mrs. Charles Bingham, Mr. and Mrs. Joseph Jefferson and others. . . . " The Admiral and Mrs. Dewey, he of Spanish-American war fame, returned on February 6 for another musicale. Other guests included Mr. and Mrs. William Rockefeller.

Two nights later there was yet another party, the first formal dinner at Whitehall. The guest of honor was Sir William Grey-Wilson, governor of the Bahama Islands, who sat with Henry at the head of a wide table. On Flagler's left was the Duke of Manchester, and on the governor's right was Dr. Woodrow Wilson, president of Princeton University.[5]

Washington's birthday was the height of the season and a fancy costume *Bal Poudre* at Whitehall was described by the Palm Beach *Daily News*.

After the formal presentation to Mr. and Mrs. Flagler, and their cordial welcome, the guests proceeded to the music room, through which they later found their way to the ballroom, and awaited the *Bal Poudre*, which opened with a graceful minuet danced by fourteen of the beauties of Palm Beach. Their natural charms were heightened by white wigs of the colonial period, ornamented with wreaths of tiny rosebuds, and Louis Quinze bows of black velvet. . . . The favors were appropriate, among them pots of cherry trees for the ladies and silver hatchets for the men; also parasols of red, white and blue for the ladies, and sashes in the same colors for the men. Other favors were sunflower pin cushions, brooches, and gold-cuff buttons and loving cups of silver having a souvenir of Whitehall on the outside. . . .

It was an arduous schedule, and after the first season, Flagler threw in the towel.

The parties continued, but often without Henry. Mary Lily adored entertaining and was an acclaimed hostess. She loved theme parties and went overboard on them. Henry began to avoid them, slipping up hidden stairs earlier and earlier.

After the first couple of years, despite all the guest rooms, the Flaglers had very few house guests. When Henry was away, or unwilling to socialize, Mary Lily would be escorted by her first cousin, Owen Kenan, a sort of ladies' man.

The social differences between the couple began to pall, and in their last few years together, Mary Lily was often restless and unhappy but stayed with Henry anyway.[6]

As FAR as is known, neither Henry nor Mary Lily kept diaries. But they did have a live-in organist, an expensive proposition but understandable when one considers there was no radio or television for home entertainment. The phonograph had been invented decades earlier, but the sound production remained primitive.[7] Movies were available, but they were silent, short, difficult to obtain and required a projectionist and a musical accompanist for each showing. One could read and swap stories, of course, and then there was the Ouija board, but presumably Henry had had enough of that.

The organist the Flaglers hired was Arthur Spalding, and what is important about him for our purposes is that he wrote wonderfully descriptive letters home to his sister in New England. He commenced his tale of the days at Whitehall on January 9, 1907, having caught the train from Lowell, Massachusetts.

Jan. 9, 1907, Hotel Alcazar, St. Augustine:
    Well, here I am on the threshold of high life! Just mention [Flagler's

private secretary J.C.] Salter's or Flagler's name down here and the servants will turn handsprings for you in the street.

Reached here about 1:30 this noon and went directly to the Ponce de Leon, sending my card in to Salter. He's a tip-top fellow about 35 years old and makes one feel at home at once. Finding that I hadn't eaten lunch, he sent me over to the Alcazar where he stays and I had the first square meal since leaving New York. (The Lord deliver you all from Southern railroad meals!) I then went back to the Ponce de Leon where Salter has his office, and he took me over to the Memorial Church, which was really the cause of my stopping here.

It is a magnificent church, given to the town by Mr. Flagler, and Dr. Anderson, one of Mr. Flagler's chums, is the chief mogul of the church and one of the trustees. It seems that the organist, a self-made musician who had never heard a good organ outside of this church, wanted a vox humana stop put in the organ, although she had never even heard one herself. So they put one in, and she immediately likened it to a nannie-goat and others who didn't know much about organs also poked fun at it, so that Dr. Anderson began to wonder whether he had had his leg pulled. Consequently he got Flagler to ask me to stop off and give what he was gracious enough to call an expert opinion. The man who put the stop in was there, and Dr. Anderson and Mr. Stout, the pastor. I tried the organ for about half an hour, besides going all through the inside of it, then walked back to Dr. Anderson's house with him, as a result of which he said he guessed he "would pay the old chap and send him on his way rejoicing."

I haven't looked around much yet but from what I have seen it's a perfect paradise with flower-beds, fountains, and palm trees. The weather seems like our late May or early June, and I can't imagine that it is January. If Flagler is as pleasant as Salter, I shan't have many scraps with him. Salter told me I could stay at the Ponce de Leon if I preferred to, but as long as he suggested the Alcazar first, I think I will follow his suggestion. He told me to have everything charged to Mr. Flagler; there seems to be nothing close about him.

Three days later, Spalding met Flagler for the first time.

Jan. 19, Hotel Royal Poinciana, Palm Beach:

I immediately aimed for Mr. Flagler, at which moment he started towards me, shaking hands very cordially, and taking me over to introduce me to his wife—an unaffected, cordial, homelike and charming woman. She invited me to sit down, and we had a very pleasant chat, becoming acquainted at once. Then "the old man" as many people call him down here, came over and we chatted pleasantly until it was time to prepare for dinner. Thus did I become a member of the household!

The people in the hall whom I did not recognize upon entering proved to be a party that had come down from St. Augustine with the Flaglers. They were Mrs. Flagler's mother, Mrs. Kenan, a sister, a sister-in-law, and several friends, among them a Mr. Van Ness, Columbia '96, who has composed several operas for college societies and is now at work on one for professionals, besides being an organist.

Before going up to dress for dinner, I asked Mrs. Flagler if she would like some music in the evening and she said she thought it would be fine. About quarter past eight I returned to Whitehall and began to fool with the organ until they should get through dinner. In a few minutes they came in and I began to play—a program similar to what I play at weddings, after which they asked for specific things which I happened to know. We kept it up until ten o'clock with time out for conversation and strolls about the court—a superb spot in the evening with electric lights below and stars overhead.

You are probably dying to know what kind of impression I made, and if you will keep this strictly within the family, I'll confess that, judging from the many things said to me and things I overheard, I made good all right. Mrs. F. said she never knew there was so much in the organ, that I used stops and combinations that Mr. Joy never used, that my touch was so different from his and that—well, on the whole, it was the most gratifying test I ever went through.

This morning upon coming in to breakfast, I found that George Ward and his wife had arrived by the night train. George seems to know everyone and to be universally popular . . .

Jan. 20, Royal Poinciana, Palm Beach:

Mr. Flagler told me last evening that he was looking for me in the afternoon as he wanted to take me automobiling. I wish he would come around this afternoon. He is certainly a fine old man—one of the gentlest and kindliest I have ever met. As we came out of the church this noon, a little girl ran up and kissed him, then walked along part way with us, holding on to his hand. He is just that grandfatherly sort of man, and he and his wife seem devoted to each other.

Jan. 21, 1907, Palm Beach:

Last evening we had an informal sing in the music room, there being no one there but the family and Mr. Van Ness. Mrs. Flagler used to sing considerably before she was married but has given it up since. Her voice now shows lack of practice, but I should judge it was pretty good in its day. After we had sung a while, Mr. Flagler suggested that I play one or two *Great Big Things* as he expressed it (he is so deaf that he can't hear the soft things that other people are always calling for), so I played the "March"

from *Tannhauser*, and the "March of the Priests" from *Athalia*, and he began
to clap before I got through either piece. He likes a lot of noise and one of
his favorites is the "Anvil Chorus" from *Il Trovatore*, which unfortunately
I haven't arranged for the organ yet.

Later, sitting on the piazza, Mrs. Flagler's brother told Mr. Van Ness
and me about the building of the house. It illustrates . . . Mr. Flagler's
wonderful determination and utter disregard of obstacles that would over-
power an ordinary man.

The house was built about five years ago and I imagine was a sort of
wedding present for Mrs. Flagler, as she has been married five years, although this is merely a surmise on my part. However, Mr. Flagler determined to erect a house of which he might be proud, but nature had not
provided a place from which he could obtain just the view of the lake that
he wanted, so his first step was to create a lot for the house by filling in a
part of the lake. The result is the house sticks right out into the lake with
a magnificent view in either direction.

The railroad track used to come across the lake right at one end of
Whitehall—the end toward the Poinciana—and partly because it was too
near the hotel and also interfered with plans for laying out the Whitehall
grounds, Mr. Flagler had the bridge and track removed to the other end of
the hotel. The track, by the way, upon which the mule car runs over to the
Breakers, is part of the original railroad.

Then Mr. Flagler wanted the house to be completed in a hurry, so at
one time there were 1,000 men working on the job. The result was that the
house was entirely finished in 13 months from the time they began to fill
in the lake, and the music room was completed including the setting up of
the organ in two weeks from the time they began to lay the floors and plaster
the ceiling.

You might imagine that the house is nothing but a gaudy display of wealth,
but it doesn't strike you so at all. In spite of its splendor, there appears to
have been most careful attention to detail given by the designer, with the
result that things harmonize wonderfully well. Mrs. Flagler says the house
is his particular pride but neither of them ever seems to boast about it, all
the foregoing facts having been obtained from her relatives.

Jan. 22, Palm Beach:

It is still difficult to believe that you are shivering in zero weather.
Yesterday was quite cool here, the mercury being down to 68 degrees at
noon so that I had to put on a vest. The Jacksonville paper predicted freezing
weather from the northern and central portions of Florida. They have a
curious kind of weather signal throughout the state. It seems that when a

frost is predicted the locomotive engineers are all informed, and as they come into villages or pass isolated farms, they blow with their whistles a certain signal which means a frost, whereupon the farmers cover up their crops and gather fire wood to prepare for it.

Jan. 25, Palm Beach:

Yesterday afternoon after finishing my letter to you, and playing the organ for a while, I went over to the baseball game and such sport I never had in my life. Both teams are colored and composed of employees of the Breakers and Poinciana hotels, who however are hired because of their baseball ability and then incidentally given employment as waiters or porters. Many of them play on the Cuban Giants team during the summer so that the quality of baseball ranked with professional white teams. The greatest sport was in listening to the coaching and watching the antics of a full grandstand back of first base. Their sympathies were pretty evenly divided between the two teams, so accordingly whenever either team would make a hit, then was the time to watch the bleachers. The crowd would yell themselves hoarse, stand up in their seats, bang each other over the head, and even the girls would go into a perfect frenzy as if they were in a Methodist camp meeting. The third baseman on the Poinciana team was a wonderful ball-player and kept the whole crowd roaring with his horseplay and cake-walks up and down the sidelines.

The more I see of Mrs. Flagler the better I like her and she is not at all the kind of woman I was prepared to see. Of course she is not perfect any more than the rest of us are, but there is nothing snobbish about her. If you treat her well and don't appear to be using her for what you can get, you can't ask for better treatment than she will give you in return.

Jan. 26, Palm Beach:

Today just two tables away from me at lunch sat Wm. Rockefeller with a party, so you see the celebrities are beginning to arrive. He showed no signs of being loaded down with tainted money and looked not unlike the rest of humanity.

Jan. 28, Palm Beach:

This morning about 10 I began to practice on the organ when Mr. Flagler came in and invited me to go for an automobile ride. He, Mr. Flagler the younger (a cousin), Mr. Kenan, a chauffeur and I were in the party. There is a garage at this end of the bridge but automobiles are not allowed around the place, in fact there are no paths wide enough for them, so we crossed over the bridge and went down the shell road towards Miami for 12 miles. This must originally have been a wonderful road but it is now somewhat worn in spots. For 7 miles after leaving W. Palm Beach there is not a turn in the

road and no hills to speak of. We had several interesting experiences with
frightened horses and ignorant drivers. One horse driven by a colored man
bolted and the driver, instead of tightening up on his reins, dangled them
up and down on the horse's back with the result that he was about to tip
him into the ditch, when Mr. Flagler, losing all patience, yelled, "Get out,
you clumsy lubber you, and lead the horse by," whereupon the driver
replied, "Ah never driv a horse befoa, sa"—a confession which he needn't
have made as it was very much apparent from his actions. We got home at
one o'clock, hungry as bears!

Feb. 3, Palm Beach:

As I went into the church today, a woman asked me if Mr. Flagler ever
went to that church and if so, where he sat. She said she wanted to see the
man as she thought he had done so much for the state of Florida. So I pointed
out his seat, she fixed it in her mind and sat down to wait for the king to
enter. What she said is absolutely true and I know of hardly a man who has
brought more pleasure to thousands of people than he has. As I keep hearing
of the condition in which this east coast was only a dozen years ago,
the things that Mr. Flagler has accomplished are miraculous and he is still
at it in his 77th year. As Mrs. Flagler says, he wouldn't be happy if he
wasn't working and accomplishing unusual things. To be sure most of the
improvements are carried out in the name of the East Coast R. R. but
he is the whole thing and almost sole owner of it—the one man who insti-
gates every improvement. Yet, he's the most modest appearing man about
the place.

Feb. 6, Palm Beach:

Last evening I went hunting for the first time—insect hunting. It began
when Mrs. Flagler spotted a mosquito reposing on my shirt stud and destroyed it with her fan, thereby committing my shirt to the laundry. She,
Mrs. Mitchell, and I were chatting in the music room, Mr. and Mrs. Percy
Rockefeller having left and Mr. Flagler having gone up to bed. Suddenly I
saw Mrs. Flagler's eyes become fixed on a dark spot on the drapery across
the room, then grow wider and wider until finally unable to stand it any
longer she crept over to the spot and gave a blood-curdling shriek which
would have made the car-mule wild with envy and which brought Mrs.
Mitchell and me to the spot and Edward the footman into the room on the
dead run. There in the folds of the drapery reposed the nearest approach
to a tarantula that I have seen yet. I was perfectly contented that Edward
was there so that my gallantry would not be put to a test. Mrs. Mitchell was
going to bravely gather it into her handkerchief, but you might as well try
to squeeze a soft-shelled crab between your fingers, so Edward was des-

patched for a broom while Mrs. Flagler withdrew to the farthest corner of the room.

Mrs. Flagler remarked this morning that she was afraid if last evening's experience should be repeated, I would think there is more insect life down here than social life, but fortunately Whitehall is well screened and swept so that an experience like that could not be expected often. I have described this in detail so that it may make you more contented with life in Lowell in February.

Feb. 23, Palm Beach:

I haven't written about the Beach Club yet. You needn't worry lest I get drawn in there, as in the first place I have no desire to enter, and in the second place, they probably wouldn't let me in anyhow. Mr. Flagler tried to close the place up a few years ago so they don't allow people closely connected with him to enter. It is kept by two men named Bradley, is just across the road from the hotel grounds, and has a fine and entirely respectable restaurant where "swell" dinners are often given. The main feature, however, are the gambling rooms where roulette is played for enormous stakes, and the money that passes hands during a season must be something appalling. A man told me that Mrs. Herman Oelrichs was gambling with one thousand dollar bills one evening this week. The gambling spirit is rampant here generally, men betting freely on every ball game and women finding it difficult to get up a bridge game unless there's a stake on the game.

Late in the season, Spalding met an unusual personality.

Feb. 27, Palm Beach:

As we watched the party leave, a very plain looking woman approached us—a woman whom you wouldn't notice in most places, but who stood out here merely because of the marked contrast to the dazzling array we had just been looking at. As she passed, Mrs. Mitchell recognized her and introduced us—Miss Lee, Daughter of Gen. Robert E. Lee. Then the Judge and Mr. Martin came up, Mrs. Flagler was brought over from the crowd she was with and we had quite a "confab." Mrs. Flagler, loyal Southerner that she is, was delighted to meet her and immediately invited her to lunch this noon. She came and I have just returned from Whitehall, having played the organ to her for about half an hour. She is a woman of sixty or sixty-five I should say and it was amusing how the Judge almost worshipped her on her father's account of course, for he told me the other day that he considered Gen. Lee the greatest general the world has ever produced.

Spalding also found that the household loosened up considerably when Flagler was on the road.

March 8, Palm Beach:

When the cat's away, the mice will play! There's a vivid illustration of that at Whitehall this week. One thing that Mr. Flagler insists on from family and guests alike is punctuality at meals, and when he is at home, I tell you, everyone gets down to breakfast promptly at nine unless he is disabled. But practically every morning since the old man has been away, the people in the house have had breakfast in their rooms, getting downstairs any time before lunch.

March 10, Palm Beach:

Things are still coming my way! Tomorrow afternoon I am going down to Miami with Mr. and Mrs. Flagler, Mrs. Mitchell, Mr. Martin, Butler and Jessie Ames, and George Ward to be gone until Friday night—the whole party going down as guests of Mr. Flagler. The particular occasion is the Dade County Fair, which lasts four days and where I shall see every kind of fruit, vegetable and flower raised in this state. It is held in a building erected several years ago by Mr. Flagler for this purpose and Mr. and Mrs. Flagler give about all the money premiums that are awarded so they are of course the heroes of the occasion and it will be great sport watching the natives shower them with attention as Mrs. Flagler says they always do. Wasn't it bully of Mr. Flagler to want me to go with them? It will be a very interesting change and a mighty jolly spree besides as we all know each other so well.

March 12, Palm Beach:

Mrs. Mitchell, George Ward, Jessie and I are going to Miami in Mr. Flagler's automobile. It is a sixty mile run and we want to get down there before dark. The rest of the party including Mr. McCreary, whom Mrs. Flagler has also invited to go, will take the 5:25 train and get there about 7:30. Everyone, including Mr. and Mrs. Flagler themselves, is enthusiastic about the trip and we ought to have a very merry lark. There will be two automobiles there for our use and motor boats on the river so that there will be something doing about all the time . . . The women folks are going to spend most of the forenoons in bed.

Last evening Mr. Martin, Mrs. Mitchell and I went over to the Beach Club to watch the fun. The gambling room is a most attractive looking room, octagonal in shape, brilliantly lighted with electricity and handsomely furnished in green. The tables extend around the room and there are two "hazard" tables and six or seven roulette tables. Of course it's a gambling den, pure and simple, but you don't experience any shock upon entering. There's no secrecy about it, no barricading the doors against the police, and of course no unseemly or boisterous conduct. Seated at the tables are men and women gorgeously dressed—the very ones that you have seen about the hotel so that no thought of violation of the law enters your head. Nor are you very deeply impressed when you see them toss $5 or even $100 bills on the table, only to have them scooped up by the banker or doubled by him according to whether you win or lose.

There's such an air of indifference about the whole thing that your first impression is no different from what it would be if you were looking at a game played with beans. But when you stay there the whole evening there's something shocking about the whole thing. The amount of money made during the season is appalling and the lowest estimate I've heard as to their net profits is $200,000.

March 14, Miami:

This is really a charming spot, and of course I am seeing it under the best possible circumstances. It is vastly different from Palm Beach and in the long run might become monotonous but for a change I like it immensely. Instead of the lake and broad ocean view, we have a beautiful view of Biscayne Bay with much boating. There's not the high pace here that prevails at Palm Beach—perhaps more restful though not so interesting.

March 15, Miami:

We have just returned at 5:30, from our outing and everyone had a great time. In the party besides our own crowd were Mr. Parsons, our host, Lord and Lady Wolverton, a Mr. Jones, a Mr. and Mrs. McDonough and Miss Harding, the New York *Herald* correspondent at Palm Beach who came way down just to write up the trip. We had a 14 mile sail down to Soldier Key, the outermost key in the bay. The key is a small one with nothing on it but a house where they serve fish dinners, the establishment being run by the hotel company. We sat down to a delicious dinner about 1:30 and I tasted more kinds of fish, right fresh from the water, than I had ever heard of before. We had clam chowder, fried crawfish, crawfish salad, boiled groupers, baked porkfish, fried red snappers, fried chicken, mashed potatoes, Saratoga potatoes, tomato and lettuce salad, asparagus on toast, ice cream, crackers and cheese, coffee, punch, and Poland Spring water. During and after lunch we had singing and mandolin and guitar playing by a colored quartet that was brought along with us.

It was a very congenial crowd, with no formality, and after lunch we had coon songs by Mrs. Flagler, rag time on the piano and popular songs by the whole crowd.

Miami is much more of a place than I had any idea of, and when you consider that only ten years ago it was wilderness, it is today the "Magic City" as they call it in Florida.

As the season wound down, Spalding summed up his experiences as he prepared for his trip home.

March 18, Palm Beach:

Many people, especially the [George] Wards, seem to think that Mrs. Flagler has the society bee in her bonnet and rejoices in all the entertainment that takes place at Whitehall, but I must confess she doesn't appear that way to me. To me she never seems happier than when she is off with a few friends whom she knows well and can act as she pleases without the restraint of all the formality and conventionality that is necessary in Whitehall functions. At any rate we all cut up merrily, even the Judge and Mr. Flagler acting as kittenish as the rest.

As for my feeling at home in Whitehall, I certainly do and feel so much like a member of the family that I shall almost hate to take their money. However, I shan't refuse it for I need it in my business. Mrs. Flagler is already talking of having me down to Mamaroneck to visit them sometime![8]

In the meantime, the twentieth century was pushing in on Henry.

On December 17, 1903, even as the Flaglers were preparing for the *Bal Poudre* at Whitehall, two men in North Carolina had gone flying on regular Standard Oil gasoline, brought to the sand dunes of Kitty Hawk, North Carolina, by sailboat in a 50-gallon drum.

The Wright brothers had made four flights in all and, curiously, no one from the town was there to see the event. The only witnesses were two men from a nearby weather station who had come over to lend a hand. The last flight ended almost in disaster when a sudden gust of wind toppled the fragile plane over. If it had not been damaged, according to biographer Fred C. Kelly, the brothers would have tried to fly to the Kitty Hawk town. Their gasoline tank, he said, still held about half a gallon, and they would have liked to use it up.

Airplanes.

When Henry Flagler was growing up, the Franklin stove was the outer edge of technology. Now, he installed electric elevators in his hotels and lit the halls of his homes with electric lights. He himself rode and drove automobiles, and other men were flying.

The years were passing, and Henry felt it was time to complete his work. He confided to his friend, the churchman George Ward, that he had decided definitely to build a railroad over the seas to Key West.

Ward replied, "Flagler, you need a guardian."

Henry laughed.

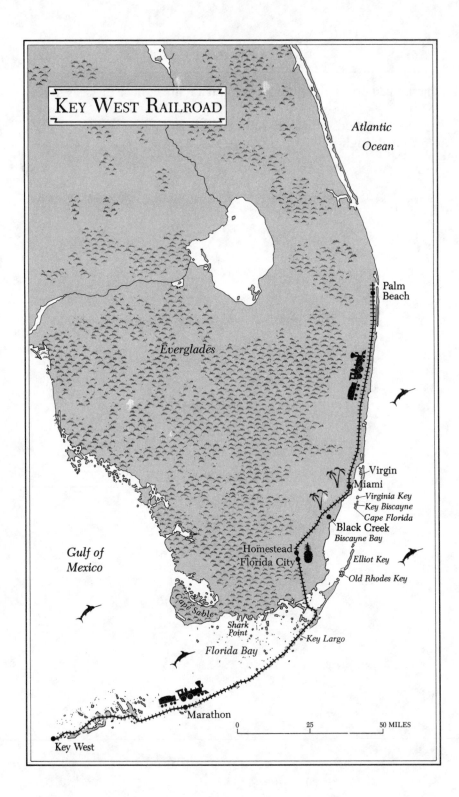

# KEY WEST RAILROAD

*Atlantic*
*Ocean*

*Everglades*

*Gulf of*
*Mexico*

Palm
Beach

Virgin
Miami
*Virginia Key*
*Key Biscayne*
*Cape Florida*
Black Creek
*Biscayne Bay*

Homestead
Florida City

*Elliot Key*

*Old Rhodes Key*

*Cape Sable*

Shark
Point

*Florida Bay*

Key Largo

Marathon

0          25          50 MILES

Key West

# CHAPTER 17

# Key West

FLAGLER was well aware of his power position in Florida. In February 1898, he had invited President William McKinley to visit him in Florida and joked, somewhat boastfully, "My domain begins at Jacksonville." His power went far beyond that of an owner of railroads, hotels and land. He was a colonizer, and in a 1901 letter to Reverend Stevens he had written, "I feel that these people are wards of mine and have a special claim upon me." Flagler invited other businessmen, most especially Rockefeller, to see his domain from their palace cars and hotel suites. He wanted to show them that he had provided for the welfare of his wards by building not only towns and cities but also schools, churches, hospitals and city halls. Although he did not own all the land in what he considered his domain, he controlled the character of the population by carefully selecting new residents for the area. His memos show a constant stream of instructions to Ingraham and other executives to be more concerned with the character of the colonists they were bringing to Florida rather than the number of them.

Henry did not see himself as a despotic baron, but rather, an enlightened lord who financed his good works and colonies by extracting coin from the rich, who paid heavily for their visits to his unusual kingdom.

He was developing an *undeveloped* region, and it was a life-giving task that Mary Harkness would have applauded. Standard Oil had been take, take, take. Take from the ground, take from the railroads, take from the producers. Florida was the reverse. There, Henry was *giving*.

In colonizing Florida, there remained one last logical step for him to take—the untamed Keys. When Flagler decided to go to Key West, it wasn't simply a matter of laying more track across Florida swamp.

What he had in mind meant crossing the open sea. If successful, it would be the greatest engineering feat in history, as bold as anything before it, including the Suez Canal and the unsuccessful French attempt to dig a Panama Canal in the 1880s.

Flagler had planned on a Key West "extension" of his railway as early as 1891. But Biscayne Bay was the key to such an extension, and he hadn't reached there with his track until 1896. The time since then had been largely absorbed by personal matters—the insanity of Ida Alice, his affair with Mary Lily, the divorce, the marriage, Whitehall. He was so absorbed in these matters that it seemed he had put his Key West ambitions aside.

Almost, but not quite. In 1899, he purchased the local newspaper and instructed his aide Parrott to keep the enterprise secret. "If it leaks out that we are interested, somebody will surely start an opposition paper in the expectation that we will buy them out."

Then in 1901, his old friend Mark Hanna of Ohio persuaded the President and the Congress to make an attempt at America's own canal across Panama, following much of the route which had defeated the French. At the time, Panama was a province of Colombia. In January 1903, the United States signed a treaty with Colombia which set aside a swath of land across Panama for the Canal. The Colombian Senate, however, refused to ratify the treaty and in November, with American backing, the province of Panama revolted and became the independent Republic of Panama.

Immediately afterward, President Theodore Roosevelt announced that the work would begin.

Flagler, however, had begun his move toward the canal a year and a half earlier.

THE IMPORTANCE of access to a deep-water harbor had been painfully impressed upon Flagler during the Spanish-American War, when the War and Navy Departments routed all troop movements and military equipment and supplies through Tampa instead of Miami because the former could accommodate ships of deeper draft.

Key West had the finest deep water harbor south of Norfolk, and an extension to Key West would put Flagler's railroad 300 miles nearer the canal than any other railroad in the United States. To protect the canal, the United States would have to have ships in the area. The

Navy was limited in its maneuverability by the availability of coal. Key West, with its good harbor, was an excellent coaling station—if it had coal. The cheapest way to ship coal was by rail. Also, Cuba was but 90 miles away with its cargoes of sugar, coffee, bananas and pineapples. Cuba itself would be a great resort, if it could be reached by comfortable trains. From Key West, such trains could easily be ferried across to Havana.

THE FIRST SURVEY of a railroad route to Key West had been made in 1866 by civil engineer J. C. Bailey for the International Ocean Telegraph Company. When the Western Union Telegraph Company obtained control of the IOT, the report came into its possession, and thence into the hands of Western Union board member Henry Flagler, who had it prior to 1894.

In that same year, Flagler made his first move toward gaining a share of the Cuban trade. He made a trip to Cuba with Sir William Van Horne, a man who was enthusiastic about the potential of railroads in Cuba. After his conversations with Van Horne, Flagler reportedly began consideration of a car–ferry link between Key West and the Cuban railroads, with connections to Miami. It was said he was not preoccupied with making money on the venture.[1]

That Flagler foresaw possibilities of developing the Keys is undeniable. As early as 1895, he was in possession of a number of them, including ownership of nearly one-half of the largest of the islands, Key Largo.

These islands, varying in size and composition, had been described as "worthless, chaotic fragments of coral reef, limestone and mangrove swamp."[2] But the soil of many keys was well suited to particular types of farming. Pineapples, bananas, and limes, as well as some vegetables, had been successfully grown in certain locations for years.

The importance of Key West as a port had increased even further after Flagler's attempts failed to dredge Biscayne Bay and make Miami a port city. Over $200,000 had been spent on the unsuccessful dredging operations. When the federal government refused to lend any assistance, Flagler abandoned the project.

ONCE he decided on Key West, Henry moved promptly. In 1902, he sent his engineers south of Miami, an area but partly explored,

with instructions to find the most feasible route for a railroad to Key
West. They surveyed routes through the Everglades with a view to
spanning the Bay of Florida with a long bridge. And they surveyed
routes over the full length of the Keys.

The man picked to lead the survey was William J. Krome, who
had attended the University of Illinois and Cornell University, and
had spent some years on railroad projects in Missouri and elsewhere.
The young Krome proved to be a brilliant engineer and capable
leader.

The surveying parties endured unbelievable hardships during their
explorations. When possible, an Indian or one of the few white settlers
in the area was employed as a guide. Even so, a number of surveyors
got lost, and nearly died. In January of 1903, Krome sent a report to
the railroad offices at St. Augustine from his temporary field camp.
He had just returned from a two-week journey through the Big Mangrove Swamp. On that expedition, the main party had been left behind, and Krome pushed on with a man named Nixon and two packers.
The man explored as far south as Barnes Sound on the east coast.
They took along two metal boats and two weeks' rations. No open-
water routes were found, so the men had to drag the heavy boats
most of the way.

The muck over which they walked seemed almost bottomless;
progress was only three miles a day. In some areas, dense cypress
growth was encountered; mosquitoes were everywhere. The party
turned north and reached the community of Cutler in three days,
after traveling along the coast. Krome had written: "I found a most
Godforsaken region in its present state."[3]

On February 22, 1903, Krome reported from Flamingo that the
expeditions had explored more territory by utilizing light 'gator boats
in the swamps, and switching to a sailboat for travel in the Bay of
Florida. Krome added: "But of keys, bays, rivers and lagoons there
is no end, and it is going to take us much longer to get a survey than
I had expected."

Krome and his surveyers conducted exhaustive studies of Cape
Sable and the surrounding area. He concluded that the eastern end
of the cape would afford the most advantageous route, since much of
it was prairie and could support a roadbed. He foresaw the possibilities
of making a good harbor on the coast of that area.

The idea of building the railroad extension through Cape Sable was eventually abandoned because the cost would have been excessive.

Finally, the engineers decided to take advantage of the natural protection provided by the Keys and outlying reefs. The railroad was to cross from the mainland to Key Largo, follow south along that island and run the length of the Upper Keys. Few people lived on the Keys, outside of Key West, and the area required extensive explorations. The longest key was 16 miles long. Channels between the Keys varied from a few hundred yards to seven miles. Because of the distances involved, towers had to be built in some places to facilitate sighting instruments.

In late 1903, a few weeks after Roosevelt's announcement of a canal, the engineers submitted their reports, maps and cost estimates. Flagler and Parrott studied the reports and at the end of winter, Flagler asked Parrott, "Are you sure this railway can be built?" Parrott answered, "I am sure." It was then that Flagler issued a famous order—"Go ahead; go to Key West."

THE FIRST requisite was an engineer of sufficient courage to undertake the project and sufficient skill to meet its difficulties. The person chosen was Joseph Carroll Meredith, who was found in Tampico where he was building a pier for the Mexican government. A noted bridge builder with considerable experience Meredith was small of stature, but resourceful and determined. From the time he assumed his position with the railroad on July 26, 1904, Meredith pushed himself and his assistants relentlessly.[4]

Meredith recalled that Flagler was disinterested in profit and the interview consisted of

. . . the inevitable and perfectly proper questions for corporations to ask of their engineers. I had done some work in Tampico Harbor, Mexico, and they sent for me to come to Florida. They told me about the Key West extension. Not a word about cost or possible profits; merely the matter of engineering feasibility. Mr. Flagler wanted either to fill in or to build a viaduct, for he hates makeshifts. Permanence appeals to him more strongly than to any other man I ever met. He has often told me that he does not wish to keep on spending money for maintenance of way, but to build for all time. [This was contrary to common practice because] a corporation, especially where the country has to grow up and the paying traffic is all in the future, will do barely enough to supply the pressing needs. They make improvements gradually, as the profit comes in. But that is not Mr. Flagler's way.

I was told to make my studies and my estimates. We had lots of problems to solve, and I was quite a long time at doing it.[5]

Krome was appointed assistant engineer and directed the forces in the field. R. W. Carter was the chief of design. Miss Marie Stephens was the only woman employed in the enterprise, as Meredith's stenographer.

BEFORE the work was under way, however, opposition came from the U.S. government, which was already looking into Flagler's Standard Oil connections. Now surveyors declared that the 156 miles of rail line (from Miami), with its many causeways and concrete viaducts, would block the Gulf Stream and change the climate of south Florida. Although the plans called for hundreds of arches along the causeway, permitting water to surge beneath the track, the government demanded miles of deep-water bridges. Eventually, 18 miles of such bridges were built.

In 1904, while the government negotiations were going on, Flagler extended his railroad 30 miles south to a backwoods community called Homestead. After the railroad came, there bloomed fine winter crops, groves of oranges, grapefruit, kumquats, limes, avocados and papayas, and extensive fields of tomatoes and potatoes.

The construction of the Key West Extension began from Homestead in May 1905 with a small force of laborers, By the following February, there were 4,000 men engaged.

FLAGLER and other officials made numerous inspection tours along the proposed route. Such a trip was made on a three-decked paddle-wheeler, the *Biscayne*, which left Miami on July 28, 1905.

Arriving at the scene of early construction operations, the *Biscayne* tied up to a houseboat and its passengers were transferred to shore. This first stop was at a camp of 300 men doing fill work. Mosquitoes became so unbearable that the touring officials retreated to their boat, which anchored in the bay for the night. Even in open water, however, they did not escape mosquitoes.

Aboard the *Biscayne* was New York engineer Russell Smith who found it strange to be aboard a steamboat running

. . . over the proposed site of a railroad nearly 200 miles in length. . . . Under all these southern waters the wonderful little coral has built a solid rock floor until it has almost driven the water off entirely and added many square miles of dry land to the state of Florida. In thousands of places it has come up above the surface and formed reefs and keys, to which the wind and wave have carried seeds of tropical growth, and now they are densely wooded with mangrove, palmetto and coconut trees, making an almost impassable jungle.

Going over shoals and through such narrow channels that the boat touches both sides at once, the bottom of the sea is always visible, with its jelly-like sponges and beautiful branching coral. A huge manatee or "seacow" passed, about eight feet in length with . . . myriads of beautiful strange fish, varying in size from the little sharp-nosed gar to large porpoises, which continually played about the bow of the boat and swam for miles without apparent moving of a hair. "Skipjacks" continually jumped out of the water and rode on the surface for hundreds of yards, just touching the surface with the tips of their tails. Flying fish left the water and flew for a quarter of a mile before returning.

Arriving at the scene of the first active operation, a comfortable houseboat came into view and to this we were tied. Taking a small boat, the party went ashore to Key Largo, where there is a camp of about 300 negroes engaged in the grubbing and grading of a small fill throughout the length of this, the largest key.

Here is experienced the most serious problem to overcome this great undertaking. The mosquitoes on this key are almost unbearable, and the problem is to persuade laborers not to run away, for it means certain death as there is no possible outlet to the mainland. The jungle was almost impassable except where the work was in progress. The mangrove tree predominates and it is curious indeed to see their roots branching down from limbs. Pineapple and citrus and lime trees are abundant and tall coconut trees, always bearing fruit, wave high in the air. The temperature is very pleasant, being cooler than the average summer day in New York.

They anchored offshore, said Smith,

. . . thinking a mile and a half from the nearest land sufficient to keep us immune from mosquitoes, but such was far from being the case and no one on board slept that night. After trying all other experiments, I lay down on a canvas cot with a double thickness of blanket, thinking this too thick for the pests to bite through.

I reckoned wrong, for they attacked from below and bit through the canvas cot. All our party were considerably relieved when the sun rose and drove the mosquitoes away.[6]

Flagler's friend Andrew Anderson had made the same trip earlier with Flagler. Anderson recalled:

On traveling with him for the first time, we went over the route of his proposed overseas railroad in a steamboat. I was astounded at the temerity and the vastness of the proposition. He had a joking way of calling his road "my road" so I said to him, "Why, Flagler, this is impossible. Nobody can build this road. Nobody can afford it. Nobody has the money nor the brains nor the grit to do it." And he said, "It is perfectly simple. All you have to do is to build one concrete arch, and then another, and pretty soon you will find yourself in Key West."[7]

It took 180 reinforced concrete arches, for example, to build the Long Key viaduct. A special cement that would harden under water was imported from Germany. Because much of the concrete work could not be interrupted, once started, all of the floating equipment was fitted with dynamos for generating electric light so that work could continue after nightfall. Being exposed to hurricanes, the great viaducts were built to withstand wind pressure four times greater than any every recorded on the keys.

Shallow-draft, stern-wheel Mississippi River steamboats were brought in to deliver supplies to the camps and men for the labor crews.

By February 1906, engineers were surveying Key Largo, first and largest of the islands that stretch 128 miles from the Florida mainland to Key West. There, they found a surprise—a large lake which had not been marked on the survey maps. Lake Surprise, as they called it, was one-half mile across, over a mile long and six feet deep. The bottom was entirely of peat. A trestle installed over the lake proved unsatisfactory due to the unstable foundation. It was decided to drain the lake, dig up the peat and fill in with rock and other material for the embankment. Two dredges spent 15 months completing the operation.

The true menace of the work, however, was not mosquitoes or alligators or quick-sand lakes.

On October 17, 1906, one of the railroad employees, William Mayo Venable, on Long Key, saw the barometer at camp dropping noticeably. It read 29.66 at 6 A.M.; 29.62 at noon; and 29.59 at 6 P.M. Clouds were observed approaching from the southeast.

A hurricane was coming.

By evening, the order was given for men on the work barges to be removed since the roughness of the water made work impossible. Equipment was anchored to mooring piles. The wind continued to build in force, making it almost impossible to walk on the decks of the floating barracks called quarterboats. Before midnight, communication between boats became impossible. The storm center passed slightly to the north of Long Key camp. Wind velocity reached an estimated 90 miles per hour.

Quarterboat number four, listed as missing, had broken its moorings during the storm and was swept out to sea. As the boat was being buffeted by high winds and tremendous waves, resident engineer Bert Parkins had gone into the hold to encourage some of the men who were huddled there. He was killed by a flying beam when the superstructure collapsed as the boat disintegrated on Alligator Reef. All those in the hold perished. But others, who had crowded on the balcony on the windward side, escaped the falling wreckage.

About 87 men survived the wreck of the quarterboat and the ordeal which followed. Many saved themselves by clinging to bits of wreckage, tables and trunks. The Italian steamer *Jenny* picked up 44 survivors the afternoon after the storm.

The tales were many of the crew of quarterboat number four. Kelly and Kennedy, two mechanics, jumped onto a barge being blown past the boat. They drifted on the barge for nearly a week before being picked up. Both men were nearly dead from hunger and exhaustion.[8] A father and son had also jumped off the boat. For hours they clung to a trunk of family possessions which somehow remained afloat. Eventually, both were forced to let go. Each managed to survive and was picked up by a passing ship, believing the other had drowned. Several days later they were joyfully reunited.

Others were not so lucky. Of 49 men swept to sea from other boats, only a man named John Russell was saved. One worker was swept away on a water barge. He saved himself by getting into an empty water tank he had unbolted from the barge and pushed into the sea. The tank, with its occupant still barely alive, was picked up several days later off Nassau. Another man, named Mullin, was aboard a cement barge blown out on the reef. He stoked the boiler and kept the lights blazing until the barge was pulled under, and then he died.[9]

At least 134 men, from various ports of the construction, lost their lives. Survivors were picked up by ships like the British steamer *Alten*, which saved 24. Survivors were landed at New Orleans and Norfolk and as far away as Liverpool, England, depending on the ship's destination.

When the hurricane cleared, Flagler immediately took precautions to guard against future storms. Refuge canals were dredged in sheltered areas. On receipt of storm warnings, floating equipment was moved to the canals from construction sites. To prevent barges from being swept to sea, many of them were sunk in the canals and raised after the storm passed.

The psychological impact on the work force was considerable. Engineer Krome wrote Flagler that, "No man has ever passed through one of these West Indian hurricanes and boasted that he had no fear of it."[10]

THERE were peculiar features to the 1906 hurricane. With the exception of Venable's instrument at Long Key, none of the barometers with which every one of their barges, pile-drivers, tugs, and the like, were equipped gave the slightest warning of the storm. It lasted hardly more than half an hour, yet during that brief spell 134 of the gang were drowned and quantities of shanties, pile-drivers and barges were washed away. Two barges loaded with coal were blown out to sea and found several days later over on the Bahamas without the loss of single pound of coal.

Mindful of the effects of the 1906 hurricane, Flagler wrote to Meredith, urging him to push construction of concrete work before the beginning of hurricane season each August.

By 1909, most workers were staying in storm-proof dormitories instead of floating camps. Bridges were reinforced against the increased volume of water that was discovered to rush through the channels when a hurricane hit. Everyone kept closer watch of barometer readings. Regular checks were made with the U.S. Weather Bureau in Washington. During the hurricane months of August, September and October, railroad families were moved from the camps to Key West or Homestead.

The 1906 hurricane caused a year's delay in construction, and

3,000 men were laid off as repair crews first assessed and then repaired the damage. About this time, Flagler was hospitalized by his old liver condition, the same malady which had sent him to Florida originally.

Noticing the inactivity and Flagler's illness, newspapers in New York and elsewhere killed him off with almost savage glee. Here is an early obituary from the New York *Journal*.

His most recent disappointment is the one which, it is rumored, was the real cause of the illness from which he is suffering in Bretton Woods, New Hampshire, and which his most sanguine friends believe will prove fatal, was brought on within the last few months, when he at last realized the futility of further carrying on his great railroad scheme in southern Florida.

It was the "railroad that goes to sea," and it has been Mr. Flagler's ambition for years to leave that to posterity as a monument to himself. He had personally supervised all of its workings; but when success seemed most sure, when hundreds of miles of the great railroad that was to connect Miami with Key West, and make the latter virtually a land city, the project had to be abandoned—temporarily, say his friends; probably for all time, say those engineers who have announced that they believe the terminal of the railroad will always be at Knight's Key, where the work has been abandoned . . .

Since early spring, not a wheel has turned in the railroad's construction, not a boatload of concrete or iron been taken South, and the thousands of men who were employed in the work have sadly packed their kit and drifted back to New York, leaving the half-built giant railroad practically deserted. And all because Mr. Flagler, man of millions, who has already sunk $20 million in the enterprise, was unable to raise a few paltry thousands in cash.

Broken in spirit and badly weakened from overwork and worry incident to the strain of raising funds, Mr. Flagler took to his bed in St. Augustine last April. He did not mend rapidly and his physician advised his removal to a cooler climate. Early in the summer he was taken to his summer home in Mamaroneck in New York's Westchester County, but was later removed to the Mount Washington Hotel in Bretton Woods, N.H., when symptoms of a general nervous breakdown asserted themselves. There he is constantly watched over by his personal physician, Dr. [Owen] Kenan, two trained nurses and his beautiful wife, who has given up all thoughts of opening Whitehall, their magnificent home in Palm Beach, this winter.

Thinking that Flagler was down, the New York *American Examiner* also leaped at the chance to kick him.

He disinherited his son, after giving him a hotel in St. Augustine, which gossip said was in itself a sort of revenge, as the hotel in question had notoriously been running behind in its accounts for years at the rate of

$20,000 a year. So surely has Harry Flagler gone out of his father's life that for years past he has been taught to forget that he is the sole heir . . .

Young Mr. Flagler's thirst for notoriety has died out since the Seeley dinner. Here is what was written about him at the time which aroused the ire of his sire:

"Young Mr. Flagler is a bright, handsome young man, who, when a child, had an especial fondness for paper dolls, with which he used to play for hours. He doted on those fluffy gauze skirts, and evidently still retains his fondness for the ballet. Mr. Flagler had toy theaters in those days and was stage manager, director, impressario and 'angel' all rolled into one, to say nothing of being dressmaker, carpenter and a dozen other persons of minor importance. His puppets danced at his pleasure, just as readily as did 'Little Egypt' at the request of Mr. Herbert Seeley at the famous dinner."

Such articles give insight into Flagler's hatred of newspapers and his desire to own them so he could control what was printed.

Meanwhile, down in the Keys, work resumed, but in 1909 another hurricane struck, with winds clocked up to 125 miles per hour. Miles of embankment were washed away, but the completed concrete viaducts withstood the test. At least three girders on Knight's Key Bridge were blown off the piers because an insufficient number of anchor bolts had been used. Four thousand feet of track were ripped out north of Jewfish Creek.[11]

Despite short notice, construction crews were better prepared for the hurricane of 1909, but the tugboat *Sybil* capsized in Bahia Honda Channel, with the loss of 13 lives. The only survivor of the crew was found unconscious under an overturned wheelbarrow on shore. He could not explain how he got there.

Yet another hurricane hit the railroad the following year, in October 1910. It was described by natives at the time as the worst in history. But the engineers and foremen were warned in time and the equipment had been secured. A telegram was received in Krome's office at Marathon, advising that a hurricane would hit the Keys some time that night. Krome ordered all trains off on the sidings. Rain came down in torrents, and the wind blew with tremendous force. One mechanic at nearby Boot Key called on the telephone to report the key was under a foot of water. He was ordered by Krome to seek shelter at Marathon, which was on higher ground. The storm washed out some sections of track and damaged a few pieces of machinery, but the crews at Marathon had taken adequate precautions.

Damage to railroad property was kept at a minimum, and only one life was lost.

In the meantime, Flagler ran into problems with the federal government. His railroad was being accused of using slave labor.

# CHAPTER 18

# Water, Liquor and Mosquitoes

RECRUITING agents for the Florida East Coast Railway had a difficult task keeping a continuous supply of laborers moving down to the extension. A high turnover rate meant that replacements had to be obtained in large numbers. Men with special skills had to be found or trained and they were wary because the railroad had to contend with rumors and federal charges about alleged illegal labor practices. However, the search to find men ultimately resulted in a variety of races and nationalities being thrown together in a labor force that adapted to the work with surprising willingness.

Pay for ordinary laborers on the extension was $1.25 to $1.50 per day. Carpenters received $2 to $3 for an average 10-hour day. The men worked a six-day week, as elsewhere in the country. The pay was a bit better than the national average for non-skilled labor—$1.10 per day—and was high enough to attract thousands of workers from the United States and the Caribbean islands.[1]

Nevertheless, it was necessary to offer transportation to the Keys as an incentive for men to make the journey to the wilds of southern Florida. Passage from the big northern cities to Jacksonville, by boat or rail, was arranged by the FEC Railway Company, and workers reimbursed the company out of their construction earnings. The fare was $12 from New York, and transportation from Jacksonville to the Keys was provided free of charge.[2]

Numerous recruits took advantage of the railroad's offer of a free ticket only to jump off the train before it reached its destination. Most found work on Florida farms. About one-half of the workers recruited in New York in 1905 jumped train before reaching the work sites.[3]

ONCE the men arrived, many temptations drew them away from their work.

Flagler expressed his regret to Krome that laborers were so hard to keep and blamed the farmers for enticing most of them away to help with vegetable harvesting.

It was felt that a number of men would walk off the job if they weren't paid on schedule. Extra measures were therefore taken to ensure that the paymasters arrived on time. On paydays, many men quit to go on sprees lasting several days, until their money was gone, and they sobered up and returned to work. Others quit, went home and returned to work under a new contract after a few weeks off the job. Some workers were paid once a week, others once a month. All were paid in gold coins.

Considerable numbers of Greeks and Italians were recruited for work, but their terms of service usually remained short. The Greeks were excellent divers and were employed for the underwater work. After 1907, Spanish laborers from Cuba, northwest Spain and the Minorcan Islands also made up a significant portion of the labor force. They were originally attracted by the high wages paid for cement work on the Long Key viaduct. This Spanish labor was considered by FEC executives to be reliable and particularly suited to carpentry and bridgework. Most of the laborers spoke only Spanish. Nearly all of the Spaniards came to work and returned to their homes without setting foot on the mainland of the United States.

One of the largest and most dependable groups of laborers came from the Cayman Islands, British Caribbean possessions. Each year, mostly in January, hundreds of these men arrived at the Keys in their own vessels. Caymanders, as they were called, always worked steadily until two weeks or so before Christmas, when nearly all would quit to go home for the holidays. A mixture of Bahamian and West Indian, many had sandy complexions and red or blonde hair, and quite a few had Negroid features. Two-thirds of them had a surname of either Jackson, Sands or Eubanks. They were particularly adept at handling barges and other watercraft.

The largest group of laborers was composed of transients, chiefly from the Bowery in New York. A great many of them were referred to as "down-and-outers." Surprisingly, they proved to be reliable laborers. A record of those possessing special skills was kept, when possible. The lists included lawyers, doctors, pharmacists, preachers, teachers and salesmen. On the Key West railroad, all of them started at the roughest kind of menial labor.[4]

There were three problems directly related to maintaining the quantity and quality of laborers: water, liquor and mosquitoes. The task of the engineers and foremen was to get enough of the first and to do away with the other two.

Workmen were quartered in houseboat barracks until the hurricane of October 1906. The larger houseboats quartered up to 200 men. Each man was given board and lodging in addition to a salary. The camp mess halls served meals which were, according to one visitor, "substantial, wholesome, bountiful and decidedly appetizing." In addition, all personnel received free medical and hospital care. Each camp had a first aid station, and if a patient needed more specialized attention he was sent immediately to a company hospital at Key West or Miami. Throughout the building of the extension, careful enough attention was given to sanitation so that there was never an epidemic among the laborers.

MAINTAINING the water supply was the most critical problem.

Attempts to locate fresh water on the islands were unsuccessful. The only natural source of fresh water found on the Keys was a few ponds of rain water. Virtually all water had to be hauled from the mainland. Not only was it necessary to provide fresh water for crews, but it had to be pure. Sickness and epidemics from bad water could have seriously delayed the entire project. Because water had to be provided for locomotives and stationary steam engines as well as for human consumption, requirements were enormous—4.5 million gallons or 700 carloads per month.

At first, water was hauled from Miami to the Keys by steamboat. Later it was hauled from Manatee Creek in the Everglades, but this proved to be an undependable source. During one day, a northwest wind blew water out of the nearby bay, making it impossible for the boats and water barges to get near shore. Finally, water was obtained from deep wells near Homestead and shipped to the Keys in cypress tanks, mounted two to a flat car. Each tank held about 3,500 gallons. After 1907, at Marathon and other points, water was transferred from the railway cars to barges, each of which held six tanks. The barges were then towed by steamboats, like the *Wanderer*, to camps and worksites which had not yet been reached by rail.

No whiskey was allowed in the camps. And in this, as in many other things, Flagler was elitist. On the one hand, he thought that most of the lower classes could not handle strong drink. On the other hand, he himself drank in moderation, and insisted on serving liquor in all his hotels. Furthermore, he made no attempt to enforce drinking rules against his upper echelon employees, several of whom were problem drinkers. For example when W. H. Chambers, the Florida East Coast railway auditor, went on periodic drunken sprees in Jacksonville, Flagler instructed his aides to rehabilitate Chambers: "Before taking any summary steps in this matter, we must make another effort to save him."

But Flagler insisted on no drinking in the camps, a rule which was difficult to enforce. Ordinarily, laborers traveled to Miami or Key West on their days off. Key West became a lively, boisterous town when the shiploads of railroad men docked. Miami enforced a prohibition law, so railroad crews had to center their activities in North Miami. Most would come to town on Saturday nights, get drunk and end up in jail, only to be sentenced back to work on Monday morning.[5]

An old, derelict ship, the *Senator*, was anchored at Boot Key and run by a group of natives as a bar and house of prostitution—a venture which was as profitable as it was popular, which is to say a lot. The men claimed that the only way they could survive the heat and miseries of the Keys was to have an occasional wing-ding and one could build a fair argument on that side of it.

But Flagler was firm in his policy that more work got done when whiskey was kept out of the camps, and Joseph Meredith did his best to intercept the many "booze boats" that moved freely among the Keys.

The presence of mosquitoes and sand flies on the Keys was the major discomfort for work crews. Sand flies were worse during certain seasons, but mosquitoes remained a year-round problem. Prytheum powder and smudge pots were burned in camps, but these helped only temporarily. It was necessary to screen all mess halls, offices and living quarters. FEC vice president Parrott urged his employees to conserve screens and to use them even in temporary camps. The men were cautioned to be careful about where they dumped waste water so as not to start new breeding areas.

Few workers ventured outside after five o'clock at night. Many men wore gloves, screened hats and long-sleeved shirts to protect themselves from mosquitoes. Others covered themselves with oil or carried a palm-leaf switch.

Headnets were sometimes necessary to guard against the mosquitoes and other insects. The best design, said engineer Krome,

. . . was one adapted from Cape Sable squatters. It is built for use over a stiff-rimmed hat and consists of a band of canvas fitting closely around the crown of the hat. To this is sewed a strip of close mesh copper wire netting extending down the back and curving over the shoulders to the level of the chin. Cheesecloth is taped around the bottom of the copper gauze and tucked beneath the coat, which is buttoned over it.[6]

One section of the Keys remained surprisingly free of mosquitoes—the Lignumvitae Keys. It was learned that the tree of the same name, which grows on those keys, gives off an odor that repels mosquitoes. It is probable that insects drove men off the job more than any other cause.

As a relief against jungle and mosquitoes, there were special amenities. A headquarters camp at Marathon, accessible by boat, provided a rest area where engineers and other workers read or played billiards and card games. They also could play tennis, fish and explore the outer islands.

Despite such arrangements, Flagler had a difficult time keeping men on the job. Among his problems were occasional rumors of oil on the Keys, which tended to draw men away from railroad work. Krome had to track down the rumors and get the men back to work. The "oil finds" invariably turned out to be swamp gas and sulfur mixed with only traces of oil. Injured workers were often brought to Marathon for treatment.

An FEC employee, W. R. Hawkins, noted in his diary his impressions of a trainload of recruits that stopped at Marathon. "Two hundred sixty-nine [of 345 that boarded the train in New York] mostly pretty tough looking customers though most any one would look tough after a trip from New York in day coaches with no chance to wash and not much to sleep or eat."[7] Out of that single trainload, 130 men left before the train reached the construction. Some of the men who got such a free trip to Florida, and others who quit the extension force, created further difficulties for the railroad by circulating rumors about poor living conditions in construction camps. It was also alleged in Northern newspapers that FEC officials had forced some workers into a state of peonage by requiring them to repay the railroad for passage, before quitting the work.

REPLYING to its critics, the FEC released an official statement designed to quiet the accusations. It was instead a remarkable exercise in class condescension and racism, and gives an idea not only of the sort of thinking going on in America at the time, but also of Flagler's thinking.

Throughout Henry's biographical record, one finds few instances of sympathy for America's impoverished black classes. He did not dislike Negroes. He was simply indifferent to their plight. He built a school here and there. He paid them the going wages, which at $1.00 to $1.50 per day was at the bottom of the wage scale. He provided thousands of jobs. But no black ever had more than a menial position in his companies or in his households.

In the FEC statement, approved by Flagler, whites were treated no better than blacks. They were described in terms of class and described bloodlessly; as draft animals used as means to achieve an end.

Ultimately, Flagler and the capitalist class of 1907 were no better or worse than people of other times, and ultimately they should not be judged by a different time. In terms of class prejudice and race, they were but ordinary people programmed by their own society.

In the FEC statement, Flagler defines his era's perception of lower economic classes. The distinctions are finely made, even to the nomenclature of American-born "negroes" and foreign-born "Negroes"; American-born "Whites" and foreign-born "whites."

The Flagler statement explains:

From the beginning of construction work in April 1905 until the opening of the line to traffic to Knight's Key in February 1908 there was a large number of southern negroes employed on the work. These men were recruited from

Florida and Georgia, and included a large proportion of the lower type of negroes who follow railroad work and are more or less of a floating class, working only a short time in one place before they seek new fields. The efficiency of this class of labor was so low that it was found necessary to recruit white labor in the north, and the demand for negro labor in the south at that time was so great that it was impossible to build up a force sufficient to carry on the work. The largest number of negroes employed at any one time was in the neighborhood of eight hundred men.

The white laborers were recruited in New York, Philadelphia, Pittsburgh and other northern cities, and while most of it was of a class not used to the rough kind of work needed in railroad construction, and included a large portion of undesirable types, it was thought they could be educated up to our requirements.

After the recruiting of the whites, very few attempts were made to recruit negro labor and the gangs diminished so that during 1906 and 1907 the number did not run over four hundred at any time; the negroes who remained or who came in later, were of a much better grade than the first recruits, and for the clearing of the heavy jungle along the right of way the negro was far superior to the whites.

The most satisfactory results were secured through the letting of contract work, the contracts being let to individuals who would hire ten or twenty men to help them, the price being fixed in advance for the work to be done. The contractors seldom failed to make good wages and a profit on the work. The station men, or contractors, however, particularly the negroes, seldom kept their earnings very long owing to their tendency to gamble and spend their money in liquor. Once each month on the day following pay day there would be very little work done among the negro laborers, the time being spent in drinking and gambling and when their money was gone they would return to work and earn another stake. There were strict rules prohibiting the introduction of liquors into the camps, but it was undoubtedly brought in by the men themselves. There was this noticeable difference, however, the negroes were regular, but moderate drinkers while the whites who drank would get on a spree of several days before returning to work.

It was thought we could secure some labor from the British West Indies, but after a trial of this class they were found to be low in efficiency.

At various times during the progress of the work small numbers of whites from the Southern states were recruited, but the white "Cracker" of the South Atlantic and Gulf States is not adapted by training or disposition for railroad construction work; is more inclined to stick to farming or trucking and has no liking for any work that takes him away from his home and his

"Folks." This class of labor was of little service to the Extension work.

The "conch" white labor was also employed to a certain extent but it was found that while there were some exceptions, as a rule he was not adapted to the hard work of railroad construction.

At no time was there any trouble in securing all of the common labor that was needed of the above classes, but the building up of an efficient working force was a very difficult task. Considerable care was taken at the recruiting stations to select men who were physically able to perform the work required of them, but by changing names and trading tickets, a large number of undesirables secured passage to the work. The men of middle age were often more capable laborers than the younger men, but were broken down by drink and disease, and while these older men did not object to remaining in one place and doing hard work, many of them missed the opportunities to secure liquor and at pay days would visit the nearby towns and indulge in sprees.

During a part of 1907, Spanish laborers from Cuba, attracted by the high scale of wages paid on the concrete construction at Long Key Viaduct, began to enlist and since then have formed a considerable element of the labor force, and these men have been a generally satisfactory type of laborer employed on the Extension. This type work in gangs and will not permit "Soldiering" on the part of other members of their own race, the drones being eliminated by a process of their own devising. They are cleanly in their quarters and in care of their persons. To some extent they are clannish and do not mix with workers of other nationalities, but at the same time . . . they . . . can be worked in the same camp and housed in the same quarters with Irish, American or other white labor, without friction. They are "stayers" and hoard their earnings carefully, seldom leaving the work for "lay-offs" or junketing trips.

During the fall of 1905 considerable members of Greeks and Italians were recruited but their term of service was usually short, several of the gangs recruited not even reaching the scene of actual work at all.

Cubans from Key West were also tried in small numbers at various times, but were unable to endure the hard labor required of them.

Summarizing the above, I would say that our labor came from the following sources:

Southern States negroes, from Florida & Georgia.

Bahama Negro: from Nassau, Bimini, and other West Indian Islands, and from Key West.

Northern White: from New York, Philadelphia and other northern cities.

Southern White: from Georgia and Florida.

"Conch" white from Key West, the Keys and southern Florida mainland.

Spanish white, originally from Northern Spain to us by way of Cuba and Key West.

Small numbers of Greeks, Italians, Cubans and West Indies whites.

Despite his class and race distinctions, Flagler was insistent that all his workers receive not only adequate care, but the best possible care. As early as August 1905, he had instructed Parrott:

I have this morning read with a great deal of interest N.Y. *Herald's* report of an interview with Mr. Theodore P. Shonts, member of the Panama Canal Commission who was advising on care for workers in the tropics. In the article, Shonts lays very great stress upon the importance of providing proper facilities for housing, feeding and caring for the employees. While we have no condition such as exists on the Isthmus, it occurs to me that whoever is in charge of that work should look carefully into the question of everything pertaining to the health and proper care of the force we employ.[9]

Parrott replied that what the men had was good enough.

. . . With reference to the quarters for our men; no very elaborate quarters are necessary; the greatest difficulty we have to contend with is the insect pests—mosquitoes, etc., which at times become very troublesome. Fortunately we are nearing the cooler season when it is hoped these conditions will improve.[10]

In December of the same year, a reporter for the Brooklyn *Eagle* went down to have a look and telegraphed back that not only were the laborers well cared for, "but the Brooklyn boys are romancing the island girls," an observation that may not have proved reassuring to the Brooklyn girls. The reporter found further that the FEC maintained a hospital camp for emergencies at each station in the islands and a main hospital at Miami and any man taken sick is furnished with hospital service free of all expense:

Some of the boys came down here evidently to get their passage paid without any intention of working for the company. A number got employment in Miami with local concerns and we are out the cost of their passage. It is these fellows that often stop men at the railroad station and on their way to the works and fill their ears with all sorts of false stories . . .

. . . The men are housed free by the company in comfortable quarters. They buy their own food, sold at the commissary department at reasonable prices, and can live well on $2.50 per week . . .[11]

Eighteen months later, F. S. Spofford of the Chicago *Daily News* made a similar inspection:

. . . I doubt if there could be found better conditions for the common laborer in any engineering work than exist along this extension.

I spent two days in these camps, mingled with the men, ate their food, inspected their quarters, and I must say that on every hand were evidences of the greatest consideration for their welfare. . . . [The engineers know] that the best way to get a good day's work out of a man is to feed him well, give him a good place to sleep, and, in short, treat him decently. What criticism could be passed on a menu like this: fresh meat, good vegetables, good bread, creamery butter, genuine coffee, rice pudding, and all in plenty. I am certain that such a meal is no exception. Pure water and ice are supplied to every camp. The bedding was clean and I saw no evidence whatever of insanitary conditions. The camps are under almost military discipline without encroaching upon natural liberties. There is no rowdyism, no drunkenness; in fact, no liquor is sold in or near the camps. . . . The percentage of sickness has been much lower than that in the regular Army of the United States.[12]

Despite such praise, a New York federal grand jury indicted the engineers in charge of the extension. According to affidavits from government witnesses, once recruited workers left Miami, the dock gates were locked behind them, preventing their return to that city without railway permission. They were forcibly detained on the job and not allowed off the islands. Some who did escape were arrested by local authorities on vagrancy charges and returned to the job in chains as state convicts. The construction camps were described as hellholes. Such testimony was hard to corroborate, however, and federal prosecutors delayed trial while they attempted to gather more evidence.

With much difficulty, the railroad succeeded in bringing the case before a jury in November 1908. After a week of shaky prosecution testimony, the judge directed the jury to return a verdict of acquittal, and he rebuked the prosecuting attorney for making charges on a flimsy foundation of hearsay.[13]

Although the federal investigators found the charges to be without foundation, they had made their scars on the people at Whitehall. Flagler's organist Spalding wrote home to his family in Lowell, saying:

I am sending you a copy of this morning's Palm Beach *Daily News*, containing a splendid editorial on Mr. Flagler. I imagine it was called forth by an outrageous article that appeared in the *Cosmopolitan* entitled "Slavery as it appears today in Florida" or something of that kind and containing a picture of Mr. Flagler as the man who the article says is largely responsible for the cruel conditions that exist. It is a base libel, at least as far as Mr. Flagler is concerned, and a cruel blow to deal at such sensitive and kind-hearted people as the Flaglers. The truth is that Mr. Flagler has spent thousands of dollars in merely improving the living conditions of the laborers along the extension, and they live in far better houses than they ever knew before or will know after they leave the employ of the East Coast Railway.

The article is simply a sample of the hysterical raving that is now going all over the country against men of capital, and alas, probably will either be believed as gospel truth or else passed over unread. The injustice and cruelty of such articles become apparent when we know the persons at whom they are aimed and find them to be as sensitive as the rest of us even though they are in the limelight much of the time.

Spalding added that Mrs. Flagler cried her eyes out the afternoon she read the article.

FLAGLER was pleased with the acquittal but puzzled over the sudden halt to the case. Why hadn't the judge allowed the FEC men to fully explain themselves? Flagler was suspicious that the whole thing was somehow part of a government attack on Standard Oil and suspected that Teddy Roosevelt was behind it. "There is an air of mystery about this thing that we do not understand," he told a friend.

He hated Roosevelt with an almost paranoid intensity, although the two had been friends in New York and Flagler had supported his election to the governorship in 1898. Almost immediately after his inauguration, however, Roosevelt had instituted a tax on corporate franchises, an act Flagler regarded as a betrayal. Their relationship had gone downhill since. When Roosevelt began to attack Standard Oil, Flagler wrote an associate, "I have no command of the English language that enables me to express my feelings regarding Mr. Roosevelt. He is shit." In November 1901, less than two months after Roosevelt became President, he held a meeting with Flagler's aide Parrott. Parrott passed on the details of the meeting to his boss and suggested a Flagler–Roosevelt meeting might repair the quarrel.

Flagler hotly rebuffed the invitation: "I . . . note the account of your meeting with President Roosevelt; also your desire that I should stop in Washington and make a call upon him. I don't believe there is a man in America who dreads such a thing as much as I do. I am glad you saw him, for I am sure I don't want to do it."

When Roosevelt announced after leaving office in 1909 that he was going on safari in Africa, Flagler wrote: "I am glad that Teddy is going to Africa soon, for I want to spare him the humiliation of knowing that he has been all wrong in his persecution of the Standard. I would like to keep him swelled up as much as possible, so that when a lion swallows him, he won't be able to disgorge him."

It was Roosevelt, however, who had the last bite.

During the previous 20 years, there had come to light many of the secret Standard Oil contracts and arrangements engineered by Flagler and Rockefeller. Prodded by Roosevelt administration lawsuits, the U.S. Supreme Court in 1911 ordered the breakup of the various companies which made up the Standard Oil Company. The absolute monopoly of Standard was thus finished, although the constituent companies continued to operate through centralized policies and management.

# CHAPTER 19

# Eyewitness

I N 1909, Henry Flagler was visited by one of the premier financial writers of America. His name was Edwin LeFevre, and LeFevre went in with preconceived notions. He expected Flagler to be one of those men who appeared at church on Sunday in a silk hat, carrying a gold-headed cane, giving dimes to urchins and standing around to be marveled at. Flagler, too, had his prejudices. He thought this LeFevre fellow, for all his high reputation, was nothing more than an elevated newspaperman. Even before they met, the two had taken a dislike to each other right away. They hadn't wasted any time on it.

Lefevre, 39 years old at the time of his Whitehall visit, was considered the nation's leading analyst of Wall Street conditions.

He was a native of Panama, with distinguished parents. His mother, Emilia de la Ossa LeFevre, was the daughter of the chief justice of the Panama Supreme Court and niece of the president of Panama. Edwin's father, Henry L. LeFevre, was an American Panama agent of the Pacific Mail Steamship Company and had been a Union naval officer during the American Civil War.

After taking an engineering degree at Lehigh University, Edwin LeFevre switched careers and became a reporter on the New York *Sun*, and then a free-lance specialist on financial affairs.[1]

Despite his prejudices, or perhaps because of them, LeFevre approached the Flagler interview cautiously—first inspecting the system of hotels and railroads, then sounding out key assistants. Only at the end of his trip did he walk up the steps of Whitehall to find Flagler sitting on the porch.

I saw an old man with a high forehead rising in straight lines from the temples. His hair is of a clean, glistening silver, like the cropped mustache and the eyebrows. They set off his complexion, which is neither ruddy nor baby-pink, but what one might call a virile red. He has a straight nose and a strong chin. The head is well shaped. The eyes are a clear blue—some might say violet. They must have been very keen once; today their expression is not easy to describe—not exactly shrewd nor compelling nor suspicious; though you feel they might have been all of these, years ago. Withal, you are certain that it is not age which has mellowed them; the change is more subtle; it is from within—eyes that gleam but never flame. Between his eyebrows there is an inverted V, deep-wrinkled; you think of it as a sort of chronic frown, which disappeared decades ago. A handsome old man! Under his fourscore years his shoulders have bowed slightly, but there is no semblance of decay.

You see in his face good concentration; good observation, without undue alertness; meditation without self-abstraction; attentiveness without tension; indomitable will without stubbornness; a steady-gaited man, deliberate not from age nor from indifference, but from temperament and life habit.[2]

His article, from *Everybody's* magazine, reflects his changing attitude on the trip. It begins snobbishly then mellows to cynicism as he talks with Flagler aides; and finally dissolves to respect as he meets the object of his journey.

"It is only as you approach St. Augustine that the car window messages begin to interest you. Among clumps of verdure you watch a glimpse of red-tiled roofs and Spanish towers; the 'Ponce de Leon' and the 'Alcazar.' " "Flagler," LeFevre adds sarcastically, "and his hotels!"

And a beautiful dome, dominating as the Duomo of Florence, though without the sea of Florentine roofs about it: the Memorial Church, perhaps the most beautiful small church in America. More Flagler!

You stop in St. Augustine to rest before proceeding south. It is an old town, St. Augustine: "The oldest city in the United States," they are careful to tell you. Also they point out a dozen "oldest" houses, none particularly interesting, and the old Spanish fort and the old slave market—which probably wasn't a slave market at all. In point of fact, the spirit of the place does not bear down very heavily on you with the weight of antiquity. No huge ash-sifter has been shaken over it, covering everything with the fine dust of disintegrated centuries, as in the medieval towns of Europe. Nevertheless, something here is different; I think it is because everywhere you see palms.

And utilizing to the utmost this palm *motif* are the Flagler hotels. They fit, these beautiful edifices, Spanish in architecture and gorgeously successful in the utter un-Americanness of their environment and general effect. Barely twenty years old, they look as if they had always been there, in that precise spot. They "belong," very decidedly.

And the crowd that you see is a crowd of all kinds of people, who are not altogether pleasure-hunting nor exclusively health seeking, neither prosperous looking nor shabby. In all the hotels you see more grayheads than black or brown or blond. They tell you, on the slightest provocation, how many years they have been coming down here for the winter. And you gather, before your first day has passed, that Florida is not merely a Fashionable Fad. It is a National Institution.

If you are a motorist you will see the Ormond Beach, return thanks to the Maker thereof, and refuse to use the rest of your railroad ticket, for you have here the most wonderful speedway in the world; that, smooth, just hard enough, and swept clean every day by the mighty broom of the tide. The Ormond Hotel is between the beach and the Halifax River. It is comfortable, and more homelike, than any other Flagler hotel, and the grounds have a more exotic look than in St. Augustine. You drive to Daytona along beautiful roads, past orange groves and the cottages of the winter residents, through streets bordered by trees heavily hung with Spanish moss. Beautiful places, Daytona and Ormond, with river and ocean "views"; but you must push southward to Palm Beach.

Flagler's Palm Beach awes even LeFevre, a sophisticated world traveler.

It is the heart of our Riviera. The train stops at the very gates of the Royal Poinciana—the largest wooden building in the world used exclusively for hotel purposes. You notice long, colonnaded porches and no architectural pretensions—a hotel that has grown by means of additions as it grew in popularity.

If the Royal Poinciana Hotel neither awes you by its size nor charms you by its architecture, the grounds completely delight you. Yesterday a swamp was here, today you see the wizardry of the dollar. To make a lawn here was more difficult than it would have been to spread a sheet of solid silver on this spot, or on the golf links, where Mr. Flagler's engineers dumped thousands of carloads of earth. Lawns you have seen before; but not these curious trees and strange shrubs with polychromatic leaves; uncanny screw pines with clumps of exposed roots like writhing serpents upholding the trunk; the gaudy crimson blossoms of the hibiscus that suggest the red lights on a Christmas tree; palms of divers kinds, borders of century plants grown to huge size. And over it all the azure splendor of the Florida sky canopying a scene of so exotic a beauty that you are not merely miles, but whole worlds away from New York.

Hither comes the ultra-fashion of the great cities to wear its summer gowns six months ahead of time: to see and to be seen. The crowd alone is worth the trip. You get to know [couturieres] Doucet and I'aquin better than you know your pastor, and a trip through the hotel corridors in the evening is merely a journey from Paris to Palm Beach . . .

LeFevre found that the rich didn't walk.

In an Ethiopian propelled wheel chair you go forth to see Palm Beach; no horses are allowed here. The hotel is on Lake Worth, and you take the drive along the shore. Bluebill ducks swim about and dive with an air of doing it for your benefit. You see the garfish poking their noses into everything; the oldest of extant fishes, unchanged and "unevoluted" these hundred thousand years, they now help to intensify the feeling of being in a strange world. . . . The lake shows curious patches of varying blueness. . . . There is now sky: only a stupendous turquoise incandescence; and along the horizon a paler strip— crushed jewels and vaporized silver—otherwise you could not tell where the sky began or water left off. And where you should see clouds, you see instead soft whitenesses, glinting like new snow in bright sunlight. . . .

On both sides of the Lake Drive grow coconut palms, graceful, lithe, almost animate. You see them gazing at themselves in the mirror of the lake, perennially fascinated by their beauty. But others distinctly lean away from the water; veritable women in the act of fleeing, suddenly metamorphosed into palms. . . . Along the glaring white road, through tennels of verdure, the noiseless wheel chair carries you, each strange tree adding impressions of a land utterly foreign. It is as if your soul were receiving mysterious little taps—tap! tap! tap!—psychic hammer strokes that numb other thoughts and lull our senses into the Floridian mood.

You return and drive through palm bordered streets to the "Jungle Trail"— a man-made labyrinthine road, cut tunnel-like through banks of vegetation; past weird, misshapen trees . . . on out to the "Breakers," the other Flagler hotel, and the pier. . . . The ocean is very blue, save near the horizon, where it is green. There is the smell of the sea and the roar of the sea— that and the sky and its eternal azure challenge to the water.

Leaving Palm Beach, LeFevre finds the remainders of Flagler's domain as exotic as a Gauguin landscape.

It is a place, Palm Beach, unlike any other in the world. And only the other day it was merely sand and marsh and brush, with a few palms that grew from coconuts which drifted ashore from the wreck of a West Indian schooner. Only that and the blue sky and the blue lake and the blue ocean. And Flagler came and saw what there was. And then he saw what there would be.

You push on to Miami, in what was, till recently, the southernmost section under Flagler development. It is not so picturesque a place as Palm

Beach. But it impresses you as being infinitely more useful. It is a business town, but the business is fruit growing and therefore you see no smoke belching factory chimneys. The roads are absolutely white—literal streaks of blinding glare in the sunlight. You are no longer warm, you are hot. Where nothing was, a few years ago, you see streets, brick buildings, hotels, banks, churches, schools, cottages not of "resorters" but of residents. It is no longer an experiment; it is a fact—proved less by the money spent by Flagler than by the money earned by the farmers and fruit growers. The Royal Palm—the local Flagler hotel—strikes you as the only "resort" feature here.

You push southward. Seen from the car windows, the Keys are shoreless islands of verdure, for all the world suggesting a flooded meadow with clumps of trees rising above the flood. The water itself is the greatest charm, with its varying shades of blue and green, according to the depth. In many places it shows chalky white, especially after a storm, which stirs up the marl in the bottom. You see no habitations; no sign of human life until you stop at Long Key, from which the famous viaduct starts. Long Key is now the most popular fishing camp in Florida, with its comfortable, homelike hotel.

The white coral beach and the coconut palms recall to your mind *South Sea atolls*. And you sit on the porch of your cottage, and look across the waters that shade from light green to blue; and you see the Gulf Stream like a clearly defined sapphire streak, and you are confronted by the might of the invincible ocean—until, happening to turn, you see the concrete viaduct built into that same invincible ocean.

It is Flagler's railroad.

When I was down there a year ago, the late J. C. Meredith, construction engineer, had his headquarters at Knight's Key. In and out of the construction camps he flitted in his launch, his binoculars to his eyes, like a general observing the movements of his troops on the battlefield. You could see telephone poles sticking out of the water in the shallow places, for all the world like lines of skirmishers and scouts. On the deck of his launch, inspecting the work, he explained remarkable achievements in a remarkably matter-of-fact way. Then he spoke about himself:

"It was very strange, at first, for me to work for Mr. Flagler, on account of his point of view. With him it is never a case of *How much will it cost?* nor of *Will it pay?*—which are the inevitable and perfectly proper questions for corporations to ask of their engineers . . .

"I was told to make my studies and my estimates. We had lots of problems to solve, and I was quite a long time at it, and I knew how much he desired to see the work rushed, but I never heard a word from him; not one request for haste. When the report was ready, Mr. Parrott and I took it to Mr. Flagler. He heard how we proposed to do it. We stopped before we came to the estimates of cost. And Mr. Flagler stood up and looked at us and said: 'Well, let's get to work!' It was the most serious work he had planned to do in Florida. Perhaps he felt the occasion called for some comment, for he looked at me and said very quietly: 'I want to see it done before I die.' That is all he said."

The engineer was an unemotional, deliberate man of the von Moltke type. He paused and looked at me. Then he said, very earnestly, "Mr. LeFevre, there isn't one of us who wouldn't give a year of his life to have Mr. Flagler see the work completed!"

It is to be doubted whether mere figures can give an adequate idea of the magnitude of Flagler's work. He has spent $41,000,000 in Florida; that is, his investment in incorporated enterprise amounts to that, divided roughly as follows: $18,000,000 in the old railroads, including the development of towns, $10,000,000 in the Key West Extension, $12,000,000 in hotels, and $1,000,000 in steamboat and outside enterprises. This sum does not include his charities, churches and divers donations, for neither he nor any one else has kept the figures. The value of the taxable property in the counties *exclusively* reached by the Flagler roads has increased over fifty millions since he began. And there are today only about 25,000 acres under cultivation for fruit and vegetables out of a total of about 3,500,000 acres now available for such cultivation. Flagler has *made* the East Coast of Florida.

The construction of the Ponce de Leon Hotel began in 1885. The house opened in December 1888. The Alcazar was completed shortly after. The Ormond Hotel was purchased in 1890, and enlarged from time to time. The Royal Poinciana at Palm Beach, originally a five-hundred-room house, was opened in February 1894; it now has 2,000 rooms. The Breakers was completed in 1895, destroyed by fire in 1903, and entirely rebuilt on the old site. It is a four-hundred-room house. The Royal Palm at Miami was completed and opened for the season of 1896–97. At Nassau, the Colonial, a four-hundred-room house, was opened in 1899. Flagler purchased other property there, including the Hotel Victoria, from the English Government. The Continental, at Atlantic Beach, Florida, a two-hundred-room summer hotel, opened in May 1901. His railroad carried one million passengers in 1908.

Steamship service was first inaugurated to Nassau in 1895 by the Florida East Coast Steamship Company, owned by Flagler. In 1896 the Key West line was opened, and, in the winter of that year, the operation was extended

to the Havana line. There is now a daily service. In 1902 the Florida East
Coast Steamship Company was consolidated with the Plant Steamship Company. Flagler owns one half of the stock of the consolidation.

AT THIS point in the article, LeFevre lets us know that he is beginning
to stand in awe of Flagler.

George W. Perkins, of J. P. Morgan & Co., said not long ago, "I can
understand how, for instance, James J. Hill built his railroad into the uninhabitable prairies, for he knew what the soil was capable of, and it was a
country similar to what men elsewhere were used to. But that any man
could have the genius to see of what this wilderness of waterless sand and
underbrush was capable and then have the nerve to build a railroad here,
is more marvelous than similar development anywhere else in the world."

For you must remember that Flagler owns the hotels and the railroad.
He has never done any promoting. He has never asked any one to buy stock
in his company. He has "incorporated" himself in order to be business-like
in his spending. The magnitude and the picturesqueness of the work, its
absolutely unique quality, grow the more it is studied. It was not merely a
rich man's hobby, nor strictly a commercial enterprise. Why, then, is this
work at all? To explain this you must explain Flagler himself.

IN INTERVIEW after interview, LeFevre found that nobody knows
Flagler.

In the Standard Oil offices you hear: "A fine man!" or "A wonderful man!"
But nobody can visualize an adjective. Being in Florida, you naturally turn
to the Flagler lieutenants. Your credentials entitling you to their confidence,
they speak very frankly. You are immediately struck by the curious note of
apology in their voice and manner—as though they expected derision or
skepticism. They simply despair of making you believe that anybody could
possibly be as nice as Flagler is to all his employees. The *esprit de corps* is
amazingly strong. He gives them a free hand. By putting them on their
honor, he also puts them on their mettle, though, after all, their chief motive
force appears to be personal loyalty.

I wish to make it very clear that I cherish no deathless illusions about
men rich or poor; that, having spent my working life in Wall Street, I cannot
be accused of unfamiliarity with either modern business methods or the
personality of the great captains of industry. And now, I deliberately state
that Mr. Flagler's subordinates in Florida, in charge of interests representing
an actual cash outlay of more than forty millions of dollars, when deciding
disputes or settling any manner of business matters, always act, not for "the
good of the company" or its profit, but invariably as they think Mr. Flagler
would personally act. And Mr. Flagler always decides in favor of what is

just and fair and kind. I cannot say as much of any other "big man," though
it must be remembered that while other corporations have no souls, this
one has, and it belongs to Henry M. Flagler.

Only the other day an old carpenter, who had been in Mr. Flagler's
employ from the early St. Augustine days, was striken with locomotor ataxia.
Well, without consulting Mr. Flagler they simply pensioned off the man,
who is now provided for to the end. They wished to spare their chief the
sorrow of learning of the man's misfortune, and they did what they knew
he would have done. And this merely one of many such instances. I consider
this more remarkable than the green enchantment of Palm Beach or the
gray grandeur of the Long Key viaduct.

He has had these same men in his employ many years. It may show that
his judgment in the first instance was good. But you are surprised to hear
that he never once has praised them to their faces; never expressed pleasure
or gratification in their wisdom or success or fidelity to duty; never patted
them on the back, never called them by their first names. And yet they all
love him! He never gives positive orders. He expresses his views or wishes;
but he also *asks* their *views* and invites suggestions. If theirs are better, he
promptly says: "That's better than mine. We ought to do that!" That is as
near a positive order as he ever gives, and yet he is a man of decision and
indomitable will.

Flagler's Florida lieutenants told pretty much the same stories. If I quote
one, it is because that is substantially what all said.

"It is natural that I having worked under him for years, should think that
Mr. Flagler is not only a very good man but a great man. He has the faculty
of clear logical reasoning and a perception so keen and quick that he unerr-
ingly detects the flaw anywhere at a glance.

"He is very careful and studies a thing thoroughly before he acts. Once
he is convinced it can be done he goes ahead without regard to the time of
[sic] the profit. Fifty months or fifty years are all the same to him, so far as
*profits* are concerned. And he is never impatient and never discouraged."

ON HIS TRIP, LeFevre also interviewed Flagler's friend, the Reverend
George Ward, who told the journalist:

I should say that he is the most modest man in the world. When the people
wanted to call the new town of Miami "Flagler," he refused, and asked that
it should keep its old name—and he had built the town. Why, this year—
1909—when the committee wanted to give him a box at the Ponce de Leon
celebration in St. Augustine, he wouldn't accept it, preferring to go on the
grandstand with the crowd. They literally forced him to take the box—and
you know what St. Augustine owes to him. The vestrymen of the Memorial
Church had to wait until some meeting at which he was not present to vote

a pew to him in perpetuity; he did not wish to accept it, preferring to be like any other pewholder—and he had built the church.

He never swears. I think "Thunder!" is his strongest expletive. And I have yet to hear him call any one a "damned fool." The nearest he comes to it is: "Now, wouldn't you think a man would have more sense than that?"

He has none of the steam-roller tendencies which I hear people accuse other big men of. For instance, when he was about to build the Alcazar, which, like the Ponce de Leon, is situated on marshy ground which he filled in, the Methodist Church stood near by. It was an old building that would have been dear at $4,000, land and all. He told the congregation that if they would let him have the site, he would build them a nice church anywhere else they wished. They agreed, thinking he would deal fairly by them. They hoped that he might spend as much as $5,000 on it. Well, he built the Methodist Church and parsonage at a cost of $84,000 and gave it to them, free and clear. And that is characteristic of him.

One time, when in New York, he received a letter from a cripple here who was about to be foreclosed, a man too old and sickly to start life anew elsewhere with any likelihood of success. Mr. Flagler telegraphed me to go to the man's relief. The cripple lived in a settlement miles and miles from anywhere. To get to it I had to go up the river a long distance in a launch, and the rest of the way over trails. There weren't even roads, and Mr. Flagler knew it. While on the way, a second telegram reached me saying that he had sent the money in gold certificates to Titusville. You see, he feared the mortgagee might be some ignorant backwoodsman who would not want to take my check.

In the towns he has built he has begun work on a church and a schoolhouse at the same time that he began his railroad station. He says he has done this for the sake of the women. This is a level country and settlers can live where the women-folk can have neighbors and their children schooling, while the men can ride to their plantations on bicycles. The church is the social center of the place. In towns with the development of which he has nothing to do, he always responds to appeals for schools and for churches—without respect to denomination.

His religion? He is a Presbyterian, but not narrow. Some of his best friends, I've heard him say, are in the Catholic hierarchy. I remember when the Memorial Church was building he ordered some palmettos from a distance, to plant about it. They did not reach St. Augustine until the very Sunday morning of the dedication. When I told him, early in the morning, that the palms had arrived, he said: "What can be better than to plant them on the day of the dedication?" And so his laborers broke the Sabbath. Some of the congregation predicted a short life for the Sabbath-desecrating palmettos. Years afterward, one Sunday morning, Mr. Flagler and I came out of the church. He looked at the palms and said to me: "Every one of the wicked things lived!"

Over the entrance to the Palm Beach cemetery he has placed this inscription: *Anything so universal as death must be a blessing.* Also this, from the 121st Psalm: *The Lord shall preserve thy going out and thy coming in from this time forth, and even for evermore.*

I tell you, it is difficult to convey to strangers or visitors how he has worked for Florida and for the people he has brought to the East Coast. He wants them to find work, to make money. He has never gone into anything that local capital would or could do. Nobody else would build the railroad, because it would not pay, nor the hotels; nor the waterworks and electric light plant in Miami; and so he did. But he won't, for instance, even run the stage line in St. Augustine, nor permit his hotels to do a livery business, because other people can make a living at it.

Kindly and considerate as he is, he is also the most self-repressed man living.

Finally, at Whitehall, LeFevre met Flagler and he decided that despite all his efforts, Flagler was a stoic who had endured intense and unexplained suffering.

You realize that you are before a man who has suffered and has never wept; who has undergone intense pain and has never sobbed; who has never bent under stress and has never hurrahed! When a man has one or another group of salient traits, you place him in a certain pigeonhole of human classification. Your great man is apt to be one with certain faculties over-developed, and classifies easily. But Flagler is not like any one else and withal is not eccentric.

He is without redeeming vices, without amiable inconsistencies, without obsessions. He simply does not "classify." You cannot accurately *adjectivize* him. He does not defy analysis; he baffles it. It is as if the soul of him, condensed, compressed by environment, or heredity, or some great natural force—not by self-effort—had been molded into a statue, full of vitality, yet immobile; a statue with veins. Whether they run red blood you cannot tell; but you are certain it is not ice water. What color is it, then?

That is the mystery of the soul of Henry M. Flagler.

LeFevre felt ill at ease, standing awkwardly on the shaded flagstones of the Whitehall courtyard. Flagler attempted to make him comfortable.

"Sit here, on this lounge beside me," Flagler courteously told LeFevre. "I will let you have my good ear . . . " and then he smiled, "although it is none too good at that."

He made room for me beside him, the first time I saw him.

I asked him many questions. He answered every one promptly; I received no definite impression of the man. It does not often happen. Silence is the best guard against self-betrayal. With this man it was speech. And yet he was frank.

The conversation ran like this:

"Do you do thus and so?"

"Sometimes."

"Do you like this?"

"Oh, yes."

"Are you fond of that?"

"Yes, somewhat." Always with a quiet voice, neither bored nor interested.

"How did you build your system?"

"Oh, it's one of those things that just happen . . . I happened to be in St. Augustine and had some spare money."

"You must have thought a good hotel was needed."

"I suppose so," very simply.

"You think ten times to one of talking?"

"I've talked you black and blue."

"But you do think ten times more than you speak?"

"I suppose so." There is no weariness in the "I suppose so." It isn't languid, it isn't tired, no indifference, no interest. He accepts facts without thrills.

"How did you achieve your success in business?"

"All I can say is by working six days a week." He does not seem to have any maxims or business aphorisms.

"How do you manage to have such health at your age?"

"When I answer friends who ask me that same question, they laugh. But I mean it. When I was young I was too poor to indulge in bad habit. By the time I was able to afford them, it had become a fixed habit to live simply."

Only now and then are you made conscious that he is of an earlier generation. Thus, in answer to another question:

"I have studied the price men pay for success—the loss of health or of character or of reputation. And I find that all men who win success, no matter how they win it, are always met with envy. That accounts for many of the attacks you mention."

"Why should that be?"

"Poor human nature, I suppose." He has not grasped the reason for muckraking.

On a trip to Indian River, years ago, he met a squatter, a Jerseyman who had gone south for his health and was growing all manner of fruits and vegetables, including pineapples, of which he had secured the slips on a trip he once made to the Bahamas.

"He told me," said Flagler, "that the apple Eve tempted Adam with must have been a pineapple. When I saw how this man was growing all sorts of sub-tropical fruits, I thought that what he could do others could do, and that it ought to pay. I decided to give them a chance to do it by building a railroad. It was forlorn-looking country. If I hadn't seen that Jerseyman, I'd never have believed it could be done. But I decided it was a good thing."

"And you were right."

LeFevre was the only interviewer who ever got Flagler to talk about his parents in detail. Like the letter to the unknown Philadelphia pastor in 1901, Flagler reveals surprising intimacies to a stranger. It seems he wanted his story told and understood.

My mother died in 1861. I was then thirty-one. The local paper published the customary obituary notice, and I got several copies and sent them to friends back in New York State, who had known mother. I told my father about it and asked him if there was any one else to whom he thought I ought to send a copy of the paper. He thought a long time—quite a long time. Finally he said: "Yes, you might send a copy to Mrs. So-and-So," somewhere out in Indiana, I think. I did so; and asked him if he thought of any one else. Again he thought—a long time—and at last he said: "Yes. You might send a copy to Mrs. —" another name in Kansas. I did so and asked him if these ladies knew mother well. "I think so," he said. "Who are they, father," I asked him; and he said: "They are my sisters." Several years afterward, when a cousin in Canandaigua was getting up a history of the Flagler family, I learned for the first time that my father was one of twelve children. So I suppose I inherited from him my dislike of speaking about myself.

LeFevre continued:

I asked him what the "M" in his name stood for, and he replied: "Morrison. My mother was Scotch. The first time I ever used my middle name was ten years ago, when the Governor of the Bahamas wished to know, on account of a contract between myself and the British Government. He cabled me: 'How do you spell it?' and I didn't know, I wasn't sure whether there was one 'r' or two." He was only seventy years old and had never thought about his middle name!

In "Whitehall," during the visit, I remarked on the charming color scheme of, I think, the drawing room, and I learned it was his own suggestion to his decorators.

"How did the idea come to you?"

"I don't know. I just thought it would look well."

"You have the aesthetic sense well developed?"

"I don't know." And then he told me that he had differed with his architects only once. It was about the height of the ceiling in the great hall. They wanted it higher, to secure the right proportions.

"But I wanted to feel at home, and so I made them put it eight feet lower. I can come here and sit down and feel that it is my home. The Italian ambassador told me that I had something the Old World had not; and that was a palace to be lived in. That was what I wanted—a home." And characteristically, it was built in eight months. He himself decided everything.

I remember, after he had shown me through "Whitehall," and I had congratulated him on its beauty, that he led me to a panel of Honduras mahogany that hung, picture-like, from the wall; a beautiful slab of wood, exquisite in color and marvelously grained. He turned to me and said: "I often look at this house that I built and had decorated by artists. Then I look at this panel. I am going to put on it: 'What God hath wrought.' "

But all this did not give me the insight into the man that I desired. The clues came later.

"Mr. Flagler, which do you enjoy more, planning work or doing it?"

"There isn't much fun in work if you don't accomplish something."

The second was: "Which do you consider the hardest thing you have done in Florida?"

"Building the Ponce de Leon. Here was St. Augustine, the oldest city in the United States. How to build a hotel to meet the requirements of nineteenth century America and have it in keeping with the character of the place—that was my hardest problem. The Alcazar I built because it was suggested to me that there were many nice people who might not be able to afford to pay the rates the Ponce de Leon would have to ask, and yet wished to enjoy St. Augustine. To provide accommodations for them we built the Alcazar as a two-dollar-a-day house. It is every bit as good as the Ponce de Leon."

After several interviews at Whitehall, LeFevre met Flagler again in St. Augustine and explored why Flagler had seemed to have changed his goals in middle life, from the rapacity of building Standard Oil to the philanthropy of building Florida. Said LeFevre:

On the night of the Ponce de Leon celebration in St. Augustine last spring, I met him in the courtyard of the hotel. He was standing by the fountain. The sky was like the inside of a huge, hollow turquoise—blue, luminous, thinly washed with silver. The moon was very bright, so near the earth that it seemed more neighborly than in the North. A mist as of vaporized moon-metal enveloped the buildings and made them unforgettably beautiful. The grounds were illuminated; you could have sworn the lights were captive fireflies. The palms resembled ghosts of women with disheveled hair. The fountain splashed droningly. You heard no other sound.

For perhaps five minutes he [Henry] stood there; at length he turned to me and murmured:

"This is beautiful! Beautiful!"

At that moment, in the midst of Flagler's reverie, an understanding came to LeFevre, washing over him like breaking waves.

I walked back twenty years, to the beginning of the second youth of Henry M. Flagler.

Past his half-century, Flagler, a clear-headed, calm-eyed man, found himself enormously rich. The profits of the oil business had been put back into the business. But the inevitable day came when there was no need for further investment. The money-making machine was not only perfect; it was permanent. The only concern of its engineers was now personal: What to do with the profits? His yearly income was in itself princely fortune—and growing princelier. Outside investments must be sought. John D. Rockefeller became the richest man in the world. Flagler says: "If it wasn't for Florida, I'd be quite a rich man today."

. . . In all his life he has never been in Europe, nor even in California. He told me once: "If ever the Lord made a man who hated traveling, I am that man!" But he had read books, he was fond of history. His thirst for information made him interested in beautiful and strange places, even though he preferred to imagine what they were like rather than to visit them. He had grown up with his own country. And in Ohio, where he lived from boyhood till middle age, he had seen about him only the new, the raw, the man-made things of today. Yet antiquity and the works of antiquity had for him a peculiar fascination. You must bear in mind also that there is a well-developed vein of sentiment in him. He himself probably is not aware of it; but he has it. Nor does it show inconsistency.

And so this man of fifty-five, so rich that his most serious problem was how to invest his income, this man who had read a great deal and *had never traveled*, went to St. Augustine. It was the oldest city in the United States. He saw the old slave market, he saw the old Spanish town; he saw the old city gates! He saw what you and I saw when we went to Pompeii or first gazed at the Pyramids! He saw palms—*palms!*—this man who had grown up in Ohio amid the wheat. St. Augustine was a magic pool, he steeped his soul in the glamour and romance of antiquity.

It was to him, logically enough, the most interesting place he had ever seen, the most unusual, the most un-American. Why didn't more people come to it? This Spanish city was three hundred years old; and the city of Cleveland, Ohio—why he was as old as Cleveland, almost.

The reason why more people didn't come to St. Augustine was that the hotel accommodations were not first class. Nobody would build hotels, because they might not pay. Flagler had more money than he knew what to do with. He decided to build a hotel. He thought it might pay, when people learned about St. Augustine. They might take a long time to learn. But what did that matter to a man with his millions?

And so, while it was business—for he felt sure of eventual success—it wasn't Standard Oil business. And it wasn't altogether play. It was the new point of view that made it seem like a whim to so many people at the time and that makes it still arouse suspicions among some. Remember he said: "My hardest problem was the Ponce de Leon: How to build a hotel *to meet the requirements of nineteenth-century America and yet be in keeping with the character of the place!*" He gave the commission to a firm of then unknown young architects—Carrere & Hastings. He set no limits to cost. It was built by day's labor—as a rich man might build his own house if he really were interested in a home. The best site for such a hotel was certain swamp. Maria Sanchez Creek ran through what is now the Alcazar. So even the ground was built by him that his scheme might go through in its artistic entirety.

With the building of the Ponce de Leon and the Alcazar, Flagler began to emancipate his mind from the thralldom of the Oil Trust, to awaken his dormant aesthetic sense and exercise it by erecting hotels and creating resorts. In doing so, Flagler had shifted from the center of his point of view—which had been making money. He now had time to look at the blue sky and the wonders of the earth and they began to hold meaning for him.

By transforming a streak of rust and right-of-way through a wilderness into an efficient railway; by developing sandy wastes, sparsely settled, into a productive country with a self-supporting population, Flagler had found a way not only to pacify his guilts but also to satisfy his dormant creative needs. He became interested in agricultural development. He saw great possibilities in orange growing. He decided to extend and improve his railroads—not gradually, as the profits justified, but at once, for he had the money and no need to wait for profits. So he had engineers survey a line for a railroad, and built into undeveloped jungle. And people came and planted orange trees.

In the worst frost on record, he promptly went to the scene in order to consider intelligently what to do. And there he saw for himself how people whom his railroad had induced to come here and invest money and devote time and labor to develop the country, had lost. He saw for himself human suffering, he met his fellow-men close enough to look into their eyes. He reverted to his first youth, to the time when he was very poor, before he was even a partner in a country store. It was then that his philosophy of life began to crystallize, slowly at first, more rapidly as he saw more and more of men. Work brought wealth. And wealth brought responsibility. Having great wealth, he decided there was but one thing to do: Extend his railroad still farther south, where orange growers would be less at the mercy of weather.

FLAGLER'S reaction to the frost, said LeFevre, was a major career turning point.

Logical, clear-sighted, immune from greed, and free from emotionalism, a six-days-a-week worker from his youth, realizing the value of opportunity to men, he now reached the conclusion that the best way to help others was to help them to help themselves. The desire to help he might long have had; it was intensified, made definite, but the sight of the distress caused by the blighting of the oranges.

That is why Flagler decided to push south; and *there* it was that he found the Magic Fountain of his Second Youth!

He built the Palm Beach hotel to get passenger traffic. He did not care so much for the tourists as for the fruit growers now. Therefore in Palm Beach he did not take the interest in the Royal Poinciana Hotel, architecturally, that he did in the Ponce de Leon. He gratified his love of beauty with the marvelous grounds, in the making of a garden spot.

And again the frost came. When orange trees were killed, perversely, in what up to that time had been a section safe from "freezes" somebody showed him a spray of lemon blossoms from near Miami. The lemon tree is even more delicate than the orange. So he carried his railroad to Miami. He built the town. He felt safe there. He would see a city below the frost belt. He laid it out, when he should have been thinking of the City Beautiful. But had he not found his Second Youth?

When Cuba became a republic, it was evident that under American influences it would develop fast. Friends tried to induce him to build a chain of Flagler hotels on the Island; but he declined. I myself think it was too much of a money-making scheme to move him. His views were more serious; if he worked at all, he would do a man's work; not merely a capitalist's. But he did think of extending the railroad to Key West. When it became certain that the United States would build the Panama Canal, he sent for his engineers. And the amazing railroad among the Keys followed.


LeFevre found Flagler unique among capitalists. It was not money which spurred him but building and creation.

I do not know whether I have succeeded in making clear what I mean by saying that in Florida Henry M. Flagler found his Second Youth and was able to do a work that only youth ever does. It is an amazing work, even in this land of rapid development. Where others have *helped*, he has *formed* growth. That it is a work of vast importance is obvious. That it is unique is due to the impossibility of finding a man of Flagler's mind and Flagler's wealth and Flagler's business experience, having the attitude of Flagler toward his fellow-men. To my mind his most remarkable exploit was the changing of his own point of view, of his attitude toward his fellow-men, so completely, at so advanced an age. You must admit that he has done as a man in his prime does. It is easy to give; it is not easy to give as Flagler has given—money and service. And if the magnitude of his accomplishment grows the more you ponder it, so does the man's character appear more remarkable the more you reflect. It is therefore not so difficult, after all, to visualize the man as he is today, at eighty years, *in the flower of his Second Youth.*

In the end, LeFevre was totally fascinated with Flagler.

LeFevre turned to the aged Flagler, who had done so much and had talked so little, and asked him impatiently:

"Doesn't this sky get into your soul? Doesn't that glow light it? Don't you love that water, that line of trees, that sky? Isn't *this* the real reason why you do things here?"

Flagler turned to him, hesitated, then, very slowly, very quietly, Henry said: "Sometimes, at the close of day, when I am fortunate enough to be alone, I come here." Henry faced Lake Worth and was silent. Then he spoke again: "I look at the water and at the trees yonder and at the sunset." He turned and placed his hand on LeFevre's shoulder. Then, earnestly, almost wistfully, he said: "I often wonder if there is anything in the other world so beautiful as this."

Slowly, LeFevre began his exit, turning occasionally to look at Flagler, "a tall, sturdy figure, snow crowned, looking at the lake over whose mid-day turquoise dusk had spread a silver rug—wrinkled in places, for the night winds had come.

"I did not say good-by to this man. The sun had said it for me."

LeFevre found Flagler to be unknowable. He found him to be modest, wise and unassuming. A man who with his unique energies provided life opportunities for thousands, ultimately millions of people. Yet, finally a man who kept a lonely secret, who, despite all his virtues, had in his seventy-ninth year, by choice, one friend in the world—Anderson in St. Augustine.

There are, however, other rewards on earth than friendship, and Flagler was about to enjoy one of them, called glory.

# CHAPTER 20

# Paid

"I don't know of anyone who has been successful, but
that he has been compelled to pay some price for success.
Some get it at the loss of their health; others forego the
pleasures of home and spend their years in the forests
or mines; some acquire success at the loss of their
reputation; others at loss of character, and so it goes.
Many prices are paid."
—HENRY FLAGLER

FLAGLER's health was fading rapidly.
By the fall of 1911, the Key West Extension was nearing
completion. The major bridge projects were opened or in the
final stages of construction, and other sections of the line were being
finished or strengthened. Project director William Krome kept an
account book showing what phases of work up and down the line
were ahead of or behind schedule. Engineers became increasingly
aware of the deadline of January 1, 1912. FEC aide James Parrott
hoped to let Flagler ride into Key West on his eighty-second birthday,
which fell on January 2, 1912.

Rumors were circulating in Key West that Flagler would ask the
engineers to resign if the line were not completed by the first of
January. Although the rumors were untrue, the work force was doubled in less than a month. It was not too difficult since wages were
higher and most of the dangerous work was already done.

The last track was laid by the deadline, but it was decided to officially open the extension on the 22nd, thus allowing the crews time
to strengthen the trestle work and get the line in the best possible
shape.

Early in the morning of the 21st, Henry and Mary Lily left Whitehall and boarded their private car for the trip to Key West, a journey

of more than 250 miles. Elsewhere in Florida, other special trains began their journey en route to Key West.

At 10:43 A.M., January 22, the first New York to Key West train arrived with the Flaglers aboard. After this came a "super" train, including 13 Pullman cars of American and foreign officials, including Assistant Secretary of War Robert Shaw Oliver, who represented President Taft. An astounding seven more trains arrived during the day bringing foreign diplomats, military officers and other guests. Governor Albert Gilchrist of Florida arrived on one of the later trains. Park Trammell and J. W. Watson, candidates for Florida governor, were also in town to make speeches. Representatives of the embassies and legations of Italy, Mexico, Portugal, Costa Rica, Ecuador, Guatemala, San Salvador and Uruguay were present.

The Fifth Atlantic Fleet was in port, with the cruisers *Washington*, *North Carolina*, *Birmingham* and *Salem* making rendezvous at Key West. Key West guardsmen, Navy militia men and a U.S. Coast Guard company were also on hand.

When Flagler stepped from the train he was greeted by Key West Mayor F. N. Fogarty and handed a solid gold facsimile of the Western Union telegram inscribed with congratulations from every employee of the FEC.

One thousand children and 10,000 other citizens greeted Flagler's train, the Extension Special. For many Key Westers it was the first train they had ever seen. Henry was welcomed with the roar of bursting bombs, shrieks of whistles and marching bands. Old and feeble but cheerful, Flagler made a brief speech including the remarks, "Now I can die happy. My dream is fulfilled."

Without false modesty, he reminded the crowd of his accomplishments:

On the first day of December 1885, we commenced the digging of the excavation for the foundation of the Hotel Ponce de Leon in St. Augustine. At that time St. Augustine had a population of from 1,500 to 2,000 persons. There were but 12 houses on the line of the railroad between Jacksonville and St. Augustine. There was no house, no habitation, between St. Augustine and what is now East Palatka . . . Ormond may have had 150 inhabitants, Daytona 150 . . . Rockledge existed, practically only existed . . .

The 66 miles intervening between Palm Beach and Miami was practically an unbroken wilderness. I traveled over it riding behind a mule and a cart, fortunately that had lumber springs under the seat. Palm Beach had three houses, two families living in two of them and an old bachelor in the third house. Coconut Grove perhaps had three or four houses—nothing south of that. Today there is a very large population and that whole country is filled with an industrious, prosperous people, and thousands of comfortable homes exist where desolation existed only 25 years ago.

Now, I do not believe that I am indulging in fanciful ideas when I say that in ten years the city of Key West will have a population of 50,000 people, and I am going to try to live that ten years.[1]

After that speech, Henry was escorted to a platform to be serenaded by a group of school children who scattered roses before him. In this moment of triumph, tears welled from the old man's eyes. "I can hear the children," he said sadly, "but I cannot see them." He was nearly blind.

GOVERNMENT officials and military brass took turns trying to outdo each other in praising Flagler and his great accomplishment. The three days and nights of frantic celebration that followed included receptions, banquets, dances, concerts, boat rides, inspection tours and fireworks. A Cuban circus performed as did a Spanish opera company. There were also baseball games, parades, motion picture shows, an aviation demonstration and a carnival.

Streets were decorated in American flags and bunting. Homes were arranged with palm and coconut fronds hanging on the veranda. Everyone was in a festive mood and quite optimistic about the future of their city. They had spent much money for the celebration, but expected to be rewarded for their efforts by new businesses and a general economic boom brought about by Henry and his railroad.

ON THE 24th of January, Flagler returned by train to Whitehall where he enjoyed the traditional afternoon of sports by the staffs of the hotels. There were sack races, three-legged races, potato races and other games which kept the grandstand in continual laughter.

Three days later he wrote to James Parrott in St. Augustine:

The last few days have been full of happiness to me, made so by the expressions of appreciation of the people for the work I have done in Florida. A large part of this happiness is due to the gift of the employees of the Florida East Coast Railway. Their loyalty and devotion is evidenced by the beautiful gift they sent me, and for which I beg you will express to them my most sincere thanks. I greatly regret that I cannot do it to each one in person.

The work I have been doing for many years has been largely prompted by a desire to help my fellow men, and I hope you will let every employee of the Company know that I thank him for the gift, the spirit that prompted it, and for the sentiment therein expressed.[2]

Henry was frail, but he carried on as ever, showing attentions to his wife with an anniversary gift and a note saying, "To my darling wife in loving remembrance of the day you became my wife and the many happy days you have given to me since our marriage. May the dear Lord reward you for what you have done for me." With characteristic formality, he signed it, as he always did, *HM Flagler*, as if she might have forgotten who he was.

The summer of 1912, as all the summers since 1881, was spent in part at Satan's Toe. He still went to the office.

Recalled his secretary, Warren Smith:

Mr. Flagler used to come to the office several times a week while living at Mamaroneck, being met at Grand Central by Waddy Thompson, and conducted through the subway maze to Wall Street Station, and so on into the building. One day the 26 Broadway elevators failed, and we had been telephoned word that Mr. Flagler was walking up. This, at his high age. We tried to stop him, even sent a chair to one of the landings, where he could rest, but he persisted in coming the rest of the way immediately by foot, and arrived none the worse for wear apparently, at our 18th floor office!

In this period, despite LeFevre's remark that Flagler didn't engage in homilies and axioms, we find him giving amazingly clichéd lectures on how the younger generation might succeed in business. He recommended thrift, stoicism and self-denial, characteristics which hadn't been particularly noticeable in the young Henry Flagler of Ohio—he who danced on hotel tables, ran up beer tabs, bought his way out of the Civil War draft and indulged himself in fast horses and good times.

Nevertheless, he freely gave his advice to young men in a series of newspaper interviews. A typical excerpt:

There are hundreds of thousands of young men all the time but only a few of them ever come to great success. Why is it? I have been given many answers. But who supports all the saloons in this country? Certainly not the rich. And the theaters? Not the wealthy, but the men who get from $500 to $5,000 a year. It is improvidence that stands in the way of the average American.

I hesitate to say it, but I recollect when I wore a thin overcoat and thought how comfortable I should be when I could afford a long, thick Ulster. I carried a lunch in my pocket until I was a rich man. I trained myself in the school of self-control and self-denial. It was hard on Flagler, but I would rather be my own tyrant than have some one else tyranize me.

For these last summers, when Henry and Mary Lily weren't at Mamaroneck, they would be at the Hotel Mount Washington in Bretton Woods, New Hampshire.

"There were but two trains a day in and out of Bretton Woods," recalled his secretary Warren Smith, "which also brought the mail. Mr. Flagler waited for each and was very active in handling all reaching him.

"Mr. Flagler carried on his person a little black book, recording various donations made. . . . The calls upon him [for donations] were tremendous and he gave me the mention of being able to handle them, without making them feel offended . . ."

Flagler was inconsistent in how he reacted to charities and people in need. For example, when informed of a problem at the Memorial Church in St. Augustine, he immediately wrote to contractor John McGuire:

"Dr. Anderson tells me that the gutters of the Memorial Church are leaking badly; that the roof needs some repairs, and that the ball on the cross looks as though the soldered joint had opened. I wish you would make these repairs at the earliest moment possible and send the bill to me. . . ."[3]

At nearly the same time in early 1910, he investigated then rejected a request for help from the widow of a retired FEC employee. In a series of letters to McGuire, he advised that he had paid $236 in funeral costs for the dead retiree but declined any further assistance to the widow:

. . . I feel that I have done now all I ought to do for her, and as she has two sons and a daughter living at the North, it seems to me they ought to provide for her house rent and living expenses if she wants to stay in St. Augustine, or else she could go North and live with them. . . .

. . . You may give Mrs. Ackerman her house rent until the first of May, and this letter of the daughter will put you in a better position to talk with

Mrs. Ackerman about her going North. . . . You may continue the pension formerly paid Alec Ackerman to his wife until May 1st.[4]

His birthdays and Christmases continued to be the biggest holidays of his year and, recalled secretary Smith, "on such occasions he received hundreds of congratulatory messages from the United States and abroad—each of which he insisted he personally acknowledge. He was frequently heard to remark, 'most of my friends are Catholics and I'm a Protestant . . . Most of my associates are Democrats, and here I am a Republican. . . .' "

Henry was growing frailer, and several months after the Key West celebration he informed Beardsley:

"To relieve myself of writing by my own hand as much as possible, I have today given Warren E. Smith verbal instructions to sign any checks coming from this office over my signature, with his last initial attached, and this will be your authority for recognizing and making payment account such drafts when they are presented."[5]

JANUARY 2, 1913, was Henry's last birthday, and it was his final season at Whitehall. Normally, to avoid the heat and mosquito season of Palm Beach, he and Mary Lily would stay until a week or so after Washington's Birthday, February 22, then move up by train to the cooler climate of St. Augustine, where they'd stay until mid-May. They'd then go farther north, by train or yacht, to Mamaroneck.

In the winter of 1913, however, perhaps because of Henry's increasing frailty or perhaps because of cooler weather, they prolonged their stay at Whitehall.

They had closed most of the house and sent the staff away. During the daytime Henry used a large downstairs bathroom reserved for male members of the household and visitors. The bathroom was appointed with the latest in design, including doors equipped with pneumatic devices that closed them automatically. The room also had a narrow marble threshold with a short but steep flight of marble steps leading down to the large restroom with its urinals and stalls. If the automatic closing device was set with too much force, and if one paused a moment on the narrow threshold, the door closed with sufficient speed and strength to give one a sharp shove down the stairs and onto the hard, tiled floor.

Those doors may have been the cause of Henry Flagler's death.[6]

On March 15, 1913, he was found sprawled headlong at the bottom of those stairs. Presumably he had entered the bathroom, paused at the top of the stairs and then been shoved by the automatically closing doors. He was unconscious and, because he, Mary Lily and a few servants were the only people in the house, he had been on the floor for several hours before he was found.

He had a broken hip and other complications.

"When Mr. Flagler fell," said Warren Smith, one of the staff still present,

Dr. Owen Kenan was on the spot, in charge at Whitehall. Fortunately, guesting at the [nearby Royal Poinciana] hotel, was a Dr. Newton Shaffer, orthopedic surgeon from New York, who was consulted. Mr. Flagler was ordered to bed with sandbag reinforcement. He even tried to get out of this. As the weather grew hotter, and the hotels closed, Mr. Flagler was transferred to a company beach cottage. In fact our own staff plus Dr. Ward and the Bemis family were likewise accommodated at the Beach.

To care for Flagler, several merchants agreed to remain on the island despite the closing of the season. These included Western Union manager William W. Scott, and the owner of the drug store, Dr. George Merriam. "But," said Smith, "Mr. Flagler, with two male nurses in attendance, was growing weaker and Mrs. Flagler telegraphed Harry Harkness, his son, to come down, which he and his wife did, and rooms were opened up for them at The Breakers."

HARRY HARKNESS FLAGLER hadn't seen his father since his own wedding in 1894. He had never been to Whitehall. He had never met Mary Lily.

After an absence of nearly 20 years, he recalled that he was quivering with emotion, but determined to do something for his father.

"He had been moved to a cottage on the oceanfront belonging to the hotel. This was because of the extreme heat. When I heard of his critical condition, I telegraphed offering to go to him if he wanted me. I was not allowed to do so while there was a chance of his recognizing me. He was kept constantly under drugs and was practically in a coma the three or four days after my arrival until his death."

At no time during the several visits of Harry Harkness did Flagler indicate he recognized his only son and his only surviving offspring.[7]

Mary Lily stayed at Henry's bedside for the last three or four nights, despite the entreaties of Owen. Owen wanted a nurse, but Mary Lily refused.

Flagler's secretary Smith said the old man was so heavily doped he was out of his mind:

"I happened to be on the porch of the Flagler cottage when I heard Mr. Flagler call for me, from his nearby bedroom. He said, *'Send in my boy Martin.'* He always called me that, because of his difficulty in hearing. *'I want to give him $35,000—same as Dr. Ward.'* The attendants just laughed at that and said, 'He's packed with Hyoscine and out of his mind.' "

WHEN word got out that Flagler was gravely ill, financial speculators did everything possible to discover his condition, including bribes to telephone and telegraph officials to intercept information. To counter this, Flagler's lieutenants used a code to communicate with Standard Oil headquarters in New York. The last message sent said *Suspenders Orton Holoow Scranton Says Pansy.* Translated: *HMF condition critical. He is sinking fast. Dr. Casselberry says cannot live more than tonight.*

Flagler died the next morning, at 10 A.M., May 20, 1913.

AS HE HAD requested, Henry was buried in St. Augustine, at the Memorial Church, in a sheltered tomb beside his first wife, Mary Harkness Flagler, and their daughter, Jennie Louise Flagler Benedict, and Jennie's baby.

The services were conducted, and the eulogy was given, by his friend, the Reverend George Ward, who said that Henry, ever the fighter, went unwillingly to his grave.

When he lay stricken down by that cruel fall, he asked one day, "Doctor, do you think that was just fair of God? I was old and blind and deaf, was it fair to make me lame?" And later—"Was this a part of a plan to make me see my helplessness?" But, thank God, the day came when he thrust his hand in mine and said, "Doctor, I do not want to go, but I can say, and honestly, I am ready to do His will."

. . . it broke me down, for to yield a will like that was the supreme sacrifice . . .

I often wonder what Eternity must mean to him . . .

Flagler died with one piece of work undone—a railroad around Lake Okeechobee. A Flagler biographer, Walter Martin, regarded it as "the most important of all the branch lines of the Florida East Coast Railway."[8]

The line was known as the Okeechobee Division and was begun in 1911, only two years before Flagler's death. By the time it was finished, in 1915, it serviced one of the richest agricultural sections in the nation, the Florida Everglades.

The last conversation Flagler had with his longtime aide, Ingraham, did not concern their many accomplishments together, but the progress of the Okeechobee line. Said Ingraham:

The last time I saw him, stretched out on his bed of suffering at Palm Beach, before his death, I had just returned from a trip to Okeechobee . . . He asked me to tell him about it, and I showed him some pictures and he gave me his last words on this subject, which were: "I hope you will succeed. I am sorry I have not been there. I wish I could go, I hope to go, but I am afraid I will never see that great lake and that great country."

He then put his hand on mine and said: "When were you at Miami?" I said: "I was there yesterday and the day before, came up from there this evening." He said: "Well, what about it, what are they doing?" I told him some things that were going on, and I told him that it was truly a magic city.

He said: "No, it is not a magic city. It is a city of eternal youth. Those men and women there are like boys and girls. They have never been hurt and they know no fear."[9]

THERE was no eulogy from Flagler's old partner and friend, John D. Rockefeller. Simply a few clichés spoken by Rockefeller to the press. Nor did Rockefeller attend the funeral.

DESPITE Flagler's massive celebrity, he died an unknown man. He had an almost excessive modesty and a personality so elusive as to be unseizable. His sole intimates were his wives; the friend of his boyhood, Dan Harkness; and the friend of his manhood, Andrew Anderson. The friends of his youth, the relatives, the business associates, the men who headed his forces down the coast of Florida did not know him. They knew some of him, but no one knew all of him.

He left many memorials, but the truest of them is long gone. It is this:

ONCE the Key West rails were laid, he liked to ride the line below Miami, ride in the engineer's cab and pull the cord and whistle his way through the keys.

In the days of the steam locomotive, many an engineer had his own way of sounding his whistle. Folks living along the railroad could tell the name of the engineer the moment he came within hearing distance. Some could make it sound off like a steam calliope in a circus parade.

Regulations banned unnecessary locomotive whistling on the mainland. But all restrictions seemed to end once a train, especially a freight, passed south of Jewfish Draw. If there were rules, no one on the keys was mean enough to tell Henry Flagler to enforce them; so the boys often broke loose. When Uncle Henry asked the engineer to play "Long Caleb McGee" or "Old Dan Tucker," he played it. And when Henry was in the cab, he played it for himself. It was loud and strong yet sweet and he could hear it well.

They kept playing the songs for 20 years after Henry was dead. They played until the steam locomotives themselves were no more.

# EPILOGUE

AFTER Flagler's death, Mary Lily alternated her residences between Whitehall, her permanent suite at the Plaza Hotel in New York and the home of the Pembroke Joneses in Newport. Sometime in 1915 or 1916 she was contacted by an old beau, Robert Worth Bingham, who was then practicing law in Louisville, Kentucky. They were married in November 1916, but Mary Lily lived only eight more months, dying of an apparent heart attack while in their Louisville home.

Bingham inherited $5 million, some of which he used to buy a string of daily newspapers, which were consolidated into the present Louisville *Courier-Journal*. The remainder of Mary Lily's estate, worth more than $100 million in 1917 dollars, went to her brother and sisters and to a favored neice, Louise Clisby Wise.

Miss Wise also inherited Whitehall and Kirkside. She preferred Kirkside and St. Augustine to Palm Beach and consequently Whitehall was left vacant for seven years. She sold it, and in 1926 ten storeys were added behind it, and the proud mansion became a luxury hotel. It remained as such until 1959, when Mrs. Jean Flagler Matthews (1910–1979) purchased the property.

Mrs. Matthews, daughter of Henry Flagler and one of Henry Flagler's three surviving granddaughters, said that

. . . during my years of growing up, rarely was the name of Henry Morrison Flagler mentioned. I knew from my sister that there had been an estrangement between father and grandfather, but not until I rented a house in Miami Beach did I begin to know of grandfather's accomplishments. That was in 1938–1939. In 1940, when I came to Palm Beach, many questions were asked, so I scurried around to the libraries in order to have some idea of his many accomplishments. The more I learned, the more I gazed at Whitehall and started the mind thinking about what should be done. One day, while mulling on the problem, I heard that a spa was going to open at Whitehall, and that the Marble Hall would be used for dressing room cubicles—that did it. The next morning I attended a board meeting . . . and during the Treasurer's Report, leaned over to my then lawyer and said, "I want to acquire Whitehall as a memorial to grandfather." He looked at me as if I were crazy. . . . It all happened in the nick of time, as hammer and chisel were about to be lowered.

Whitehall opened as a museum, with an appropriate Restoration Ball on February 6, 1960.

FLAGLER'S Key West railroad died in one terror-filled night in 1935. On September 2, Labor Day, while people watched with sickening apprehension, winds rose and barometers plunged to 26.35 inches—the lowest sea-level reading ever recorded in the Western Hemisphere.

At 8:20 that evening a rescue team—11 cars hastily sent from Miami and already loaded with refugees—reached Islamorada, on Upper Matecumbe Key. Winds by then screamed at nearly 200 miles an hour. The engineer, backing up to avoid a time-consuming turn-around, was blinded by waves surging across the track. At first he missed the little station where hundreds more waited.

He pulled forward and people struggled toward the cars. Then a monstrous wave—survivors estimated it at 20 feet high—smashed in from the sea, engulfing the fleeing islanders and sweeping the cars from the track.

Next morning, the Keys began counting their dead. Roughly half the bodies found were those of construction workers, victims of the Great Depression who were helping to build a highway parallel to the railway. Some 41 miles of the railroad had been smashed into a jumble of twisted rails and washed-out roadbed, drowning hundreds of World War I veterans who had gone down to pick up Depression wages of $30 a month working on the federal highway.

As a railroad, Flagler's dream was dead.

In another form, however, it lived on. Florida persisted with its highway, using Flagler's roadbed much of the way. The railroad's viaducts, bridges and roadbed were used as the foundation of the overseas highway. In 1938, the last broken link was closed and U.S. 1 was at long last open from Maine to Key West.

As for the main business, the Flagler System of hotels and railroads, Flagler named James Parrott of Oxford, Maine, as his successor president under his will, but Parrott took office prior to Flagler's passing. However, Parrott died in Maine five months after Flagler;

and William Beardsley was elected to the office. The companies prospered under him.

The Florida East Coast Railway, when finally completed, consisted of 764 miles of track. Flagler tied up a large portion of his fortune in the railroad, advancing the funds throughout the period of construction. It was estimated that he spent upwards of $35 million on the building of his railroad alone. The hotels and mansions were extra.

Flagler didn't even attempt outside financing until 1909, when he borrowed $12 million because of the immense cost of building the Key West Extension. With a first mortgage on the railroad line being posted as collateral, bonds were sold to brokers in the North and East.

During Flagler's lifetime, the road was still in the stage of promotion and construction. The value of the properties rose from $5.5 million in 1894 to $15 million in 1914, though the gross revenues rose very slowly. The year of Flagler's death the railroads collected about $5 million. The total net profit from 1892 to 1914 was a mere $9,531.

Flagler said he didn't expect to make a dollar off his railroad and he came very close to that prophecy.

Following Mary Lily's death, Will Kenan and his two sisters owned the Florida East Coast Railway until it went bankrupt during the Depression. Ed Ball, a bit of a robber baron himself and in command of the Alfred I. duPont estate, slowly bought the railroad's bonds until he had acquired a controlling interest—purchasing $26 million worth of bonds for less than $4 million.

Despite the loss of the FEC, however, the Kenans did not go broke. Will Kenan died in 1965, leaving an estate which included a $160 million bequest for an educational trust. The two sisters died shortly afterwards, leaving estates of $160 million each.

BESIDES the Florida East Coast Hotel Company, the Florida East Coast Railway Company and the Model Land Company, the Flagler System also included the Miami Electric Light Company, the West Palm Beach Water Company, various smaller land companies and later the Florida East Coast Car Ferry Company. Flagler also purchased controlling interests in various Florida newspapers during his lifetime, including the Miami *Herald*, the St. Augustine *Record*, the

Miami *News*, the Palm Beach *Daily News* and the (Jacksonville) Florida *Times-Union*.

DEVELOPMENT of the cactus-scarred snakepit called Miami Beach was begun a year before Flagler's death by millionaire Carl Fisher. The sale of Fisher's auto headlight business—Prest-O-Lite Corporation of America—had left Fisher with $5.6 million to play with, and he decided Miami Beach would be his sandbox.

Fisher loaned $50,000 at 8 percent interest plus a "bonus" of 150 acres to an 81-year-old Quaker farmer, John Collins, to complete a bridge linking Miami Beach with the mainland. Fisher also bought an additional 60 acres from the brothers J. N. and J. E. Lummus, who both headed local banks. Fisher agreed to build streets and sidewalks and fill the mangrove swamps by dredging sand from the bottom of Biscayne Bay.

While the Lummuses would sell land only to people who were "white and law abiding," Fisher aimed for an even more exclusive crowd. He wanted other newly rich industrial magnates, shunned by Palm Beach's upper crust, to vacation in Miami Beach. Several of them did, including Harvey Firestone and Alfred duPont.

Fisher may have been more particular than the Lummuses, but they all had the same aim—to sell land. Even Fisher's incredible Flamingo Hotel—with its private docks, bathhouses, broker's office and fluffy extras (40 milk-producing Guernsey cows, gondolas steered by Bahamians wearing brass earrings)—was simply a tool to lure prospective land buyers.

Until 1920 the lots sold slowly. But by 1924, first Miami and then the rest of the state experienced an unprecedented explosion in land values, which firmly established Miami Beach.

HARRY HARKNESS FLAGLER, having finally graduated from Columbia at age 26 in 1897, blossomed following Flagler's death and became one of the most important figures in the New York musical world of the twentieth century. He was president of the Symphony Society of New York and the Philharmonic-Symphony Society. He was successively the principal financial supporter of the orchestra of each organization.

Owen Kenan, Flagler's doctor and Mary Lily's cousin, said that Harry Harkness Flagler was the nicest gentleman he had ever met.

"Harry Harkness never saw Mary Lily or Flagler during the 13 years of the marriage. Instead of having a knockdown fight, Harry kept them inside."

After Henry Flagler's death, Owen used to see Harry in Flagler's office, a place he had never dared to venture during the last 20 years of Flagler's life.

In a lengthy and laudatory obituary, the *New York Times*, on July 1, 1952, said of Harry:

. . . although those who knew Mr. Flagler well found him possessed of evident business capacity, he never engaged in business and kept aloof from the affairs of the Standard Oil Company. Nor did he show interest in the large . . . holdings . . . of his father in Florida. His temperament was artistic and as early as 1903 he became secretary of the Permanent Fund Orchestra, which planned the development of the Philharmonic Society.

Having reorganized the Symphony Society of New York and its orchestra, Mr. Flagler served as its president from 1914 to 1928 and made himself responsible for its entire financial backing. After its merger with the Philharmonic Society, he became president of the new group and continued to see that money was provided to keep the organization alive and up to its high musical standard. During the depression years, he made possible the very existence of the New York Philharmonic Symphony Orchestra.

Harry's wife, Anne Lamont, died in 1939 at their home in Millbrook, New York. Harry died June 30, 1952, of a heart attack at age 81.

He and Anne were survived by three daughters: Mrs. Melbert B. Cary of New York City; Mrs. Flagler Harris of Philadelphia; and Mrs. Flagler Matthews of Rye, New York.

WITHIN a few years of his death, Henry Flagler was largely forgotten by history. Rockefeller—who had exceptionally talented sons and grandsons, highly publicized and effective philanthropies and who lived 24 years longer than Flagler—became synonymous with Standard Oil. In the many histories and biographies written on Rockefeller and the great Standard Oil machine, Flagler has been given only a few sentences, if that.

Flagler's even greater contribution, the development of the state of Florida, has also been overlooked. No one in American history, with the possible exception of Brigham Young, has been so singly responsible for the creation of a state. Yet the Flagler name is unknown outside of Florida, and inside the state his contributions are mentioned in a few paragraphs here and there in textbooks and other histories. He is mostly identified as the founder of Palm Beach.

In the 73 years since his death, this is but the second biography written on Flagler. The other is Walter Martin's *Florida's Flagler*, published by the University of Georgia in 1949 and long out of print.

In his lifetime, and in the few years that followed, Flagler's contemporaries, his friends and working partners gave him ample recognition for his contributions. Rockefeller, for example, was quick to give Flagler credit for creating Standard Oil. Men like James Ingraham were almost in awe of what he had accomplished.

In an address given in 1920 in Miami, when Miamians still knew what Flagler had done for them, Ingraham noted that Flagler's reaction to the great freeze of 1895 had restored confidence in the state.

Because other people, other territories, other banks, other corporations had realized that if Mr. Flagler had faith in Florida that it would pay them to have faith, too, and carry on the works in their territories, and they did, and the freeze instead of being, as we first thought, a great disaster, ruining the principal industry of the state, brought about an expansion of the very great amount of resources in the State, the rehabilitation of some, building up of others, to such an extent that Florida was stronger after the freezes by far than before.

The effect of the loans to the people to enable them to carry on again was marvelous. It gave them courage, it kept them from drifting away. That it was needed I assure you was absolutely true. I saw some of the direst suffering that Mr. Flagler's money relieved, which I could not have believed possible had I not seen it, and much of the welfare of this county, in fact the backbone of this county, lay in the strength of the men and women who stuck to their work, went on with their plantings and brought about a renewed condition of confidence in this territory.

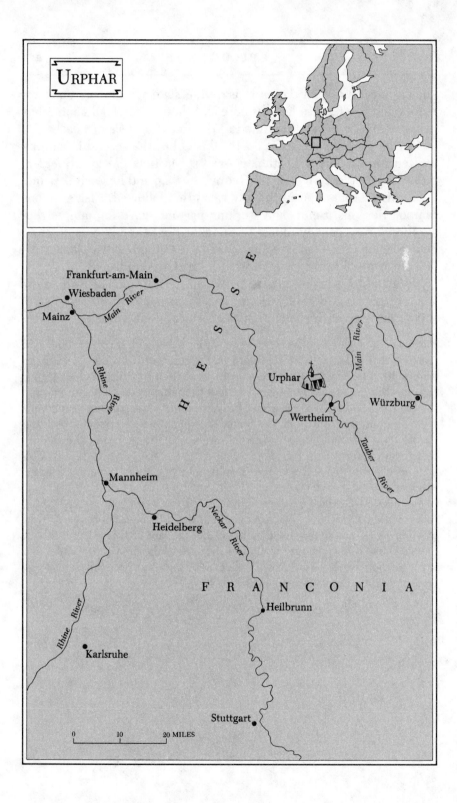

URPHAR

Frankfurt-am-Main
Wiesbaden
Mainz

Main River

Rhine River

HESSE

Urphar

Wertheim

Würzburg

Main River

Tauber River

Mannheim

Heidelberg

Neckar River

Rhine River

FRANCONIA

Heilbrunn

Karlsruhe

Stuttgart

0     10     20 MILES

# APPENDIX A

# The Immigrants

An immense slide of humanity washed along the shores
of England.
—CONRAD WEISER, linguist

T HE story of Henry Flagler begins hundreds of years earlier
and involves one of the great untold sagas in American history—the immigration of the Palatine Germans. The Palatines
represented a mixture of faiths, some Roman Catholics and many
more Lutherans and Calvinists. Hard-working and inventive, the Palatines would add strength, power and resilience to a young America.

Henry's ancestors have been traced back to the early fifteenth
century in Franconia, a province in southwest Germany. The family
name, in its original form of Flegler, was found in the town records
of Urphar, a hamlet near the meeting of the Tauber and Main rivers
whose merged waters flow westward to the Rhine. This village, just
north of the legend-haunted forest called Oden Wald and 40 miles
southeast of the city of Frankfort, seems to be the first home of the
Fleglers.[1]

The name Flegler seems to have arisen from some local hostilities
known as the *Flegler-Krieg*, or Flegler War. One of the leaders, a
certain Count Gunther, specialized in recruiting "husky and unmarried youths of stainless character," usually illiterate but enthusiastic
farmhands who gladly gave up their dawn-to-dusk labors for a chance
to pillage their neighbors. Ordered to bring their own weapons, the
farmhands grabbed the first thing at hand—a threshing tool called a
flail, or *flegel* in German, which quickly proved to be a deadly weapon
in close-range combat.

Many of Count Gunther's flailers were listed on his payrolls simply
as "Wilhelm, flegler," just as might be listed "Johann, cook," or
"Heinrich, carpenter." When the war was over, the various Fleglers,

Cooks and Carpenters took the names home with them, and Flegler became a surname.

As far as is presently known, Johann Flegler was the first direct ancestor of Henry Morrison Flagler. A harried and beleaguered revolutionary, Johann arrived in Urphar in 1526 as a refugee of the Peasant's War, a predictably bloody and unsuccessful revolt of the poorer classes against their betters. Obtaining protection from the local count, Johann married an Urphar girl and the line that eventually produced Henry Flagler began.[2]

Urphar and the surrounding area was known as the Palatinate, derived from "count palatine," a title used in the Roman, Byzantine and Holy Roman empires. In feudal hierarchy, a count palatine was something higher than a duke and less than a king. Thus, by naming real estate after a ruler's title, a palatinate was similar to a duchy or a kingdom.[3]

Situated between France and Germany, the Palatinate of the Rhine, the Flegler palatinate, was the highway of armies and the frequent field of battle. During the centuries, every great city of the Palatinate of the Rhine above Cologne was taken and sacked at least once.

The worst of the terrors came after 1688 when Louis XIV, the self-styled Sun King, ordered the devastation of the Palatinate. Thus began the War of the Palatinate which was to last 24 years, until 1712. Throughout those years, time and again, Louis' Catholic armies swept through the Protestant Palatinate, leaving death, ruin and despair in their wake.

The historian Thomas Macaulay reports that half a million people were uprooted by Louis' army. "Soon the roads and fields which then lay deep in snow were blackened by innumerable men, women, and children flying from their homes. Many died of cold and hunger, but enough survived to fill the streets of all the cities of Europe with lean and squalid beggars, who had once been thriving farmers and shop-keepers."[4]

Caught up in this general devastation was a carpenter named Zacharra Flegler, a direct descendant of Johann. Born in Urphar on October 7, 1676, Zacharra was christened the following day in Jacob's Church. From 1694 to 1700 he served in the Palatine army, doing garrison duties in various military posts.[5] At one post he met and married a girl whose name hasn't been found by historians. But the records do show they had a son, Philip Solomon Flegler, who was baptized in Jacob's Church on August 8, 1701. In 1705, a second son, Simon, was born.[6]

Sometime around 1706, Zacharra and his family, like thousands of other Palatine Germans, left their home with scant belongings. Usually traveling by night, they moved north down the Rhine to its mouth at the North Sea, the "German Ocean." From there they crossed by land to Holland, seeking temporary asylum in Rotterdam before moving on to the friendly shores of England.[7] Zacharra spent three years with his family in the suburbs of London, working as a carpenter with other Germans. In 1708, a daughter was born. Her name is unrecorded.

Few people have been the object of such kindly treatment and lavish generosity as were the first few thousand Palatines who arrived in London. But as the numbers swelled, eventually reaching 30,000, the city's charity began to pop at the seams. Conrad Weiser, then a 13-year-old Palatine refugee who would become one of America's greatest Indian linguists, described the scene as a "mass of humanity swept up onto the shores of England." A thousand army tents gave shelter to great numbers. Fourteen hundred other Palatines were lodged for months in warehouses along the Thames. Many occupied barns or empty dwellings. Often 20 to 30 men, women and children were housed in one small room. The English ruler, Queen Anne, gave of her own purse and issued calls throughout the kingdom for alms.[8]

As a group, the Palatines had no definite plan for ultimate relocation. However, Columbus' discovery of America had started the great European land hunt, and many thought the North American colonies might prove to be the land of promise. The first group of Palatines left in the spring and summer of 1709 to settle in Virginia and the Carolinas. The trip across the Atlantic took five to eight weeks and was made in ships devoid of all comfort. The bulk of the Palatines remained in London, waiting for a destination and scrounging for food and coal during the summer and fall in preparation for the winter. Among them was Zacharra Flegler and his family.

In September 1709, there arrived in England a delegation from the Province of New York, headed by Peter Schuyler, the mayor of Albany. Schuyler formally petitioned to the British Lords of Trade and Plantations that some Palatines be sent to New York. It would be good for the Germans, he said, and good for the English colonies, which desperately needed population.[9]

The Germans were needed because English colonists were discouraged by the cold winters of North America, being accustomed to the mild climate of Great Britain, whose islands are warmed by the North Atlantic Drift.[10] However, the warmth of England doesn't reach far across the channel. And the Germans of the Palatinate were accustomed to the exact kind of miserable winters which prevailed in North America.

Schuyler argued "that they be sent to settle upon Hudson's River in the Province of New York, where they may be useful to this kingdom particularly in the production of naval stores and as a frontier against the French and their Indians . . ."[11]

The idea of producing naval stores was particularly appealing to the Lords of Trade.

England was fast becoming the undisputed mistress of the seas, and thus needed a reliable source to supply her ships with masts and timber as well as tar, pitch, rosin, hemp and iron. A Swedish monopoly largely controlled the market of naval stores and had driven prices up to the point where the British government was forced to look elsewhere for supplies.

It was thought that the forests of New York might provide an answer—and here was Schuyler volunteering the Palatines to cut the wood. In this effort, Schuyler was joined by Robert Hunter, the newly appointed "Captain General and Governor in Chief of the Provinces of New York and New Jersey" and adjacent territories.

An ambitious and self-educated Scot of humble parentage, Hunter agreed to lead a contingent of 3,000 Palatines to New York, where, he said, would be found "great numbers of Pines fit for production of turpentine and tar, out of which rozin and pitch are made."[12] For the Palatines' passage, the Lords of Trade and Plantations allocated five pounds, ten shillings a head (about $125 in 1986 American dollars). In return, the Palatines were required by written contract to settle on certain lands in the colonies, where they were to reside until profits from the venture fully reimbursed the queen and the government. Following such compensation, each household would be granted the use of 40 acres, free of taxes, rents or other charges, for seven years.

Between December 25 and December 29, 1709, Zacharra Flegler, his family and the other New York-bound Palatines boarded 10 merchant ships moored at St. Katherine's Docks, just east of the Tower of London on the Thames.[13] The ships, each filled to capacity, were ordered to be at the "buoy of the Nore," 50 miles seaward from London, on or before January 2, 1710.[14] From there, as weather permitted, this fleet would sail to New York. The ships were to be accompanied by a navy escort for protection against French warships, privateers and marauding pirates.

The government had done its job, but after the rendezvous, the ships' captains and owners delayed sailing for four months. Holding the Palatines hostage on the crowded ship, the masters demanded a "foul weather" shipping bonus. During this time the ships rode at anchor along the southern coast of England, within sight of land at Cornwall, and the Palatines aboard were subjected to appalling miseries. They were confined to spaces that had been designed only for freight and baggage. Many could neither breathe fresh air nor see the light of day. Children died in great numbers. Letters written in April told of 80 deaths in one vessel and 100 sick in another. Thomas Benson, a surgeon, said that in his ship 330 people, nearly all of the ship's passengers and crew, were sick at one time. Finally, the government acquiesced, and the convoy and merchant ships left Plymouth on April 10, 1710, heading west into the Atlantic.[15]

The fleet was composed of top-heavy crafts, built neither for speed nor sensitive handling in rough seas. The quarters were so miserable and generally uninhabitable that ships destined for voyages to distant lands carried a crew more numerous than necessary in expectation of a high death rate from epidemics and exposure.

A typical transatlantic voyage of the era combined "hunger, thirst, sickness, cold and other sufferings . . ." said one passenger.

The galleon is never clear of a universal raging itch; the ship swarms with little vermin bred in the biscuit, so swift that they not only run over the cabin, beds, and the very dishes we eat on, but insensibly fasten upon the body. Abundance of flies fall into the dishes of broth, in which also swim worms of several sorts. On fish days the common diet was old rank fish boiled in fair water and salt; at noon we had kidney beans, in which there were so many maggots that they swam at the top of the broth and the quantity was so great that I doubted whether the dinner was fish or flesh. An infinite number of rats were glad to make our prey to feed on; and as they were ensnared and taken, a well grown rat was sold for 16 shillings as a market rate. Before the voyage did end a woman great with child offered 20 shillings for a rat, which the proprietor refusing, the woman died."[17]

The two deadliest enemies of voyagers were typhus and scurvy, both of which struck hard at the Palatine fleet.[18]

The sick-bays and surgical quarters were a horror. Space for hospitalization was allotted at the fore end of the waist, which was enveloped in steam from nearby pots of boiling salt beef and pork and the effluvia from overhanging toilets. The ship's surgeons brandished an array of operating instruments, which included "dismembering knives and saws, trepans for skull boring, mallets and chisels, cauterizing irons, incision shears, teeth pullicans, forcers and punches." The patients who survived were sturdy indeed.[19]

Although all North Atlantic voyages of the era were hazardous, those of the Palatines were especially terrible. Not only were the Palatines racked by disease, but they were also assaulted by a series of storms with lashing gales and mountainous waves uncommon for the month of May.

While shivering sailors handled stiff canvas aloft, panic-stricken families huddled below decks in semidarkness, packed so closely they could scarcely stand or sit. Day in and day out, for weeks on end, they lay, one body touching another, amid the wail of hungry infants feeding at the breasts of emaciated mothers. All were tossed about on rancid straw, soaked with vomit, urine and excrement. Once a day, for subsistence, they were handed down a thin, watery gruel by a crew which had nothing better for itself.

The storms scattered the fleet, leaving each ship to fight its way west without support from its neighbors. Finally the weather cleared around the first of June and six of the ships, scattered across the horizon, found each other and once again formed a fleet. On June 5, 1710, the fleet hove into view of Montauk Point at the eastern tip of Long Island. Steering South by Southwest, the small flotilla coasted Rockaway Point, then began its turn north, passing the Dutch settlement of Breuckelin (Brooklyn) on its starboard. On June 13, the *Lyon*, with Governor Hunter aboard, arrived at Nutten Island (now Governor's Island) at the tip of Manhattan. He was at once taken to New York port headquarters, his fellow passengers being detained in quarantine. On June 16, Hunter wrote the London Lords of Trade:

"I arrived here two days ago. We still want three of the Palatine ships and those arrived are in a deplorable sickly condition . . ." A few weeks later he wrote, "All of the Palatine ships separated by the weather are arrived safe except the *Herbert* frigate, where our tents and arms are. She was cast away on the east end of Long Island on the 7th of July . . . We have lost 470 of our number."[20] Among the dead were Zacharra Flegler's wife, son Simon and infant daughter. The sole survivors of the Flegler family were Zacharra and his nine-year-old son Philip Solomon.

MEANWHILE, on the quarantined area of Nutten Island, a tent city had been raised to house the suffering German community. During the first weeks of the quarantine, Palatines died by the hundreds. One coffin maker reported that "business was never better" and petitioned the city that he be paid 59 pounds, 6 shillings sterling for the burial of 250 Palatines.

The Palatines were told they would be settled in five villages on the eastern shore of the Hudson and two on the western shore. Those on the east would establish the community of Germantown; those on the west were absorbed into the existing town of Saugerties.

Zacharra and his group were among the first Palatines to arrive in America. But many more were to follow in the next 40 years. They would come initially from London and later directly from the Palatinate in Germany. And for the next century afterward, all Germans coming to America, whether from the Palatinate or other provinces, would be called Palatines.

# America, 1710-1830

I was born in Hope, near Canandaigua, New York, in 1830. I realize how this country has grown when I remember that in the year I was born there were exactly 24 miles of railroad in all the United States. My father was a Presbyterian clergyman.

—HENRY FLAGLER

ALTHOUGH the Palatines didn't expect to be received with parades and flying banners, they did expect to be received. Instead, after leaving their ships and erecting tents on Nutten's Island, they found themselves shunned, in quarantine because of the typhus. New York City, barely a shout away, had closed its doors, and its City Council, spurred by resentful and fearful citizens, protested vigorously the nearby presence of more than 2,000 typhus-exposed immigrants.

The threat of contagion was understandably of grave concern to a city of fewer than 6,000 inhabitants, which included 1,000 slaves. Sympathetic to the plight of his Palatine charges, Governor Hunter was stymied as to how to get them off the island. Then he decided to attack the New Yorkers at a particularly vulnerable point—their liking for money.

EVEN THEN, New York was primarily a community of trade, rather than a manufacturing center. Developed as an outlet for the rich agricultural lands of the upper Hudson River and the Mohawk Valley, New York had been founded as a trading post by the Dutch West Indies Company. Trade had been its inhabitants' chief occupation from the day Peter Minuit landed with his company of settlers in 1626 and drove a shrewd bargain with the Indians for the purchase of Manhattan Island for 60 guilders ($24). Also from the first days, New Amsterdam, as the Dutch renamed Manhattan, had an easy religious tolerance and a relaxed style of life, which was partly due to the fact that New York, unlike New England, hadn't been founded as a sanctuary for religious refugees.

To win support from the New Yorkers, and to relieve some of the problems among the refugees, Governor Hunter offered orphaned Palatine children for adoption and apprenticeship in the city. The plan, in its original form, not only found a home for the orphans, but was a means by which the Palatines were introduced to the New Yorkers. With care and training, the Palatines would become useful in agriculture and trades vital to the general community. Given the choice between the risks of typhus and the gift of free labor, the New Yorkers quickly opted for the latter.

Hunter did not only place orphans, but also children whose parents were still living. In so doing, however, he separated many families. One Palatine parent is quoted as saying, "He took away our children from us without and against our consent.[1]

Of the 74 children apprenticed by the governor to tradesmen, craftsmen and farmers, more than one was destined to rise to fame. Among them was John Peter Zenger, who at 13 was taken from his widowed mother, Hannah Zenger, apparently with her consent, and bound to William Bradford, an enterprising New York printer and founder of the *New York Gazette*. Zenger later went on to establish his own newspaper, the *Weekly Journal*, in which his anti-administration editorials caused him to be jailed for libel. During the celebrated trial that followed, Zenger was defended by Alexander Hamilton, who established truth as a defense in cases of libel. Zenger was acquitted, and freedom of the press gained a foothold in America.

Despite the apprenticeship policies, however, the New York City Council refused to let the remainder of the Palatines out of quarantine. Time passed and on August 15, 1710, a Lutheran minister on Nutten Island recorded the marriage between Zacharra Flegler and Anna Gertrauda Huen, the daughter of Dietrick Huen, who had died on the voyage over.

Governor Hunter finally despaired of winning over the New York City Council. He decided instead to bypass the city and ship the Palatines directly up the Hudson to a 6,000-acre "camp" on the west side of the river. Located about 90 miles north of New York City, in Ulster County, the camp was near a stream called Sawyer's Kill. At this point in history, more than 80 years after the founding of the

New York colony, farms and hamlets extended from Manhattan 160 miles up the Hudson to Albany, the latter proclaimed by its citizens to be the oldest continuously existing community in the United States.[2] The widely spread population, however, was thin and sparse and few communities had more than a dozen families.

The land was rich in forests, and Governor Hunter wrote, "I myself have seen Pitch Pine enough upon the river to serve all Europe with Tar."[3]

Beginning in early October 1710, 1,200 Palatines were removed from Nutten Island in boats and taken upriver to the Ulster tract. Among them was the Flegler family. Zacharra carried with him bags of seed for wheat, peas, onions and other vegetables. He had been carrying them since he had left Germany more than four years earlier.[4]

Despite the deadly trip and the loss of their family, Zacharra and Philip looked upon their new home and found it compatible with many of their Eurpean ways, but also a wonder in its own right. European beasts of burden—oxen, horses and donkeys—fared well, as did milk and wool-producing animals. Although the Germans had brought fowl with them, they were happy to discover the turkey, pigeon and partridge in America. And though the Germans could grow every important European crop except the wine grape in the new land, corn, tobacco and the potato proved to be important—and enjoyable—additions.[5]

Then there were the trees.

Wherever the man and boy walked, they were beneath or near the shade of trees, and, although neither of them knew it, they were in a forest which reached without break from Quebec to Florida and westward across the unexplored Appalachians.

The American woods were alive with wildlife. Pigeons darkened the skies. At sunset they would roost in the trees, piling up on one another to such a height and weight they would break down main branches. Nothing seemed to frighten them, and men and boys simply went among them with a stick and knocked them on the head.

As for meat, there were deer, elk, moose and bear. Later, pushing up the Hudson, Zacharra and Philip would thrill at the sight of valleys filled with buffalo, their ears deafened by the thunder of their run.

Even more countless was the bounty of the waters—bass, trout, perch, chub, sturgeon, clams, oysters, scallops, mussels, lobster. Lobsters six feet long were taken from the waters off New York by the

Dutch. In the ocean were more than 200 species of edible fish, including mackerel, haddock, hake, flounder, mullet, cod and sheepshead.[6]

Endless thickets of wild plum and blackberry stretched for miles along streams and open clearings. A boundless profusion of wild fruit that Europeans had never seen—or tasted—before. Vast groves of ruby crabapple, golden persimmon, black and white mulberry, and wild cherry.

But these were not to be had easily.

The Palatines were allotted plots about 40 × 50 feet in which to build huts and plant gardens. Hunter reported that "each family hath sufficient lot of good arrable land . . . have built themselves comfortable huts and are now employed in clearing the ground. In the Spring I shall set them to work in preparing the trees."[7]

The trip upriver had been too trying, however, for Zacharra's new wife, and she died a few weeks after their arrival. For the second time within a year, Zacharra was a widower.

The houses built by Zacharra and his fellow Palatines were quite primitive, usually a one-room log cabin with mud filling in the spaces between the logs and a fireplace which both heated the room and cooked the food.

It took the entire winter to clear the land, plant gardens and build the cabins. Almost immediately, the widows and widowers began to pair up. The unions were dictated not only by emotional need but by economic necessity as well. Survival depended upon the family unit with its well-defined labors for the males and females, the young and the old.

Accordingly, in the spring of 1711, Flegler married his third wife, Anna Elizabetha Schultz, the childless widow of George Schultz of Darmstadt who had died enroute to America. In the next three years, Anna bore two children to Zacharra—Anna Magdelena Elizabetha, born September 9, 1712, and Simon, born February 16, 1714.[8]

Meanwhile, work began on the Great Tar Enterprise.

The Germans began eagerly, as they were anxious to fulfill the terms of their contracts and get on with their own lives. However, they, and their English landlords, were blissfully unaware that the New York pine couldn't produce tar and pitch in paying quantities. The result was that although more than 1,000 people felled and prepared some 15,000 trees that spring and summer, with Palatine children industriously gathering pine knots for fuel, barely 60 barrels of tar were produced.[9]

Learning of this, the London board first ordered a reduction in the subsistence allowance, and then eliminated it entirely, which left the Palatines completely on their own. Ulrich Simmendinger, a Palatine, wrote in his journal: "Each one received his freedom to the extent that he might seek his own bread in his own way until the Queen should again need his services."[10]

WITH the removal of British protection the Palatines became exposed to the harassment of their belligerent and resentful English neighbors and the rigors of a harsh, uncompromising wilderness. The English pioneers, through beatings and barn burnings, broke up the Palatine community. Having no access to police or military protection the Germans dispersed in all directions. Many went to lower Pennsylvania. Some migrated to the "Mohawk's Valley." Others fled westward into the Catskills, where today may be found traces of ancient Palatine cemeteries.

In the dead of winter, in 1712–1713, about 30 families walked across the icy Hudson to rejoin their fellow countrymen in Germantown on the east bank of the Hudson. Among them were the Fleglers: Zacharra, 11-year-old son Philip Solomon, Zacharra's wife Anna, and four-month-old Elizabetha. Moving from settlement to settlement, earning their keep with Zacharra's carpentry skills, they wandered for four years.

Eventually, in 1717, they found a place to their liking in Dutchess County, about 60 miles north of New York City, on lands owned by a friendly Rhinelander named Henry Beekman. Zacharra leased and eventually bought a farm of about 600 acres on fertile low-rolling hills with an unbroken view in all directions. On the property was a gushing mountain stream which debouched into a pond in front of the main entrance to the house.[11]

Despite its beauty, the property had already been spoiled by men. Zacharra and Anna found no virgin woods but, rather, great stands of barren stumps. The trees had been burned down by Indians seeking to drive out game. However, much wildlife still remained; local histories recorded 100 types of birds and 90 kinds of fish.[12]

Although the ground was sometimes rocky, the soil was, for the most part, productive and fertile. There were few comforts and no luxuries. In the back country, away from the river, households were locked in the ice of winter for a period of three to five months. Eking out an existence on the barest necessities of clothing, shelter and food, the Palatines' chief task was staying alive.

Travel was either by water or on foot, unless one was fortunate enough to have a horse. Women and children rode behind the man on a pillion or pad with straps and a single stirrup.[13]

Mail was carried between Albany and New York mostly on foot. In winter the postman went up the Hudson by skating when the ice was good. In warm weather, mail moved in sailing boats without a fixed schedule.[14]

The house in Dutchess County was Zacharra's last homestead. In 1719, the last of his children, Zacharias, was born. In March 1720, Zacharra died. The former German soldier, English carpenter and New World pioneer was 44 years old. His son, Zacharias, the great grandfather of Henry Morrison Flagler, would become the most prolific of the Fleglers, fathering 16 children, most of whom grew to adulthood, bought farms and stayed their lives in Dutchess County.[15]

They were not without enemies. The Palatine immigrants encountered hostilities from the most surprising sources. In 1751, for example, Benjamin Franklin asked, "Why should the Palatine Boors be suffered to swarm into our settlements, and, by herding together, establish their language and manners, to the exclusion of ours? . . . Aliens who will shortly be so numerous as to Germanize us, instead of our Anglifying them?"

Nevertheless, Zacharra Flegler had planted the family seed in America. His son Zacharias would be its caretaker, nurturing it through the turbulence of the eighteenth century and the American Revolution.

Indeed, the fighting during the revolution was largely concentrated around the Fleglers and the Hudson Valley, where some 92 of the war's 308 battles took place. For example, the British failure to capture West Point, less than 50 miles from Zacharra's farm and supported by Palatine troops and forts, destroyed the British initiative for the rest of the war.

Following the war, as the nation began its constitutional government under President George Washington, the family name was changed from Flegler to Flagler by Solomon Flegler, Zacharias' eighth child, born in 1760. Solomon was the father of Isaac Flagler, who would become the father of Henry Flagler.

Born April 22, 1789, Isaac was raised on his father's farm and learned the Palatine values of hard work and religion, which he would in turn pass on to his son.

Like most American farming families, the Flaglers were nearly self-sufficient. They depended upon their own labor and land for food and sold extra produce to the few townsfolk. With the cash thus obtained, they could pay the millers who ground their meal and sawed their logs, the blacksmiths who forged their tools, the merchants who imported their coffee, tea, sugar, molasses, salt and luxury goods, and the professionals who tended their legal and spiritual needs.

Salted meat and cornmeal, which could be kept all year, dominated the winter menus, relieved by dried corn, hominy, beans and occasional wild game which could be slaughtered and hung on the porch in nature's own deep freeze. For the children, there was milk. Summer brought fresh produce, although leafy vegetables were rare, as they spoil too easily. Many farmers didn't plant them because of the need for constant care, preferring wild greens or vegetables that could be stored, such as turnips, pumpkins and beans. They raised orchard fruits more for cider and brandy than for eating, and picked and ate wild berries and crab apples to make pies.[16]

The kitchen fireplace, with its open hearth, was the center of the Flagler house. Built wide and deep to accommodate pots and ovens and joints of meat, the fireplace was crowded with equipment, including pots, skillets, and some utensils standing on trivets, which lifted the pots above the burning coals.[17]

Colonial houses offered only scant protection from the winter's cold. During that time, when farm chores were few, the Flaglers spent much of their waking hours in the kitchen.

Despite the discomforts, the Flaglers were better off than many Americans. In their house, they had a stove, a concept of heating introduced to America by the Palatines. In continental Europe, intense cold and scarce fuel had fostered the early development of stoves.[18] Immigrants from those countries brought the molds for casting stoves with them. They had the most comfortable homes in the colonies.

In the meantime, Isaac was being raised in a solid, well-to-do

German homestead which produced crop yields unlike anything known in the Old World.[19] An avid reader, he followed the exploits of the Lewis and Clark expedition, which set out in 1803 to explore lands west of the Mississippi. Following the Ohio, Missouri and Columbia rivers to the Pacific, they covered more than 8,000 miles. Later, Isaac would make long trips of his own to the West, being away from his wives and children for years at a time.

Isaac was able to witness, within a few miles of his home, some of the pivotal events of American history. In 1807, for example, Robert Fulton's *Clermont*, the first steamboat to make regular trips, arrived in Albany from New York City. It made the 150-mile trip in a record 32 hours. Another event near at hand was the construction of the Erie Canal. Begun in 1817, it was designed to connect the Great Lakes to the Hudson and thus, to the Atlantic Ocean.

Educated at local schools, Isaac began studying for the Presbyterian ministry in his teens, being ordained in 1810 at the age of 21. For much of the rest of his life, he performed more as a missionary than a minister, roaming the countrysides of New York, Pennsylvania, Indiana and Ohio, Kansas and points west, preaching and ministering to people wherever he found them, alone or assembled, on farms and in villages—unrewarded save in spiritual returns. Isaac was, as historian Robert Pierce has noted, "A Wandering Minstrel."[20]

The documented record for Isaac begins with his baptism in 1789 and then jumps to his ordination in 1810. He was assigned to the Presbyterian Church in Pleasant Valley, New York, about five miles northeast of Poughkeepsie on the Wappinger River. There, in 1813, he married his childhood sweetheart, 20-year-old Jane Ward, one of three daughters of a devout Presbyterian family.

Isaac would remain six years in Pleasant Valley, one of the longest and most peaceful tenures of his life. During this time, two children were born—Mary Esther Flagler on July 31, 1814 and Jane Augusta Flagler, on October 29, 1816.[21]

In August 1819, Isaac and his family were transferred to Marlboro, a hamlet on the west bank of the Hudson some 15 miles southwest of Poughkeepsie. Fourteen months later Jane died, leaving a grieving husband and two small children. Isaac appears to have been hard hit by Jane's death and temporarily gave up the ministry, returning to Pleasant Valley where for the next two years he farmed, wresting a hard living from the soil to support his family. He returned to his ministerial duties in 1821, and after several transfers became pastor of the Pleasant Valley Presbyterian Church.

The church had no pews, the worshippers being required to sit on planks supported on barrels. The pulpit was a high, octagonal platform set directly in front of the congregation. No hymns were sung, only metrical psalms under the direction of a choir leader.

Isaac began courting a 27-year-old parishioner, Ruth Deyo Smith, a slim, pretty young lady, with shoulder-length dark hair and the daughter of a Presbyterian minister.[22] They were married in May 1824.

A year later, Isaac became the pastor of the Presbyterian church at the hamlet of North River, located in the cold mountains of central New York. There, he and Ruth had a daughter, Anna Caroline Flagler, born May 14, 1826.[23] Seventeen months later, Ruth Deyo Flagler died. She was 30 years old. The widower Isaac was left with three daughters, two of them teenagers nearing marriage age and the other an infant.

The causes of the deaths of Flagler's two wives, one aged 27 and the other 30, weren't recorded. However, smallpox and tuberculosis, then called "galloping consumption," were common killers among persons around 30 years of age.

ISAAC continued on the move. The year 1828 found him the pastor of a church in North Romulus, a community on the northwestern tip of Lake Cayuga in Seneca County. Within a few months, Isaac met a young widow, Elizabeth Caldwell Harkness, and they were married in the fall of 1828.

Elizabeth had been married twice before. Her first husband was Hugh Morrison of Washington County, New York. Her second was David Harkness, a physician, of Bellevue, Ohio. After the death of her second husband in 1825, Elizabeth returned to New York State with her only child, David's son, Daniel Morrison Harkness. She made her home with relatives in Salem, New York, and while there she met Isaac Flagler, who at that time was serving a nearby pastorate.[24]

Shortly after their marriage, the couple moved to Hopewell, New York, near Canandaigua. There, on January 2, 1830, a son was born. They baptized him Henry Morrison Flagler. His middle name came from his mother's first husband, Hugh Morrison, it being a custom of those deadly times to name children after previous husbands or wives.

One wonders about the charm of Isaac Flagler. Why would any woman, particularly Elizabeth, twice before married and with a son of her own, take on this indigent, desultory, 39-year-old minister with three young children and a paltry income? An unsettled man, with uncertain or negligible chances of promotion in his work? Judging by his photographs, he was certainly no beauty. And judging by his wanderings, he certainly wasn't dependable.

Nevertheless, Elizabeth Flagler would spend 33 years in his bed and kitchen, seeing religion with its seams wide open.

# NOTES

## CHAPTER 1

1. "The Diaries of Zeisberger," Ohio Archaeological and Historical Publications, XXI. Zeisberger's diaries contain references to petroleum discoveries at three sites in western New York and northwestern Pennsylvania in 1768.

2. *The Early Petroleum Industry,* Paul H. Giddens, Porcupine Press, Philadelphia, 1974. Hereafter referred to as Giddens.

3. N.Y., *American Examiner,* 1907.

4. "Flagler and Florida," by Edwin LeFevre, *Everybody's,* 1906. Hereafter referred to as *Everybody's.*

5. New York *World Journal Tribune,* January 9, 1967.

## CHAPTER 2

1. Article by James B. Morrow, New York *Tribune,* December 23, 1906.

2. *Everybody's.*

3. See Herbert Aptheker, *American Negro Slave Revolts,* 1940.

4. Henry, born in Albany in 1797, was (from 1846) the first secretary and director of the newly funded Smithsonian Institution, introducing and developing many of its present activities and policies. In addition to the inventions mentioned in the text, he improved the electromagnet's strength, fitting it for practical use. His telegraph became the basis for the commercial telegraph. He discovered self-inductance, and the measure of inductance is still called the "henry." And he discovered the principle of the induced current, basic to the dynamo, transformer and many other devices. He also established the modern weather report system.

5. Hammondsport Presbyterian Church records at Flagler Museum, Whitehall.

6. Toledo *Blade,* June 4, 1910. Osborn later became clerk of the Ohio State Senate. The interracial marriage performed by Isaac Flagler was rare, but not unprecedented. The May 5, 1822, edition of the Sandusky *Clarion* reports a marriage between "William Davis an African, to Nancy Hunter, a white woman; both of Greenfield." Ohioans, at least those writing to the *Clarion,* sneered at the woman and responded with a ditty to the popular tune of "Oh, Dear, What Can the Matter Be":

> Oh, dear, what can the matter be?
> Will no one deign to marry me?
> Yes, Cupid kept his shaft not back;
> He missed the white, but hit a black!

7. Hammondsport Church records.

8. Series of weekly articles by Bellevue, Ohio, historian William Oddo, Bellevue *Gazette,* Bellevue, Ohio, 1984. Hereafter referred to as Oddo columns.

The story of the Flaglers and the Harknesses is a convoluted one. As a matter of historical coincidence, the first American-born Harkness, William, and the first American-born Flaglers were neighbors in the Albany area during the early 1700s. It is not known, however, if they had any contact. In the ensuing century, they drifted apart, the Harknesses settling in north-eastern New York near the Vermont border.

In 1815, Dr. David Harkness, then 27 years old, left eastern New York and set up a practice in Seneca County, New York, about halfway between Rochester and Syracuse. He married and had a child, Stephen, born in 1818. The mother died following complications in childbirth. Unable to care for his infant son, David boarded him with relatives in Seneca County. Almost immediately, David moved to the Ohio country, settling in Milan, a prosperous village near Toledo.

There, in 1820, he met and married a 20-year-old widow, pretty Elizabeth Caldwell, daughter of Dennis Caldwell, a local minister. They bought a brick house beside the village square, on a block lined with handsome porticoes and doorways.

Meanwhile, the medical practice was so good that David wrote to New York inviting his younger brother, Lamon, to come to Milan. Lamon, then a 19-year-old medical student, practiced with his brother for three years before setting up his own practice in a place called Amsden Corners, some 50 miles southeast of Toledo.

In 1822, David and Elizabeth had their only child, Dan, born on September 26. Three years later, David died. Elizabeth lost the house and, taking Dan, went to live with David's relatives in Seneca County. It was the first meeting of the two half-brothers, Dan and Stephen.

Shortly afterward, Elizabeth met and married Isaac Flagler.

All three of the Harknesses—Dan, Stephen and their uncle Lamon—would play major roles in Henry Flagler's career.

9. It is only after Isaac's death in 1876 that Henry speaks kindly of his father. See *Everybody's*. Both parents were removed from the Bellevue cemetery in 1976 and taken to the Flagler family cemetery at Green Haven, Dutchess County, New York.

10. *Everybody's*.

11. The area had been ceded by Connecticut to its citizens, whose lands had been burned by the British during the American Revolution, thus the name "Firelands."

The Western Reserve originally was part of the federally owned Northwest Territory, with the northeastern Ohio section claimed by the state of Connecticut.

12. Before 1800, the view of the U.S. government on land was, in effect, that it was a source of public revenue. The revenue was to be had by selling the land in great blocks to land companies that would parcel it out to individuals who would in turn pay taxes. The government also tried to sell homesteads directly, at $2 an acre, with four years to pay for a 160-acre tract. During the period 1800 to 1820, when this practice prevailed, the government had much trouble collecting its money. By 1820, individual purchasers were $21 million in arrears. To meet the situation, the government reduced the price to $1.25 an acre, payable in cash, for an 80-acre lot.

13. *Florida's Flagler*, Walter Martin, University of Georgia Press, Athens, Ga., 1949. Hereafter referred to as Martin.

14. The other partner was Judge Frederick A. Chapman, a local politician and landowner.

15. *Everybody's*.

16. New York *Journal*, 1906. The American dollar of the era was worth about $13 in 1986 currency.

17. Cleveland *Press*, December 1902, article by Jacob Waldeck, reprinted in Bellevue *Gazette*. Flagler, wrote Waldeck, "is spoken of in a kindly way by the old men who were in his set before the war. He was one of a crowd, they say, who used to walk over the table and break dishes after their spreads in the Tremont house, but they paid for the wreck." The boisterous good times also were described to the author in a September 3, 1984, interview with historian William Oddo, in Bellevue, Ohio. The Oddo interview is hereafter referred to as Oddo interview.

18. "Revelations of An Old Account Book," Hon. Thomas W. Latham, *The Firelands Pioneer*, Norwalk, Ohio, Firelands Historical Society, 1921.

19. Letter of January 28, 1852, Flagler Museum, Whitehall.

20. Republican Foster, considered a progressive economic reformer, served as Secretary of the Treasury 1891–1893. He served in the U.S. House 1871–1879 and was elected governor of Ohio in 1879 and 1881. He died in 1904 an impoverished man and his debts were made up by Henry Flagler.

## CHAPTER 3

1. *Journal of Latrobe,* Benjamin Henry Latrobe, D. Appleton & Co., N.Y., 1905.

2. *Ibid.*

3. *Ibid.*

4. *Documents Relative to the Colonial History of the State of New York, Procured in Holland, England, and France,* E. B. O'Callaghan ed., Albany, N.Y., vol. IV, 1854.

5. *Ibid.*

6. *God's Gold, The Story of Rockefeller and His Times,* John T. Flynn, Harcourt, Brace and Company, N.Y., 1932. Hereafter referred to as Flynn.

7. Giddens.

8. Undated letter found in Bissell papers, as reported by Giddens.

9. Giddens. James Townsend, president of Seneca Oil, desired to give Drake some importance among the locals and sent letters to him addressed as "colonel." For the remainder of his life, Drake was so addressed.

10. Flynn.

11. *Ibid.*

12. *Cleveland, The Best Kept Secret,* George Condon; Doubleday, Garden City, N.Y., 1967. Hereafter referred to as Condon.

13. *Cleveland, The Making of a City,* William Ganson Rose, World Publishing Company, Cleveland, Ohio, 1950. Hereafter referred to as Rose.

14. Flynn.

15. *John D. Rockefeller: A Study in Power,* Allan Nevins, Charles Scribner's Sons, N.Y., 1953. Hereafter referred to as Nevins.

16. *John D. Rockefeller, The Cleveland Years,* Grace Goulder, The Western Reserve Historical Society, Cleveland, 1972. Hereafter referred to as Goulder.

17. Rose.

18. Oil is still coaxed from the ground where Drake sank his first well. Lacking pressure to spurt upward, the greenish and golden-tinted goo is sucked from the rocks by creaking pumps that resemble iron birds pecking rhythmically in the dirt. "It is the oldest oil field in the world, and it will probably still be pumping when a lot of the others run dry," said Bernie Henderson, spokesman for the Quaker State Oil Refining Corporation in an interview with the Philadelphia *Inquirer,* August 30, 1984.

19. One hundred twenty-five years later, Pennsylvania crude, fetching $26 per barrel, made up 25 percent of the lubricating oil produced in the U.S. and an even higher percentage of the motor oil market.

20. Flynn.

21. *Ibid.*

22. Drake. Ed Drake was elected justice of the peace in Titusville in 1860 and derived an annual income of about $3,000 from fees on the rush for legal conveyances. He also became a buyer for a New York oil company, with commissions amounting to another $2,000 per year. In 1863, Drake sold his home in Titusville, left the Oil Regions, took $15,000 or $20,000 and went to

New York, where he became a partner of a Wall Street broker in oil stocks. By 1866, through speculation, he lost most of his money, and his health was bad. He began to wander the country.

In 1869, he was in New York and by accident met a Titusville man, Zeb Martin, who was startled to see that Drake walked with great difficulty and had only 60 cents in his pocket. Drake was wearing the same coat that he had worn nine years previously during the oil strike. Martin took him for a warm dinner, gave him $20 and, upon returning to Titusville, reported Drake's condition, of which no one had been aware. A public committee raised $5,000 for Drake's relief, and in 1873 the Pennsylvania legislature provided Drake with an annual income of $1,500. After his death, the money would go to his widow as long as she lived.

Meanwhile, Drake and his family had moved to South Bethlehem, Pennsylvania. His illness became more severe and after 1873 he couldn't walk and could barely use his hands, apparently because of arthritis. Suffering from excrutiating pain, he died in November 1880, a pensioner of the state.

## CHAPTER 4

1. Cleveland *Press*, December 1902.
2. The New York *World*, October 10, 1886.
3. *Ibid.*
4. U.S. Census, 1860.
5. Flynn.
6. "Civil War Draft Resistance in the Middle West," Ph.D. dissertation by Robert E. Sterling, Northern Illinois University, 1974. Hereafter referred to as Sterling.
7. *Ibid.*
8. Rose.
9. Nevins.
10. New York *Tribune*, December 23, 1906.
11. See Whitehall Letterboxes; letter from Isabella Harkness to Mary Harkness Flagler, February 14, 1862.
12. Sterling. A third future founder of Standard Oil, Sam Andrews, was exempt because of his British birth.
13. *Ibid.* The skedaddling problem was so widespread that Stanton instituted a passport system to curb the exodus of evaders. On August 8, 1862, he ordered that no citizen liable to the draft would be allowed to go to a foreign country or even to leave his county or state without a valid pass. Violators were arrested by U.S. marshals and deputies, and military police. There was no civil trial, and the writ of habeas corpus was suspended. Usually, the men were simply taken to the nearest military post and sworn into the army. Their pay would be deducted for arrest expenses, transportation costs and a five-dollar reward for the arresting officer. Serious cases were handled by a special corps of federal provost marshals, the nearest thing the United States has ever had to a Gestapo, meaning a ruthless and virtually unchecked state police force.

By order of Stanton, a special bureau of the War Department had been established to provide provost marshals for each congressional district. The marshals, having the full service of Union troops at their call, were charged with the maintenance of internal security in each congressional district. They did not have to use search warrants; they were not answerable to civilian courts, and they were not idle.

More than 300 Northern newspapers, large and small, were suppressed or suspended by provost marshals for seditious activities. A minimum of 13,535 Northern civilians were arrested and held in military prisons for months and years without trial, on charges ranging from draft evasion to sedition. (The minimum figure comes from a postwar search of War Department records. Other surveys placed the total of illegal arrests at more than 38,000.)

The harsh methods proved effective, overcoming the various modes of resistance. By war's end, Ohio had provided 205,867 men to the Union army, nearly one-fifth of its total population of men, women and children.

The first draft of men for war service began on October 1, 1862. Newspapers noted the draft had a curious effect upon some of the Ohio males. "Men who have been wearing wigs and dyeing their whiskers, passing for 38 or 39 years of age, have suddenly owned up to 45," reported one newspaper, "while young bucks who have passed with the girls for 20 have shrunk to the other side of 18." As much as $700 was paid by a draftee to a substitute to enter the service; and as the practice grew, recruiting suffered.

The Kingston (Canada) *News* observed that large numbers of Americans had sought refuge in Canada. "The promulgation of the order for an immediate draft has at once driven them over in shoals." The Chatham (Canada) *Planet* reported a steady stream of "white fugitives from Uncle Sam's plantation" debarking from every train and boat from Detroit.

14. *Ibid.*

15. Goulder. His brother William made a similar buy-out. But their younger brother Frank Rockefeller enlisted. He was only 16, but chalking an "18" on the sole of each boot, he had blithely told the recruiting officer, "I'm over eighteen!" Serving as a private for three years, he was twice wounded.

16. I was unable to find any military or draft record pertaining to either Flagler or Rockefeller, despite a search of Ohio and Michigan archives and records of the U.S. War Department. However, an article in a December 1902 issue of the Cleveland *Press* states that Flagler "provided canteens" as an alternative to military service. The article, provided by Bellevue historian William Oddo is the only contemporary reference I've seen concerning Flagler's avoidance of the draft.

Rockefeller told biographers decades later that he had bought his way out. Flagler, who was exposed to the draft in the summer of 1862 while in Bellevue, apparently bought a deferment there. He was in Michigan for the remainder of the war and exempt because of his employment in the salt industry.

Frank Rockefeller, the only Rockefeller to serve, would become a vice president of Standard Oil until 1912. But long before then, sometime in the 1860s, he became alienated from John. Although Frank renounced all business connections with Standard Oil and his brother in 1899, he was kept on the company payroll for another 13 years, presumably by decision of John.

Frank remained a resident of Cleveland, but also operated a 12,000-acre ranch in Kansas, as well as holding interests in ranches in Texas and Arizona. He would often remind people, "I am Frank Rockefeller, stock farmer—not Frank Rockefeller, brother of John D."

So bitter was his feeling toward John that he refused to speak to him during the last 15 years of his life.

17. Norwalk (Ohio) *Reflector*, August 19, 1862.

18. Bellevue *Gazette*, Oddo papers.

19. Harkness. Stephen Harkness, senior among the future Standard Oil partners, was born in 1818 in Fayette, New York. His mother died when he was two. His father, grain dealer David Harkness, then married Elizabeth Caldwell Morrison, who would later be the mother of Henry Flagler. After his father died in Ohio in 1820, Stephen was reared by his grandfather, Stephen Vander Cook, in Waterloo, New York. At 15, he was apprenticed to a harness maker and worked at that trade so well that he took over the business and built it into a chain of factories. He then sold his factories and returned to Ohio and the Bellevue area, where he was warmly welcomed by cousins, uncles and aunts. He dealt extensively in livestock and, like his

relatives, in grain and other produce—lucrative operations in war time with the government as a steady customer.

20. Article by columnist Harold V. Lappin, Saginaw *News*, Saginaw, Michigan, April 14, 1978.

21. *Ibid.*

22. *Ibid.*

23. Interview with William Oddo. Although previous accounts, some including interviews with Flagler in his later years, have Flagler leaving Saginaw in 1865 and moving directly to Cleveland, Mr. Oddo possesses documents showing that Flagler and his family returned to Bellevue. The documents include newspaper clippings and a deed wherein the Bellevue Catholic Church purchased Saginaw property from Flagler in January 1866. Flagler signed it in Saginaw, per a notary. Flagler and his family moved to Bellevue in the spring of 1866 and later that year Henry moved alone to Cleveland.

24. Appointed 1861 to fill a vacancy in the Senate, he served there until 1877, being chairman of Senate Finance, 1867, and played a leading role in government finance in the Reconstruction period. In 1880, 1884 and 1888 he was considered for the Republican presidential nomination. He was Secretary of Treasury under Rutherford B. Hayes, 1877–1881, and returned to the Senate 1881–1897. Ironically, Sherman, whose tip to Harkness helped indirectly to create Standard Oil, was the author of the Sherman Anti-Trust Act, 1890, aimed at Standard Oil. In 1897, he resigned from the Senate to provide a seat for Mark Hanna and was appointed Secretary of State by President William McKinley. Because of age and failing memory, he retired to private life in 1898.

25. Account Book.

26. Nevins.

27. Flynn.

28. Flynn.

29. Nevins.

## CHAPTER 5

1. Among the more recent settlers were the Mound Builders, who, dating from about 500 A.D., built huge earth structures in Ohio and down the Mississippi Valley. Two of the best-known mounds of the ancient culture were located in what is now downtown Cleveland at the mouth of the Cuyahoga.

In historic times, the most prominent of the Cleveland Indians were the Eries, for whom early white explorers named Lake Erie. The Eries developed great power and gained control of the southern shore of the lake from Sandusky Bay to the area of present day Buffalo, New York. Persistent war with the Iroquois, however, ended in the virtual elimination of the Eries by the mid 1600s.

2. Zeisberger's rock oil activities are mentioned in Chapter 1.

3. Flynn.

4. Father of American diplomat William Averell Harriman.

5. *Everybody's.*

6. *Cleveland City Directory,* 1866.

7. *Random Reminiscences of Men and Events,* John D. Rockefeller, Sleepy Hollow Press, Tarrytown, N.Y., 1984. Hereafter referred to as *Reminiscences.*

8. Condon.

9. Condon.

10. Rose.

11. Rose.

12. New York *Morning Telegraph*, June 11, 1911.

13. Cleveland *Leader*, May 7, 1867.

14. Oil refining was not so much a science as an art or skill. It was based on scientific principles, but success depended heavily on the experienced judgment of the man on the job.

The basic equipment consisted of stills, which were cylindrical iron tanks set in a brick frame above furnaces that heated the crude oil in the tanks. As the temperature rose, the oil began to vaporize. The vapors were collected above the stills by ducts and fed into overhead pipes, called condensers, where they cooled and condensed into liquids once again. The part of the oil which boiled off was called a "cut," or "fraction." The first fraction which vaporized was gasoline. As the still temperature rose higher, a second fraction would appear, called kerosene. The third fraction was gas oil, used chiefly to make illuminating gas. Then came heavy lubricating and fuel oils. The unvaporized residue was a tarry coke, which Rockefeller, Andrews & Flagler used as fuel to run its plants.

As distilled fractions flowed from the condensers, they passed through glass-covered "look boxes." These allowed the stillman, the "brewmaster" of the operation, to judge each product by its color with an educated eye.

A still could not be operated continuously, but had to handle crude in batches, one at a time. When a charge of crude had been vaporized, the still was allowed to cool. As soon as the heat became bearable, heavily padded still-cleaners would climb into the tanks through a manhole and furiously chip the coke away from the bottom. Then the still would be fired again and loaded with oil.

15. Martin.

16. Account Book. There have been several differing accounts of how Rockefeller and Flagler became partners. Mr. Latham, author of the Account Book, said in 1921 that his source was "W. M. Fanning, of Monroeville, who was in the employ of Mr. Harkness at the time and who related them to me."

17. The can began in 1865 when Charles Pratt hired a German inventor, Herman Miller, to improve the package in which oil and kerosene was sold. Miller invented the five-gallon tin. As early as 1868, the firm of Rockefeller, Andrews & Flagler had contracted for the manufacture of 300,000 five-gallon tins to be used in shipping refined oil abroad. The cans were packed two to a case, which could conveniently be slung across the back of a pack animal. Eventually the tins became invaluable in remote parts of the world as household utensils and as building materials.

The manufacture of the cans was one of the earliest mass production operations. By the 1880s, one plant was turning out and filling 60,000 tins a day in a continuous process.

18. "The Effects of Standard Oil's Vertical Integration into Transportation on the Structure and Performance of the American Petroleum Industry, 1872–1884," Ph.D. dissertation by Jerome Thomas Bentley, University of Pittsburgh, 1974. Hereafter referred to as Bentley.

19. Flynn.

20. Nevins.

21. Martin.

## CHAPTER 6

1. Bellevue *Gazette*, December 28, 1906.

2. Rose.

3. *Ibid.*

4. Flynn.

5. *Reminiscences.*

6. Nevins.

7. Engineer George Selden appears to have invented the automobile, as he developed a

three-cylinder internal combustion engine in 1879 and used it to power a "horseless carriage." In 1892, bicycle makers Frank and Charles Duryea of Massachusetts constructed the first gasoline automobile. Goodrich died in 1888 before the automobile era.

8. *Everybody's.*

9. Papers of Warren Smith, private secretary to Henry Flagler, Flagler Collection, Flagler Museum. Hereafter referred to as Smith papers.

10. Smith papers.

11. *Everybody's.*

12. *Reminiscences.*

13. Flynn.

14. Flynn.

15. Condon.

16. Bentley.

17. Bentley.

18. Testimony before the Ohio Legislature, March 1879.

19. Flynn.

20. *The History of the Standard Oil Company,* Ida M. Tarbell, S.S. McClure Co., 1904. Hereafter referred to as Tarbell.

21. Flynn.

22. Rose.

23. Nevins.

24. Martin.

25. Smith papers.

26. The New York *World,* October 10, 1886.

## CHAPTER 7

1 There is some confusion over whether Henry Flagler made his first trip to Florida in the winter of 1876–1877, as is maintained here, or a year later. Traditional sources, such as newspaper clippings at the time of Flagler's death and the Walter Martin biography, hold for the later date. However, in an 1887 interview with the Jacksonville, Florida, *News-Herald,* Flagler said he first came to Jacksonville "eleven years ago." In the same interview, he refers to a second visit, in 1882, due to a liver ailment, and accompanied by some "friends." Therefore, because the *News-Herald* interview is Flagler's own version, it would appear to be the best source, and I have relied on its chronology rather than the traditional texts. See Jacksonville *News-Herald,* June 20, 1887. Hereafter referred to as *News-Herald,* 1887.

2. U.S. Census, 1880.

3. George Ward Nichols, "Six Weeks in Florida," *Harper's,* October 1870.

4. *News-Herald,* 1887.

5. Nichols, "Six Weeks in Florida."

6. *News-Herald,* 1887.

7. According to Harry Harkness Flagler, this was the only home in New York City that Flagler ever owned. He did not sell it until after he moved his residence to Florida in the 1890s. The stable, however, was retained until his death. The New York city directories have the following listings for Henry Flagler:

1874—Henry M. Flagler, sec, 140 Pearl St., home Ohio.
1881—Sec, 44 Bway, home 685 Fifth Ave.
1895—Pres., 26 Bway, home 685 Fifth Ave. [business place of the Standard Oil].
1901—Pres., 26 Bway, home Florida.
1907—H26 Bway, R 500, home Florida.

8. Martin.

9. "Her father," said the Cleveland papers, "was able to afford his children every advantage in life that any child could have, and these, with the benefits of travel, were improved to the uttermost by his daughter Mary. She became as accomplished as she was lovely, and was the idol of a large and devoted circle of friends, who have watched with the deepest anxiety the too painful evidences of her failing health." See Bellevue *Evening Gazette*, May 26, 1881.

10. Walter Martin interview, August 1984.

11. Settled in the mid-1600s, it was the site of James Fenimore Cooper's marriage to Susan De Lancey in 1811 at her family's estate, the De Lancey Manor House.

12. Martin interview.

13. There is strong dispute about the relationship, if any, between Ida Alice Shourds and Mary Harkness Flagler. Most sources, including newspaper clippings from 1900 onward and Flagler biographer Walter Martin state that Ida Alice was a nurse to Mary Flagler, hired some months prior to her death.

Flagler's son, Harry Harkness Flagler, however, maintained that Miss Shourds was never a nurse to his mother, but he gave no further information. His remarks are contained in annotations to Martin's book on file at the Flagler Museum, Whitehall.

In a 1984 interview with this author, however, Professor Martin stuck to his position that Ida Alice had been a nurse to Mary Flagler and later held employment as "nurse," presumably to the children, at Mamaroneck.

In preparing his book in the late 1940s, Professor Martin said he was allowed to review a series of letters between Flagler and his friend Dr. Anderson of St. Augustine. The letters confirmed the nurse history, said Martin. Following Professor Martin's study in the 1940s, the letters were returned to their owner, Anderson's daughter, Mrs. Clarissa Anderson Gibbs of St. Augustine, but have since vanished.

14. *News-Herald*, 1887.

15. And wouldn't be until Flagler's engineers arrived to do the job.

## CHAPTER 8

1. Anderson's grandfather and John Jacob Astor were neighbors in New York City on Broadway at the corner of Liberty Street. Anderson was a shoemaker, with offices at 65 Broadway. At the time of his death in 1831, he owned large amounts of real estate in Greenwich Village plus a 45-acre farm in Harlem.

2. *News-Herald*, 1887.

3. *News-Herald*, 1887.

4. Martin.

5. St. Lucie County *Tribune*, February 9, 1912, address given January 23, 1912, at Key West by Henry Flagler.

6. *News-Herald*, 1887.

7. Martin.

8. Florida *Times Union*, January 13, 1888.

9. Julian Ralph, "Our Own Riviera," *Harper's*, March 1893. The Ponce de Leon, the Alcazar, and the Casa Monica still exist, although no longer used as hotels.

10. *Historical Statistics of the United States, Colonial Times to 1970*, U.S. Department of Commerce.

11. Martin interview. Martin's statements were based on his review of the now-missing Flagler–Anderson letters.

12. Prior to the launching of the *Alicia* in 1890, Flagler owned a sloop yacht, *Eclipse*, and a schooner yacht, *Columbia*. Flagler Museum archivist Joan Runkel says researchers have been

unable to determine what happened to the two former yachts, but the *Alicia* was sold to the U.S. government sometime in 1898, during the Spanish–American War. It was 180 feet long, had gross tonnage just over 300 tons and was designed and built by Harlan and Hollingsworth of Wilmington, Delaware.

Flagler was a member of the Larchmont Yacht Club, New York, and in 1885 he became a life member of the St. Augustine Yacht Club. After the sale of the *Alicia*, Flagler was approached several times by people wishing to sell him another yacht to which he replied, ". . . as I have had about twenty years of yachting experience and have gotten thoroughly tired of it, I do not care to commence over again."

13. Letter dated December 18, 1890; Whitehall collection; letterhead is 26 Broadway, NYC. Here is the text:

Dear John,
  I will avail myself of your [unintelligible word] and accept your offer of $150 for 2,500 shares of SO Trust. Mr. Beardsley will deliver the shares in the morning. I hope that you will make lots of money out of the purchase. I shall not regret it.

Sincerely Yours,
HM Flagler

14. Martin.
15. James Kenan was one of the first trustees of UNC and great-great-grandfather of Christopher Barbee, who gave 200 acres of his farm to UNC in the 1790s; part of it is now the center of UNC and the remainder has been sold as lots to form Chapel Hill.
16. Martin.
17. *New York Times*, April 26, 1894.

## CHAPTER 9

1. Whitehall letterbook.
2. Harry Harkness Flagler annotations, Whitehall.
3. Martin, citing Shelton Testimony, Flagler Divorce Proceedings, August 12, 1901, Circuit Court, Miami, Florida.
4. Shelton testimony.
5. Shelton testimony.
6. Letter on Royal Poinciana head to Dr. Anderson, December 31, 1895.
7. Martin.
8. *New York Times*, May 10, 1901.
9. Smith papers.
10. The other children were Jessie, Sarah and William Jr.
11. Address by Thomas Kenan III to Palm Beach Historical Society; April 20, 1972. Hereafter referred to as Kenan address.

## CHAPTER 10

1. The Gulf Stream runs barely three miles off Palm Beach with a northbound current so powerful that southbound vessels keep to its western edge to minimize resistance. As a consequence, ocean liners, rusty cargo ships and oil tankers daily pass in review almost within hailing distance of the oceanfront Palm Beach mansions.
2. Boca Raton *News*, September 23, 1973.
3. Three hundred people were killed and 90,000 left homeless in the great Chicago fire of 1871.

4. Interview with C. W. Pierce, Palm Beach *Daily News*, Historical Edition, 1936.

5. 1939 *WPA Guide to Florida*, Pantheon Books, N.Y., 1984.

6. As noted in earlier chapters, he often played the mysterious front man for Standard Oil, making million-dollar deals in secret hotel room meetings in off-the-path cities.

7. James Ingraham address to Miami Women's Club, November 12, 1920. Hereafter referred to as Ingraham address.

8. For many years, Rockefeller, known simply as "Neighbor John" among the residents, presided over an annual charity bazaar at the Hotel Ormond, attracting large crowds to bid on the odds and ends he personally auctioned. On Sunday mornings, he attended the nondenominational Ormond Union Church and after the service stood on the lawn distributing bright new dimes to children, advising them that thrift and savings would lead the way to fortune.

Every year, on the day he ordered his private railroad car north, Rockefeller placed in the hands of the local pastor an envelope with money to pay his salary and all church expenses for the ensuing year. Rockefeller delighted in the Casements and the nearby golf course.

A regular partner was humorist Will Rogers, who after losing one match said, "I'm glad you beat me, John. The last time you were beaten, I noticed the price of gasoline went up two cents a gallon." Rockefeller died at the Casements on May 23, 1937, just two years short of his one hundredth birthday. See *WPA Guide*.

9. The automobile racing tradition at Daytona began in 1903 when Alexander Winton piloted his machine at a top speed of 68 miles an hour, a world's record. The same year, R. E. Olds drove his Oldsmobile a measured mile in one minute, six seconds, or 54.5 miles per hour, a world's record for sustained speed.

10. Palm Beach *Daily News*, September 4, 1983.

11. Following the acquisition of California in 1846, the U.S. government became interested in an Atlantic–Pacific link across Central America. The first of these was the Panama Railroad, built approximately along the path of the present Panama Canal in 1848–1855. The tiny railroad was slow at best, barely able to haul passengers, let alone large amounts of cargo, and in the 1850s plans for a water connection—a canal—were begun by several nations, primarily the United States, Great Britain and France.

Permission for a canal was finally obtained by a French company, which in 1881 began construction along the railroad right-of-way under the leadership of Ferdinand de Lesseps. Disease, construction problems and inadequate financing, however, bankrupted the company in 1889. By 1891, the time of the Flagler-Browne meeting, the United States was considering not only the Panamanian Isthmus, but also the Isthmus of Nicaragua and a combination railroad-and-canal at Tehauntepec, Mexico, as proposed by the noted American engineer, James Eads.

12. Miami *Herald*, September 20, 1935, letter from Judge Jefferson B. Browne, Key West.

13. It has been traditionally reported that Flagler began planning his road to Key West in the early 1900s and his Miami venture about 1895. Judge Browne's statement and Flagler's charter applications, however, show that Henry was years ahead of his biographers.

14. Dade was later broken up into four counties: present-day Dade, Broward, Palm Beach and Martin.

15. *Old Juno*, J.E. Chillingworth, 1932. Chillingworth and some partners walked the site of old Juno in the summer of 1932 looking for ruins. All they could find among the sawgrass were a few old boards and the cement foundations of the courthouse.

In bypassing Juno, Flagler also bypassed one of Florida's better known curiosities—"The Celestial Railroad," a seven-and-a-half-mile long narrow gauge road built in 1889 to connect the tiny beach resort of Jupiter to Juno, so named because Juno was the "bride" of the older Jupiter.

To create publicity, the railroad added a couple of fictitious stops, naming them Venus and Mars. Soon they were calling the line the Celestial Railroad and for 75 cents you could make a trip out of this world. An old wood-burning locomotive pulled three or four small cars up the line and backed them down again, for the road had no switches or turntable. When Henry built his competing Florida East Coast Railway nearby however, the Celestial Railroad went into permanent eclipse.

16. Letter from Flagler to Parrott, June 11 and 18, 1895, Flagler Museum.

17. *Suntime* magazine article by Walter Martin, September 5, 1953.

18. *Ibid.*

19. Philadelphia *Press*, March 25, 1895.

## CHAPTER 11

1. Miss Geer's article was reprinted in the Palm Beach *Sun*, March 19, 1948.

2. Flagler System financial records for 1894, Flagler Museum, and *Historical Statistics of the United States*, U.S. Department of Commerce. The 1893 U.S. dollar was equivalent to $11.93 in 1986 dollars.

3. The island's exclusivity, which included official and unofficial racial discrimination against Jews and blacks, extended well into the twentieth century. In its more benign form, the exclusivity barred wheeled vehicles, with the exception of bicycles and the "Afromobiles" favored by Henry Flagler. In the later 1920s, motorcars were admitted, but even as late as 1941 there were no commercial parking lots.

As late as the 1960s, Negroes were not allowed residences on the island unless they had police identity cards and were employed as domestic servants living in servants' quarters of their employer. Indeed, until the mid-1960s, blacks were not allowed on the streets of Palm Beach after dark unless actively employed on the island. *WPA Guide;* interview with W. U. Newcome, former senior reporter for the Palm Beach *Daily News*.

4. Palm Beach *Post-Times*, April 26, 1953. Flagler was usually careful to keep his political fences mended.

In late December 1894, Governor James Stephen Hogg of Texas issued a subpoena for Flagler and other top Standard Oil executives for violation of the Texas state antitrust law by Standard Oil agents in that state.

Flagler, who regarded the Populist reformer Hogg as a radical socialist, was outraged to be included in the Texas indictments, which were related to very minor offenses by a Standard Oil distributor. The newly elected governor of Florida, Henry Mitchell, at first agreed to an extradition but later was persuaded by Flagler intermediaries to change his mind. A few months later, on April 12, 1895, Flagler wrote to the Florida governor, saying:

As this late day, I deem it proper to say to you that when I arrived in Florida last January, it was my intention to have made a trip to Tallahassee for the sole purpose of making your acquaintance . . . but it occurred to me that possibly my visit during the Legislative Session might be misconstrued and become an embarrassment to you. I have decided therefore . . . to express the hope that our "late unpleasantness" [i.e., the Texas extradition] may not, in any way, be a bar to our future acquaintance . . .

Mitchell replied warmly:

I, too, regret that it has not been our good fortune to meet each other, because it would have afforded me much pleasure to meet a gentleman of your reputation; one who has invested so much in, and done so much for, Florida. Still, I agree with you that perhaps it would be best for you not to visit Tallahassee at the present time, as your motive in doing so might be misconstrued.

If convenient, after the adjournment of the Legislature, I would like to meet you, so that we could talk over several matters.

In the meantime, I beg to assure you that there was nothing personal in the "late unpleasantness."

5. The building was enlarged in 1899 and again in 1901. It continued in use until the end of the season of 1929–1930, and was demolished in 1936.

6. Palm Beach *Daily News*, February 23, 1983.

7. Research done by Whitehall archivist Joan Runkel.

8. *WPA Guide*. The Beach Club remained in operation as a casino until the mid-twentieth century and from beginning to end, to maintain its privileged arrangement vis à vis the state gambling laws, admittance was denied to full-time Florida residents and to persons younger than 24 years.

9. Philadelphia *Press*, March 1, 1895.

10. Philadelphia *Press*, January 28, 1895.

11. Bobo Dean sold his interests in the Palm Beach newspaper in 1905 and moved to Miami where he spent the next few years attacking Flagler through the columns of the Miami *Metropolis*. His attacks ceased when merchants, eager to win Flagler's approval or otherwise objecting, boycotted the *Metropolis* and began withdrawing ads.

12. Eulogy by George Ward, Memorial Services, Royal Poinciana Chapel, March 15, 1914. A copy is on file at the Flagler Museum.

13. "The Era of Millionaires," New York *Herald*, undated clip, Flagler museum.

14. *Ibid.*

15. "The Story of a Pioneer," Florida East Coast Railway Company, St. Augustine, Fla., 1957.

16. Letter from Flagler to Parrott, August 26, 1895; Flagler Museum.

17. Interview with Charles Simmons, director of Flagler Museum.

18. After Whitehall, his $4 million Palm Beach mansion, was ready in 1902, Flagler brought the celebration there. The St. Augustinians got jealous, and after a few years Flagler and his wife, Mary Lily, moved the festivities back to the Ponce de Leon.

19. Smith papers.

20. *New York Times*, February 22, 1898.

21. Standard Oil reorganized in 1899 and made Standard Oil of New Jersey the holding company in charge of virtually all assets—pipeline companies, crude oil producing, refining, transporting and marketing organizations. Flagler was the first president of Standard of New Jersey, although he functioned more as a chairman of the board rather than a day-to-day chief executive officer.

22. Smith papers.

## CHAPTER 12

1. *Historical Facts*, Historical Association of Southern Florida. The reference is to the Freducci Map of 1514. The village, occupying the present site of the DuPont Plaza, has been thoroughly explored by archeologists.

2. *Ibid.*

3. Just east of the present-day campus of the University of Miami, in the community known as Perrine.

4. "Northern Biscayne Bay in 1776," Roland E. Chardon, and "Miami in 1876," Arva Moore Parks, *Tequesta*, XXXV, 1975.

5. *Homeseeker*, January 1901.

6. Niles *Register*, November 15, 1817.

7. Parks, "Miami in 1876."

8. *Ibid.*

9. The same Abner Doubleday who fired the Union army's first shot of the Civil War in

defense of Fort Sumter. He also is credited, somewhat shakily, as the man who invented
baseball at Cooperstown, N.Y., in 1839.

10. *WPA Guide.* Her father had two earlier marriages and four other children. His first
wife was Helen Louisa Oviatt, who died in childbirth after three years of marriage. His second
was Julia DeForest, who bore him three children. Following the death of the second wife in
1845, Ephraim married Frances Leonard, born in Woodbury, Connecticut.

At the time Sturtevant wrote his will, believed to be in 1870, he had three living children:
Warren, Wheeler DeForest (born of his second wife, Julia DeForest) and Julia.

There is no indication that Warren ever lived in South Florida. However, Wheeler was
there in the 1880s, after his father's death, making repairs on the house. He moved to Biscayne
permanently in the early 1890s and lived out his life there, a quarter of a century, dying in
1916 at the age of 77. Wheeler, who never married, and his half-sister, Julia, were close. Early
newspaper reports mention his trips into Miami to visit her, and he left his property to her
children. He and Julia shared a common middle name, DeForest, a name of which Julia was
proud. At the time of her premature death, she was planning to build a town on 1,200 acres
(near present-day Hallandale) and call it DeForest. (Miami *Metropolis*, June 24, 1898.)

11. "Biscayne Dade County," Cleveland *Herald*, September 30, 1875.

12. *Wild Life in Florida*, London, Hurst and Blckett, 1875. Cited by Parks.

13. Miami *Herald*, May 23, 1926.

14. "Miami, From Frontier to Metropolis," F. Page Wilson, *Tequesta*, XIV, 1954.

15. Coontie, also called komptie, is the name for the plant and also the flour produced
from the starch of an arrowroot, *Zamia Floridana*. Coontie flour was used to bake a heavy,
non-rising bread. The roots were pounded in water, and the white sediment was dried and
used as flour. The Seminoles regarded the coontie as sacred to the Great Spirit.

16. Miami *Metropolis*, July 25 and 27, 1906.


## CHAPTER 13

1. *Congressional Record,* August 17, 1954, remarks of Hon. George H. Bender of Ohio:

Discovered as early as 1600 by French explorers, it wasn't until 1789 that man first recorded formation of
iron ore in the Lake Superior district. . . . These early pioneers correctly reasoned that if iron could be
brought down to lower lake ports and coal brought up from the south, a great iron producing center could
be established along the shores of Lake Erie. Earliest of these practical men who had visions of mining the
ore and bringing it to Lake Erie ports were Isaac Hewitt & H. B. Tuttle, Cleveland commission merchants.
The company, known as Hewitt & Tuttle, was principally engaged in the selling of food. However, as time
went on, they became more and more interested in the selling of Lake Superior iron ores. The first shipment
of ore from the Lake Superior region to the lower lakes was made in 1852, comprising six barrels. It was
dug by hand and hauled by mule team to water, hauled by mule again around the Soo, wheel-barreled onto
a sailing ship and, legend has it, consigned to the commission firm of Hewitt & Tuttle.

The firm of Hewitt & Tuttle, forerunner of Oglebay, Norton & Co., from this small beginning started
the flood of iron ore which was to reach an all-time high of approximately 95 million tons in 1953.

2. *Biscayne Country,* Thelma Peters, Banyan Books, Miami, Florida, 1981. Hereafter referred to as Peters.

3. Memoir of Julia Tuttle's daughter-in-law, Mrs. H. E. Tuttle (hereafter referred to as
Mrs. H.E. Tuttle memoir), Gralynn Hotel, Miami, Florida, Historical Museum of Southern
Florida, Miami, hereafter referred to as HMSF. The church memberships are mentioned in
papers of the Tuttle Collection, HMSF.

4. *Ibid.*

5. *Ibid.*

6. Rose.

7. The series of letters between Julia Tuttle and John D. Rockefeller are stored at the Rockefeller Archives, Tarrytown, N.Y.

8. Mrs. H. E. Tuttle memoir.

9. Miami *News,* May 19, 1984.

10. Letter of Henry Flagler to Julia Tuttle, April 27, 1893, HMSF.

11. Miami *Herald,* July 10, 1956. Dorn went on to become an insurance executive, automobile dealer and civic leader. He helped to organize Miami's first fire department, opened its first garage, organized the first Humane Society and helped to organize the Board of Trade, which became the Chamber of Commerce.

12. Mrs. H. E. Tuttle memoir.

13. Ingraham address.

14. Letter from Henry Flagler to Julia Tuttle, April 22, 1985. Written from St. Augustine.

15. Their agreement was drawn up in contract form on October 24, 1895.

## CHAPTER 14

1. Miami *News,* September 19, 1948.

2. The railroad did put up a supply depot in Lemon City at what is now the intersection of the railroad and 61st Street in Miami.

3. Flagler collection, Flagler Museum.

4. Miami *News,* September 19, 1948.

5. *Homeseeker,* January 1910.

6. Miami *Herald,* December 5, 1937.

7. Miami *Daily News,* November 26, 1946.

8. Ingraham address.

9. Now the intersection of East Flagler Street and Second Avenue, it was then called, respectively, Twelfth Street and Avenue B.

10. Her husband later became the first mayor of Miami Beach. One of her children, J. Newton "Newt" Lummus, also became a mayor of Miami Beach and for a long time was Dade County's tax assessor.

11. From HMF on personal letterhead, 26 Broadway, N.Y., to Tuttle, August 10, 1896, HMSF.

12. *Ibid.,* August 27, 1896 and December 5, 1896.

13. Miami *Herald,* July 28, 1953.

14. When the first Florida East Coast Railway passenger train pulled into Miami on April 22, 1896, the depot was at what then was Avenue E and Twelfth Street (West Flagler Street and First Avenue).

15. Ingraham address.

16. *Ibid.*

17. Peters.

18. The lands that were once the golf course are now significant parts of Jackson Memorial Hospital, as well as Cedars of Lebanon Hospital, the county jail and public safety department, the Metro courts building, a state office building and an expressway.

## CHAPTER 15

1. Lockport, N.Y., *Union-Sun and Journal,* June 23, 1965.

2. Letter from Sterling Ruffin to Annie Carrie Ruffin Sims, his sister, Wilson, North Carolina, January 8, 1885, Flagler collection.

3. Information about Mary Lily's opium habit comes from members of the family of her

second husband, Robert Worth Bingham. It is disputed by Kenan family members. However, after she died of a heart attack in her bath in 1917, her autopsy showed large amounts of morphine and alcohol.

The statistics on drug use come from records of the U.S. Narcotics Bureau. According to those records, in 1900, one of every 400 Americans had a drug addiction. With the advent of drug restrictions, beginning in 1914, the rate decreased rapidly through World War II. At that time, military medical exams indicated a national addiction rate of one out of 6,000. The rate began to deteriorate after the war, and by 1982 had returned to the 1900 level—one of every 400 Americans.

4. Interview with Thomas S. Kenan III. Hereafter referred to as Kenan interview.

5. *Ibid.*

6. Coded dispatch from W. H. Beardsley to H. M. Flagler, St. Augustine, dated April 3, 1899, and Beardsley to W. R. Kenan, Wilmington, N.C., same date:

Dear Sir,

I beg to acknowledge receipt of certificates for one thousand shares Standard Oil Trust in name of Miss Mary Lily Kenan, which I have put in transfer, as directed by Mr. Flagler.

According to Thomas Kenan III, the stock was worth between $850 and $900 a share at the time.

7. Smith papers.

8. The storm did not abate until 1905 when the law was repealed.

9. Kenan interview.

10. Letter, HMF to Rev. Charles Stevens, Philadelphia, dictated at Mamaroneck.

11. Rates varied from town to town. In 1905 in Lake City, the rate was 35 cents per month for each 16-candlepower bulb, which was doubled if the bulb was used after midnight.

12. Bellevue *Evening Gazette*, October 29, 1903.

## CHAPTER 16

1. Kenan interview.

2. Interview, J.C. Salter, St. Augustine *Evening Record*, date unknown, St. Augustine Historical Society.

3. Smith papers.

4. *Ibid.* Flagler's private car was the Alicia, usually referred to by Flagler simply as Car 90. It replaced the Rambler, built for Flagler in 1886. Car 90 is privately owned and still in use. The Rambler is at the Flagler Museum.

5. And, of course, 13 years later to be President of the United States.

6. Kenan interview.

7. Thomas Edison invented electrical recording of sound and built the first phonograph in 1877, using a cylinder as the recording palette. In 1896, Emile Berliner patented the disc record, a lateral recording which superseded the Edison method. Orchestra recordings were not even attempted until about 1913, and even then were highly unsatisfactory.

8. The Spalding letters are part of the Flagler Collection, Flagler Museum.

## CHAPTER 17

1. John Maurer Rockwell, "Opening the Over Sea Railway to Key West," *Colliers*, January 20, 1912.

2. Ralph D. Paine, "Over the Florida Keys by Rail," *Everybody's*, February 1908.

3. Krome, Cape Sable Field Camp, January 28, 1903, to E.B. Carter, St. Augustine, FEC Collection, Flagler Museum.

4. The pace evidently was too great. He died April 20, 1909, after five years on the project.

5. Paine, "Over the Florida Keys by Rail."

6. Russell B. Smith, "Steamboat Runs over Proposed Site of Railroad," New York *Herald*, August 13, 1905.

7. Dr. Andrew Anderson, Armistice Day Speech, 1921, Anderson Collection, St. Augustine Museum.

8. Hunter, "A Railway Across the Sea."

9. *Ibid.*

10. Chapin, *Key West Extension of Florida East Coast Railway*—Official Program and Souvenir, 1912, FEC Collection, Flagler Museum.

11. "The Construction of the Key West Extension of the Florida East Coast Railway, 1905–1915," Todd M. Tinkham, 1968; a college paper on file in the Flagler Collection, Flagler Museum.

## CHAPTER 18

1. FEC statistics from FEC Collection, Flagler Museum. U.S. statistics from *Historical Statistics of the United States.*

2. Brooklyn *Daily Eagle*, December 31, 1905.

3. Krome, August 15, 1911, to A. V. Tiscornia, N.Y., FEC Collection.

4. Carlton J. Corliss, "Building the Overseas Railway to Key West."

5. Krome collection.

6. Corliss, "Building the Overseas Railway to Key West."

7. Diary of W. R. Hawkins, Marathon, entry of November 3, 1911, FEC Collection.

8. *Ibid.*

9. HMF to Parrott, August 16, 1905, FEC Collection.

10. Response from Parrott, August 23, 1905.

11. Brooklyn *Daily Eagle*, Sunday, December 31, 1905.

12. Chicago *Daily News*, May 22, 1907.

13. Krome collection.

## CHAPTER 19

1. *New York Times*, February 24, 1943. LeFevre's obituary at his death at 73. His journalism career spanned 51 years, from 1890 until 1941. In 1910, a year following his Flagler visit, the Panamanian government named him ambassador to both Italy and Spain.

2. *Everybody's*. All LeFevre quotes and excerpts in this chapter are from the LeFevre 1909 article.

## CHAPTER 20

1. St. Lucie County *Tribune*, February 9, 1912, address given January 22, 1912, at Key West, by HMF.

2. Flagler, Palm Beach, January 27, 1912, to Parrott, St. Augustine, FEC Collection.

3. FEC letterhead, HMF to J. A. McGuire, January 17, 1910.

4. Letters of March 1910, Whitehall, from HMF, Royal Poinciana, to J. A. McGuire, Flagler Collection, Flagler Museum.

5. April 19, 1912, Flagler collection.

6. The theory of how Flagler died was developed by Charles Simmons, director of the Flagler Museum, who conducted experiments with the automatic door closer.

7. Harkness notations to Martin book, Flagler Museum.

8. *Suntime* article by Walter Martin, September 5, 1953.

9. Ingraham address.


## APPENDIX A

1. From an address by Dr. Adolf Flegler, Stuttgart, to the "1971 Flegler–Flagler Meeting," held at Wertheim, Franconia, West Germany, May 20, 1971. Transcripts are at the Flagler Museum in Palm Beach, Florida. Hereafter referred to as Flegler address.

Urphar is the site of "die Jakobskirche," or Jacob's Church, a place of worship for many generations of Fleglers. The church, untouched by the centuries of war, has remained in its present form since the year 1500. Initially Roman Catholic by faith, its congregation since 1600 has been Lutheran. The church stands on the foundation of an older edifice, dating to 400 A.D., when it was a "Wehrkerche," or defense church, overlooking a Roman military road.

2. *Ibid.*

3. The name Palatinate, as a political division, disappeared from the map of Europe at the end of the eighteenth century. There were two Palatinates. The Upper or Bavarian Palatinate, near the Bohemian Forest, west of Czechoslovakia; and the Palatinate of the Rhine, which occupied about 2,800 square miles of fertile land on both sides of the Rhine. Its capital was the city of Heidelberg. It is the latter which was the home of the Fleglers.

4. Cited by Robert Pierce, "The Germanic Origin of the Flagler Family of Dutchess County," *Dutchess County Historical Society Yearbook*, 1972, Poughkeepsie, New York. Hereafter referred to as Pierce, 1972.

5. Flegler address.

6. *Ibid.*

7. *Ibid.*

8. "The Palatines," Wilhelmina Powers, *Dutchess County Historical Society Yearbook*. Hereafter referred to as Powers.

Powers tells us that the leading benefactor of the Germans was the Queen, Anne Stuart, daughter of the deposed James II, a plain sort of sovereign who seems to have been totally without ambition, and not particularly brainy. Jonathan Swift said of her that she was a person of few words and of still fewer ideas and that her usual theme of conversation concerned local weather observations.

Swift's opinion notwithstanding, the people of England liked her, calling her "good Queen Anne" for her success in annexing Scotland, for her kindness to the working classes, and possibly because she employed women in royal household positions previously held by men. Anne felt the women could do the work better, and deserved more jobs. Conrad Weiser arrived in America in 1710, his family settling along the Hudson. In his teens, the youth began living with the Mohawks in western New York. Learning their language and customs, he became the official Pennsylvania Indian interpreter and gained fame as a wise and honorable mediator between whites and Indians. He was influential in persuading the Iroquois to support the British against the French in the French and Indian Wars.

9. *Ibid.*

10. It is a common error to confuse the North Atlantic Drift with the Gulf Stream and attribute the warmth of northwestern Europe to the latter. In fact, the Gulf Stream loses its characteristics and is absorbed by the drift in the mid-Atlantic.

11. Powers.

12. *Ibid.*

13. Pierce, 1972.
14. Powers.
15. *Ibid.*
16. *Ibid.*
17. Cited by Powers.
18. In 1747, a generation after the Palatine voyage, Scottish naval surgeon James Lind obtained dramatic cures by treating scurvy-ridden sailors with lemons and oranges.
19. Powers.
20. Pierce, 1972.


## APPENDIX B

1. Pierce, 1972, and Powers.
2. The title of oldest continuous settlement usually is claimed by St. Augustine, Florida, founded in 1565. Twice, however, St. Augustine was burned, sacked and its population dispersed by English raiders—Sir Francis Drake in 1586 and Captain John Davis in 1665. The city's continuous occupation dates from just after the Davis raid. Another claimant of oldest continuous settlement is Hampton, Virginia, first settled in 1610 by the English. An even older claim can be made by the pueblo village of Acoma, which sits atop a steep-sided, 350-foot high sandstone mesa in western New Mexico. Approximately 70 acres in extent and little changed from Coronado's visit in 1540, it has been continuously occupied for at least 600 years.
3. Pierce, 1972, and Powers.
4. *Ibid.*
5. The potato, a native of South America, was a reintroduction, having been brought in the early 1500s from Inca Peru to Spain, whence it spread throughout Europe. It was returned to the Americas by European settlers in the early 1600s. Rich in carbohydrates, potassium, phosphorus and iron, it was a major source of starch, flour, alcohol, dextrin and fodder.

Corn, or maize, was even more useful. The small European grains of wheat, barley and rye required a carefully tilled and finely prepared soil. But corn, in the Indian method of primitive agriculture, could be produced among stumps, rocks and even in the forests when clearings were made by ax or fire.

Unlike all other grains, ripe corn can wait on the stalk for delayed harvesting. In much of North America, at least some of the crop will stand in perfect condition on the stalk or in the shock through winter and into the spring. This self-storage allows families time to gather other crops or to go on hunting expeditions.

Corn's versatility aided the settler. Green (immature) corn was a prized midsummer vegetable. Whole grains of ripened corn could be pitched into a campfire for subsistence on expeditions where the hunting failed. After the grains were soaked in lye, the husk could be peeled off and the corn cracked between two stones, thus making hominy—the standby of the Indian's diet. Ground corn could be made into meal, mush and bread. Bundles of cornstalks, fodder, could make a warm, dry roof for a shed or shack, to be eaten later by domestic animals. Cornhusks furnished material to stuff mattresses.
6. *American Heritage Cookbook and Illustrated History of American Eating & Drinking,* Simon and Schuster, N.Y., 1964.
7. Pierce, 1972, and Powers.
8. Flegler address.
9. Pierce, 1972.
10. *Ibid.* The political reasons for abandoning the Palatines were real. England's lifeblood, its trade with Europe, was at a standstill due to a costly war with Louis XIV and to an epidemic of the Bubonic Plague, which killed half a million people in Europe in the year 1711 alone. In

London, food was scarce, work hard to find and industry was hanging by its fingernails. The poor, with bread twice the usual price, resented any form of philanthropy beyond their neighborhoods.

11. "Over Hill: Over Dale," Robert Pierce, *Dutchess County Historical Society Yearbook*, 1972.

12. "School District #1 Town of LaGrange," Clifford M. Buck, *Dutchess County Historical Society Yearbook*, 1972.

13. When families or parties of three or more traveled, a "ride-and-tie" system was often used, whereby one or two started out on the horse, mounted in the saddle or on the pillion. The others went by foot. Those on the animal rode about a mile, dismounted, tied the horse to a tree and walked on. When the people on foot reached the tethered horse, they repeated the process.

14. Pierce, "Over Hill: Over Dale."

15. Genealogical charts, Flagler Museum.

16. *Never Done, A History of American Housework*, Susan Strasser, Pantheon Books, N.Y., 1982.

17. *Ibid.*

18. *Ibid.* The first native American stove was Ben Franklin's Pennsylvania Fireplace, introduced in 1742. As described by Strasser, it was a box formed with cast-iron plates fitting into a conventional fireplace, increasing thermal efficiency by using heat that otherwise went up the chimney. Smoke and combustion gasses passed through flues that heated the plates, which in turn radiated heat into the room. Concentrated in a small space, the fire used all the air that entered the stove, producing a hotter and more efficient flame. Because Franklin thought the watching of a fire "a pleasant thing," his stoves had front doors that could be left open.

19. *American Heritage Cookbook and Illustrated History of American Eating & Drinking.* The Europeans encountered the "intertillage system" developed by the Indians. The Indians would plant single seeds carefully, some of corn, some of peas, some of other crops, thus replenishing the soil with each planting. This was new to Europeans who planted crops by scattering seed at random, hoping some would catch and root. Fields planted Indian-style with beans, peas, squash, melons, sunflowers and corn yielded "at the least two hundred London bushelles" an acre, whereas in England "fourtie bushelles of our wheate [an acre] . . . is thought to be much," as English colonist Thomas Hariot noted admiringly.

20. "A Wandering Preacher I," Robert Pierce, *Dutchess County Historical Society Yearbook*, 1976.

21. Neither daughter married, Mary Ester dying June 6, 1844, at the age of 30; Jane dying April 28, 1849, at the age of 33.

22. Based on the portrait of her at the Flagler Museum, Whitehall, which was done in 1819 when she was 22.

23. Anna Caroline Flagler lived to be 90 years old, dying January 24, 1917.

24. Article by Clyde M. Maffin, Ontario County Historian, the *Daily Messenger*, October 18, 1967, Canandaigua, N.Y.

# INDEX